BusinessW

Fast Track

CO-AZM-733

WITHDRAWN

The Best

B   S

Fu   *ive*

Lisbon   London   Madrid   Mexico City   Milan
New Delhi   San Juan   Seoul   Singapore
Sydney   Toronto

1 2 3 4 5 6 7 8 9 0   DOC/DOC   0 9 8

ISBN 978-0-07-149653-7
MHID   0-07-149653-X

McGraw-Hill books are available at special quantity discounts to use as premiums and sales promotions, or for use in corporate training programs. To contact a representative, please visit the Contact Us pages at www.mhprofessional.com.

This book is printed on acid-free paper.

Contents

0 3 1 0 0 7 4 1 0

Full-Time MBA Programs

Executive MBA Programs

Part-Time MBA Programs

Acknowledgments

Like any collaborative enterprise, this book could not have been written if not for the hard work and dedication of dozens of people.

Dan Macsai, Kristen Lease, Sonal Rupani, Kristen Fiani, John Peabody, Josh Vittor, and Sabrina Siddiqui spent months compiling the program information, reading thousands of student surveys, and assembling the profiles that make up the bulk of this book. Sidebars were contributed by Jennifer Merritt and Kerry Miller.

The book, and the Fast Track series of which it is a part, were conceived by John Byrne, who launched the magazine's first MBA ranking in 1988. Frank Comes and Leah Spiro guided the project from beginning to end, while Ruth Mannino directed the design and editorial production of the book.

Of course there would not be a book if there had never been the rankings. The team that labors mightily to produce the magazine's B-school rankings includes Geoff Gloeckler, who manages the ranking surveys and whose patience, diligence, and creativity make the whole rankings enterprise hum; Fred Jespersen, our tireless number-crunching guru; as well as Jane Porter, Paula Lehman, John DeBruicker, and Kristen Dew. Supervising the rankings were Robin Ajello and Elizabeth Weiner.

The team that produced all the online content for BusinessWeek.com, our award-winning Web site, includes Francesca Di Meglio, Janie Ho, Jessica Sanders, Julie Gordon, Kerry Miller, Lauren Lavelle, Jeffrey Gangemi, Alison Damast, and Alina Dizik. Technical assistance was provided by Arthur Eves, Pedro Santiago, and Michael O'Malley. Phil Mintz, Martin Keohan, and Kathy Rebello supervised the online crew.

Finally, a special thanks to all the hard-working people at the programs mentioned in this book. Without their substantial help this book could not have been completed.

Introduction

In the long list of decisions that all young adults must make, deciding whether to pursue an advanced degree is easily among the most difficult and complex. The fact that you're holding this book in your hands means that you're already well on your way to choosing the potentially life-altering path that business school represents. Like all advanced degrees, an MBA, should you choose to get one, will open doors that were once closed. But unlike nonbusiness degrees, where career paths are fairly well defined from the outset, an MBA represents a ticket to many shows. It can be used to pursue any number of paths up the corporate hierarchy, bring modern management techniques to nonprofit organizations at work in the developing world, or start a new business. It can even take you to the White House. That wealth of possibilities makes choosing an MBA program significantly complex.

This guidebook is an outgrowth of *Business Week*'s rankings of business schools, which began in 1988 with our first ranking of full-time MBA programs. Since then, the magazine has launched numerous other franchises, including a ranking of executive MBA programs in 1991 and a new ranking of part-time MBA programs last year. In this book, you'll find detailed statistical profiles of more than 100 programs of all three types, including both domestic and international full-time programs, that came out on top in the most recent rankings. But this book is only the beginning. In fact, *Business Week*'s coverage of management education extends far beyond the pages of this book and of the magazine itself.

At BusinessWeek.com, you'll find a wealth of additional content. There are lengthy profiles of more than 300 schools, including expanded versions of the profiles in this book, along with interactive tools, blogs, journals of current and recently graduated MBA students, and video interviews with dozens of B-school deans, admissions officers, and placement directors. You'll also find something that cannot exist between the pages of any book or magazine: community. On our message boards, you can take part in online chats with admissions and placement professionals, connect with students and alumni who have gone through a program you're considering, seek advice about the admissions process, and make new friends. You can access the site at www.businessweek.com/bschools/.

Choosing a B-school is an intensely personal process, one that inevitably includes a great deal of introspection about career goals, financial resources, academic strengths and weaknesses, work and family demands, and myriad other factors. But for the vast majority of prospective students, it can be reduced to three questions: Why? When? and Where?

Why Apply to B-School?

By the time most prospective MBA students ponder this question, they are about 27 years old, with about five years of work experience under their belts. This means one of several things. They may be in a career that they no longer like. They may have hit a career plateau and be unable to advance without additional training. They may have been laid off. They may have caught the entrepreneurial bug and be hankering to start a business of their own. Any one of these is a legitimate reason for applying to B-school. In fact, the three main reasons people enroll in an MBA program are to jump-start a career that's stalled, head off in a new direction, or simply make more money.

One thing is virtually guaranteed about MBA programs: students will earn far more money after graduation than they did before they got their MBA. In 2006, among schools that participated in *BusinessWeek*'s ranking of full-time MBA programs, graduates who answered our survey had salaries averaging $93,400 after graduating, an increase of $31,700 over what they earned in their pre-MBA days. In 2006, that "MBA premium" of better than 50% was the best since 2000. The rea-

The Best B-Schools of All Time			
Based on 18 years of *BusinessWeek* rankings of full-time MBA programs			
1.	Northwestern	6.	Stanford
2.	University of Pennsylvania	7.	Columbia
3.	Harvard	8.	Dartmouth
4.	Chicago	9.	Duke
5.	Michigan	10.	MIT

son is simple: for corporate recruiters, graduates of these top programs add bottom-line value to their organizations. They bring analytical abilities honed by two years of classroom practice and the ability to bring fresh thinking to old problems. Many prove themselves quite adept at climbing the corporate ladder, where their impact is magnified, with compensation to match. A 2003 *Business Week* study tracking the career outcomes of nearly 1,500 alumni of the Class of 1992 from our Top 30 B-schools found that their average salaries had nearly tripled—from $56,600 in their first post-MBA job to more than $155,200 ten years out. Average total compensation, includ-

> *The three main reasons people enroll in an MBA program are to jump-start a career, head off in a new direction, or simply make more money.*

ing bonuses, was a staggering $387,600. The typical alumnus from the study had three different post-MBA employers and four promotions since graduation ten years earlier. (See "What's an MBA Really Worth?" page xix.)

One reason that MBA earning power stays strong over time, and a compelling reason for undertaking an MBA in the first place, is the value of the specific MBA brand. When you graduate from Harvard Business School, for example, you don't just graduate with a cookie-cutter MBA. You graduate with the same MBA that propelled generations of Harvard alumni to the top echelon of corporate power, every one of them with a lifetime of achievement that reflects back on their alma mater. In effect, when employers hire a Harvard graduate, they're making a calculated gamble that that person will show the same kind of extraordinary promise. If nothing else, a Harvard MBA—or an MBA from any other well-known program, for that matter—guarantees that you'll stand out from the crowd. After all, just getting into Harvard, which turns down 85% of all applicants, is something of an accomplishment in itself. Research has shown that during the recruiting process, the prestige factor counts for more than anything else—surpassing in importance even the candidate's skills and abilities. "The more prominent the school, the higher the salaries" notes Violina P. Rindova, an assistant professor of strategy at the University of Maryland who coauthored the research.

OK, now we know why you should get your MBA. But there are also compelling reasons why you shouldn't. One thing to consider is timing, which we'll get into in more detail a little later. Applications to B-school are a countercyclical phenomenon: they tend to increase when the economy is contracting, and decrease when the economy is firing on all cylinders. A big increase in applications during an economic slowdown often results in a glut of new MBA graduates two years later, just as the economy is heating up again—and a lot of competition among them for the best jobs. So a slowing economy by itself isn't an adequate reason to get an MBA, and getting one at such a time is a strategy that could backfire at graduation. Bottom line: if you're out of work and a slowing economy will make it difficult for you to find a high-paying job—or any job at all, for that matter—then B-school might be a good use of your time. If you're gainfully employed in a job you enjoy, you'll probably want to think twice before you give it all up for B-school, or at least give serious thought to a part-time or executive MBA program that allows you to continue working.

Another bad reason for applying to B-school is the notion that an MBA is a sure-fire ticket to the corner office. It's not. A 2006 *BusinessWeek* study found that only about a third of the highest-paid executives at S&P 100 companies—chief executive officers and their top deputies—have MBAs. Of the more than 250,000 living alumni of *BusinessWeek*'s top 10 MBA programs, only 71 made it into the ranks of the highest-paid. Among the CEOs who made it to the top without the help of an MBA are Frederick W. Smith at FedEx Corp., Steven A. Ballmer at Microsoft, and H. Lee Scott at Wal-Mart. The main reason that an MBA is not a ticket for admission into the ranks of top executives is the way in which such personnel decisions get made at the highest levels. "In the pure Darwinian world we live in, pedigrees mean nothing," says Peter D. Crist, chairman of Crist Associates, a Hinsdale, Illinois, executive search firm. "It's instinct, it's hard work, and it's raw intelligence." (See "Is the MBA Overrated?" page xx.)

An MBA is a big investment—in money, time, and effort—so before you apply, it's important to consider whether the program will actually teach you anything that you don't already know. If you received an undergraduate business degree and have spent five years learning on the job in a midlevel managerial or consulting position, it might not. A better use of your time might be an extremely targeted nondegree executive education program or—if you're contemplating a career switch—a degree that will better prepare you for the nonbusiness side of your new position, such as science or medicine. Some universities now offer joint programs that would be a good fit in such a situation—such as the nondegree executive education program in biotechnology now offered by Northwestern University's Kellogg School of Management and the medical school at Johns Hopkins University.

When Should I Apply to B-School?

The answer to this question is more complicated than it seems. There is no perfect time to attend B-school, so the question that you, as a prospective student, need to answer is when most of the planets will be aligned in your favor. Since the process of applying to B-school can easily take more than a year—from the initial research and taking the GMAT to completing the applications and awaiting the admission decisions—timing should be something that you give serious thought to long before you make a commitment to B-school. You should think of this as a two-step process. In the first stage, you're deciding whether B-school is even possible given your marital status, where you are in your career, and what kind of financial resources you have at your disposal. If you decide that it is, then you need to decide how to time your application to maximize your chances of getting into the best possible program.

B-school is not just a huge commitment for you; it's a major hassle for everyone around you, especially (if you have them) your spouse and children. (See "Can Your Relationship Survive B-School?" page xxii.) At the very least, much of the free time that you would otherwise use for family events—from spending time with your spouse to going to school plays—will be spent studying. Should you decide to attend a school far from home, you'll have an additional decision to make: will you uproot your family, or will you commute home on weekends? If your spouse or children are opposed to your B-school plans, you may want to shelve them for a while, or limit yourself to part-time or executive programs closer to home. But your family is only one piece of the puzzle. If you're employed, a full-time program will require you to quit, while a part-time or executive program may eat into some office hours. Since the total cost of a two-year full-time program, including forgone salary, can easily top $300,000, you need to investigate your financial resources as well. Do you have adequate savings? Are you eligible for financial aid? How much debt are you comfortable taking on? All this needs to be taken into consideration.

In 2006, graduates who answered our survey had salaries averaging $93,400 after graduating, an increase of $31,700 over their pre-MBA days.

So your family is onboard, your resignation letter is written, and money isn't a problem. What's next? The next step is deciding how to get into the best program and how long it will take you to polish up your application. You want to make sure that your credentials—especially your GMAT scores, work experience, and undergraduate grades—are exactly what the top B-schools are looking for. When all these ducks are in order, the time is perfect to apply.

At this point, there's nothing you can do about your undergraduate grades, but GMAT scores are another matter entirely. It's worth taking the test early in the decision-making process in order to find out where you stand relative to the requirements for the schools you'd like to apply to. If your heart is set on a top 10 school, prepare to sharpen your No. 2s: GMAT scores for those programs averaged 707 in 2007, and anything below 650 is likely to rule out most applicants. If your first score is below 700, it's worth the added expense and effort to take a GMAT preparation course and retake the test to increase your grade. Another option is to scale back your expectations a bit. There are many top 30 B-schools, including the University of Maryland's Robert H. Smith School of Business and Washington University's Olin School of Business, where GMAT scores average about 650 and applicants with scores below 600 are routinely accepted.

Even more important than GMAT scores is work experience. It's not just the amount, but the quality of the work experience that matters. So put your résumé under a microscope. How much postundergraduate work experience do you have? Students at top 30 schools who responded to the *Business Week* survey in 2006 had nearly five years' experience on average—anything less and you might want to delay the application process. The one exception: a small, but growing, number of MBA programs that are beginning to reach out to "early career" applicants with fewer than three years of work experience, and in some cases none at all. (See "B-Schools: You Don't Have to Wait," page xxiv.)

While time on the job is important, it's not the only thing that admissions directors look for. Have you managed a team? Have you held a leadership position? Do you have a record of extraordinary accomplishment that will make your application stand out? If so, it may not be necessary for you to wait until you have the requisite five years' experience. But if you're expecting a promotion or a big increase in responsibilities, or if a pet project is about to reap big dividends for your company, it may be smart to delay your application until that happens.

Finally, consider the economy. As noted earlier, MBA applications tend to increase when the economy slows down. After a three-year decline, application volume has been on the rise since 2004, with two out of three programs reporting a year-over-year increase in 2007. (See "MBA Applications Surge," page xxiv.) Some top B-schools have also reduced class size for a variety of reasons, including new resource-intensive curriculums. (See "More Crowding at Top B-Schools," page xxv.) The result: many MBA programs are getting pickier about whom they'll admit. In 2006, one out of every five applicants to the top 10 B-schools received an offer of admission; at Stanford, it was one out of 10 in 2006 and one out of 13 in 2007. In such an environment, it becomes more difficult for all but the very best applicants to get in. However, when applications decline, as they do when the economy is growing, a larger percentage of applicants is accepted, making it easier for students with less than perfect credentials to get a foot in the door.

> *"The more prominent the school,"* notes University of Maryland researcher Violina P. Rindova, *"the higher the salaries."*

So you've taken the GMAT twice and your score now tops 700. You have five years of work experience, four of it spent in a managerial role, during which you launched a new and highly successful business for your company. Applicant volume has been trending upward, making it harder to get in, but you're confident of your credentials. If you're ready to take the plunge, there's only one question left: when to actually submit the application. The rule of thumb here is, the earlier, the better. Most schools have final application deadlines between March and June, but you should plan to submit your application no later than early January for fall admission. The competition is generally tougher in the early rounds, but applications that are not immediately accepted are reconsidered in later rounds—in effect, you get two bites at the apple instead of one. This also leaves you plenty of time to visit campuses, set up interviews, and decide whether you'll accept an offer of admission if one is made.

Where Should I Apply?

For many prospective students, the search for programs to apply to begins and ends in one place: the rankings. (See "The Best B-Schools of All Time," page x.) That's a big mistake. While the rankings are important, they are far from the only thing that matters when choosing a program, and in many cases the program that is right for you is not necessarily the one that is most highly ranked. There are important differences between full-time, part-time, and executive programs, and between domestic and international programs. There are some schools, like the University of Chicago Graduate School of Business, that focus on quantitative skills, and others, such as Northwestern University's Kellogg School of Management, that have teamwork and communication skills at their core. After graduation, some programs funnel students into big financial services companies, some have deep recruiting relationships with Big Four accounting firms, and others serve as incubators for tomorrow's entrepreneurs. All this should be factored into your decision.

Luckily, you are already in possession of the tools you need to parse the pros and cons of more than 100 programs of all types. In the profiles that follow, and in those available at BusinessWeek.com, you'll learn the things you need to know in order to determine if a program is right for you. These include the top functional areas for graduates, the biggest on-campus recruiters, leading areas of study, teaching methods, even prominent faculty. You find out about average class size, the number of business electives, and how students rated everything from teaching quality to career services to the curriculum.

To narrow the field, a good place to start is deciding what type of program is right for you. If you haven't already chosen a full-time, part-time, or executive MBA program, there are important distinctions to consider, starting with the basic program format. Full-time programs are complete immersion experiences. In most cases, you will proceed through the program with a "cohort" of students, attending many of the same classes, working together on long-term projects, and taking part in extracurricular activities. You'll also bond with classmates in a way that frequently results in the creation of extensive postgraduation networks that are critical to career success—one of the most valuable parts of any MBA program.

If your heart is set on a top 10 school, prepare to sharpen your No. 2s: GMAT scores for those programs averaged 707 in 2007.

Part-time programs are increasingly popular because they allow students to remain employed. But because they usually meet only a few times per week, they also take longer to complete—typically anywhere from three to six years. And since students in many cases don't proceed through the program in cohorts, the relationships forged during the program are frequently not as intense or long-lasting. To complete and succeed in a part-time program requires a level of self-discipline that many already overworked employees just can't muster.

Executive MBA programs, originally designed to enhance the management skills of high-potential executives, generally meet on weekends, so face time with professors and classmates is limited. What's more, EMBA programs are changing. At one time, companies would foot the entire bill for executives they enrolled; today, only about a third of all EMBA students are entirely company sponsored. And such support, when offered, usually comes with strings attached—a promise to remain on the job for at least two years postgraduation. The result: a lot of the people who are enrolling in EMBA programs are job-hoppers or career switchers—in short, they aren't all that different from those that you'd find in full-time or part-time programs.

If you've settled on a full-time program, there's one other decision you need to make: should you stay in the United States to get a degree or go overseas to do so? Each has its advantages. In the United States, you'll find the best management education available anywhere. The value of a degree from a top-ranked U.S. school such as Wharton, Stanford, or MIT is almost incalculable—in virtually any country in the world, such names are instantly recognizable as centers of academic excellence and powerful brands in their own right. At best, though, only about a third of the students you'll encounter in these programs come from outside the United States. At many international programs, particularly those in Europe, that figure is likely to be two-thirds or more—in effect, every classroom is the business equivalent of the United Nations. Such classroom diversity is an attractive asset for U.S.-based students who are seeking a global perspective in the classroom and hoping to launch their careers overseas after graduation. As a result, the number of American students signing up for overseas MBAs, while still only a tiny fraction of all U.S. MBA students, has nearly doubled in recent years. Another major attraction of leaving the United States to study: many European MBA programs can be completed in 18 or only 12 months, essentially cutting the price in half.

Once you've decided on the program format and location, the hard work of matching up individual programs with your goals and aspirations begins. If you know what your major will be, finding schools that list that specialty as either a leading area of study or a top functional area for graduates is a fairly simple matter. But then it's time to dig deeper. For example, let's say that you've got your heart set on both a top 10 full-time MBA program in the United States and a career in consulting. At No. 1–ranked University of Chicago, 22% of the graduates go on to careers in consulting, and the top 15 recruiters include such giants of the industry as McKinsey, Booz Allen Hamilton, BCG, Bain, and Accenture. So far, so good.

But post-MBA pay is the lowest among the top 10 schools, just $95,000. And the school, which is well known for its analytical rigor, might not be the best fit for someone looking for a program that emphasizes soft skills such as communication. Put it in the maybe pile. How about No. 3–ranked Kellogg? Post-MBA pay is significantly higher—$105,000—and more graduates go on to consulting careers. Many of the same top firms recruit there, including McKinsey, which hired more graduates at Kellogg than it did at Chicago. What's more, judging from the student comments, the curriculum is more teamwork focused, and the culture is marked by camaraderie and collegiality. Put that in the probably pile.

A big increase in applications during an economic slowdown often results in a glut of MBA graduates two years later— and a lot of competition for the best jobs.

As you continue your homework, you'll probably want to expand your analysis well beyond career outcomes and major strengths. Are small classes important to you? What about a large selection of electives? Teaching quality? Internships? You'll also want to listen closely to the student voices you hear, both in the student comments section of the profiles in this book and in the online forums. Do these sound like people who have enjoyed their experience and gotten a lot out of it? Or do they sound unhappy? You may even consider things that are completely unrelated to B-school. Are you happier in a city? If so, Columbia, New York University, Chicago, or any of the other large urban campuses might be a good choice. If you're more of a nature buff, a program like Dartmouth's Tuck School—an intimate program tucked away in the New Hampshire mountains—might be better. (See "A Small B-School Can Be a Big Plus," page xxv.)

For the most part, all B-school curriculums are variations on the same pedagogical theme. No matter where you go, a large part of the instruction you receive will involve case studies, each an in-depth analysis of a company that requires students to bring all their knowledge to bear on a problem. You will also probably take basic courses in accounting, finance, marketing, statistics, and economics, as well as electives that depend largely on your major. (Chicago, where there are no mandatory courses except for a special orientation program, is an exception; students there are allowed to pursue advanced studies if they already know the basics.) But even within that basic framework, there is great variation. Schools such as Harvard and Darden, for example, focus on teaching general management rather than narrow technical specialties. As a result, their graduates tend to fare well in fields like consulting. Other schools have niche programs designed to give them a national profile. Babson, for example, has developed a renowned program in entrepreneurship, while Vanderbilt has a program in e-commerce, and Michigan State offers training in supply chain management.

Indeed, the vast number of choices can seem paralyzing at first. The number of programs, in the United States and abroad, accredited by the American Association of Collegiate Schools of Business now approaches 550, up from 322 ten years ago. But that's actually a good thing. With so many permutations on the MBA theme, your chances of finding a program that truly meets your needs are quite good. And your chances of finding one that will help you achieve your career goals—whether you want to be an analyst at a top financial services firm, a strategy guru at one of the top consulting companies, or the next Steve Jobs—are excellent.

Of course, the key word here is *help*. No MBA program will hand you the career of your dreams on a silver platter. At best, it will give you the tools you need to realize your ambitions. Everything else? Well, that's up to you.

About the Profiles

The programs profiled in this book are those that were ranked by *BusinessWeek*. For the full-time programs, we included the top 30 domestic and top 10 international schools from our 2006 ranking, as well as an additional 13 "second-tier" schools. Also included are the top 25 executive MBA programs and the top 30 part-time MBA programs (five from each of six geographic areas) from our 2007 rankings. The rankings are based on student surveys conducted by *BusinessWeek* with the help of Cambria Consulting Inc., as well as additional information gathered by the magazine staff. For additional information about our ranking methodologies, visit our Business School Rankings & Profiles page at http://www.businessweek.com/bschools/rankings/ and click on the FAQ.

Most of the statistical information in the profiles was provided by the schools themselves. When schools declined to provide the information and we relied on

BusinessWeek survey data, this is footnoted. The remainder of each profile is based on *BusinessWeek* research, including surveys of students, recruiters, and executive MBA directors. In almost all cases—such as GMAT scores and work experience—the numbers represent averages, not medians. In most cases, the data concerning students reflect either the newest entering class or the most recent crop of graduates.

Some of the statistics in the profiles might not be familiar to all readers. Selectivity is the percentage of applicants accepted. Yield is the percentage of accepted applicants who enroll. Post-MBA salary increase is simply the difference between the average salary students had when they entered the program and the average salary they received upon graduation. Total first-year compensation includes average salary, signing bonus, and other guaranteed compensation—among graduates who reported receiving each form of pay. The percentage of students who are minorities is based on U.S. citizens and permanent residents only, and includes African Americans, Asian Americans, Hispanic Americans, Native Americans, and other ethnicities.

Program costs are another complicated area. For executive MBA programs, total cost is simply tuition and all required fees. For part-time MBA programs, we list tuition per credit hour, as actual costs will depend on how many credits are taken each semester. For full-time MBA programs, we've calculated a total cost figure that includes tuition and fees, living expenses, and forgone salary for the entire length of the program. Annual living expenses are also broken out separately and include room and board and all other miscellaneous expenses (excluding tuition and fees) that a student is likely to incur.

Each profile also includes letter grades based on responses to individual questions (or groups of questions) in our ranking surveys. Since these grades represent only a fraction of the entire survey, it's possible for highly ranked programs to have some poor grades and vice versa. In each category, the top 20% earned an A+, the next 25% received A's, the next 35% were awarded B's, and the bottom 20% got C's. No D's or F's are awarded.

The Best MBA Articles from *BusinessWeek* and BusinessWeek.com

What's an MBA Really Worth? (September 22, 2003)

Once the holy grail of business education, the MBA has become increasingly tarnished over the past two years. The credential that came of age in the late 1980s and early 1990s as business became the "it" profession has been taking its lumps right along with corporate America. Then, last year, Stanford University business professor Jeffrey Pfeffer turned up the volume. In a controversial paper, he argued that since there had never been a measure of the long-term value of the degree, there was no way to really know if a pricey B-school education was worthwhile.

Well, hold onto your hat, Professor Pfeffer. The Class of 1992 gives B-school a big thumbs up. In *BusinessWeek*'s exclusive survey of MBA alumni, nearly 1,500 alums of the Class of 1992 from our Top 30 B-schools report high levels of satisfaction with their careers and say they owe much of that success to their MBA experience.

Overwhelmingly, they say that earning the degree was worth it. Some 89% say that they would go for the MBA again if they had it to do over. And nearly 80% said that they would attend the same school. There's no question that the MBA catapulted most of the class into the upper reaches of American society. Today, the members of the Class of 1992 earn an average salary of more than $155,200—up from the average $56,600 they earned in their first post-MBA job. Add in the $232,400 in average bonus and other compensation—buoyed partly by windfalls earned by alumni working in banking and finance—and compensation for the class last year was $387,600. Compare that to today's average salary for a person with only a college degree—about $43,400—and the MBA premium comes into focus.

As a group, the Class of 1992 ended up in a truly commanding position. They're loaded with management responsibilities—on average, they oversee 93 people each—and as a group they have started hundreds of companies that created nearly 100,000 jobs. Some 22% ended up in banking, 16% in technology, 15% in consumer goods or manufacturing, and 12% in consulting. On average, they've had three different post-MBA employers, along with four promotions, since graduation. And about 25% have switched fields since their first post-MBA job.

Across the board, alumni said that they had counted on the fabled alumni networks but had been largely disappointed. When it comes to advice, job leads, and lifelong connections, alumni gave their schools low marks. Even schools like Harvard and Stanford, tight-knit Dartmouth and Kellogg, and techno-giant MIT scored only slightly above the average. Looking back, many alumni saw their training as too grandiose—overly focused on being a CEO, rather than the more likely middle-manager role—and not practical enough to prepare them for tackling everyday problems. "At a minimum," says one, "I wish someone had told me this would be one of the biggest challenges, and then given me some tips."

—Jennifer Merritt

Is the MBA Overrated? (March 20, 2006)

In the executive pantheon, David K. Zwiener might be considered a minor god. As a graduate of No. 1–ranked Kellogg School of Management at Northwestern University, the executive vice president at Hartford Financial Services Group Inc. is one of 47,000 living alumni of one of the world's most prestigious MBA programs. But he has an unusual distinction: in 2004, his $3.7 million pay package made him one of only three Kellogg MBAs among the 500 highest-paid executives in the Standard & Poor's 100-stock index that year. "It opens that first door for you," Zwiener says of MBAs in general, and his in particular. "After that, it's up to you."

Zwiener's experience points to a little realized fact about the MBA: it gets you only so far. In fact, for those seeking a job at the very top of the corporate hierarchy, it's not even a requirement. *Business Week* research has found that fewer than one out of three executives who reach those lofty heights do so with the help of an MBA. And if you think a sheepskin from a top school is a necessity, think again. Only half of the executives with MBAs went to the top 10 schools in the 2004 *Business Week* ranking.

Business Week examined the five highest-paid executives at each of the S&P 100 companies in 2004, the most recent year for which data are available. We then tracked their

Of the more than 250,000 living alumni of Business Week's top 10 MBA programs, only 71 made it into the ranks of the highest paid executives at S&P 100 companies.

educational credentials, obtaining information on 441. Finally, we calculated the pay for all 500 executives and combined those data with statistics about each school's alumni base as well as company performance for 2002–2004. Some startling numbers came to light. Only 146 of the 500 executives reported having MBAs, a surprising number considering the hundreds of thousands of B-school alumni with enough experience to qualify them for top jobs. What's more, only 71 received MBAs from top 10 B-schools, and two-thirds of those executives have degrees from just three institutions: Harvard Business School, Stanford University's Graduate School of Business, and the University of Pennsylvania's Wharton School.

Headhunters say that while an MBA may help someone land a first job after graduation, the career benefits from that moment on are almost nonexistent. "In the pure Darwinian world we live in, pedigrees mean nothing," says Peter D. Crist, chairman of Crist Associates, a Hinsdale (Illinois) executive search firm. "It's instinct, it's hard work, and it's raw intelligence."

In such a world, a credential that makes people better managers should confer an evolutionary advantage. But *Business Week's* research calls that premise into question. An examination of company performance for 2002–2004 shows that outfits run by CEOs with MBAs do, in fact, have a modestly better return on equity than those run by non-MBAs. But median shareholder return for the MBA-run companies was significantly worse—7.4% versus 9.9% for outfits run by non-MBAs. Researchers at Pace University came to similar conclusions but went a step further. They examined the 2000–2002 performance of all companies listed on the New York Stock Exchange that were run by CEOs with U.S. undergraduate degrees and discovered that those with MBAs from top schools performed no better than those with less prestigious degrees. "If you go to Harvard, you're more likely to meet successful people who will enable you to do well," says Aron A. Gottesman, an associate finance professor at Pace. "You're not necessarily a better manager."

—Louis Lavelle

Can Your Relationship Survive B-School? (February 13, 2007)

There's a reason the MBA has earned a reputation as "the divorce degree."

B-school students are typically older than other professional degree seekers (27, on average), and a higher percentage of them (about one-third) are married or seriously committed. Some of them have children. That means that applying to B-school, and then to jobs, can be an emotional roller coaster for two. Combined with the financial strain of going from two paychecks to one (or none), the round-the-clock nature of a full-time MBA program—from morning classes to late-night pub crawls—can put serious stress on relationships.

Even dual-career households that are used to competing demands on their time can hit the skids when it comes to adjusting to a partner's new student schedule. And partners can start to resent students' "community building" activities when they're the ones getting up at 6 a.m. to go to work or get the kids off to school. "Sometimes you would like to be cheered for," says Heather Cody, whose husband, Preston, is a first-year student at the University of Texas at Austin. "But for two years you're the cheerleader for your student."

Being forced into a supporting role is psychologically burdensome for many partners, says Betsy Howell, a therapist and life coach who runs partner support groups at Dartmouth's Amos Tuck School of Business. "Women come here thinking, 'O.K., this is good for my husband's career. I'll come. I'll put up with it.' But then they become kind of angry, depressed, and upset because their dreams are all on hold and life is kind of circling around the husband."

To prevent frustrations from mounting into serious problems, Howell emphasizes that good communication is crucial. Setting aside a regular "date night" is a strategy that works for many couples, she says, as is making a "wish list" of activities they would like to do together. Many partners also say that getting involved in B-school events that are open to partners is a worthwhile experience. In the end, says Jennifer Jaax, wife of Grant, a second-year at UNC Kenan-Flagler, the experience is what you make of it: "It has been very challenging, but very eye-opening. Really, this has been two of the best years of my life."

—Kerry Miller

B-Schools: You Don't Have to Wait (August 7, 2006)

When Jonathan Bankard decided to apply to Harvard Business School last year, the Brown University senior heard the same thing from pretty much everyone: "You won't get in." After all, they told him, everybody knows you need years of full-time work experience to get into business school. But Bankard, who had worked or interned every summer since he was 13, been a teacher's assistant at two business courses at Brown, and founded his own start-up tech company, figured he might as well give it a shot, and his parents—and ultimately, Harvard—agreed.

Bankard's father had himself gone straight from undergraduate work to Harvard Business School back in 1966, when close to a third of his classmates did so as well. Things have changed a bit since then: not only do Harvard B-schoolers no longer wear suits to class, but students straight out of college make up only about 1% of enrollment there, as at most other top programs, where the average student has between four and six years of work experience. But that might not be the case for long.

While undergraduates applying to B-school is hardly a new phenomenon, now more schools, including Harvard, Stanford, Wharton, and Chicago, are making a greater effort to reach out to "early career" applicants with less than three years of work experience, including students like Bankard who apply directly from undergraduate programs. While the number of college seniors admitted to top B-schools is likely to remain a tiny percentage of the total (the University of Rochester is an exception), many admission directors hope the renewed focus on younger applicants will eventually help expand the entire applicant pool by bringing in more people (in particular, more women) applying one to three years into their careers.

One reason that work experience requirements have risen over the years—and the number of nonexperienced hires has dropped—is competition. Older applicants fetch higher salaries at graduation, and higher salaries often result in better rankings. Another reason is the changing nature of B-school education. As students became more experienced, B-schools came to rely less on teachers teaching students and more on students teaching each other. However, applying early often has benefits for individuals. Since early-career applicants generally draw smaller salaries than they will later in their careers, a break for B-school is less of a financial sacrifice. And, especially for women, it reduces the chances that career and family will be put in direct conflict. Companies, too, see benefits. Some top consulting firms and investment banks would rather see their entry-level analysts apply to B-school after two or three years instead of

For women, applying early reduces the chances that career and family will be put in direct conflict.

going elsewhere first to gain more experience, while other companies prefer hiring MBAs with only a few years of experience, before they've been molded to another company's corporate culture.

Since even the most academically gifted students may not be ready to begin an MBA program, many schools are using deferred admission programs to cherry-pick the best without sacrificing work experience. Harvard, Stanford, and MIT all have such programs. In 2005, the University of Texas's McCombs School of Business launched a new deferred admission program called Jump Start. Companies including Deloitte Consulting and JPMorgan Chase agree to hire the students for three years, and McCombs offers candidates deferred admission to the MBA program.

—Kerry Miller

MBA Applications Surge (August 15, 2007)

Demand for admission to U.S. graduate business schools has risen, and the growing number of applicants is entering what some say is the most competitive pool in recent years.

The Graduate Management Admissions Council (GMAC) reported Aug. 15 that applications to business schools are being buoyed by a confident outlook on the economy and increasing demand from employers for management degrees. In turn, schools are choosing from a pool of applicants who are equally or better qualified academically than last year's class. The majority of the group's member schools are in the U.S. Nearly three in five full-time master's and MBA programs reported that their applicants are of better quality than those seen last year, according to the GMAC survey.

Nearly two-thirds (64%) of full-time MBA programs reported an increase in application volume compared to 2006. The boom in applications mirrors an increase in registration volume for the GMAT—the B-school entrance exam—which this year jumped by 6.2% within the U.S. and 21% outside the U.S.

One of the key movers in the growing number of applicants is demographics, says Rachel Edgington, director of market research and analysis for GMAC. A cohort of students dubbed "millennials"—those from the generation born in or after 1982—fueled much of the growth in domestic applications this year, Edgington said. "This younger generation is a much larger pool then the past generation and they are starting to enter into the application pool," Edgington said. "Just in sheer size, they are much larger."

Fifty-six percent of full-time MBA programs said application volume from domestic candidates was up this year, a significant reversal from recent years where growth was flat. Applications from students abroad, particularly those in India and China, remain strong. India is fueling most of the growth in international applications seen by full-time programs in the U.S., with 64% of B-schools reporting India as the country from which they received the greatest number of applications.

Another area showing considerable growth is part-time MBA programs, where more than two in three programs reported an increase in applications over 2006. Women and minorities are driving the increase in part-time application volume, which is expected to continue.

—**Alison Damast**

More Crowding at Top B-Schools (February 4, 2007)

Rounds three and four are shaping up to be tough ones for this year's applicants to some top-ranked B-school programs. Admissions directors say that application volume is up, compared with recent years—as much as 30% at some schools. And several B-schools have announced that their classes this fall will be smaller than in years past.

New curriculum implementation at Stanford's Graduate School of Business and Yale School of Management means that both schools are accepting fewer applicants this year. Stanford Admissions Director Derrick Bolton says that the class size in the past few years has been around 378, but this year admissions will be bringing it back down to the official target size of 360. This is because of the extremely resource-intensive nature of the new curriculum, which includes small seminar classes and one-on-one advising. At Yale, Admissions Director Bruce Delmonico is aiming for a class size of 195. This includes 30 to 40 students who deferred from last year's class in order to take full advantage of the new curriculum.

But Stanford and Yale aren't the only schools where applicants might feel the pinch. At Virginia's Darden School, Assistant Director of Admissions Wendy Huber says that this year, admissions is aiming for a class size more on a par with previous years—310 to 315—compared with last year's larger-than-average class of about 332 students. Admissions Director Carol Swanberg says that Syracuse's Whitman School is downsizing to strengthen its class profile. And it won't take effect this year, but Columbia's business school is considering shrinking its class size by about 60 students for "various reasons."

—**Kerry Miller**

A Small B-School Can Be a Big Plus (January 22, 2007)

The advantages of going to a large business school in an urban area appear obvious to many applicants. After all, the thinking goes, big cities are where big business is done (not to mention the restaurants, the nightlife, and the healthy population of old college buddies to ease the transition). And a bigger school, it stands to reason, often means more of everything—more resources, more elective choices, more classmates with whom to network, and so on.

If that line of thinking sounds familiar—and admissions consultants such as Clear Admit's Graham Richmond say it's quite common—you might want to take a step back and consider that the experience of attending B-school in a town like Charlottesville, Virginia, Hanover, New Hampshire, or Ithaca, New York, has its own upside. While many of those advantages are of the more intangible variety (how do you put a value on school spirit?), satisfied alumni say that the small-town, small-school experience can bring big-time payoffs.

So what, exactly, is the small-school advantage? In a word: community. Students say it's easier to form close bonds with classmates at a small school like Tuck or UNC's Kenan-Flagler, where each graduating class is kept to under 300 people, compared with larger ones like Harvard and Wharton, where the graduating class size is roughly triple that. David Pyke, a Tuck professor and associate dean who has also taught at Wharton, says that smaller schools are more conducive to student-faculty interaction, for the same reason.

The more remote locations of small schools like Cornell and Darden can also be advantages—and not just because of the lower cost of living. The lack of outside distractions can give students a chance to immerse themselves more fully in the B-school experience. Says Richmond: "Spending two years in a place like Hanover really gives students the chance to unplug and devote themselves entirely to academic study and MBA community events."

It can be difficult for urban schools to instill a sense of community when students don't live on campus and have all the diversions of urban life, including existing social networks. When students have made the commitment to pack up their lives and move to "the middle of nowhere," they're typically more open to forging new bonds with classmates quickly, in part because they have fewer options. That sense of community often continues long after graduation, if alumni giving rates are any measure. At Tuck, for example, a hefty 65.1% of alumni donated this past year—more than double the giving rate at most top-ranked B-schools.

—**Kerry Miller**

B-SCHOOL BY THE NUMBERS

Salaries
Among ranked full-time MBA programs, domestic and international

Highest

School	Base Salary
IMD	$121,000
IESE Business School	$118,160
Stanford University	$117,681
Harvard University	$115,665
University of Pennsylvania	$110,550

Lowest

School	Base Salary
HEC Montréal	$67,500
University of Western Ontario	$79,800
University of Toronto	$83,067
University of Maryland	$83,165
University of Rochester	$84,137

Total Compensation
Base salary, signing bonus, and other guaranteed compensation
Among ranked full-time MBA programs, domestic and international

Highest

School	Total Compenstion
Stanford University	$209,407
Harvard University	$205,659
Columbia University	$181,448
Dartmouth University	$179,298
IMD	$171,000

Lowest

School	Total Compenstion
York University	$91,580
HEC Montréal	$95,235
University of Maryland	$96,914
Purdue University	$106,082
University of Toronto	$106,230

Post-MBA Pay Hike
Among ranked full-time MBA programs, domestic and international

Highest

School	% Increase
IESE	174.2
Michigan State	124.2
University of Notre Dame	117.1
Yale University	98
University of North Carolina at Chapel Hill	95.9

Lowest

School	% Increase
MIT	24.3
Columbia University	27.6
Harvard University	29
University of Pennsylvania	29.2
HEC Montréal	33.9

Selectivity
Among ranked full-time MBA programs, domestic and international

Most Selective

School	% of Applicants Accepted
Stanford University	7.9
University of California at Berkeley	14
Harvard University	14
Yale University	15
Columbia University	16

Least Selective

School	% of Applicants Accepted
Queen's University	65
HEC Montréal	62
ESADE	48
Vanderbilt University	47
University of Notre Dame	44

Annual Tuition and Fees

Among ranked two-year full-time MBA programs, domestic and international

Most Expensive

School	Tuition and Fees
University of Pennsylvania	$49,722
Harvard University	$48,738
Duke University	$46,622
Stanford University	$45,921
Carnegie Mellon University	$45,640

Least Expensive

Michigan State University	$26,358
York University	$28,500
Purdue University	$33,462
Indiana University	$34,850
University of Notre Dame	$37,145

Total Program Costs

Tuition, living expenses, and forgone salary for entire program
Among ranked full-time MBA programs, domestic and international

Most Expensive

School	Total Cost
Harvard University	$325,928
MIT	$318,336
University of Pennsylvania	$315,060
Columbia University	$315,008
London Business School	$307,508

Least Expensive

HEC Montréal	$89,535
University of Western Ontario	$140,125
Queen's University	$144,726
Michigan State University	$158,729
INSEAD	$159,730

Years to Recoup MBA Investment

Based on post-MBA pay hike and total program cost
Among ranked full-time MBA programs, domestic and international

Fastest Return

School	Years to Pay Back
IESE Business School	2.3
Michigan State University	3.3
University of Notre Dame	3.9
IMD	4.0
York University	4.3

Slowest Return

School	Years to Pay Back
MIT	15.1
Columbia University	13.6
University of Pennsylvania	12.6
Harvard University	12.5
Cornell University	11

STILL CAN'T DECIDE?

Get more insight with the award-winning resources of the BusinessWeek B-Schools Channel.

CUSTOMIZE YOUR SEARCH
- Compare B-schools based on criteria you select using interactive tables.

TAP INTO YOUR COMMUNITY
- Connect with thousands of other applicants, students, and alumni.
- Chat with BusinessWeek editors in live Q&A sessions.
- Hear what school is really like from MBA bloggers.

DIG INTO THE DETAILS
- Scan exclusive rankings of the top full-time, part-time, and executive MBA programs.
- Get application tips and interview techniques from admissions officers.

Go to businessweek.com/bschools/

Babson College

F. W. Olin Graduate School of Business
2006 Ranking: Second tier (U.S.)
231 Forest St.
Babson Park, MA 02457
E-mail address:
    mbaadmissions@babson.edu
Web address: www3.babson.edu/mba/
For more info: Call the main
    switchboard at (781) 239-4317

☑ B4UGO

Applicants accepted: 57%
Average GMAT score: 631
Average years' work experience: 4.9
Average post-MBA salary increase:
    66.3%
Average total first-year
    compensation: $116,634

Why Babson?

While not an elite Top 30 program, Babson is widely regarded as the premier school for entrepreneurship studies, with innovation and entrepreneurial thinking informing every aspect of the program. While many graduates go on to lead start-up ventures, many others use the entrepreneurial skills honed here to succeed in a corporate environment. Stressing the practical application of business ideas, the first-year curriculum is built around a series of four cross-disciplinary "modules" designed to hone basic skills. As part of one module, students work with artists in fields such as music, writing, sculpture, and dance to get their creative juices flowing. In the second year, students can choose from more than 80 electives. Selected courses, known as "intensive electives," can be completed in just three days of highly concentrated study.

Babson is a private institution. Established in 1951, Babson's full-time MBA program is accredited by the Association to Advance Collegiate Schools of Business (AACSB). Babson also offers a part-time MBA program.

Headlines

April 30, 2007: Babson investment team wins CFA Institute's Global Investment Challenge

April 11, 2007: President Brian Barefoot to step down in 2008

February 9, 2007: Babson business incubator accepts 12 student start-up projects

November 15, 2006: Babson partners with B-school in Brazil

"I would highly recommend Babson to anyone."

Famous MBA Alumni

Robert Davis, former CEO of Lycos, managing general partner at Highland Capital Partners

William D. Green, chairman and CEO of Accenture

James Palermo, vice chairman of Mellon Financial Corp.

 Who Are My Classmates?

Full-time enrollment: 409
Women: 29%
International: 33%
Minority: 24%
Average age: 28
Accepted applicants enrolled: 49%

"The faculty exceeded my expectations."

The 411

Annual tuition and fees: $34,240
Annual living expenses: $22,733
Total program cost, including forgone salary: $221,368
Classes begin: September
Application deadlines: Mid-January (international), Mid-April (U.S.)
Application fee: $100

Cliff Notes

Leading areas of study: Consulting, Entrepreneurship, General Management, International Business, Marketing
Average class size, core courses: 52
Average class size, electives: 28
Number of electives: 84
Teaching methods: Case studies (55%), team projects (35%), lectures (5%), simulations (5%)

But What's It *Really* Like?

Graded by students:
Overall ranking: **B**
Teaching quality: **A**
Career services: **C**

Graded by recruiters:
Overall ranking: **B**
Accounting: **A**
Analytical skills: **A**
Communication: **A**
Finance: **B**
General management: **A**
International business: **B**
Marketing: **A**
Operations/production: **A**
Teamwork skills: **A**

Bling

Average pre-MBA salary: $53,711
Average post-MBA salary: $89,315
Graduates with job offer by graduation: 80%
Companies recruiting on campus: 46
Top functional areas for graduates: Consulting, Finance/Accounting, General Management
Biggest recruiters: Irving Oil, Fidelity, EMC, Ocean Spray, Devonshire Investors

The Good, the Bad, and the Ugly: Students Speak Out

"Babson is an incredible place; people are collaborative, innovative, and pleasant to be around. I would highly recommend it to anyone."

"A relative weakness of the program is the career office. They've overhauled it recently, and I think the changes will eventually bear fruit, but for this year the recruiting and job placement weren't as quick as many had hoped."

"Recruiting and job placement weren't as quick as many had hoped."

"My experience at Babson opened my eyes to careers that were off my radar prior to my MBA. Babson sparked my love for entrepreneurship, the understanding of the company as a whole, from birth to transition, and from product or service to management. I learned more than I expected to learn, and the social network was outstanding."

"The faculty greatly exceeded my expectations in their real-world experience with business and their willingness to commit time outside of class to their students. Even now, months after graduation, I am in contact with professors who are always happy to give direction and advice."

"Having come from a teaching background, I have been particularly impressed by Babson's innovative curriculum. Professors teach cases in pairs during the first year, providing a well-rounded perspective on the issues of the day. In addition, students engage in consulting projects that run in parallel with the learning experience. Above all, the spirit of entrepreneurship here is incredible! Babson develops an irrepressible culture of venture creation and provides attainable models of success through its faculty and alumni."

"I think Babson is the leader in integrated curriculum and getting students to think holistically about how operations, finance, accounting, and marketing affect one another."

"Babson has a great reputation in the Boston area. Unfortunately, that reputation has not expanded across the United States, which has made job searching with global companies more difficult."

"Every company I've interviewed with has an appreciation for the creative, outside-the-box thought process that Babson students possess. Babson produces students that can excel in virtually every business situation while a number of the top programs produce cookie-cutter thinkers to fill the ranks of the McKinseys and Goldman Sachses of the world."

 **Where to Stay**

Courtyard by Marriott
342 Speen St.
Natick, MA 01760
(508) 655-6100

Hampton Inn
319 Speen St.
Natick, MA 01760
(508) 623-5000

Doubletree Guest Suites
550 Winter St.
Waltham, MA 02451
(781) 890-6767

 Where to Eat

China Sky
11 Forest St.
Wellesley, MA 02481
(781) 431-2388

Legal Sea Foods
50-60 Worcester Rd.
Framingham, MA 01702
(508) 766-0600

Bertucci's (Italian-American)
150 Worcester Rd.
Framingham, MA 01702
(508) 879-9161

 Things to Do

Danforth Museum of Art
123 Union Ave.
Framingham, MA 01702
(508) 620-0050

Roger's Pub
Park Manor Central on campus
Babson Park, MA 02457
(781) 239-5500

CHECK OUT BUSINESSWEEK.COM FOR MORE:

Admissions Q&A: Babson's dean of graduate admissions, Kate Klepper, describes what it takes to get your foot in the door.

Video View: Dean Mark Rice discusses the changing face of entrepreneurship studies at Babson.

B-School Blogs: Check in with MBA student bloggers from Babson.

Search & Compare: Conduct a side-by-side analysis of the schools on your short list to see how Babson stacks up.

Expanded Profile: More Babson facts and stats.

Access all the B-schools content on BusinessWeek.com by subscribing to MBA Insider.

Carnegie Mellon University

David A. Tepper School of Business
2006 Ranking: 16 (U.S.)
5000 Forbes Ave.
Pittsburgh, PA 15213
E-mail address:
   Mba-admissions@andrew.cmu.edu
Web address: www.tepper.cmu.edu
For more info: Call MBA admissions at
   (412) 268-2272

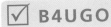

B4UGO

Applicants accepted: 30%
Average GMAT score: 696
Average years' work experience: 4.2
Average post-MBA salary increase:
   62.2%*
Average total first-year
   compensation: $131,648
*Based in part on *BusinessWeek* survey data.

Why Carnegie Mellon?

A perennial member of the top 20 MBA programs, Tepper is known for the intensity, focus, and diligence of its students and faculty. Tepper distinguishes itself with popular finance and marketing programs and its small, intimate class structure. Innovation is a buzzword here. Dean Ken Dunn encourages students to embrace Tepper's interdisciplinary approach to learning, which includes such innovations as a "management game" that simulates the multifaceted task of managing a real company in real time. Tepper provides a reliable investment in its students' futures—90% of students get job offers before graduation, along with a median post-MBA salary approaching $100,000. That's on a par with many higher-ranked schools.

Carnegie Mellon University is a private institution. Established in 1949, Tepper's full-time MBA program is accredited by the Association to Advance Collegiate Schools of Business (AACSB). Tepper also offers part-time and executive MBA programs. For details on Tepper's part-time MBA program, see page 321.

 Headlines

May 18, 2007: Kenneth B. Dunn reappointed to second five-year term as dean

January 3, 2007: Tepper announces new PNC professorship in computational finance

October 19, 2006: Average GMAT score for new MBA students hits all-time high: 696

October 11, 2006: Bosch Institute endows five new faculty chairs at Tepper

---

"An exceptional finance program with great faculty."

Famous MBA Alumni

Paul Allaire, former chairman and CEO of Xerox

David Coulter, former chairman and CEO of Bank of America

Larry Kurzweil, president and COO of Universal Studios Hollywood

 ## Who Are My Classmates?

Full-time enrollment: 319
Women: 25%
International: 32%
Minority: 43%
Average age: 28
Accepted applicants enrolled: 46%

"The thing that I enjoyed most was the collaborative atmosphere."

The 411

Annual tuition and fees: $45,640
Annual living expenses: $20,360
Total program cost, including forgone salary: $252,102*
Classes begin: August
Application deadlines: None
Application fee: $100

*Based in part on *BusinessWeek* survey data.

Cliff Notes

Leading areas of study: Entrepreneurship, Finance, Manufacturing and Technology, Management, Marketing, Strategy
Average class size, core courses: 82
Average class size, electives: 30
Number of electives: 142
Teaching methods: Lectures (50%), case studies (25%), simulations (15%)

But What's It *Really* Like?

Graded by students:
Overall ranking: **B**
Teaching quality: **A**
Career services: **B**

Graded by recruiters:
Overall ranking: **A**
Accounting: **C**
Analytical skills: **B**
Communication: **C**
Finance: **B**
General management: **C**
International business: **C**
Marketing: **C**
Operations/production: **A+**
Teamwork skills: **B**

 ## Bling

Average pre-MBA salary: $60,051*
Average post-MBA salary: $97,394
Graduates with job offer by graduation: 90%
Top functional areas for graduates: Finance/Accounting, Consulting, Marketing/Sales
Biggest recruiters: Booz Allen Hamilton, Deloitte, Merck & Co., A.T. Kearny, Constellation Energy Group

*Estimate based on *BusinessWeek* survey data.

The Good, the Bad, and the Ugly: Students Speak Out

"Carnegie Mellon has an exceptional finance program with great faculty, and it also happens to have a great reputation among financial firms. My personal experience has helped cement that belief as well."

"The Tepper experience has been unbelievable—beyond my wildest expectations. I'd recommend it to anyone who would listen to me."

"The Tepper School of Business offers a superb experience, with intimate classes and a vast array of opportunities. Although Pittsburgh may not be the cultural epicenter of the world, the environment at Tepper allows students to grow, explore, and, more than anything, devote time to professional development."

> ## "The small size limits the variety of classes."

"One area I feel the school could improve is by creating a slightly more flexible academic schedule—now that the class size is much smaller. Some classes should definitely be longer than one quarter. The mini system has plenty of merits, but it is not the only way."

"Pittsburgh isn't exactly the best city in the nation, in my opinion (though the beer here is really cheap). But the campus itself is beautiful."

"The thing that I enjoyed most about CMU was the collaborative atmosphere. All classmates are your friends and can be counted on for support whenever needed. Everyone is trying to help each other."

"The MBA experience at Tepper was filled with surprising discoveries about myself, others, and the world we live in. It was an extremely rewarding experience that went by in a flash but has left me changed forever."

"The study-abroad opportunity is exceptional. Tepper partners with a top-notch business school in Germany to give Tepper students a well-rounded international education. Applying to the study-abroad program is highly recommended."

"For most career tracks, the program offers great opportunity to gain valuable tools. However, the small size limits the variety of classes. While I would recommend the program to most candidates, I don't think it will satisfy every possible career aspiration."

"The Tepper School of Business works hard to incorporate technology into its curriculum, but falls short."

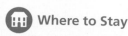 **Where to Stay**

Wyndham Garden Hotel
3454 Forbes Ave.
Pittsburgh, PA 15213
(412) 683-2040

Holiday Inn at University Center
100 Lytton Ave.
Pittsburgh, PA 15213
(412) 682-6200

Residence Inn by Marriott
3896 Bigelow Blvd.
Pittsburgh, PA 15213
(412) 621-2200

 Where to Eat

Primanti Brothers Restaurant (American)
3803 Forbes Ave.
Pittsburgh, PA 15213
(412) 621-4444

Mad Mex (Tex-Mex)
370 Atwood St.
Pittsburgh, PA 15213
(412) 681-5656

Aladdin's Eatery (Middle Eastern)
5878 Forbes Ave.
Pittsburgh, PA 15217
(412) 421-5100

 Things to Do

Pittsburgh Zoo & PPG Aquarium
One Wild Place
Pittsburgh, PA 15206
(412) 665-3640

The Andy Warhol Museum
117 Sandusky St.
Pittsburgh, PA 15212
(412) 237-8300

CHECK OUT BUSINESSWEEK.COM FOR MORE:

Admissions Q&A: Laurie Stewart, executive director of MBA admissions, on what makes an applicant Tepper material.

Interview Tips: Get the lowdown on what it takes to land a spot at Tepper.

Video View: Dean Kenneth Dunn discusses his plans for Tepper.

Search & Compare: Find out how Tepper stacks up against other top schools.

Expanded Profile: Find more stats and facts on Tepper in the school's online profile.

Access all the B-schools content on BusinessWeek.com by subscribing to MBA Insider.

Columbia University

Columbia Business School
2006 Ranking: 10 (U.S.)
216 Uris Hall
3022 Broadway
New York, NY 10027
E-mail address:
   apply@gsb.columbia.edu
Web address: www.gsb.columbia.edu
For more info: Call the main
   switchboard at (212) 854-5553

 **B4UGO**

Applicants accepted: 16%
Average GMAT score: N/A
Average years' work experience: 4.8
Average post-MBA salary increase:
   27.6%*
Average total first-year
   compensation: $181,448

*Based in part on *BusinessWeek* survey data.

Why Columbia?

Widely recognized for excellence in entrepreneurship, finance, general management, and international business, Columbia's location gives students ample opportunity to network in New York City, one of the world's premiere business capitals. This pays off during recruiting season, when students are wooed by the financial giants and top consulting firms that call the city home. Two years after taking over as dean in 2004, Glenn Hubbard introduced an innovative program in Social Intelligence designed to enhance students' leadership abilities. And in 2008, there will be a new curriculum. Half the core will be replaced by a new "flexible core"—in management, economics, or operations—allowing students to pursue career interests as part of their required courses.

Columbia University is a private institution. Established in 1916, Columbia's full-time MBA program is accredited by the Association to Advance Collegiate Schools of Business (AACSB). Columbia also offers an executive MBA program. For details on Columbia's executive MBA program, see page 213.

 Headlines

May 25, 2007: Columbia graduate wins $100,000 in seed capital

May 9, 2007: Collaboration with Harlem Children's Zone announced

August 16, 2006: Columbia launches Social Intelligence program

May 11, 2006: Three alumni pledge $45 million for curriculum and faculty development

---

"Dean Hubbard is shaking things up."

Famous MBA Alumni

Sallie L. Krawcheck, chair and CEO of Citigroup Wealth Management

Rochelle "Shelly" Lazarus, chair and CEO of Ogilvy & Mather Worldwide

Henry Kravis, founding partner of Kohlberg Kravis Roberts & Co.

 Who Are My Classmates?

Full-time enrollment: 1,220
Women: 33%
International: 40%
Minority: 26%
Average age: 28
Accepted applicants enrolled: 77%

> *"I had some excellent professors and a few who were not worth my time."*

The 411

Annual tuition and fees: $43,908
Annual living expenses: $29,556
Total program cost, including forgone salary: $315,008*
Classes begin: September
Application deadlines: March (International), April (U.S.)
Application fee: $250

*Based in part on *BusinessWeek* survey data.

Cliff Notes

Leading areas of study: Consulting, Entrepreneurship, Finance, General Management, Strategy
Average class size, core courses: 65
Average class size, electives: 44
Number of electives: 146
Teaching methods: Case studies (40%), lectures (40%), team projects (15%)

But What's It *Really* Like?

Graded by students:
Overall ranking: **A**
Teaching quality: **B**
Career services: **A**

Graded by recruiters:
Overall ranking: **A+**
Accounting: **A+**
Analytical skills: **A+**
Communication: **A+**
Finance: **A+**
General management: **A+**
International business: **A+**
Marketing: **B**
Operations/production: **A**
Teamwork skills: **A**

 Bling

Average pre-MBA salary: $84,040*
Average post-MBA salary: $107,265
Graduates with job offer by graduation: 88%
Top functional areas for graduates: Finance/Accounting, Consulting, Marketing/Sales
Biggest recruiters: McKinsey, Citigroup, Goldman Sachs, Deutsche Bank, Booz Allen Hamilton, JP Morgan Chase
*Estimate based on *BusinessWeek* survey data.

((•)) The Good, the Bad, and the Ugly: Students Speak Out

"The administration is generally open to hearing what students have to stay. They support our efforts and help us effect change."

"If you want to work in New York, there is no better place to go to school. You have a distinct advantage over any other school, provided you can capitalize on the exposure."

"My experience with core classes was definitely mixed. I had some truly excellent professors who made me glad I was spending the money I was, and I had a few who were so bad they were simply not worth my time."

"Core classes are a little hit-or-miss."

"Dean Hubbard has brought a fresh mindset and new perspective to the school, which was needed after 15 years under the previous dean. He is shaking things up, which is good, and he's making some great improvements."

"The professors were outstanding and there were far too many opportunities to even take advantage of."

"The student body is very individualistic. Despite school efforts to build community, the 'I' is more prevalent than the 'we.'"

"In addition to having top-quality guest speakers, we have a large base of adjunct professors who teach courses while working. One of my professors, for example, was the chief investment officer at one of the largest hedge funds in the world. He held office hours at his office in midtown Manhattan."

"Columbia's greatest asset, access to New York City, is also one of its greatest liabilities. Everyone is extremely proud of the school, but nobody likes to stick around after classes, as there is always so much to do in the city."

"Columbia has a wonderful group of diverse and intelligent students that make the school a very special place. So many people help others unselfishly and without hesitation."

"Core classes are a little hit-or-miss. I would like to see a greater global focus because the current curriculum is still very much U.S.-centric."

"The electives available for second year students are magnificient. Many of the topics are very advanced and tailored for specific industries."

"Before Columbia, my world was finance, and I did not even give a second thought to other industries. After my MBA, I feel as if my eyes have been opened to the rest of the world."

Where to Stay

The Lucerne Hotel
76th St. & Amsterdam Ave.
New York, NY 10024
(212) 875-1000

On the Ave Hotel
2178 Broadway
New York, NY 10016
(212) 362-1100

The Belleclaire Hotel
250 W. 75th St.
New York, NY 10024
(212) 362-7700

 Where to Eat

Dinosaur Bar-B-Q
646 W. 131st St.
New York, NY 10027
(212) 694-1777

Le Monde
2885 Broadway
New York, NY 10025
(212) 531-3939

Meridiana
2756 Broadway
New York, NY 10025
(212) 222-4453

 Things to Do

Madame Tussauds Wax Museum
234 W. 42nd St.
New York, NY 10036
(800) 246-8872

Top of the Rock
30 Rockefeller Center
New York, NY 10020
(212) 698-2000

CHECK OUT BUSINESSWEEK.COM FOR MORE:

Admissions Q&A: Linda Meehan, director of MBA admissions, describes the ideal Columbia applicant.

Sample Application Essays and Interview Tips: Get the lowdown on what it takes to get in.

Careers Q&A: Columbia's Regina Resnick on matching students with the right companies.

Search & Compare: Do a side-by-side analysis of Columbia versus other top B-schools.

School Tour: Check out the campus before planning your visit.

Access all the B-schools content on BusinessWeek.com by subscribing to MBA Insider.

Cornell University

Johnson Graduate School of
   Management
2006 Ranking: 13 (U.S.)
111 Sage Hall
Ithaca, NY 14850
E-mail address: mba@cornell.edu
Web address: www.johnson.cornell.edu
For more info: Call the admissions
   office at (607) 255-4526

☑ B4UGO

Applicants accepted: 25%
Average GMAT score: 680
Average years' work experience: 4.8
Average post-MBA salary increase:
   34.2%
**Average total first-year
   compensation:** $143,272

Why Cornell?

Cornell's highly respected full-time MBA program attracts a student body with a diverse set of qualifications. This program is particularly popular with career changers. Some top areas of study are consulting, finance, entrepreneurship, and portfolio management. A highly selective school, Johnson chooses 30 exceptional candidates to participate in the Park Leadership Fellows Program, which pays for tuition and expenses. Cornell is located in charming Ithaca, a city with weekly farmer's markets and small downtown shops. Without the distractions of big city life, students form closer relationships and a more meaningful alumni network, making it easier to find a job after graduation. "Johnson School is a tight community where you know all [the students] in your class, not just the 50 or so in your specific cohort," one student writes.

The Johnson School is a private institution. Established in 1946, its full-time MBA program is accredited by the Association to Advance Collegiate Schools of Business (AACSB). The Johnson School also offers an executive MBA program. For details of Cornell's executive MBA program, see page 217.

 ## Headlines

June 14, 2007: Joe Thomas named interim dean for Johnson School

April 11, 2007: Cornell launches joint business-engineering program

September 29, 2005: Johnson receives top national Hispanic education award

September 12, 2005: Alumni give $1.5 million, up 15%; participation rate tops 26%

> *"The facilities and infrastructure are superlative."*

Famous MBA Alumni

Jim Morgan, chairman and CEO of Applied Materials, Inc.

Rich Marin, chairman and CEO of Bear Stearns Asset Management

H. Fisk Johnson, chairman and CEO of S.C. Johnson

 ## Who Are My Classmates?

Full-time enrollment: 565
Women: 28%
International: 26%
Minority: 33%
Average age: 27
Accepted applicants enrolled: 49%

"The collaborative community still amazes me."

The 411

Annual tuition and fees: $42,700
Annual living expenses: $21,260
Total program cost, including forgone salary: $273,910
Classes begin: August
Application deadlines: October 10 to March 19
Application fee: $200

Cliff Notes

Leading areas of study: Consulting, Entrepreneurship, Finance, Marketing, Portfolio Management
Average class size, core courses: 70
Average class size, electives: 35
Number of electives: 106
Teaching methods: Lectures (30%), case studies (30%), team projects (20%)

But What's It *Really* Like?

Graded by students:
Overall ranking: A
Teaching quality: A
Career services: A

Graded by recruiters:
Overall ranking: A
Accounting: C
Analytical skills: A
Communication: A
Finance: A
General management: B
International business: B
Marketing: A
Operations/production: C
Teamwork skills: A+

 ## Bling

Average pre-MBA salary: $72,995
Average post-MBA salary: $97,985
Graduates with job offer by graduation: 90%
Top functional areas for graduates: Finance/Accounting, Marketing/Sales, Consulting
Biggest recruiters: Citigroup, General Electric, Deloitte Consulting, JP Morgan, McKinsey, Microsoft

The Good, the Bad, and the Ugly: Students Speak Out

"The students at Johnson came from incredibly diverse backgrounds. I found those experiences enriching in a way that students from more homogenous schools could never understand. I was on projects with people who were as likely to have worked in the Peace Corps as on Wall Street."

"In terms of challenges, location is the largest challenge for Johnson and recruitment. The school is working hard to address this and create a long-term sustainable pipeline for students. I obtained my nontraditional MBA job through the alumni network. I found the alumni to be an amazing resource."

> *"Location is the largest challenge for Johnson and recruitment."*

"I came to the school with a lot of expectations, and most of these have been met. In several cases, the school has far exceeded them. The facilities and infrastructure available in Sage Hall are superlative and unsurpassed, in my opinion. The school fosters a very team-driven environment while equally stressing leadership and individual achievement."

"My only concern—that making connections with investment banks from Ithaca would be difficult—proved to be unfounded. We've got alumni all over Wall Street, and our connections are improving."

"I am glad I went to a school in a small community like Ithaca. Speaking with friends at big city schools, I know my classmates and I formed stronger bonds than they did. Those bonds should influence better connections throughout our careers."

"While overall very positive, I think that there are opportunities for improvement in the core, specifically in the Managing and Leading Organizations class. I saw a hodgepodge of topics with no common theme other than that they were research areas in which the professor specialized."

"The collaborative community at the Johnson School still amazes me. I have never experienced that kind of help and support from everyone anywhere else."

"The excellent research facilities, accessibility of faculty, very collaborative environment, student-run hedge fund, and student-run venture capital fund make Cornell's MBA program an excellent choice."

"I could not have asked for a better experience than the one I had at Cornell. The faculty is topnotch, students are friendly and outgoing, the facilities are nice, and I had numerous job opportunities."

Where to Stay

The Statler Hotel
130 Statler Dr.
Ithaca, NY 14853
(800) 541-2501

A Comfort Woods Guesthouse
971 Comfort Rd.
Danby, NY 14883
(607) 277-1620

Annie's Garden Bed & Breakfast
220 Pearl St.
Ithaca, NY 14850
(607) 273-0888

 Where to Eat

Blue Stone Bar & Grill
110 N. Aurora St.
Ithaca, NY 14850
(607) 272-2371

Asian Noodle House (Chinese)
204 Dryden Rd.
Ithaca, NY 14850
(607) 272-9106

Sangam Indian Curry
Downtown Ithaca Commons
Ithaca, NY 14850
(607) 272-6716

 Things to Do

Taughannock Falls State Park
Rte. 89
Trumansburg, NY 14886
(800) 456-CAMP

King Ferry Winery
Cayuga Wine Trail
King Ferry, NY 13081
(315) 364-5100

CHECK OUT BUSINESSWEEK.COM FOR MORE:

Admissions Q&A: Randall Sawyer, director of admissions, talks about what makes a good fit at the Johnson School and offers advice on when to apply.

Sample Application Essay and Interview Tips: Read a sample essay that worked for a Johnson applicant, and learn how to ace the interview.

School Tour: See what life at Cornell is like through this photo essay.

MBA Journal: The Cornell MBA experience—from application through the recruiting process—through the eyes of a student.

Video View: Former Dean Bob Swieringa discusses business and technology.

Financial Aid Q&A: Ann Richards, financial aid director, discusses costs, scholarships, fellowships, and sponsorships.

Access all the B-schools content on BusinessWeek.com by subscribing to MBA Insider.

Dartmouth College

Amos Tuck School of Business
  Administration
2006 Ranking: 11 (U.S.)
100 Tuck Hall
Hanover, NH 03755
E-mail address:
  tuck.admissions@dartmouth.edu
Web address:
  www.tuck.dartmouth.edu
For more info: Call the admissions
  office at (603) 646-3162

Why Dartmouth?

Dartmouth's internationally renowned full-time MBA program is the choice of those who want a solid business foundation in a close-knit community. While Tuck offers a general management curriculum to all its students, the leading areas of focus are accounting, consulting, finance, and marketing. The 32-week core, longer than most other MBAs, features courses in decision making, leadership, and management communication, while 75 electives allow students to tailor the program to their interests. The highly selective school boasts small classes that create a personal learning experience in a friendly environment. The campus, nestled in the hills of New Hampshire, is "perfect for the person who wants to be able to play outside when they aren't hitting the books," as one student observes.

☑ B4UGO

Applicants accepted: 19%
Average GMAT score: 713
Average years' work experience: 5.3
Average post-MBA salary increase: 76.9%
Average total first-year compensation: $179,298

Dartmouth College is a private institution. Established in 1900, Tuck's full-time MBA program is accredited by the Association to Advance Collegiate Schools of Business (AACSB).

 ## Headlines

March 26, 2007: Paul Danos reappointed for a fourth term as dean

February 13, 2007: Societal leadership program added to MBA curriculum

February 17, 2006: Tuck launches European initiative to attract international students

October 4, 2005: Tuck raises $100,000 for Hurricane Katrina disaster relief

"The small size makes the experience special."

Famous MBA Alumni

Peter Dolan, former CEO of Bristol-Myers Squibb

Jeffrey Swartz, president and CEO of Timberland Co.

Steve Roth, chairman and CEO of Vornado Realty Trust

 Who Are My Classmates?

Full-time enrollment: 500
Women: 35%
International: 36%
Minority: 25%
Average age: 28
Accepted applicants enrolled: 51%

"Our professors are leaders in their fields and always take time with students."

The 411

Annual tuition and fees: $43,293
Annual living expenses: $25,507
Total program cost, including forgone salary: $259,000
Classes begin: September
Application deadlines: October to April
Application fee: $220

Cliff Notes

Leading areas of study: Accounting, Consulting, Finance, Marketing, Strategy
Average class size, core courses: 60
Average class size, electives: 34
Number of electives: 75
Teaching methods: Case studies (50%), lectures (23%), team projects (20%)

But What's It *Really* Like?

Graded by students:
Overall ranking: **A**
Teaching quality: **A+**
Career services: **A**

Graded by recruiters:
Overall ranking: **A**
Accounting: **B**
Analytical skills: **A**
Communication: **A**
Finance: **B**
General management: **A**
International business: **A**
Marketing: **A**
Operations/production: **B**
Teamwork skills: **A+**

Bling

Average pre-MBA salary: $60,700
Average post-MBA salary: $107,406
Graduates with job offer by graduation: 96%
Top functional areas for graduates: Finance/Accounting, Consulting, Marketing/Sales, General Management
Biggest recruiters: McKinsey, Lehman Brothers, Bain, Beacon Capital Partners, Oliver Wyman

The Good, the Bad, and the Ugly: Students Speak Out

"The overall balance is excellent. The small size makes the experience special [and] the accessibility of faculty is amazing as well. The career office is always helpful with great advice. And the great alumni network is always there to help you."

"Tuck is an amazing place. However, it is a Petri dish socially to the point that it can become unhealthy. With no other outlet besides your classmates (because of the location in a small college town), it can be overwhelming."

"I was amazed by the quality and support of the rest of the community for those of us with kids—it made Tuck a lot easier to get through!"

"Tuck is a Petri dish socially to the point that it can become unhealthy."

"I believe that Hanover, New Hampshire, is a huge asset to Tuck, as living there allows you to focus on learning and getting to know your classmates, two of the most important aspects of an MBA experience."

"Our professors are leaders in their fields, and always take time to speak with students and nurture their learning."

"The small school with a smaller outreach of employers has not worked well for my job search, as I am still looking for a job. I believe the smaller size/scale also affects the academic caliber of a school."

"If you're looking to improve your overall leadership abilities and develop solid interpersonal and academic business skills to be the best business leader you can be, then there's no other choice but Tuck."

"The career development office relies too much on the fact that Tuck has outstanding and responsive alumni and does not generate many new opportunities."

"I think the connection with my classmates and other generations of graduates is the thing I will take away. I loved my experience and would recommend it to anyone."

"Tuck has been a transformative experience. The strong general management core combined with leadership training has made me ready to tackle almost anything."

Where to Stay

The Hanover Inn
2 S. Main St. (on campus)
Hanover, NH 03755
(603) 643-4300

Courtyard by Marriott
10 Morgan Dr.
Lebanon, NH 03766
(800) 321-2211

The Hampton Inn
104 Ballardvale Dr.
White River Junction, VT 05001
(802) 296-2800

 Where to Eat

Canoe Club
27 S. Main St.
Hanover, NH 03755
(603) 643-9660

Lou's Restaurant
30 S. Main St.
Hanover, NH 03755
(603) 643-3321

Murphy's Ón The Green
11 S. Main St.
Hanover, NH 03755
(603) 643-4075

 Things to Do

Dartmouth Skiway
39 Grafton Tpke.
Lyme Center, NH 03769
(603) 795-2143

Hood Museum of Art
6034 E. Wheelock St.
Hanover, NH 03755
(603) 646-2808

CHECK OUT BUSINESSWEEK.COM FOR MORE:

Placement Q&A: Richard McNulty, director of career development, on what makes Tuck graduates stand out.

Video View: Dean Paul Danos talks about early admissions and new classes on ethics and job hunting.

Admissions Q&A: Admissions director Kristine Laca talks about reapplication, GMAT scores, and postgraduation work experience.

Sample Application Essays and Interview Tips: Read sample essays that worked for Tuck applicants and find out how to ace the interview.

School Tour: Discover what life is like at Dartmouth through photos.

Access all the B-schools content on BusinessWeek.com by subscribing to MBA Insider.

Duke University

Fuqua School of Business
2006 Ranking: 9 (U.S.)
One Towerview Dr.
Durham, NC 27708
E-mail address:
admissions-info@fuqua.duke.edu
Web address: www.fuqua.duke.edu
For more info: Call MBA admissions at
(919) 660-7700

 **B4UGO**

Applicants accepted: 31%
Average GMAT score: 690
Average years' work experience: 5.4
Average post-MBA salary increase:
85.5%
**Average total first-year
compensation:** $147,997

Why Duke?

Duke's full-time MBA is one of the South's leading programs. Recruiters rave about graduates' communication, teamwork, and analytical skills, while students give the program high marks for teaching quality and career services. With nearly a dozen specializations—including international business and corporate social responsibility—the program sends the bulk of its graduates on to jobs in the financial services, consulting, and consumer products industries. Unlike those in other programs, Duke's courses are taught in six-week terms, allowing students to take five or more electives by the end of their first year—an advantage when applying for summer internships. The arrangement permits students to explore, without sacrificing face time with faculty. Students average more than five years of work experience, and graduate with jobs paying close to $100,000 a year.

Duke University is a private institution. Established in 1962, Fuqua's full-time MBA program is accredited by the Association to Advance Collegiate Schools of Business (AACSB). Fuqua also offers a global executive MBA program. For details on the executive MBA program, see page 221.

 ## Headlines

April 27, 2007: 34 first-year students disciplined in cheating scandal

February 20, 2007: Duke to receive $10 million for financial aid

January 10, 2007: Duke University names Blair Sheppard new dean of Fuqua

October 12, 2005: Duke announces exchange program with Chinese B-school

"The program has been everything I expected and more."

Famous MBA Alumni

Kerrii Anderson, president and CEO of Wendy's International
Melinda Gates, co-chair of the Bill & Melinda Gates Foundation
Mary Minnick, executive vice president and president of marketing, strategy, and innovation for Coca-Cola

Who Are My Classmates?

Full-time enrollment: 826
Women: 36%
International: 40%
Minority: 32%
Average age: 29
Accepted applicants enrolled: 46%

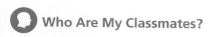

"Fuqua is clearly experiencing some growing pains."

The 411

Annual tuition and fees: $46,622
Annual living expenses: $15,950
Total program cost, including forgone salary: $230,154
Classes begin: September
Application deadlines: November 1, January 3, March 3
Application fee: $185

Cliff Notes

Leading areas of study: Entrepreneurship, Finance, General Management, Leadership, Marketing
Average class size, core courses: 66
Average class size, electives: 45
Number of electives: 90
Teaching methods: Case studies (30%), lectures (30%), team projects (20%)

But What's It *Really* Like?

Graded by students:
Overall ranking: A+
Teaching quality: A+
Career services: A+

Graded by recruiters:
Overall ranking: A+
Accounting: B
Analytical skills: A+
Communication: A+
Finance: A+
General management: A+
International business: A
Marketing: A+
Operations/production: A
Teamwork skills: A+

Bling

Average pre-MBA salary: $52,505
Average post-MBA salary: $97,384
Graduates with job offer by graduation: 87%
Top functional areas for graduates: Marketing/Sales, Finance/Accounting, Consulting
Biggest recruiters: Johnson & Johnson, Bank of America, Deloitte Consulting, McKinsey, Accenture, Citigroup

"All of the deans have an open-door policy and sometimes have open lunches in the cafeteria. They really have a handle on the pulse of the school and work quickly to remedy any issues that occur."

"Leaving Fuqua, I think I have a strong alumni network."

"Fuqua is clearly experiencing some growing pains. My first year, this was very clear. But I think the school has made some very strong strides within in the past 12 months and has greatly improved its core teaching quality, leadership focus, and general curriculum."

"My classmates were some of the most intelligent, impressive, driven, helpful, supportive, and talented people I will ever know. You can stop any one of them anytime and ask for help, and you will get ten times what you expected."

"Leaving Fuqua, I think I have a strong alumni network that I will be able to depend upon when figuring out my future career path."

"There weren't enough interesting kids—people who had taken the time to venture outside their comfort zone geographically, academically, or otherwise. Besides the international students, most of my classmates contributed little in terms of alternative perspective."

"I am in an incredible position to make a true difference when I return to my job because of the leadership, communication, and relationship-building skills I gained at Fuqua."

"Since Fuqua is so much younger than its peers, its structure is a lot less formal. And this pays off: Students are able to take many entrepreneurial initiatives and run with them, making the school, and our experience, better in the process."

"The program has been everything I expected and more. I have made friends for life, achieved my job search goals, and learned about a highly diverse range of subjects, including finance, real estate, marketing, entrepreneurship, leadership, teamwork, interpersonal skills, and myself."

"At Fuqua, the level of cooperation is impressive, even by 'enlightened' B-school standards. When preparing for a competitive (forced curve) test, our entire section met, and volunteers stepped up for each section of the test and explained it. Note takers compiled and then distributed the resulting 14 pages of material. My classmates dramatically increased my understanding of the material."

Where to Stay

Washington Duke Inn & Golf Club
3001 Cameron Blvd.
Durham, NC 27705
(919) 490-0999

Millennium Hotel Durham
2800 Campus Walk Ave.
Durham, NC 27705
(919) 383-8575

Brookwood Inn at Duke University
2306 Elba St.
Durham, NC 27705
(919) 286-3111

 Where to Eat

Blue Corn Café
716 9th St.
Durham, NC 27705
(919) 286-9600

Metro 8 Steakhouse
746 9th St.
Durham, NC 27705
(919) 416-1700

Magnolia Grill
1002 9th St.
Durham, NC 27705
(919) 286-3609

 Things to Do

Nasher Museum of Art
2001 Campus Dr.
Durham, NC 27705
(919) 684-5135

Sarah P. Duke Gardens
426 Anderson St.
Durham, NC 27705
(919) 684-3698

CHECK OUT BUSINESSWEEK.COM FOR MORE:

Admissions Q&A: Liz Riley, director of MBA admissions, describes what Fuqua is looking for in an applicant.

Sample Application Essays and Interview Tips: Get the lowdown on what it takes to get in.

School Tour: Planning a visit? Check out the campus first, using this slide show.

Careers Q&A: Sheryle Dirks of Fuqua's Career Management Center talks about how she customizes recruiting for students.

Expanded Profile: All the stats on Fuqua's admissions, academics, and job placement, plus more student comments.

Access all the B-schools content on BusinessWeek.com by subscribing to MBA Insider.

Emory University

Goizueta Business School
2006 Ranking: 23 (U.S.)
1300 Clifton Rd., Suite 214
Atlanta, GA 30322
E-mail address:
   admissions@bus.emory.edu
Web address:
   www.goizueta.emory.edu
For more info: Call general information
   at (404) 727-6270

☑ **B4UGO**

Applicants accepted: 39%
Average GMAT score: 685
Average years' work experience: 4.8
Average post-MBA salary increase:
   81.4%
Average total first-year
   compensation: $129,920

Why Emory?

Aiming to produce "principled leaders for global enterprise," Goizueta has built a program around the twin ideas of leadership and ethics. Leadership training starts before day one (with an overnight retreat and ropes course) and is incorporated throughout the program through required courses and activities. But the centerpiece is the Advanced Leadership Academy, a yearlong program that includes an Appalachian Trail hike, a leadership assessment, and an innovation competition. Ethics isn't a single course, as it is elsewhere. Goizueta's seven core values are incorporated throughout the curriculum, from admissions to team activities to classroom discussions. For the impatient (at least those with undergraduate business or economics degrees), Goizueta offers a popular, fast-paced, one-year MBA program.

Emory is a private institution. Established in 1919, Goizueta's full-time MBA program is accredited by the Association to Advance Collegiate Schools of Business (AACSB). Goizueta also offers part-time and executive MBA programs. For details of Goizueta's part-time MBA program, see page 333. For details on Goizueta's executive MBA program, see page 225.

 Headlines

May 8, 2007: Goizueta launches new real estate program

April 27, 2006: Goizueta's art collection gets new home in research center; 180 pieces on view, including works by Dali, Warhol, Picasso

September 28, 2005: New $33.4 million Goizueta research center dedicated

July 1, 2005: Lawrence "Larry" Benveniste takes the helm as Goizueta dean

"Goizueta has made incredible strides in the area of leadership."

Famous MBA Alumni

Duncan Niederauer, CEO of the New York Stock Exchange
John Chidsey, CEO of Burger King Corp.
Paul Amos, president and COO of Aflac Inc.

 ## Who Are My Classmates?

Full-time enrollment: 331
Women: 31%
International: 43%
Minority: 23%
Average age: 28
Accepted applicants enrolled: 48%

"The experience at Goizueta is amazing and unforgettable."

The 411

Annual tuition and fees: $39,455
Annual living expenses: $22,984
Total program cost, including forgone salary: $227,458
Classes begin: August
Application deadlines: November 1 to March 1
Application fee: $150

Cliff Notes

Leading areas of study: Consulting, Finance, General Management, Marketing, Strategy
Average class size, core classes: 55
Average class size, electives: 30
Number of electives: 56
Teaching methods: Case studies (35%), lectures (35%), team projects (20%)

But What's It *Really* Like?

Graded by students:
Overall ranking: **A**
Teaching quality: **A**
Career services: **A**

Graded by recruiters:
Overall ranking: **C**
Accounting: **C**
Analytical skills: **B**
Communication: **B**
Finance: **C**
General management: **B**
International business: **C**
Marketing: **B**
Operations/production: **C**
Teamwork skills: **C**

 ## Bling

Average pre-MBA salary: $51,290
Average post-MBA salary: $93,060
Graduates with job offer by graduation: 83%
Top functional areas for graduates: Finance/Accounting, Consulting, Marketing/Sales
Biggest recruiters: Bank of America, Deloitte, Ernst & Young, IBM, A.T. Kearney, Citigroup

The Good, the Bad, and the Ugly: Students Speak Out

"The leadership program at Goizueta was simply amazing. It is truly the program's forte, and I don't think there is another program out there that can come close. I am extremely proud to have participated in the program and hope that it continues to grow. My experiences changed me, and I honestly believe the efforts of the academy touched lives."

"Goizueta needs to work on diversity and making it less of an ornamental factor and more a part of the actual experience. I hate to admit that the rumors I heard while applying to the school about the southern frat boy culture were confirmed by my experience."

"The rumors I heard about the southern frat boy culture were confirmed."

"Goizueta is a wonderful school that has distinguished itself in both academic quality and leadership development. This is a combination that the employers I spoke with find extremely attractive."

"The size of the program at Goizueta was ideal for me. It allowed me to build personal relationships with a large number of students and allowed a better and closer interaction with the professors."

"Goizueta has made incredible strides in the area of leadership. As a participant in the Leadership Academy, I feel that Goizueta has gone above and beyond the usual 'contrived' leadership activities you see in so many corporate training activities and has truly thought outside the box about what a leader is and how to develop one."

"I feel that maybe there are too many classes for a two-year MBA student. If there were only four classes every semester, students would have more time to do many things that are more important than the fifth class."

"The experience at Goizueta is amazing and unforgettable, which not only empowered me to land a job in my dream industry and dream city, but also gave me the precious opportunity to forge lifelong friendships and broaden my perspectives on so many things."

"I found the career center not very able or ready to help me. I really needed some career guidance, and I did not feel that they were interested in putting forth the effort."

Where to Stay

Emory Conference Center Hotel/ Emory Inn
1615 Clifton Rd.
Atlanta, GA 30322
(800) 933-6679

Wyndham Midtown Atlanta
125 10th St. N.E.
Atlanta, GA 30309
(404) 873-4900

Four Seasons Atlanta
75 14th St.
Atlanta, GA 30309
(404) 253-3853

 Where to Eat

Sotto Sotto (Italian)
313 N. Highland Ave.
Atlanta, GA 30307
(404) 523-6678

Watershed (gourmet sandwiches)
406 W. Ponce de Leon Ave.
Decatur, GA 30030
(404) 378-4900

The Flying Biscuit Café (organic, vegetarian)
1655 McLendon Ave.
Atlanta, GA 30307
(404) 687-8888

 Things to Do

Carter Presidential Center
One Copenhill Ave.
Atlanta, GA 30307
(404) 331-0296

The World of Coca-Cola
55 Martin Luther King Jr. Dr. S.W.
Atlanta, GA 30303
(404) 676-5151

CHECK OUT BUSINESSWEEK.COM FOR MORE:

Admissions Q&A: Julie R. Barefoot, associate dean and director of MBA admissions, discusses why leadership is so important for Emory applicants.

Interview Tips: Get the lowdown on how to impress the Goizueta admissions representatives.

Sample Essays: Discover the dos and don'ts of admissions essay writing.

Expanded Profile: Check out *BusinessWeek*'s online profile for more info about Emory.

Access all the B-schools content on BusinessWeek.com by subscribing to MBA Insider.

ESADE Business School

Escuela Superior de Administración y
   Dirección de Empresas
2006 Ranking: 7 (non-U.S.)
Av. Esplugues, 92-96
Barcelona, Spain E-08034
E-mail address: mba@esade.edu
Web address: www.esade.edu
For more info: Call general information
   at 34-93-280-61-62

☑ B4UGO

Applicants accepted: 48%
Average GMAT score: 650
Average years' work experience: 5
Average post-MBA salary increase:
   89.7%
Average total first-year
   compensation: $124,250

Why ESADE?

Though rooted in scenic Barcelona, ESADE's full-time MBA program offers a global learning experience. Drawing attendees from more than 40 countries, the school offers electives such as International Finance Simulation and China as a Consumer Country, and touts a curriculum emphasizing "international vision." Moreover, because courses are offered in English and Spanish—and attendees are constantly exposed to both languages— many students graduate with improved communication skills. Recruiters are taking note. In 2006, they gave ESADE graduates straight A pluses in international business, general management, and seven other areas.

ESADE is a private institution. Established in 1976, ESADE's full-time MBA program is accredited by the Association to Advance Collegiate Schools of Business (AACSB), the Association of MBAs (AMBA), and the European Quality Improvement Sys-

tem (EQUIS). ESADE also offers part-time and executive MBA programs. For details on ESADE's executive MBA program, see page 229.

 Headlines

June 18, 2007: ESADE announces collaboration with Art Center College of Design

April 25, 2007: Bain, Citigroup, and Deloitte among those attending career fair for finance and consulting

February 21, 2007: ESADE summer school offers three new marketing programs

January 22, 2007: ESADE establishes Institute for Social Innovation

"More than worth every dime."

Famous MBA Alumni

Javier Ferrán, partner at Lion Capital
Ignacio Fonts, vice president and general manager of HP Inkjet Division
Ferran Soriano, vice chairman of FC Barcelona

 Who Are My Classmates?

Full-time enrollment: 235
Women: 33%
International: 82%
Minority: N/A
Average age: 28
Accepted applicants enrolled: 58%

> *"ESADE needs to improve its Career Services."*

The 411

Annual tuition and fees: $37,310
Annual living expenses: $22,000
Total program cost, including forgone salary: $174,820
Classes begin: September
Application deadline: June 30
Application fee: $142

Cliff Notes

Leading areas of study: Corporate Social Responsibility, Entrepreneurship, Finance, General Management, Marketing
Average class size, core courses: 50
Average class size, electives: 20
Number of electives: 50
Teaching methods: Case studies (30%), lectures (25%), team projects (20%)

But What's It *Really* Like?

Graded by students:
Overall ranking: **A**
Teaching quality: **A**
Career services: **B**

Graded by recruiters:
Overall ranking: **A**
Accounting: **A+**
Analytical skills: **A+**
Communication: **A+**
Finance: **A+**
General management: **A+**
International business: **A+**
Marketing: **A+**
Operations/production: **A+**
Teamwork skills: **A+**

 Bling

Average pre-MBA salary: $44,800
Average post-MBA salary: $85,000
Graduates with job offer by graduation: 76%
Top functional areas for graduates: Consulting, Finance/Accounting, Management, Marketing/ Sales
Biggest recruiters: Novartis, Delta Consulting, Everis Consulting, Johnson & Johnson, Accenture

The Good, the Bad, and the Ugly: Students Speak Out

"I would recommend [ESADE only for students who] are planning on living in Spain or a classic European country, as the name of ESADE would be valid only in these countries and no place else."

"ESADE is more than worth every dime and every day spent there. It is only unfortunate that it has to end."

"There is a 'can do' attitude at the school: No problem is too large or too small to be tackled and solved in class or work groups."

"Many students speak three languages fluently upon graduation."

"As an American, I had not been taught to be as successful a team player as many of my classmates who were from other countries/cultures. While at ESADE, I worked hard on these skills, and it has helped me to gain trust and momentum faster with my peers and coworkers."

"ESADE needs to improve its Career Services. There's a lack of contacts and an unpleasant attitude toward students and companies."

"Students are just as likely to speak Spanish as English during breaks, and a great many students speak three languages fluently upon graduation."

"ESADE should increase the number of relationships with companies outside of Europe (particularly in the United States) and improve the core finance classes."

"The fact that the program is dual-language (English and Spanish) makes it even more enriching. Furthermore, the internationality of the student body makes the whole MBA experience unique."

"The MBA program has nearly the same subjects, including contents and cases, as the ESADE Bachelor in Economics. [Students have] problems getting jobs because of internal competition with the School of Economics and the new one-year MBA."

"ESADE really encourages a cooperative environment. I also liked that the administration and career services personnel were always available and willing to talk."

"Even though I'm not from Spain, I was able to get a job there, and that's in part due to ESADE's reputation."

"ESADE met all of my expectations and was everything that I wanted it to be. I learned more about culture and its impact on business in the last two years than in the previous 10."

 **Where to Stay**

Hotel Arts
Marina 19-21
Barcelona, ES 08005
34-93-221-10-00

Design Hotels: Casa Camper
Carrer Elisabets 11
Barcelona, ES 08001
(800) 337-4685

Design Hotels: Grand Hotel Central
Via Laietana 30
Barcelona, ES 08003
(800) 337-4685

 Where to Eat

Inopia
Carrer de Tamarit 104
Barcelona, ES 08015
34-93-424-52-31

Ca L'Isidre
Carrer Les Flors 12
Barcelona, ES 08001
34-93-441-11-39

La Clara
Gran Via de les Corts Catalanes 442
Barcelona, ES 08015
34-93-289-34-60

 Things to Do

Museu Picasso (Picasso Museum)
Montcada 15-23
Barcelona, ES 08003
34-93-356-30-00

Museu de la Xocolata (Chocolate Museum)
Comerç 36
Barcelona, ES 08003
34-93-268-78-78

CHECK OUT BUSINESSWEEK.COM FOR MORE:

Careers Q&A: Camila de Wit Giesemann, director of Career Services, on how ESADE lands jobs for graduates.

School Tour: Get a tapas-style taste for the ESADE campus with this photo slideshow.

Search & Compare: See how ESADE stacks up against other schools on your short list.

MBA Forums: Share your thoughts with other ESADE hopefuls.

Expanded Profile: More ESADE facts, stats, and insights.

Access all the B-schools content on BusinessWeek.com by subscribing to MBA Insider.

Georgetown University

Robert Emmett McDonough School of
  Business
2006 Ranking: 22 (U.S.)
3520 Prospect St. N.W., Suite 215
Washington, DC 20057
E-mail address: MBA@georgetown.edu
Web address: www.msb.georgetown.edu
For more info: Call the MBA program
  office at (202) 687-4200

☑ B4UGO

Applicants accepted: 35%
Average GMAT score: 677
Average years' work experience: 5.2
Average post-MBA salary increase:
  66.7%
**Average total first-year
  compensation:** $127,040

Why Georgetown?

Georgetown has always made a point of
casting its gaze *over* Capitol Hill and
across the ocean. McDonough follows
this trend, offering a truly global brand of
business education. With 30% international students, the student body isn't
exactly the United Nations of B-schools,
but the curriculum is another matter.
Global business concerns are woven
throughout first-year courses, while
McDonough's Global Integrative Experience, a required second-year course,
allows students to focus entirely on one
internationally based company, culmi-
nating in a nine-day foreign residency
during which students help solve real-life
business problems. Two out of three graduates end up in finance or consulting,
with salaries averaging about $90,000.

  Georgetown University is a private
institution. Established in 1957,
McDonough's full-time MBA program
is accredited by the Association to
Advance Collegiate Schools of Business
(AACSB). McDonough also offers part-

time and executive MBA programs. For
details on Georgetown's executive MBA
program, see page 233.

Headlines

Spring 2009: New $100 million MBA
facility set to open

March 29, 2007: Kimberly-Clark hon-
ored for support of Georgetown
Healthcare Leadership Institute

June 16, 2005: George Daly named
dean of McDonough School of Business

June 6, 2005: McDonough names
Anne Jones new director of career management

*"The curriculum and
professors are highly
underrated."*

Famous MBA Alumni

Michael Chasen, cofounder, president, and CEO of Blackboard Inc.
Jeffrey Stump, senior vice president of Marsh USA
Timothy Tassopoulos, senior vice president of Chick-fil-A

 ## Who Are My Classmates?

Full-time enrollment: 487
Women: 33%
International: 32%
Minority: 26%
Average age: 28
Accepted applicants enrolled: 46.4%

"Georgetown's MBA emphasizes collaboration and integrity."

The 411

Annual tuition and fees: $37,800
Annual living expenses: $24,302
Total program cost, including forgone salary: $232,310
Classes begin: August
Application deadlines: November 30 to April 25
Application fee: $175

Cliff Notes

Leading areas of study: Finance, General Management, International Business, Marketing, Strategy
Average class size, core courses: 66
Average class size, electives: 44
Number of electives: 96
Teaching methods: Lectures (35%) case studies (25%), team projects (25%)

But What's It *Really* Like?

Graded by students:
Overall ranking: B
Teaching quality: A
Career services: B

Graded by recruiters:
Overall ranking: B
Accounting: C
Analytical skills: B
Communication: C
Finance: C
General management: C
International business: B
Marketing: C
Operations/production: C
Teamwork skills: C

 ## Bling

Average pre-MBA salary: $54,053
Average post-MBA salary: $90,082
Graduates with job offer by graduation: 87%
Top functional areas for graduates: Finance/Accounting, Consulting, Marketing/Sales
Biggest recruiters: Citigroup, JPMorgan Chase, Booz Allen Hamilton, American Airlines, Johnson & Johnson

The Good, the Bad, and the Ugly: Students Speak Out

"The Georgetown experience was life-changing for me, especially the Global Integrative work/study-abroad program."

"I think the curriculum and professors are highly underrated relative to other schools. The modular system is absolutely fantastic and really forces professors to [create] content-rich classes. In addition, the professors are dedicated to the students and occasionally invite us over for big dinners."

> ## "The facilities are probably the school's weakest point."

"I learned more about business in my first year at Georgetown than I thought I would learn over the course of the program. The community created at this school is, in my humble opinion, truly without peer in the United States. Furthermore, the changes our new dean is making should exploit the best things about this community and minimize the negative aspects of the school."

"In my opinion, the facilities, which are way too small, are probably the school's weakest point. The workload could be considered as a weakness as well, since it can be very difficult to deliver [academically] and at the same time try to find jobs (or internships)!"

"The school is going through many changes, and the students are taking an active role in developing the different action plans to improve the program. The community and student involvement in extracurricular activities is outstanding."

"Georgetown's MBA program emphasizes collaboration and integrity. It was an invaluable experience, and I believe that Dean Daly will do great things for the school in terms of offering vision for the future and effective leadership, which is what was missing."

"If I had to choose all over again, I would still choose Georgetown, and I think the place will only continue to improve. Before I arrived, we went several years without a true dean, but we now appear to have a winner in George Daly. Our facilities will improve with our new building."

"One aspect of the program that stands out is the Global Integrative. It gives us grads an opportunity to leverage our academic learning to address a real-world problem in an international setting. It will stay with me for a long time."

Where to Stay

The Georgetown Inn
1310 Wisconsin Ave.
Washington, DC 20007
(202) 333-8900

The Fairmont Washington, DC
2401 M St.
Washington, DC 20037
(202) 429-2400

Key Bridge Marriott
1401 Lee Hwy.
Rosslyn, VA 22209
(703) 524-6400

 Where to Eat

Leopold's Kafe & Konditorei (German/Austrian)
3318 M St.
Washington, DC 20007
(202) 965-6005

Ching Ching Cha (Chinese)
1063 Wisconsin Ave.
Washington, DC 20007
(202) 333-8288

Pizzeria Paradiso—Georgetown (Italian)
3282 M St.
Washington, DC 20007
(202) 337-1245

 Things to Do

Blues Alley (jazz club)
1073 Wisconsin Ave.
Washington, DC 20007
(202) 337-4141

Dumbarton Oaks Gardens
1703 32nd St. N.W.
Washington, DC 20007
(202) 339-6401

CHECK OUT BUSINESSWEEK.COM FOR MORE:

Admissions Q&A: Admissions Director Monica Gray discusses the common pitfalls prospective students should avoid.

Interview Tips: Find out how to win over the admissions representatives at McDonough.

School Tour: Check out life on campus before planning a visit to McDonough.

Search & Compare: See how Georgetown stacks up against other top schools.

Expanded Profile: Want more? Dig deeper into the Georgetown program using its online profile.

Access all the B-schools content on BusinessWeek.com by subscribing to MBA Insider.

Harvard University

Harvard Business School
2006 Ranking: 4 (U.S.)
Soldiers Field
Boston, MA 02163
E-mail address: admissions@hbs.edu
Web address: www.hbs.edu/mba
For more info: Call the MBA admissions
    office at (617) 495-6128

Why Harvard?

Acclaimed for strong performance in corporate social responsibility, entrepreneurship, general management, leadership, and strategy, Harvard's full-time MBA program attracts students who have their sights set on the upper echelon of business, nonprofits, and government agencies. At the birthplace of the case-study method, HBS students can take full advantage of a case-based curriculum that challenges them to solve real-world problems. While there's no shortage of Type A personalities—it's almost an admission requirement—don't believe the rumors about cutthroat competition. "I expected my fellow students to be self-centered, Master-of-the-Universe types right out of *Bonfire of the Vanities*," one HBS attendee recalls. "But I was pleasantly surprised at how bright, and friendly most of them were."

Harvard University is a private institution. Established in 1908, the HBS full-time MBA program is accredited by the Association to Advance Collegiate Schools of Business (AACSB).

 B4UGO

Applicants accepted: 14%
Average GMAT score: 713
Average years' work experience: 4
Average post-MBA salary increase: 29%*
Average total first-year compensation: $205,659

*Based in part on *BusinessWeek* survey data.

 Headlines

June 6, 2007: 10 HBS leadership fellows take nonprofit, public-sector jobs

April 3, 2007: HBS and Kennedy School of Government announce new joint degree program

February 21, 2007: Seven faculty members, including management guru Michael Porter, win research awards

April 24, 2006: Jay Light named ninth dean of HBS

"Worth every penny of tuition."

Famous MBA Alumni

George W. Bush, U.S. president
Meg Whitman, former president and
    CEO
    of eBay
Rick Wagoner, chairman and CEO
    of General Motors

 ## Who Are My Classmates?

Full-time enrollment: 1,808
Women: 36%
International: 33%
Minority: N/A
Average age: 27
Accepted applicants enrolled: 89%

"Apart from serving as career insurance, HBS made me a better citizen of the world."

The 411

Annual tuition and fees: $48,738
Annual living expenses: $24,562
Total program cost, including forgone
    salary: $325,928*
Classes begin: September
Application deadlines: October 2,
    January 3, March 12
Application fee: $235

*Based in part on *BusinessWeek* survey data.

Cliff Notes

Leading areas of study: Corporate
    Social Responsibility, Entrepreneur-
    ship, General Management,
    Leadership, Strategy
Average class size, core courses: 90
Average class size, electives: 90
Number of electives: 95
Teaching methods: Case studies
    (80%)

But What's It *Really* Like?

Graded by students:
Overall ranking: **A+**
Teaching quality: **A+**
Career services: **A+**

Graded by recruiters:
Overall ranking: **A+**
Accounting: **A**
Analytical skills: **A+**
Communication: **A+**
Finance: **A+**
General management: **A+**
International business: **A+**
Marketing: **A+**
Operations/production: **A+**
Teamwork skills: **B**

 ## Bling

Average pre-MBA salary: $89,664*
Average post-MBA salary: $115,665
Graduates with job offer by graduation:
    96%
Top functional areas for graduates:
    Finance/Accounting, Consulting,
    Marketing/Sales
Biggest recruiters: BCG, Fidelity,
    JPMorgan Chase, McKinsey, UBS

*Estimate based on *BusinessWeek* survey data.

The Good, the Bad, and the Ugly: Students Speak Out

"Apart from serving as a career insurance policy that will enable me to take entrepreneurial risks in the future, I believe my experience at HBS has made me a better citizen of the world. I've been exposed to things on a global scale that I never understood before matriculating."

"The quality of students is second to none."

"My one criticism of the school is its lack of coursework on climate change, the most critical issue facing humanity. The school was willing to adjust its operations to be more environmentally friendly, but student efforts to integrate new ideas into the curriculum usually fell upon deaf ears."

"If you believe in the case method, I truly believe there is no better school in the world for management training than Harvard Business School. The access to thought leaders is unmatched by other institutions, and the overall quality of the students is second to none."

"The biggest negative at Harvard Business School is the overwhelming number of opportunities. There isn't enough time in the day to pursue all your interests here."

"The alumni network has been the most amazing part of this experience—I had over an 80% response rate from alumni that I contacted (including one who put me in touch with all the right people for my summer internship, even though he had not met me)."

"I expected to gain technical expertise at business school, but I ended up gaining a holistic view of how organizations work and a diverse group of dynamic friends all over the world—which I think is more valuable in the long run."

"HBS had to use a crowbar to pry my fingers from its door at graduation."

"Harvard Business School provided everything I could have hoped for in a business education. I have the job I wanted, in a great location, and my degree prepared me to excel during my internship and the recruiting process. An outstanding institution, and worth every penny of tuition."

"There was only one teaching assistant for courses like finance and accounting for the whole class (900 students). Only around 30 to 50 attended the practice sessions. Still, this 1:50 ratio made it a bit challenging for learning."

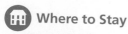 **Where to Stay**

Harvard Square Hotel
110 Mount Auburn St.
Cambridge, MA 02138
(617) 864-5200

The Inn at Harvard
1201 Massachusetts Ave.
Cambridge, MA 02138
(617) 491-2222

Sheraton Commander Hotel
16 Garden St.
Cambridge, MA 02138
(617) 547-4800

 Where to Eat

Charlie's Kitchen
10 Eliot St.
Cambridge, MA 02138
(617) 492-9646

16 Garden Street Restaurant
16 Garden St.
Cambridge, MA 02138
(617) 547-4800

Grafton Street Pub & Grill
1230 Massachusetts Ave.
Cambridge, MA 02138
(617) 497-0400

 Things to Do

Freedom Trail (sightseeing tour)
15 State St.
Boston, MA 02109
(617) 242-5642

New England Aquarium
Central Wharf
Boston, MA 02110
(617) 973-5200

CHECK OUT BUSINESSWEEK.COM FOR MORE:

Chat: Admissions Director Deirdre Leopold fields questions from prospective applicants.

Sample Application Essays and Interview Tips: Get the lowdown on what it takes to get in.

School Tour: Check out the campus before visiting.

Placement Q&A: HBS career services guru Timothy Butler on the importance of a good coach.

Search & Compare: See how Harvard stacks up against the competition.

Access all the B-schools content on BusinessWeek.com by subscribing to MBA Insider.

HEC Montréal

École des Hautes Études Commerciales
2006 Ranking: 10 (non-U.S.)
Registrar's Office
3000 chemin de la Côte Ste-Catherine
Montréal, QC (Canada) H3T 2A7
E-mail address: mba@hec.ca
Web address: www.hec.ca/mba
For more info: Call general information
at (514) 340-6000

 B4UGO

Applicants accepted: 62%
Average GMAT score: 600
Average years' work experience: 6.9
Average post-MBA salary increase:
33.9%
**Average total first-year
compensation:** $95,235

Why HEC Montréal?

With one of the lowest tuition costs among top-tier international programs, HEC Montréal's full-time MBA is a bargain. Beyond forging close ties with classmates from across the globe—60% of full-time students are from outside of Canada—attendees can choose from 11 concentrations and nearly 100 specialized courses. But that's not all. Unlike most U.S. programs, which take two years to complete, HEC's is short and sweet—just 12 months. And in keeping with the school's worldwide focus, classes are offered in English, French, and occasionally Spanish. Recruiters don't give HEC high marks, and starting salaries for graduates are low for a top-tier school. Still, HEC graduates are hired by such well-known companies as Deloitte, Ernst & Young, and Johnson & Johnson.

HEC Montréal is a public institution. Established in 1968, its full-time MBA program is accredited by the Association to Advance Collegiate Schools of Business (AACSB), the Association of MBAs (AMBA), and the European Quality Improvement System (EQUIS). HEC Montréal also offers part-time and executive MBA programs.

 Headlines

November 1, 2006: HEC Montréal to celebrate 100th anniversary in 2007

September 19, 2006: Over $1 million in scholarships awarded to 50 students

August 24, 2006: HEC Montréal names new director Michel Patry

April 5, 2006: MBA students post 95% pass rate on SAP certification exam

*"A very demanding
and thorough
program."*

Famous MBA Alumni

Thierry Vandal, CEO of Hydro-Québec

Louis Roquet, CEO of Desjardins Capital de Risque

Yannis Mallat, CEO of Ubisoft Canada

 ## Who Are My Classmates?

Full-time enrollment: 172
Women: 33%
International: 45%
Minority: N/A
Average age: 31
Accepted applicants enrolled: 67%

> *"This school caters to Québec students, not international ones."*

The 411

Annual tuition and fees: $5,500 (resident), $22,135 (nonresident)*
Annual living expenses: $17,000*
Total program cost, including forgone salary: $72,900 (resident), $89,535 (nonresident)
Classes begin: August
Application deadline: March 15
Application fee: $75

*Total for program.

Cliff Notes

Leading areas of study: Finance, General Management, International Business, Management, Information Systems, Marketing

Average class size, core courses: 35
Average class size, electives: 22
Number of electives: 95
Teaching methods: Case studies (45%), lectures (25%), team projects (15%)

But What's It *Really* Like?

Graded by students:
Overall ranking: B
Teaching quality: B
Career services: B

Graded by recruiters:
Overall ranking: C
Accounting: B
Analytical skills: C
Communication: N/A
Finance: B
General management: B
International business: C
Marketing: N/A
Operations/production: N/A
Teamwork skills: B

$ Bling

Average pre-MBA salary: $50,400
Average post-MBA salary: $67,500
Graduates with job offer by graduation: 37%
Top functional areas for graduates: Finance/Accounting, Marketing/Sales, Consulting
Biggest recruiters: Bombardier, TD Bank, Royal Bank of Canada, Canadian National Railway, SAP Canada, Deloitte

The Good, the Bad, and the Ugly: Students Speak Out

"Because the English program at HEC Montréal is fairly new, the school is having trouble attracting good teachers who are fluent in English, which takes away from the quality of the program."

"HEC Montréal is a very demanding and thorough program. Students come here and learn in a truly outstanding and highly international environment."

"The age of all my colleagues was too low, and the work experience almost absent."

"HEC Montréal has a strong culture that engages all students, especially in the intensive MBA program."

"The evaluation criteria should be reevaluated. A grading curve is applied by the majority of professors, but it doesn't always follow the same criteria. This sends a mixed message to students."

> *"I learned about tolerance, leadership, and teamwork."*

"HEC Montréal is very customer-oriented. It focuses on improving student satisfaction, and every piece of our opinion is usually viewed as very important."

"This school caters to Québec students, not international ones. It is also very poorly known outside the province of Québec."

"The HEC Montréal MBA was a fantastic experience. Its courses are taught by some well-known and experienced Québec businesspeople, it provides the opportunity to consult at several businesses, and its fast-paced format improves your ability to lead and work effectively in a team."

"As a Canadian in a program with a large number of international students, I felt that the amount of work I was required to do as part of a team was much more than my teammates. Correcting English and trying to understand exactly what my colleagues meant took up a lot of my time."

"This MBA experience has changed my life. It has not only helped me land a job, but also influenced me as a person. I learned about tolerance, leadership, and teamwork, and I feel I am a more mature and more responsible person."

"I learned so much more than I anticipated. I wish I could renew this experience every 10 years."

Where to Stay

Le Saint-Sulpice
414 rue St-Sulpice
Montréal, QC H2Y 2VS
(877) 785-7489

Le Germain
2050 rue Mansfield
Montréal, QC H3A 1Y9
(514) 849-2050

Auberge de La Fontaine
1301 rue Rachel est
Montréal, QC H2J 2K1
(514) 597-0166

 Where to Eat

Au Pied de Cochon (The Pig's Foot)
536 rue Duluth est
Montréal, QC H2L 1A9
(514) 281-1116

L'Express
3927 rue St-Denis
Montréal, QC H2W 2M4
(514) 845-5333

**Chez Schwartz Charcuterie
Hébraïque de Montréal**
3895 bd. St-Laurent
Montréal, QC H2W 1X9
(514) 842-4813

 Things to Do

McCord Museum of Canadian History
690 Sherbrooke St. W.
Montréal, QC H3A 1E9
(514) 398-7100

**Le Jardin Nelson (The Nelson
Garden Treasure)**
407 Pl. Jacques Cartier
Montréal, QC H2Y 3B1
(514) 861-5731

CHECK OUT BUSINESSWEEK.COM FOR MORE:

School Tour: Thinking of visiting HEC Montréal? Peruse this *BusinessWeek* photo essay first.

Search & Compare: See how HEC Montréal stacks up against other top international B-schools.

MBA Forums: Connect with other HEC Montréal hopefuls.

Expanded Profile: Drill down into HEC Montréal 's placement data and other stats.

Access all the B-schools content on BusinessWeek.com by subscribing to MBA Insider.

HEC School of Management

2006 Ranking: Second tier (non-U.S.)
1 rue de la Libération
Jouy-en-Josas, France 78351
E-mail address: admissionmba@hec.fr
Web address: www.mba.hec.edu
For more info: Call admissions
coordinator Isabelle Rainaud at 33-1-
39-67-71-67

✅ B4UGO

Applicants accepted: 20%
Average GMAT score: 660
Average years' work experience: 5.4
Average post-MBA salary increase: 121.1%
Average total first-year compensation: $160,063

Why HEC Paris?

With nearly 90% of participants hailing from outside of France and 55 nationalities represented, HEC Paris boasts one of the most diverse MBA programs on the planet. At 16 months, it's longer than some European programs, allowing students ample time to sample the 95 electives on offer and to take the compulsory French lessons. During the second half, students choose from seven tracks—including negotiation skills, group dynamics, and an international exchange. Only about half of all students have jobs at graduation, but many score positions at top companies—such as McKinsey, Lehman Brothers, and Johnson & Johnson—with starting salaries north of $100,000.

HEC Paris is a public institution. Established in 1969, its full-time MBA program is accredited by the Association to Advance Collegiate Schools of Business (AACSB), the Association of MBAs (AMBA), and the European Quality Improvement System (EQUIS). HEC

Paris also offers part-time and executive MBA programs.

Headlines

March 16, 2007: Joint certificate program in fashion and luxury graduates its first class.

May 13, 2006: Abu Dhabi's Institute for Enterprise Development links up with HEC Paris

February 8, 2006: HEC Paris partners with Ecole Polytechnique to create new economics and management institute

August 12, 2005: HEC Paris sets up program in China

"Intellectually challenging and highly demanding."

Famous MBA Alumni

Sydney Taurel, chairman and CEO of Eli Lilly

Henri de Castries, chairman and CEO of AXA Group

Pascal Cagni, vice president of Apple Europe, Middle East, Asia

 **Who Are My Classmates?**

Full-time enrollment: 135
Women: 31%
International: 87%
Minority: N/A
Average age: 29
Accepted applicants enrolled: 60%

"HEC's student body is exceptionally international."

The 411

Annual tuition and fees: $55,167*
Annual living expenses: $23,685*
Total program cost, including forgone salary: $142,185
Classes begin: September
Application deadlines: December 7 to May 26
Application fee: $185
*Total for program.

Cliff Notes

Leading areas of study: Corporate Social Responsibility, Entrepreneurship, Finance, General Management Leadership
Average class size, core courses: 45
Average class size, electives: 30
Number of electives: 95
Teaching methods: Case studies (30%), team projects (30%)

But What's It *Really* Like?

Graded by students:
Overall ranking: **B**
Teaching quality: **B**
Career services: **B**

Graded by recruiters:
Overall ranking: **C**
Accounting: **N/A**
Analytical skills: **B**
Communication: **N/A**
Finance: **N/A**
General management: **C**
International business: **C**
Marketing: **B**
Operations/production: **N/A**
Teamwork skills: **N/A**

$ Bling

Average pre-MBA salary: $47,500
Average post-MBA salary: $105,041
Graduates with job offer by graduation: 52%
Companies recruiting on campus: 108
Top functional areas for graduates: Finance/Accounting, General Management, Consulting
Biggest recruiters: BNP, Citigroup, LVMH, Johnson & Johnson, McKinsey

⟨⟨⟩⟩ The Good, the Bad, and the Ugly: Students Speak Out

"There are criticisms that HEC Paris can be too 'French-centric,' but the administration is very successful in bringing more multinational companies on campus for recruiting events."

"I am especially happy with the MBA program at HEC, as its student body is exceptionally international (80% non-French) and there is a lot of emphasis on teamwork. As a result, you can learn from the previous experiences, cultural differences, and expertise of others."

"The school is not well known outside France."

"The job environment in France is stagnant, which affects the school's capacity for job placement. The school is still perceived as French, and its brand is not well known outside France."

"The HEC Paris MBA program was my first choice from the beginning because of the quality, structure, and length of the program, the international student body, and the positive impression I had from my visit to the campus and conversations with students."

"HEC Paris was a great and valuable experience, and the school has a great atmosphere that can also be seen in the organization of its MBA Tournament, the largest annual gathering of international business school students!"

"The major weakness of HEC is its unwillingness to devote resources to helping students stay in France and work after their studies are done. Once you've arrived and committed to pay your tuition, the school administration claims their role is to educate you, not relocate you to France. The dichotomy between what they say when they woo you and what they say when you're there is painful."

"The MBA at HEC surpassed all my expectations: it was intellectually challenging and highly demanding. I befriended some of the most interesting people I have ever met."

"HEC Paris has to grow in order to match other schools in the international arena, particularly in its brand recognition. Lehman Brothers, for example, has only just 'discovered' us and now offers summer and permanent jobs."

"HEC has a good core program. The student body is diverse, and one gets to learn about international practices. Its weakness is the career services support offered, which makes job-hunting more of a struggle than it should be."

Where to Stay

Hotel Saint-Louis
75 rue St-Louis-en-l'Ile
Paris, FR 75004
33-1-46-34-04-80

Galileo Hotel
54 rue Galilee
Paris, FR 75008
33-1-47-20-66-06

Hotel Torcadéro La Tour
5 bis rue Massenet
Paris, FR 75116
33-1-45-24-43-03

 Where to Eat

Le Rich
14 rue Cadet
Paris, FR 75009
33-1-48-01-87-87

P'tit Bouchon Gourmand
5 rue Troyon
Paris, FR 75017
33-1-40-55-03-26

La Coupole
102 bd. du Montparnasse
Paris, FR 75014
33-1-43-20-14-20

 Things to Do

Sacré Coeur
Parvis du Sacre Coeur
Paris, FR 75018
33-1-53-41-89-00

Musée d'Orsay
62 rue de Lille
Paris, FR 75343
33-1-40-49-48-14

CHECK OUT BUSINESSWEEK.COM FOR MORE:

Admissions Q&A: Admissions Director Isabelle Cota answers questions about the international MBA program.

Sample Application Essays: Find out how to score a spot at HEC Paris.

School Tour: Bonjour! Check out the HEC Paris campus through *Business-Week*'s online photo essay.

Search & Compare: See how HEC Paris stacks up against other top B-schools on your short list.

Video View: Associate Dean Valerie Gauthier discusses how HEC Paris is blending the U.S. and European models of management education.

MBA Forums: Connect with other HEC Paris hopefuls.

Access all the B-schools content on BusinessWeek.com by subscribing to MBA Insider.

Indiana University

Kelley School of Business
2006 Ranking: 18 (U.S.)
1275 E. 10th St.
Suite 2010
Bloomington, IN 47405
E-mail address: mbaoffice@indiana.edu
Web address: www.kelley.indiana.edu
For more info: Call general information at (812) 855-8100

☑ B4UGO

Applicants accepted: 34%
Average GMAT score: 656
Average years' work experience: 4.9
Average post-MBA salary increase: 72.8%
Average total first-year compensation: $118,400

Why Indiana?

The most unusual feature of the Kelley full-time MBA is its eight industry-focused academies. From consulting to marketing to investment banking, the academies blend advanced coursework, special projects, and direct contact with top executives—as well as almost guaranteed placement both for summer internships and after graduation. With seven majors and nearly 90 electives, students have the ability to create a custom-tailored MBA experience that ends with a business simulation designed to put all their new skills to the test in a competition against teams of other students. At about $35,000 a year (half that if you're a Hoosier), Kelley is the least expensive program in *Business-Week*'s top 20. Kelley has been part of that elite group since 2000.

Indiana University is a public institution. Established in 1935, Kelley's full-time MBA program is accredited by the Association to Advance Collegiate Schools of Business (AACSB).

Kelley also offers an online MBA program.

Headlines

May 17, 2007: Phillip Cochran named associate dean

October 31, 2006: Kelly's entrepreneurship programs receive national recognition

September 5, 2006: New MBA program chair and associate chair named

July 28, 2005: Dan Smith appointed Kelley dean

"The best-quality MBA education at a very affordable tuition."

Famous MBA Alumni

Cheryl Bachelder, former president of KFC
John Chambers, president and CEO of Cisco Systems
Alan Graf, CFO of FedEx

 Who Are My Classmates?

Full-time enrollment: 444
Women: 28%
International: 42%
Minority: 18%
Average age: 28
Accepted applicants enrolled: 56%

"The program is highly demanding academically."

The 411

Annual tuition and fees: $18,510 (resident), $34,850 (nonresident)
Annual living expenses: $11,400 (resident), $11,500 (nonresident)
Total program cost, including forgone salary: $162,806 (resident), $195,686 (nonresident)
Classes begin: September
Application deadlines: November 15 to April 15
Application fee: $75

Cliff Notes

Leading areas of study: Consulting, Entrepreneurship, Finance, Marketing, Supply Chain Management
Average class size, core courses: 79
Average class size, electives: 38
Number of electives: 87
Teaching methods: Case studies (35%), lectures (30%), team projects (20%)

But What's It *Really* Like?

Graded by students:
Overall ranking: B
Teaching quality: A+
Career services: B

Graded by recruiters:
Overall ranking: A
Accounting: A
Analytical skills: A
Communication: A
Finance: A
General management: A
International business: A
Marketing: A+
Operations/production: B
Teamwork skills: A+

 Bling

Average pre-MBA salary: $51,493
Average post-MBA salary: $89,000
Graduates with job offer by graduation: 91%
Top functional areas for graduates: Finance/Accounting, Marketing/Sales, Consulting
Biggest recruiters: Johnson & Johnson, Cummins, General Electric, Citigroup, Eaton

⟨⟨⟩⟩ The Good, the Bad, and the Ugly: Students Speak Out

"I understand that there are several programs that are ranked higher than Kelley, but I honestly cannot imagine that the quality of the education is any better. The program is highly demanding academically, and I have found myself better educated than my counterparts at higher-ranked schools."

"My goals when I went to graduate school were to (1) find a new direction for my career and get an awesome job in that field, (2) develop leadership skills, (3) learn a new subject (business rather than engineering), and (4) travel the world. I was able to accomplish these goals and, even beyond that, add contacts from a network of unbelievable individuals. I could not have asked for more."

"Not the best school for a consulting or investment banking career."

"My biggest concern for the school is the lower enrollment levels adopted. The school should consider increasing enrollment by about 25% to maintain a critical mass for recruiters to include it as a focus school."

"I cannot say enough about the 'Kelley spirit.' The support I received from my peers is something I will always value."

"Indiana University at Bloomington provides the best-quality MBA education at a very affordable tuition. Further, the college town setting provides a high quality of life for students and their families that is not available in the larger metropolitan areas."

"The faculty was extremely knowledgeable and friendly—it was as easy to ask your finance professor a tough question as it was easy to ask him out for a drink/dinner."

"I loved the teamwork and camaraderie at Indiana. Many times students, faculty, and staff went above and beyond to make the MBA program as inclusive and rewarding for the students as possible."

"It is really a top program for a few career paths, such as marketing or corporate finance. But it is probably not the best school for someone looking for a consulting or investment banking career."

"Kelley really taught me how to think and solve problems that I had never encountered. The faculty and other students are outstanding, and everyone is interested in making your 2 years the best they can be. The workload is extremely heavy, which was a little frustrating sometimes, but overall it was a great experience."

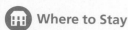 **Where to Stay**

Hilton Garden Inn Bloomington
245 N. College Ave.
Bloomington, IN 47404
(812) 331-1335

Grant Street Inn
310 N. Grant St.
Bloomington, IN 47408
(812) 334-2353

Scholars' Inn
717 N. College Ave.
Bloomington, IN 47404
(812) 332-1892

 Where to Eat

Gratzie (Italian)
106 W. 6th St.
Bloomington, IN 47401
(812) 323-0303

The Trojan Horse (Greek)
100 E. Kirkwood Ave.
Bloomington, IN 47408
(812) 332-1101

Nick's English Hut (pub)
423 E. Kirkwood Ave.
Bloomington, IN 47408
(812) 332-4040

 Things to Do

Oliver Winery
8024 N. State Rd. 37
Bloomington, IN 47404
(800) 25-TASTE

Fourwinds Resort & Marina
9301 Fairfax Rd.
Bloomington, IN 47401
(800) 824-2628

CHECK OUT BUSINESSWEEK.COM FOR MORE:

Admissions Q&A: Jim Holmen, director of admissions and financial aid, fields questions on the application process.

Sample Application Essays: See what it will take to get accepted at Kelley.

Video View: Dean Dan Smith discusses what prospective students ought to be looking for in an MBA program.

Search & Compare: Find out how Kelley stacks up against other top schools.

Expanded Profile: Need more? You'll find all the details on Kelley in its extended online profile.

Access all the B-schools content on BusinessWeek.com by subscribing to MBA Insider.

INSEAD

The European Institute of Business
Administration
2006 Ranking: 6 (non-U.S.)
Boulevard de Constance
Fontainebleau, France 77305
E-mail address: mba.info@insead.edu
Web address: www.insead.edu
For more info: Call general information
at 33-1-60-72-40-00

☑ B4UGO

Applicants accepted: N/A
Average GMAT score: 701
Average years' work experience: 5.9
Average post-MBA salary increase:
48%*
**Average total first-year
compensation:** $126,500†

*Based in part on *BusinessWeek* survey data.
†Base salary and signing bonus only.

Why INSEAD?

INSEAD calls itself "the business school for the world," and with good reason. With campuses in France and Singapore (the former is the flagship), and more than 70 different nationalities in the classroom, the school offers a truly international experience. Though U.S. B-schoolers typically spend two years securing a full-time MBA, INSEAD offers the same credential in just 10 months—one of the most accelerated programs in the world. Moreover, three out of four students receive job offers by graduation (many from top firms like McKinsey and BCG), and the average starting salary exceeds $100,000. The faculty, with 33 nationalities represented, wins raves from students

INSEAD is a private institution. Established in 1959, its full-time MBA program is accredited by the Association to Advance Collegiate Schools of Business (AACSB), the Association of MBAs (AMBA), and the European Quality Improvement System (EQUIS).

INSEAD also offers an executive MBA program. For details on INSEAD's executive MBA, see page 237.

 Headlines

March 20, 2007: INSEAD establishes 3D "virtual campus" on Second Life Web site

February 16, 2007: INSEAD partners with the World Economic Forum's Global Leadership Fellows Program

May 3, 2006: European Entrepreneurship Accelerator launched by INSEAD and IESE

December 16, 2005: J. Frank Brown new dean of INSEAD

*"INSEAD is a great
place to network."*

Famous MBA Alumni

Mika Salmi, president of global digital media at MTV Networks
Daniel Lalonde, president and CEO of LVMH Watch and Jewelry USA
Sir Lindsay Owen-Jones, chairman and former CEO of L'Oréal

 ## Who Are My Classmates?

Full-time enrollment: 887
Women: 24%
International: 89%
Minority: N/A
Average age: 29
Accepted applicants enrolled: N/A

"Career Services wasn't very helpful."

The 411

Annual tuition and fees: $65,880*
Annual living expenses: $21,870*
Total program cost, including forgone salary: $159,730†
Classes begin: August
Application deadlines: October 3 to April 3
Application fee: $270

* Total for program.

† Based in part on *BusinessWeek* survey data.

Cliff Notes

Leading areas of study: Corporate Social Responsibility, Entrepreneurship, General Management, International Business, Leadership
Average class size, core courses: 75
Average class size, electives: 35
Number of electives: 80
Teaching methods: Case studies (30%), lectures (30%), team projects (20%)

But What's It *Really* Like?

Graded by students:
Overall ranking: **A+**
Teaching quality: **A+**
Career services: **A**

Graded by recruiters:
Overall ranking: **A+**
Accounting: **B**
Analytical skills: **A**
Communication: **A+**
Finance: **A**
General management: **A+**
International business: **A+**
Marketing: **A**
Operations/production: **C**
Teamwork skills: **A**

Bling

Average pre-MBA salary: $71,980*
Average post-MBA salary: $106,500
Graduates with job offer by graduation: 76%
Top functional areas for graduates: Consulting, Finance/Accounting, General Management
Biggest recruiters: McKinsey, Bain, BCG, Booz Allen Hamilton

*Estimate based on *BusinessWeek* survey data.

The Good, the Bad, and the Ugly: Students Speak Out

"The students here are so diverse. At a dinner party, it's common to speak to a group of friends in several languages."

"INSEAD is a great place to network and meet people, and, in addition to course and group work, an intense and dynamic social life is part of the experience."

"INSEAD's diversity is amazing."

"One caveat: students coming from outside the EU (except the United States) might face some difficulties in finding jobs because of language and visa requirements."

"Coming to INSEAD has been one of the best decisions I've made. It's been a place where, on top of acquiring business skills, I have had the opportunity to learn about myself, my goals, and my preferences."

"INSEAD's diversity is amazing. Because there is such a variety of locations, students, and professors, we're challenged on many different levels and come away with a new understanding not only of business, but of life."

"INSEAD is a great school for MBA experience and learning, but definitely not for career changers (especially those with inferior experience levels)."

"The intensity of the one-year program builds much stronger bonds between classmates."

"Career Services wasn't very helpful. But the education at INSEAD is so brilliant, and the student/alumni network so good, that we don't really need Career Services. We can very well get the jobs ourselves."

"Many schools advertise the importance of global business, but deal with it only in the context of the American business environment. True diversity is having participants who have lived and worked in 73 countries—like INSEAD."

"One crucial advantage that INSEAD has is its two campuses. The ability to spend time both in Singapore and in France within the same MBA program adds a lot of international perspective to the program, especially since the Far East is currently a very important place for many businesses."

"There are a few courses—like Kevin Kaiser's finance course, Michael Brimm's Leading People and Groups, or F. Bartholome's Psychological Issues in Management course—which alone would be worth the tuition in my opinion."

 **Where to Stay**

L'Aigle Noir
27 Place Napoléon Bonaparte
Fontainebleau 77300, FR
33-1-60-74-60-00

Hôtel Napoléon
9 rue Grande
Fontainebleau 77300, FR
33-1-64-22-20-39

Londres
1 Place du Général de Gaulle
Fontainebleau 77300, FR
33-1-64-22-20-21

 Where to Eat

Au Bureau
12 rue Grande
Fontainebleau 77300, FR
33-1-60-39-00-01

Pizza Pazza
1 rue Bouchers
Fontainebleau 77300, FR
33-1-60-72-05-61

Chez Bernard
3 rue Royale
Fontainebleau 77300, FR
33-1-64-22-24-68

 Things to Do

Château de Fontainebleau
Place du Général de Gaulle
Fontainebleau 77300, FR
33-1-60-71-50-70

Forest of Fontainebleau
4 rue Royale
Fontainebleau 77300, FR
33-1-60-74-80-22

CHECK OUT BUSINESSWEEK.COM FOR MORE:

Admissions Q&A: Associate Admissions Director Johanna Hellborg describes the ideal INSEAD applicant.

Search & Compare: Does INSEAD have the goods? See how it stacks up against other top B-schools.

School Tour: Scope out INSEAD's scenic campus with this photo essay.

Video View: Dean Frank Brown defends the one-year MBA program.

Sample Application Essays: See how current INSEAD students made the grade.

Access all the B-schools content on BusinessWeek.com by subscribing to MBA Insider.

IMD

International Institute for Management
  Development
2006 Ranking: 4 (non-U.S.)
IMD MBA Office
Ch. de Bellerive 23, P.O. Box 915
1001 Lausanne, Switzerland
E-mail address: mbainfo@imd.ch
Web address: www.imd.ch/mba
For more info: Call general information
  at 41-21-618-01-11

 B4UGO

Applicants accepted: 28%
Average GMAT score: 680
Average years' work experience: 7.3
Average post-MBA salary increase:
  56.5%
**Average total first-year
  compensation:** $171,000

Why IMD?

Consistently ranked among *Business-Week*'s top 5 international programs, IMD's full-time MBA offers an intimate learning experience (each incoming class has just 90 attendees) with a forward-thinking curriculum. In addition to taking classes on global business, students benefit from IMD's "real world, real learning" approach: case study discussions, leadership exercises, hands-on projects, and intensive personal coaching are common throughout. At just 11 months, the Swiss program is fast and intense—great for more experienced students, but less so for those who need a brush-up on the basics. And there's always the "cha-ching" factor: 92% of students receive job offers by graduation—from high-profile companies like BCG and McKinsey—and their average starting salary exceeds $120,000, one of the highest among top-ranked programs.

IMD is a private institution. Established in 1972, IMD's full-time MBA program is accredited by the Association to Advance Collegiate Schools of Business (AACSB), the Association of MBAs (AMBA), and the European Quality Improvement System (EQUIS). IMD also offers an executive MBA program. For details, see page 245.

 Headlines

February 6, 2007: IMD announces record female enrollment

January 23, 2007: IMD reduces and offsets its carbon emissions

June 24, 2006: New research building inaugurated at IMD

September 2, 2005: Shell and IMD partner to develop future business talent

> *"IMD is a
> hidden jewel."*

Famous MBA Alumni

Mark Cornell, president and CEO of Moët Hennessy USA
Jürgen Fischer, president of Hilton International's Commercial Operations Group
K.Y. Lee, chairman of BenQ Corp.

 ## Who Are My Classmates?

Full-time enrollment: 90
Women: 24%
International: 97%
Minority: N/A
Average age: 31
Accepted applicants enrolled: 86%

"More focused, intense, and personalized than other programs."

The 411

Annual tuition and fees: $67,912*
Annual living expenses: $30,753*
Total program cost, including forgone salary: $175,961
Classes begin: January
Application deadlines: February 1 to September 1
Application fee: $300
*Total for program.

Cliff Notes

Leading areas of study: Entrepreneurship, General Management, International Business, Leadership, Social Responsibility
Average class size, core courses: 90
Average class size, electives: 45
Number of electives: 9
Teaching methods: Case studies (40%), team projects (35%)

But What's It *Really* Like?

Graded by students:
Overall ranking: A
Teaching quality: A
Career services: A+

Graded by recruiters:
Overall ranking: B
Accounting: B
Analytical skills: C
Communication: B
Finance: B
General management: B
International business: B
Marketing: B
Operations/production: A
Teamwork skills: B

Bling

Average pre-MBA salary: $77,296
Average post-MBA salary: $121,000
Graduates with job offer by graduation: 92%
Top functional areas for graduates: Consulting, Marketing/Sales, General Management
Biggest recruiters: Shell, Schindler, BCG, Medtronic, McKinsey

⟨⟨⟩⟩ The Good, the Bad, and the Ugly: Students Speak Out

"IMD integrates learning hard-core academic subjects with just-as-essential (perhaps more so) interpersonal skills, dealing with teams, leadership skills, and time management."

"IMD owns its reputation: I worked hard and slept less than five hours per night. The principle is similar to that of martial arts training: when your body is tired and your nerves are weak, your mind gets educated."

"The program can be a little too intense at times."

"IMD is a hidden jewel in a stunning location that will only continue to grow stronger. The school is investing in new buildings, teaching staff, and exercise facilities, among other things."

___

"The program can be a little too intense at times."

___

"The intensive personal coaching helped me learn a lot about myself—and I could immediately apply and practice those teachings in a risk-free environment."

"What I found at IMD was a program focused on practical education and geared toward global business leadership—the exact qualities employers say they look for in recruiting new candidates."

"With its small class sizes and highly talented professors, IMD is able to exceed expectations on all fronts. The program was incredibly challenging, but the professors were so well coordinated with one another that it felt as though they knew exactly how far they could (and should) push us."

"IMD's program seemed to me to be more focused, intense, and personalized than other programs I considered (i.e., INSEAD, IESE, and LBS). The small class size and higher-than-normal average age of participants make it a great fit for more mature and experienced candidates."

"IMD is not for everyone. For those who are looking to make a career change, to earn lots of money as a merchant banker, or to have one last hoorah before facing the real world, this is not the place. But if someone is looking for a big internal transformation in developing their personal capabilities as well as their leadership potential, IMD is for that student."

"If you want to be challenged academically, grow emotionally, and develop your own leadership skills, my advice would be only IMD."

 **Where to Stay**

Mövenpick Radisson Hotel
Avenue de Rhodanie 4
1007 Lausanne, CH
41-21-612-76-12

Hôtel Au Lac
Place de la Navigation 4
1006 Lausanne, CH
41-21-617-14-51

Hôtel du Port
Place du Port 5
1006 Lausanne, CH
41-21-612-04-44

 Where to Eat

Chalet Suisse
Rte. du Signal 40
1018 Lausanne, CH
41-21-312-23-12

Le Pinocchio
Avenue de la Harpe 16
1007 Lausanne, CH
41-21-616-40-37

Le Bistrot Louis
Place de l'Europe 9
1003 Lausanne, CH
41-21-213-03-00

 Things to Do

Olympic Museum
Quai d'Ouchy 1
1001 Lausanne, CH
41-21-621-65-11

Boat trip to France (30 minutes)
Compagnie Générale de Navigation
sur le lac Léman
Avenue de Rhodanie 17
1007 Lausanne, CH
41-84-881-18-48

CHECK OUT BUSINESSWEEK.COM FOR MORE:

Admissions Q&A: Admissions Director Katty Ooms Suter discusses how to score a spot at IMD.

School Tour: Seeking something Swiss? Get a taste with *BusinessWeek*'s IMD photo essay.

Search & Compare: See how IMD stacks up against other top B-schools.

Video View: Program Director Sean Meehan discusses his makeover of IMD's yearlong MBA course.

MBA Forums: Connect with other IMD hopefuls.

Expanded Profile: Still not satisfied? Check out IMD's complete online profile for more facts, statistics, and student comments.

Access all the B-schools content on BusinessWeek.com by subscribing to MBA Insider.

MIT

Sloan School of Management
2006 Ranking: 7 (U.S.)
50 Memorial Dr.
Room E52-126
Cambridge, MA 02142
E-mail address:
  mbaadmissions@sloan.mit.edu
Web address: www.mitsloan.mit.edu
For more info: Call general information
  at (617) 258-5434

☑ B4UGO

Applicants accepted: 20%
Average GMAT score: 705
Average years' work experience: 5.8
Average post-MBA salary increase:
  24.3%*
Average total first-year
  compensation: $161,676
*Based in part on *BusinessWeek* survey data.

Why MIT?

Nobody comes to MIT for "soft" skills like teamwork and communication— they come for the operational tools that will allow them to get things done. A unique 13-week course structure features 6 weeks of coursework on either side of a "Sloan Innovation Period"— an intense week of experiential leadership training and exposure to cutting-edge faculty research. Once students complete the first-semester core, they are free to choose from 130 electives and design a program of their own choosing. Several specialized programs are also available, including a new entrepreneurship and innovation program. Sloan's 20,000 alumni include giants in the worlds of business and global affairs—from former Hewlett-Packard CEO Carleton "Carly" Fiorina to former Israeli prime minister Benjamin Netanyahu. More than 650 have gone on to found companies.

MIT is a private institution. Established in 1914, the Sloan full-time MBA is accredited by the Association to Advance Collegiate Schools of Business (AACSB).

 Headlines

June 12, 2007: Interim dean named to replace outgoing Dean Richard Schmalensee

April 25, 2007: Groundbreaking planned for new management facility

February 2, 2007: Sloan's new Laboratory for Sustainable Business committed to countering global warming

March 9, 2006: Legendary General Electric CEO Jack Welch to teach at Sloan

"MIT's Career Development Office was fantastic."

Famous MBA Alumni

Philip M. Condit, former chairman and CEO of Boeing
William A. Porter, founder of E*TRADE
Kofi Annan, former secretary-general of the United Nations

 Who Are My Classmates?

Full-time enrollment: 746
Women: 30%
International: 36%
Minority: 34%
Average age: 28
Accepted applicants enrolled: 66%

> *"MIT has the most incredible entrepreneurial community in the world, bar none."*

The 411

Annual tuition and fees: $44,556
Annual living expenses: $27,726
Total program cost, including forgone salary: $318,336*
Classes begin: September
Application deadlines: October 30, January 15
Application fee: $230

*Based in part on *BusinessWeek* survey data.

Cliff Notes

Leading areas of study: Entrepreneurship, Finance, General Management, Manufacturing and Technology Management, Strategy
Average class size, core courses: 66
Average class size, electives: 40
Number of electives: 130
Teaching methods: Case studies (33%), lectures (33%)

But What's It *Really* Like?

Graded by students:
Overall ranking: **A+**
Teaching quality: **A**
Career services: **A**

Graded by recruiters:
Overall ranking: **A**
Accounting: **B**
Analytical skills: **A+**
Communication: **B**
Finance: **B**
General management: **A**
International business: **A**
Marketing: **C**
Operations/production: **A+**
Teamwork skills: **B**

 Bling

Average pre-MBA salary: $86,886*
Average post-MBA salary: $107,990
Graduates with job offer by graduation: 93%
Top functional areas for graduates: Consulting, Finance/Accounting, Marketing/Sales
Biggest recruiters: McKinsey, Bain, BCG, Booz Allen Hamilton

*Estimate based on *BusinessWeek* survey data.

The Good, the Bad, and the Ugly: Students Speak Out

"One thing that's been impressive is how much I have learned from my fellow students. With diverse backgrounds, they all have different academic training, problem-solving skills, leadership styles, and goals. And because MIT's program is so small, there's essentially zero competition among students!"

"If you want a fluff program, look somewhere else."

"MIT's physical infrastructure lags behind that of other top schools."

"I went into the MIT program looking for a career change as well as an industry change. MIT's Career Development Office was fantastic at helping me to achieve these goals. I was offered and accepted my dream job—a more senior position than I had hoped for in one of my first-choice companies."

"MIT community members were the largest supporters and investors in my start-up. MIT has the most incredible entrepreneurial community in the world, bar none."

"MIT Sloan offers a wonderful environment with great students who work well in teams. They don't exhibit some of the stereotypical MBA student behavior of overcompetitiveness."

"Though certainly the exception to the general responsiveness and respect at MIT Sloan, there is one high-level administrator who does not value student input and appears to fear change."

"The administration is highly responsive to student feedback, often soliciting it through focus groups and direct contact with students at school events. The results are nearly real-time. Some problems that arose at the end of my core semester experience were addressed and corrected for the very next class."

"If you want a fluff program where you don't learn much and just party, look somewhere else. MIT Sloan is rigorous."

"As an international student, the quality and diversity of the student body, the access to renowned faculty, and the opportunities to interact with leading companies, business leaders, and investors in the world have been incredible. On a recent study trip to Asia, we met an ex-president, an ex-chief of staff, and other senior government officials and business leaders."

Where to Stay

Hotel at MIT
20 Sidney St.
Cambridge, MA 02139
(617) 577-0200

Hyatt Regency Cambridge
575 Memorial Dr.
Cambridge, MA 02139
(617) 492-1234

Sheraton Boston Hotel & Towers
39 Dalton St.
Boston, MA 02199
(617) 236-2000

 Where to Eat

Scollay Square
21 Beacon St.
Boston, MA 02108
(617) 742-4900

Pad Thai Café
1116 Boylston St.
Boston, MA 02215
(617) 254-6232

Sel de la Terre
255 State St.
Boston, MA 02109
(617) 720-1300

 Things to Do

New England Aquarium
Central Wharf
Boston, MA 02110
(617) 973-5200

Faneuil Hall Marketplace
4 South Market Building
Boston, MA 02169
(617) 523-1300

CHECK OUT BUSINESSWEEK.COM FOR MORE:

Admissions Q&A: MIT's Rod Garcia describes the ideal applicant.

Sample Application Essays and Interview Tips: Advice on how to write the essay and nail the interview.

Video View: Watch Dean Richard Schmalensee discuss his plans for integrating tech teaching tools and expanding international programs.

School Tour: Check out the MIT Sloan campus before you visit, using this photo essay.

Expanded Profile: Everything you ever wanted to know about MIT Sloan, and then some.

Access all the B-schools content on BusinessWeek.com by subscribing to MBA Insider.

McGill University

Desautels Faculty of Management
2006 Ranking: Second tier (non-U.S.)
1001 Sherbrooke St. W.
Suite 300
Montréal, QC (Canada) H3A 1G5
E-mail address: mba.mgmt@mcgill.ca
Web address: www.mcgill.ca/mba
For more info: Call general information at (514) 398-4066

☑ B4UGO

Applicants accepted: 33%
Average GMAT score: 645
Average years' work experience: 4.4
Average post-MBA salary increase: 83%
Average total first-year compensation: $96,465

Why McGill?

McGill's Desautels Faculty of Management is as multinational as its hometown of Montréal—which, apart from being a bustling Canadian business center, is officially bilingual. With more than half of its student body hailing from 25-plus countries, and two-thirds of its faculty coming from abroad, the school touts a full-time MBA curriculum that "naturally leans toward advancing an understanding of global issues." In the classroom, students learn from theories and case studies alike, and professors emphasize collaboration and teamwork. Mean starting salaries hover around $85,000, and some recent graduates have received job offers from high-profile companies such as IBM and Fidelity Investments.

McGill University is a public institution. Established in 1963, its full-time MBA program is accredited by the Association of Universities and Colleges of Canada (AUCC). McGill

also offers part-time and executive MBA programs.

Headlines

February 12, 2007: McGill conference focuses on sustainability

October 19, 2006: B-school marks 100 years of management education

November 17, 2005: McGill B-school receives $22 million donation

July 5, 2005: B-school names Peter Todd new dean

"The professors are of top caliber."

Famous MBA Alumni

Darren Entwistle, CEO of TELUS Corp.

Seymour Schulich, chairman of Newmont Capital Ltd.

Wong Ngit Liong, chairman and CEO of Venture Corp. Ltd.

 Who Are My Classmates?

Full-time enrollment: 202
Women: 53%
International: 36%
Minority: N/A
Average age: 27
Accepted applicants enrolled: 52%

"Less financial resources are dedicated to the MBA program."

The 411

Annual tuition and fees: $3,351 (resident), $22,024 (nonresident)
Annual living expenses: $17,180
Total program cost, including forgone salary: $137,062 (resident), $174,408 (nonresident)
Classes begin: September
Application deadlines: March 1 (international), June 1 (domestic)
Application fee: $100

Cliff Notes

Leading areas of study: Finance, International Business, Manufacturing and Technology Management, Marketing, Strategy
Average class size, core courses: 45
Average class size, electives: 30
Number of electives: 79
Teaching methods: Case studies (30%), lectures (30%), team projects (20%)

But What's It *Really* Like?

Graded by students:
Overall ranking: C
Teaching quality: B
Career services: B

Graded by recruiters:
Overall ranking: B
Accounting: C
Analytical skills: A
Communication: B
Finance: B
General management: C
International business: B
Marketing: B
Operations/production: N/A
Teamwork skills: A

 Bling

Average pre-MBA salary: $48,000
Average post-MBA salary: $87,850
Graduates with job offer by graduation: 51%
Top functional areas for graduates: Finance/Accounting, Consulting, Marketing/Sales
Biggest recruiters: RBC Capital Markets, BMO Capital Markets, CIBC, Imperial Oil, Fidelity

The Good, the Bad, and the Ugly: Students Speak Out

"The proximity of the school to an urban city center was very useful. It made practitioner visits more frequent and made conducting real-life consulting projects easier."

"During my two years at the McGill MBA, the people I have met have made a lasting impression on me. I am sure that I will be talking to them in the future on both a personal and a professional level."

"It represents a huge advancement in my career and my personal life. This was the toughest challenge I ever took on, but I am greatly satisfied with my learning experience and with the final outcome."

"McGill's low tuition makes it a bargain."

"I believe that the strength of the school is its ability to integrate different cultures. It has done a great job of selecting people with similar mentalities who are competitive, but in a healthy way."

"The administration treats the MBA program a few notches lower than the Bachelor of Commerce program. While both programs are very good, it appears that less financial resources are dedicated to the MBA program, whether for marketing/positioning the B-school or attracting better teaching faculty."

"The professors are of top caliber, and that, coupled with a diverse selection of courses, makes the learning experience a pleasure and a challenge simultaneously."

"McGill's low tuition makes it a bargain."

"I am concerned about the facilities (i.e., classrooms, buildings, etc.) of the program and how they fall short of a number of other MBA programs in Canada."

"The school is incorporating many exciting changes that better align the program with entrepreneurial and corporate needs. Most importantly, environmental, fiscal, and social responsibility elements are being integrated into the MBA experience in very creative ways—many of which are being driven by students themselves."

"The program offers an extremely attractive range of electives, and the fellow students and staff are top notch."

"The McGill MBA is a fantastic value for the money. The large number of international students adds so much to the program. Teachers are exceptional and dedicated."

Where to Stay

Meridien Château Versailles
1659 Sherbrooke St. W.
Montréal, QC H3H 1E3
(514) 933-8111

Sheraton Four Points
475 Sherbrooke St. W.
Montréal, QC H3A 2L9
(514) 842-3961

Kempinski Ritz-Carlton Hotel
1228 Sherbrooke St. W.
Montréal, QC H3G 1H6
(514) 842-4212

 Where to Eat

Sakura (Japanese)
2114 rue de la Montagne
Montréal, QC H3G 1Z7
(514) 288-9122

Commensal (vegetarian)
1204 McGill College Ave.
Montréal, QC H3B 4J8
(514) 871-1480

Il Cortile (Italian)
1442 Sherbrooke St. W.
Montréal, QC H3G 1K4
(514) 843-8230

 Things to Do

Montréal Museum of Fine Arts
1380 Sherbrooke St. W.
Montréal, QC H3G 2T9
(514) 285-2000

Montréal Botanical Garden and Biodôme
4101 Sherbrooke St. E.
Montréal, QC H1X 2B2
(514) 872-1400

CHECK OUT BUSINESSWEEK.COM FOR MORE:

Search & Compare: Find out if McGill makes the grade.

MBA Forums: Connect with other McGill hopefuls.

Expanded Profile: Still have questions? Check out McGill's full profile online.

Who's Hiring: Use this interactive feature to find out who's recruiting on campus.

Access all the B-schools content on BusinessWeek.com by subscribing to MBA Insider.

Michigan State University

Eli Broad College of Business
2006 Ranking: 29 (U.S.)
215 Eppley Center
East Lansing, MI 48824-1121
E-mail address: mba@msu.edu
Web address: www.mba.msu.edu
For more info: Call general information
at (517) 355-7604

☑ B4UGO

Applicants accepted: 29%
Average GMAT score: 633
Average years' work experience: 4.5
Average post-MBA salary increase:
124.2%
**Average total first-year
compensation:** $108,483

Why Michigan State?

Broad's academic claim to fame is its top-notch supply chain management specialization. Students also praise the program's emphasis on leadership and teamwork. Students get plenty of hands-on experience, from the Team Leadership Lab, which places student teams in high-stress military simulations, to the Financial Analysis Laboratory, which allows students to experience life inside an actual trading room facility. Aspiring consultants even have the opportunity to deal with clients on real projects outside of the classroom. With a total cost that is roughly half that of MIT or Stanford, and one of the biggest post-MBA salary increases around, MSU students can repay their B-school investment in a scant four years—one of the best ROIs in the United States.

Michigan State is a public institution. Established in 1960, Broad's full-time MBA program is accredited by the Association to Advance Collegiate Schools of Business (AACSB). Broad

also offers part-time and executive MBA programs.

 ## Headlines

July 1, 2007: Cheri Speier appointed associate dean for MBA program

October 23, 2006: Michigan State cracks *BusinessWeek*'s Top 30 after two-year absence

August 29, 2005: MBA students start school year with new honor code

August 29, 2005: Broad offers new programs in strategic management

---

*"Great value when
you consider
postgraduation
salaries."*

Famous MBA Alumni

James M. Cornelius, CEO of Bristol-Myers Squibb

Robert A. Chapek, president of Walt Disney's Buena Vista Worldwide Home Entertainment

Toichi Takenaka, president and CEO of Takenaka Corp.

💬 Who Are My Classmates?

Full-time enrollment: 174
Women: 28%
International: 40%
Minority: 22%
Average age: 28
Accepted applicants enrolled: 57%

"An incredible supply chain/operations management education."

The 411

Annual tuition and fees: $18,908 (resident), $26,358 (nonresident)
Annual living expenses: $14,655
Total program cost, including forgone salary: $143,828 (resident), $158,729 (nonresident)
Classes begin: August
Application deadlines: November 12 to May 12
Application fee: $85

Cliff Notes

Leading areas of study: Finance, Human Resource Management, Leadership, Marketing, Supply Chain Management
Average class size, core courses: 33
Average class size, electives: 21
Number of electives: 78
Teaching methods: Case studies (45%), lectures (25%), team projects (20%)

But What's It *Really* Like?

Graded by students:
Overall ranking: B
Teaching quality: B
Career services: A

Graded by recruiters:
Overall ranking: B
Accounting: B
Analytical skills: C
Communication: C
Finance: B
General management: B
International business: B
Marketing: B
Operations/production: A
Teamwork skills: B

💲 Bling

Average pre-MBA salary: $38,351
Average post-MBA salary: $85,974
Graduates with job offer by graduation: 94%
Top functional areas for graduates: Operations/Logistics, Finance/Accounting, Marketing/Sales
Biggest recruiters: Chevron, Motorola, Bank of America, Johnson & Johnson, United Technologies, General Motors, Intel

"Michigan State provides a small, inclusive environment where leadership and teamwork are emphasized. The faculty, administration, and students are very supportive, and the quality of education is top notch. Additionally, the cost of the school is reasonable and a great value when you consider post-graduation salaries."

"There's too much hand-holding and not enough technical skills acquired during the program."

"The program provided exposure to numerous executives in different industries, which provided for different perspectives on thought-provoking issues. The program was very supportive when it came to the job search."

"Too much hand-holding and not enough technical skills."

"If you want to go into investment banking, I wouldn't recommend this school. If you are more operationally focused, regardless of function, this is an excellent school."

"MSU's focus on teamwork, business ethics, and leadership differentiates our program from others and serves as a very strong competitive advantage for our students. MSU also provides valuable practical experience to students, such as running the students' consulting company, Spartan Consulting, leadership lab projects with undergraduate students, and real securities portfolio management."

"Unfortunately, my strong belief is that in 20 years the school will be exactly the same in terms of facilities, curriculum, IT systems, administration, and faculty. This is in large part due to a lack of leadership from Dean Duncan, the MSU bureaucracy, and a lack of funding."

"Although it is true that many desirable companies do not recruit on campus, we still had the opportunity to meet, interview, and get jobs and internships with them through several career fairs, and our travel expenditures were partially funded by the school."

"I would strongly recommend this program for those who want an incredible supply chain/operations management education. My marketing, finance, and human resource management classmates have a similar passion about the quality of education they received, but they recognize that even these classes have a strong operations/supply chain management influence."

 Where to Stay

Kellogg Hotel & Conference Center (MSU)
55 S. Harrison Rd.
East Lansing, MI 48824
(517) 432-4000

Radisson Hotel Lansing
111 N. Grand Ave.
Lansing, MI 48933
(517) 482-0188

University Quality Inn
3121 E. Grand River Ave.
Lansing, MI 48912
(517) 351-1440

 Where to Eat

OMI Sushi (Japanese)
210 Mac Ave.
East Lansing, MI 48823
(517) 337-2222

India Palace (Indian)
340 Albert Ave.
East Lansing, MI 48823
(517) 336-4150

Flats Grille (diner)
551 E. Grand River Ave.
East Lansing, MI 48823
(517) 332-8888

 Things to Do

Abrams Planetarium
Michigan State University
East Lansing, MI 48824
(517) 355-4676

Burgdorf's Winery
5635 Shoeman Rd.
Haslett, MI 48840
(517) 655-2883

CHECK OUT BUSINESSWEEK.COM FOR MORE:

Expanded Profile: Get all the basics on Broad, from student demographics to career outcomes, and more.

Interview Tips: Figure out how to sail through the interview process.

Admissions Q&A: Admissions Director Esmeralda Cardenal explains why Broad looks for leaders and team players.

School Tour: Planning a campus visit? Find out what facilities are available at Broad with this photo essay.

Search & Compare: Still undecided? Use this interactive tool to do a side-by-side analysis of all the programs on your short list.

Access all the B-schools content on BusinessWeek.com by subscribing to MBA Insider.

New York University

Leonard N. Stern School of Business
2006 Ranking: 14 (U.S.)
44 W. 4th St.
New York, NY 10012
E-mail address:
  sternmba@stern.nyu.edu
Web address: www.stern.nyu.edu
For more info: Call the admissions
  office at (212) 998-0600

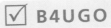 **B4UGO**

Applicants accepted: 18%
Average GMAT score: 700
Average years' work experience: 5
Average post-MBA salary increase:
  47.5%
**Average total first-year
  compensation:** $159,888

Why NYU?

Stern's highly selective full-time MBA program attracts students who want to be at the heart of the business world. Among the 15 highest-ranked programs in the nation for more than a decade, Stern's academic strengths are its finance, marketing, accounting, and entrepreneurship programs. With a location that gives students access to hundreds of companies, business leaders, and an active alumni network in a city regarded as the nation's premier MBA job market, students are able to make connections to launch their careers. In addition to the diversity and international perspective gained on campus, students can study in another country without taking a whole semester abroad through "Doing Business In . . . ," a two-week program in Argentina, Denmark, Australia, or Korea.

NYU is a private institution. Established in 1900, Stern's full-time MBA program is accredited by the Association to Advance Collegiate Schools of Business (AACSB). Stern also offers part-time and executive MBA programs. For details on Stern's part-time MBA program, see page 357. For details on its executive MBA program, see page 249.

 Headlines

May 14, 2007: Stern and Tisch Schools announce a joint MBA/ MFA degree

March 6, 2007: Stern team wins MBA real estate case competition

August 15, 2005: Derivative Research Program wins $300,000 Nasdaq grant

March 22, 2005: NYU's student-run social venture fund first in nation

*"The school is full of
high achievers, yet
amazingly friendly."*

Famous MBA Alumni

Tom Freston, former president and CEO of Viacom, Inc.
Richard S. Fuld Jr., chairman and CEO of Lehman Brothers Holdings, Inc.
Robert Greifeld, president and CEO of Nasdaq Stock Market, Inc.

 Who Are My Classmates?

Full-time enrollment: 838
Women: 42%
International: 38%
Minority: 47%
Average age: 28
Accepted applicants enrolled: 57%

"Quality faculty in marketing, management, and operations."

The 411

Annual tuition and fees: $42,422
Annual living expenses: $27,622
Total program cost, including forgone salary: $271,248
Classes begin: September
Application deadlines: November 15, January 15, March 15
Application fee: $175

Cliff Notes

Leading areas of study: Accounting, Entrepreneurship, Finance, Marketing, Media/Entertainment
Average class size, core courses: 53
Average class size, electives: 44
Number of electives: 135
Teaching methods: Team projects (30%), case studies (25%), lectures (20%)

But What's It *Really* Like?

Graded by students:
Overall ranking: **A+**
Teaching quality: **A+**
Career services: **A+**

Graded by recruiters:
Overall ranking: **A**
Accounting: **A+**
Analytical skills: **A**
Communication: **A**
Finance: **A+**
General management: **A**
International business: **A+**
Marketing: **A**
Operations/production: **B**
Teamwork skills: **A+**

 Bling

Average pre-MBA salary: $65,580
Average post-MBA salary: $96,738
Graduates with job offer by graduation: 90%
Top functional areas for graduates: Finance/Accounting, Marketing/Sales, Consulting
Biggest recruiters: Lehman Brothers, Citigroup, American Express, Deutsche Bank, JPMorgan Chase

The Good, the Bad, and the Ugly: Students Speak Out

"The school is full of bright people who are high achievers, yet amazingly friendly and down to earth. My interaction with my fellow students far exceeded my expectations."

"Time needed to keep up with coursework was massive."

"The Stern full-time MBA experience is affected by the large part-time program. On one hand, since there are so many part-time students, it allows the school to offer more electives than it could have otherwise. However, during the second year of the program, two-thirds (I counted) of the electives are offered only at night."

"I am trying to start my own venture, and Stern has provided me with a number of invaluable contacts. Although the public may still perceive Stern as a finance-focused school, it is diversifying. Stern has quality faculty in marketing, management, and operations. The most valuable asset of Stern is really the students."

"The quality of opportunities outside of finance positions drops considerably. After sharing experiences with classmates, the consensus is that the Office of Career Development does minimal work. Once investment banking recruiting is finished, so is the office's work for the year."

"I've found that the young alumni of Stern are an extremely tight-knit community—it is great as a Stern student to feel that there are so many alumni out in the workplace who are working so hard to pull more Stern students into their respective companies."

"Time needed to keep up with coursework was massive during the first year. Recruiting events and networking events took up way too much time and made it virtually impossible to keep up with some homework."

"I have made the best friends of my life while at Stern and have been able to be involved in all aspects of student life through student government. I am blown away by the attention given to student life by the deans. I don't want to leave!"

"NYU is a great place to go for anyone trying to get a finance job in New York. Even if one is trying to get a non-finance job, it is appealing because the location gives you access to so many companies. It would be difficult to network with these companies outside of New York."

Where to Stay

W New York—Union Square
201 Park Ave. S
New York, NY 10003
(212) 979-5052

Holiday Inn Manhattan Downtown
138 Lafayette St.
New York, NY 10013
(212) 966-8898

Washington Square Hotel
103 Waverly Pl.
New York, NY 10011
(212) 777-9515

 Where to Eat

Mamoun's Falafel
119 MacDougal St.
New York, NY 10012
(212) 674-8685

Patsy's Pizzeria
67 University Pl.
New York, NY 10003
(212) 533-3500

Spice (Thai)
60 University Pl.
New York, NY 10003
(212) 982-3758

 Things to Do

Sing Sing Karaoke
9 St. Mark's Pl.
New York, NY 10003
(212) 387-7800

Washington Square Park
Fifth Ave. at Waverly Pl.
New York, NY 10003

CHECK OUT BUSINESSWEEK.COM FOR MORE:

Admissions Q&A: Isser Gallogly, admissions director, offers advice for Stern applicants.

School Tour: Get a feel for Stern's Greenwich Village location with this photo essay.

Sample Essay and Interview Tips: Read an application essay that worked for a Stern student and get advice on making a good impression.

Placement Q&A: Gary Fraser, dean of students and former assistant dean of career development, talks about career options, salaries, and internships.

MBA Journal: Read about what a recent graduate's life was like at Stern.

Access all the B-schools content on BusinessWeek.com by subscribing to MBA Insider.

Northwestern University

Kellogg School of Management
2006 Ranking: 3 (U.S.)
Donald P. Jacobs Center
2001 Sheridan Rd.
Evanston, IL 60208-2001
E-mail address: MBAadmissions@
kellogg.northwestern.edu
Web address: www.kellogg.
northwestern.edu
For more info: Call general information
at (847) 491-3300

Why Northwestern?

With nine top-three *BusinessWeek* rankings since 1988, the Kellogg MBA is one of the premier programs in the nation. Recognized for strong performance in entrepreneurship, general management, and marketing, the school prides itself on a collegial atmosphere and dedication to teamwork. Kellogg students can take advantage of an always-evolving curriculum as well as specialized programs in biotechnology, real estate, media, and social enterprise. In a typical year, 93% of students graduate with at least one job offer—but usually more—and the average graduate leaves with a job paying $100,000 or more.

Northwestern University is a private institution. Established in 1908, Kellogg's full-time MBA is accredited by the Association to Advance Collegiate Schools of Business (AACSB). Kellogg also offers part-time and executive MBA programs. For details on its executive MBA program, see page 253.

☑ B4UGO

Applicants accepted: 24%
Average GMAT score: 704
Average years' work experience: 5.3
Average post-MBA salary increase:
56.3%
Average total first-year
compensation: $163,570

 Headlines

May 9, 2007: Kellogg holds leadership workshop for women

March 30, 2007: More than 400 Kellogg students and faculty return from global research trips

February 16, 2007: Kellogg and the Urban League announce venture to aid African American entrepreneurs

December 19, 2006: Kellogg Finance Department receives $1 million grant for capital markets education

*"An outstanding
mix of smart,
down-to-Earth people."*

Famous MBA Alumni

Jim Scherr, CEO of the U.S. Olympic Committee
Gregg Steinhafel, president of Target Stores
Bob Eckert, chairman and CEO of Mattel, Inc.

 **Who Are My Classmates?**

Full-time enrollment: 1,200
Women: 34%
International: 34%
Minority: 33%
Average age: 28
Accepted applicants enrolled: 57%

"Kellogg doesn't encourage enough independent thinking."

The 411

Annual tuition and fees: $43,935
Annual living expenses: $24,691
Total program cost, including forgone salary: $269,880
Classes begin: September
Application deadlines: October 19, January 11, March 7
Application fee: $225

Cliff Notes

Leading areas of study: Entrepreneurship, Finance, General Management, Marketing, Strategy
Average class size, core courses: 55
Average class size, electives: 45
Number of electives: 250
Teaching methods: Case studies (30%), lectures (30%), team projects (25%)

But What's It *Really* Like?

Graded by students:
Overall ranking: **A+**
Teaching quality: **A**
Career services: **A+**

Graded by recruiters:
Overall ranking: **A+**
Accounting: **A+**
Analytical skills: **A+**
Communication: **A+**
Finance: **A+**
General management: **A+**
International business: **A+**
Marketing: **A+**
Operations/production: **A+**
Teamwork skills: **A+**

$ Bling

Average pre-MBA salary: $66,314
Average post-MBA salary: $103,652
Graduates with job offer by graduation: 93%
Top functional areas for graduates: Consulting, Finance/Accounting, Marketing/Sales
Biggest recruiters: McKinsey, Bain, BCG, Booz Allen Hamilton, Morgan Stanley

The Good, the Bad, and the Ugly: Students Speak Out

"The feeling of family is palpable, and I have no doubt that my fellow classmates, as well as the Kellogg community at large, would be there for me, both personally and professionally, at a moment's notice."

"The Career Management Center has not been helpful for anyone I know here pursuing searches outside the traditional investment banking, consulting, or brand management roles."

"The Kellogg of tomorrow will not be the same as the Kellogg of today. The school is continually refining its curriculum and extracurricular activities to provide the most relevant business school experience. Best of all, these changes are largely driven by the students."

"The feeling of family is palpable."

"Be it Yahoo, Google, eBay, Dell, or Microsoft, I was able to make substantial connections with the companies I was targeting through the Kellogg Career Center, on-campus recruiting, and Kellogg alumni."

"I think Kellogg places too much emphasis on teamwork and cooperative culture and doesn't encourage enough independent thinking."

"Kellogg has an outstanding mix of smart, down-to-earth people. At no point did I ever experience someone who wouldn't help with an assignment or prepping for an interview."

"As someone who is passionate about entrepreneurship, it was unfortunate to see this as the weakest aspect of Kellogg."

"The fact that Kellogg recruits very different types of people—from the social, extroverted 'marketing' stereotype to the analytical 'finance' stereotype—makes the experience that much more challenging, because one is constantly exposed to different ways of excelling."

"Overall, I was very impressed by the courses, and I strongly believe I am part of the 'Kellogg family' forever, given the close relationship between the school, students, and alumni."

"Kellogg needs to update its core curriculum to include more analysis of current business trends."

"Kellogg has the most amazing culture—a smart, talented, and diverse student body that is full of energy and comaraderie. It makes learning and experiencing these two years together both rewarding and a lot of fun."

Where to Stay

Omni Orrington
1710 Orrington Ave.
Evanston, IL 60201
(847) 866-1248

Hilton Garden Inn
1818 Maple Ave.
Evanston, IL 60201
(847) 475-6400

Best Western University Plaza
1501 Sherman Ave.
Evanston, IL 60201
(800) 381-2830

 Where to Eat

Tommy Nevins Pub
1450-1458 Sherman Ave.
Evanston, IL 60201
(847) 869-0450

Koi
624 Davis St.
Evanston, IL 60201
(847) 866-6969

Prairie Moon
1502 Sherman Ave.
Evanston, IL 60201
(847) 864-8328

 Things to Do

Chicago Botanical Garden
1000 Lake Cook Rd.
Glencoe, IL 60022
(847) 835-5440

**Architectural Tours (with the
Chicago Architecture Foundation)**
224 S. Michigan Ave.
Chicago, IL 60604
(312) 922-3432 x241

CHECK OUT BUSINESSWEEK.COM FOR MORE:

Admissions Q&A: Beth Flye, assistant dean and director of admissions, describes the ideal Kellogg applicant.

Sample Application Essays and Interview Tips: Get the lowdown on what it takes to get in.

Video View: Dean Dipak Jain discusses the recent uptick in the MBA job market.

School Tour: Check out the campus before visiting.

Careers Q&A: Career Services Director Roxanne Hori explains why job prospects for Kellogg graduates are strong.

Access all the B-schools content on BusinessWeek.com by subscribing to MBA Insider.

Ohio State University

Max M. Fisher College of Business
2006 Ranking: Second tier (U.S.)
2100 Neil Ave.
Columbus, OH 43210
E-mail address: mba@fisher.osu.edu
Web address: www.cob.ohio-state.edu
For more info: Call the MBA program
office at (614) 292-8511

 **B4UGO**

Applicants accepted: 29%
Average GMAT score: 662
Average years' work experience: 4.3
Average post-MBA salary increase:
105%
**Average total first-year
compensation:** $114,283

Why Ohio State?

Fisher attracts students who are looking for a personalized MBA experience, but with the added advantages of a larger school. Students can choose from more than 130 electives to customize their program. Coursework is almost evenly split among case studies, lectures, team projects, and experiential learning. While virtually all graduates have jobs within three months of graduation, some say that recruiting is heavily concentrated among companies in the Midwest, and recruiters overall give the school only mediocre grades. That said, students can expect a post-MBA pay hike of more than $40,000, allowing them to recoup their entire MBA investment in about six years—half the time it takes a Wharton graduate to get out of the red.

Ohio State University is a public institution. Established in 1933, Fisher's full-time MBA program is accredited by the Association to Advance Collegiate Schools of Business (AACSB). Fisher also offers part-time

and executive MBA programs. For details on its part-time MBA program, see page 361. For details on its executive MBA program, see page 257.

 Headlines

June 11, 2007: Student-run investment fund chalks up 28.5% return

May 5, 2007: Steve Mangum named acting dean

April 30, 2007: Fisher Dean Joseph Alutto named interim university provost

April 11, 2006: Big Four accounting firm opens recruiting office on campus

*"I am impressed with
the quality of my
classmates."*

Famous MBA Alumni

David Rader, executive vice president and CFO of Frito-Lay North America
Jeffrey Montie, executive vice president of Kellogg, president of Kellogg North America
Clayton Daley Jr., CFO of Procter & Gamble

Who Are My Classmates?

Full-time enrollment: 277
Women: 26%
International: 31%
Minority: 20%
Average age: 27
Accepted applicants enrolled: 63%

"The close relationship between students and professors is really strong."

The 411

Annual tuition and fees: $21,183 (resident), $35,337 (nonresident)
Annual living expenses: $13,149
Total program cost, including forgone salary: $150,424 (resident), $178,762 (nonresident)
Classes begin: September
Application deadline: May 30
Application fee: $60 (U.S.), $70 (international)

Cliff Notes

Leading areas of study: Finance, Marketing, Operations Management, Strategy, Supply Chain Management
Average class size, core courses: 70
Average class size, electives: 32
Number of electives: 132
Teaching methods: Case studies (25%), lectures (25%), team projects (25%)

But What's It *Really* Like?

Graded by students:
Overall ranking: B
Teaching quality: B
Career services: C

Graded by recruiters:
Overall ranking: B
Accounting: B
Analytical skills: B
Communication: B
Finance: B
General management: B
International business: B
Marketing: B
Operations/production: B
Teamwork skills: A

Bling

Average pre-MBA salary: $40,895
Average post-MBA salary: $83,817
Graduates with job offer by graduation: 76%
Top functional areas for graduates: Finance/Accounting, Marketing/ Sales, Consulting, Operations/Logistics
Biggest recruiters: Nationwide, Abbott, Limited Brands, Wipro Technologies, Deloitte, Emerson, Procter & Gamble

⟨⟨⟩⟩ The Good, the Bad, and the Ugly: Students Speak Out

"I am impressed with the quality of my classmates. Whatever group project we might be working on, they could always be depended on to come through with quality work."

"The diversity of company recruiters was somewhat limited because of the small class size in comparison to other top programs. In addition, the employers are mostly limited to the Midwest, especially Ohio."

"The Center for Entrepreneurship at the Fisher College of Business is an amazing resource worthy of any amount of time you might spend in further investigations. In addition, the local entrepreneurial community is vibrant, engaged, and willing to help students . . . a remarkable and underrated feature of the Fisher MBA and Columbus."

"The diversity of company recruiters was somewhat limited."

"I believe if you could move Fisher to the East Coast or West Coast, its reputation would be much higher. The close relationship between students [and between] students and professors is really strong. Even though it's a small B-school, we have a lot of student organizations."

"I do not feel the program offers adequate support for women or minorities. Additionally, there are not enough options for dual degrees. Those who are quiet or introverted [may be] left behind."

"Fisher's small size combined with the resources of Ohio State University create a unique opportunity for those students who are willing to leverage the opportunity the pairing creates. Things are not delivered on a platter here, but if you can dream it, you can do it."

"In five years I think OSU will be able to compete with the top 15. The school is working on bringing in additional employers, top-notch students and faculty, and improving the student experience."

"I love the intimacy among students and professors, the interaction in class, and the support from all the faculty members. The majority of Fisher's coursework is team-oriented, and I learned how to be a good team member and team leader. Overall, my MBA experience far exceeded my expectations."

"Although the program has extremely high-quality professors and is relatively inexpensive, it admits a large number of low-quality candidates (e.g., candidates who have no work experience), and the curriculum is relatively rigid."

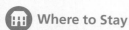 **Where to Stay**

The Blackwell
2110 Tuttle Park Pl.
Columbus, OH 43210
(614) 247-4000

**University Plaza Hotel &
Conference Center**
3110 Olentangy River Rd.
Columbus, OH 43202
(614) 267-7461

Fairfield Inn and Suites
3031 Olentangy River Rd.
Columbus, OH 43202
(614) 267-1111

 Where to Eat

**The Buckeye Hall of Fame Café
(American)**
1421 Olentangy River Rd.
Columbus, OH 43212
(614) 291-2233

The Happy Greek
1554 N. High St.
Columbus, OH 43201
(614) 291-7777

Bistro 2110
2110 Tuttle Park Pl.
Columbus, OH 43210
(614) 247-4000

 Things to Do

Wexner Center for the Arts
1871 N. High St.
Columbus, OH 43201
(614) 292-3535

Union Station Video Café
630 N. High St
Columbus, OH 43201
(614) 228-3546

CHECK OUT BUSINESSWEEK.COM FOR MORE:

Admissions Q&A: Find out what the Fisher admissions office is looking for in an applicant.

Video View: Fisher Dean Joseph Alutto describes the program's strengths and weaknesses.

Expanded Profile: More facts, more statistics, and more graduate comments.

Return on Investment: See how long it will take to repay your MBA investment at Fisher compared to other schools.

Search & Compare: Size up all the programs on your short list using this side-by-side analysis tool.

Access all the B-schools content on BusinessWeek.com by subscribing to MBA Insider.

Pennsylvania State University

Smeal College of Business
2006 Ranking: Second tier (U.S.)
200 Business Building
University Park, PA 16802
E-mail address: smealmba@psu.edu
Web address: www.smeal.psu.edu/mba
For more info: Call the main
 switchboard at (814) 863-0474

☑ B4UGO

Applicants accepted: 30%
Average GMAT score: 650
Average years' work experience: 4.8
Average post-MBA salary increase:
 121%*
**Average total first-year
 compensation:** $107,282
*Based in part on *BusinessWeek* survey data.

Why Penn?

At Smeal, semesters are broken up into a 7-1-7 format: two seven-week modular classes broken up by an "Immersion Week," an intensive learning experience that takes place in a business setting. Smeal aims to give MBA students a global experience. That effort starts with a first-year course designed to broaden their worldviews by taking them to foreign destinations such as Chile, Turkey, and China to explore the global economy. But it doesn't end there. International cases are included in virtually every class, and about a third of the students in each class come from outside the United States. Second-year electives and a capstone strategy course all have a strong international flavor, too. Smeal is also big on leadership. It is one of a handful of schools that offers personalized leadership assessment and individual coaching.

Smeal is a public institution. Established in 1959, Smeal's full-time MBA is accredited by the Association to Advance Collegiate Schools of Business

(AACSB). Smeal also offers part-time and executive MBA programs.

 Headlines

February 27, 2007: First-years depart for immersion experience in Chile, China, and Turkey

February 6, 2007: 40 companies—including Dell, IBM, and Pfizer—to attend supply chain career fair

January 1, 2006: Dean Judy Olian decamps for UCLA; James B. Thomas named as replacement

September 30, 2005: New business building dedicated

"I would choose Smeal again in a heartbeat."

Famous MBA Alumni

John Arnold, CEO of Petroleum
Products Corp.
J. David Rogers, CEO of J.D. Capital
Management LLC
James Stengel, global marketing offi-
cer for Procter & Gamble

Who Are My Classmates?

Full-time enrollment:171
Women: 33%
International: 35%
Minority: 18%
Average age: 28
Accepted applicants enrolled: 61%

"Finance majors had to do a lot of networking to secure employment."

The 411

Annual tuition and fees: $18,520
(resident), $30,122 (nonresident)
Annual living expenses: $16,428
Total program cost, including forgone
salary: $145,110 (resident),
$168,314 (nonresident)*
Classes begin: August
Application deadlines: December 1,
February 1, April 15
Application fee: $75

*Based in part on *BusinessWeek* survey data.

Cliff Notes

Leading areas of study: Entrepreneur-
ship, Finance, Marketing, Strategy,
Supply Chain Management
Average class size, core courses: 43
Average class size, electives: 24
Number of electives: 45
Teaching methods: Case studies (30%),
team projects (25%), lectures (20%),
experiential learning (20%)

But What's It *Really* Like?

Graded by students:
Overall ranking: C
Teaching quality: B
Career services: B

Graded by recruiters:
Overall ranking: B
Accounting: N/A
Analytical skills: B
Communication: B
Finance: C
General management: B
International business: B
Marketing: B
Operations/production: B
Teamwork skills: B

Bling

Average pre-MBA salary: $37,607*
Average post-MBA salary: $83,098
Graduates with job offer by graduation:
85%
Top functional areas for graduates:
Finance/Accounting, Marketing/
Sales, Operations/Logistics
Biggest recruiters: Dell, DuPont, Air
Products & Chemicals, Capital
One, IBM, Pfizer, Walt Disney

*Estimate based on *BusinessWeek* survey data.

The Good, the Bad, and the Ugly: Students Speak Out

"Looking back with 20/20 hindsight, I would choose Smeal again in a heartbeat over every other highly ranked school I was accepted to. Smeal delivered on every aspect I needed from a graduate business program, and I also graduated debt free."

"The classes are small and intimate; the faculty members are accessible, and they remember your name long after the class has ended and throughout the remainder of your education. The new business building is spectacular, and Happy Valley is alive and well with the resurgence of its football program. Not a bad way to spend two years, in my opinion."

"I didn't see as many technology-related classes as I expected. A few professors and their classes didn't provide value, and the curriculum is a little old-fashioned, without integration of different disciplines that are cross-applied in the real business world."

"Ivy League quality at state tuition!"

"I am still amazed at how much the faculty and staff are engaged in the program, as well as how enthusiastic and driven my classmates were."

"Other majors had no problem with on-campus recruiting, but because of the size of the class, finance majors had to do a lot of networking/traveling on their own to secure employment. That being said, I could have never imagined that a school's alumni would be so helpful."

"Smeal's MBA program is decent, and I learned a lot."

"Penn State offers the best communications program that I am aware of, as well as the only private-investor student-run mutual fund in the country."

"The Smeal MBA program provides an extensive, well-rounded education. Ivy League quality at state tuition!"

"Another important aspect of Penn State is the number of MBA students who get graduate assistantships and can sustain themselves. In my class alone, almost 75% of the class has GAs, which is great because you not only get an entire tuition exemption but also get a monthly wage for 20 hours."

"Penn State's Nittany Lion Fund is a truly unique learning experience. This $3 million mutual fund is entirely student run. The result is a real-world experience and an excellent network of contacts."

Where to Stay

Nittany Lion Inn
200 W. Park Ave.
State College, PA 16803
(814) 865-8500

Penn Stater Hotel
215 Innovation Blvd.
State College, PA 16803
(814) 863-5000

Atherton Hotel
125 S. Atherton St.
State College, PA 16801
(800) 832-0132

 Where to Eat

Fuji & Jade Garden
418 Westerly Pkwy.
State College, PA 16801
(814) 861-3226

Gingerbread Man
130 Hiester St.
State College, PA 16801
(814) 237-0361

India Pavillion
222 E. Calder Way
State College, PA 16801
(814) 237-3400

 Things to Do

Earth & Mineral Sciences Museum
16 Deike Building, Pollock Rd.
University Park, PA 16802
(814) 865-6336

**Penn State Downtown
Theatre Center**
146 S. Allen St.
State College, PA 16802
(814) 863-0493

CHECK OUT BUSINESSWEEK.COM FOR MORE:

Admissions Q&A: MBA Admissions Director Michele Kirsch dishes on what Smeal wants.

Interview Tips: How to ace the required interview.

School Tour: Planning a visit? Check out the Penn State campus first, using this online slide show.

Expanded Profile: Everything you ever wanted to know about Smeal, and then some.

Who's Hiring: Interested in a specific company? Find out if it recruits at Smeal.

Access all the B-schools content on BusinessWeek.com by subscribing to MBA Insider.

Purdue University

Krannert School of Management
2006 Ranking: 24 (U.S.)
2020 Rawls Hall
100 S. Grant St.
West Lafayette, IN 47907
E-mail address:
    masters@krannert.purdue.edu
Web site address:
    www.krannert.purdue.edu
For more info: Call admissions at (877)
    622-5726

✓ B4UGO

Applicants accepted: 32%
Average GMAT score: 662
Average years' work experience: 4.1
Average post-MBA salary increase:
    76.7%
Average total first-year
    compensation: $106,082

Why Purdue?

"Work hard, work right, work together"
—this simple mantra prevails at Krannert, where the emphasis is on teamwork. Throughout the program, group
projects are tackled by carefully crafted
teams made up of students with varying
backgrounds. And learning isn't limited
to the classroom. Student teams com-
mercialize new technologies, engage in
computer simulations, run an investment fund, and consult with companies
on real problems. A Friday lecture series
brings top executives to campus to
enhance students' understanding of
emerging business issues. Like many
public programs, Krannert is a bargain
for Indiana residents, who will spend
less for the entire program than most
Top 30 schools charge for a single year.
And nine out of ten graduates have a job
at graduation.

Purdue University is a public institution. Established in 1962, Krannert's

full-time MBA program is accredited
by the Association to Advance Collegiate Schools of Business (AACSB).
Krannert also offers part-time and executive MBA programs.

 Headlines

September 12, 2006: 120 employers to
attend student-run career fair

May 25, 2006: International business
program gets $1.4 million grant

February 22, 2006: Krannert launches
programs with three Chinese universities

February 10, 2006: Krannert combines
MBA and executive education programs into one administrative body

"You really get your
money's worth."

Famous MBA Alumni

Joe Forehand, retired chairman and CEO of Accenture

Marshall Larsen, president, chairman, and CEO of Goodrich

Venu Srinivasan, chairman and managing director of TVS Motor Co.

🗨 Who Are My Classmates?

Full-time enrollment: 277
Women: 23%
International: 46%
Minority: 22%
Average age: 28
Accepted applicants enrolled: 45%

"It's the boot camp of MBA schools."

The 411

Annual tuition and fees: $18,064 (resident), $33,462 (nonresident)

Annual living expenses: $10,780

Total program cost, including forgone salary: $153,316 (resident), $184,112 (nonresident)

Classes begin: August

Application deadlines: November 1 to May 1 (U.S.), December 1 to February 1 (international)

Application fee: $55

Cliff Notes

Leading areas of study: Consulting, Entrepreneurship, Finance, Marketing, Operations Management

Average class size, core classes: 55

Average class size, electives: 32

Number of electives: 71

Teaching methods: Case studies (45%), lectures (20%), team projects (16%)

But What's It *Really* Like?

Graded by students:
Overall ranking: B
Teaching quality: B
Career services: B

Graded by recruiters:
Overall ranking: B
Accounting: B
Analytical skills: B
Communication: B
Finance: B
General management: B
International business: C
Marketing: C
Operations/production: A+
Teamwork skills: C

💲 Bling

Average pre-MBA salary: $47,814

Average post-MBA salary: $84,506

Graduates with job offer by graduation: 89%

Top functional areas for graduates: Finance/Accounting, Consulting, Marketing/Sales, Operations/Logistics

Biggest recruiters: General Motors, Cummins, Emerson, Procter & Gamble, Raytheon

The Good, the Bad, and the Ugly: Students Speak Out

"The Krannert experience has been outstanding. First, I have learned a great deal, especially in analytical processes. Second, teamwork has been emphasized, and it has proven most helpful. Third, the overall culture and environment are very conducive to success, from an A-class facility to the personal responsiveness of faculty and administrative staff."

> ## *"The program could have placed greater emphasis on current issues."*

"Learning at Krannert was great; so were the professors. However, most students were immature and selfish. Coming from the military, where cooperation was a great factor, the attitude of most of the students was a shocker!"

"I thoroughly enjoyed my experience at Krannert, but my one complaint with the students is their lack of willingness to commit to things outside of the classroom. As a student leader for the school, it was always very challenging to get students to commit to anything that took time and did not involve

their getting a job or receiving an A in a class."

"I truly recommend Krannert for everyone. It is the best school for people who are concerned about integrity and like to work hard. We all 'work hard, work right, work together!'"

"The core curriculum and many electives emphasized quantitative skills and frameworks above, and often to the exclusion of, any deeper discussions. I felt the program could have placed greater emphasis on current issues and business problems."

"Krannert is a great program to go through—you really get your money's worth. It's the boot camp of MBA schools. The workload will drive you to work as a team and build relationships that will last a lifetime. The teachers are top notch, especially in the field of finance."

"Even if I had no job offers after completion of my degree, I would not hesitate for an instant to reaffirm that my decision to come to Krannert was by far one of the best decisions of my life."

"Purdue has a cost/benefit ratio that can't be beat, with assistantships available for almost everyone so that the cost of school is almost nothing."

 Where to Stay

Union Club Hotel
101 N. Grant St.
West Lafayette, IN 47906
(765) 494-8900

Hilton Garden Inn
356 E. State St.
West Lafayette, IN 47906
(765) 743-2100

University Inn
3001 Northwestern Ave.
West Lafayette, IN 47906
(765) 463-5511

 Where to Eat

Scotty's Brewhouse
352 E. State St.
West Lafayette, IN 47906
(765) 746-3131

Bruno's (European)
212 Brown St.
West Lafayette, IN 47906
(765) 743-1668

McGraw's Steak, Chop & Fish House
2707 S. River Rd.
West Lafayette, IN 47906
(765) 743-3942

 Things to Do

Wolf Park
4004 E. 800 N.
Battle Ground, IN 47920
(765) 567-2265

Tippecanoe Mall
2415 Sagamore Pkwy. S.
Lafayette, IN 47905
(765) 448-6176

CHECK OUT BUSINESSWEEK.COM FOR MORE:

Admissions Q&A: Admissions Director William "Jamie" Hobba discusses the application process at Krannert.

Interview Tips: Get the lowdown on how to impress the admissions officers at Krannert.

School Tour: Planning a visit? Check out the Purdue campus first, using this photo essay.

Video View: Dean Rick Cosier discusses the importance of a global education.

Expanded Profile: Want more? You'll find it in Krannert's online profile.

Access all the B-schools content on BusinessWeek.com by subscribing to MBA Insider.

Queen's University

Queen's School of Business
2006 Ranking: 1 (non-U.S.)
Goodes Hall, Room 414
Kingston, ON (Canada) K7L 3NG
E-mail address:
   queensmba@business.queensu.ca
Web address: www.business.queensu.ca
For more info: Call full-time MBA
   information at (613) 533-2302

☑ B4UGO

Applicants accepted: 65%
Average GMAT score: 642
Average years' work experience: 4.6
Average post-MBA salary increase:
   43.7%
Average total first-year
   compensation: N/A

Why Queen's?

A top-ranked program since 2002, the Queen's 12-month MBA is both unusually intense and deeply satisfying, owing to the near-constant interaction between students and faculty. Unlike most B-schools, where new teams form for each class, Queen's students belong to a single team for the entire year, much as they would on the job. The teams are assigned to 15- by 20-foot "offices" where they learn how to solve problems and resolve differences in a way that can't be taught in a classroom. Students can concentrate in consulting and project management, marketing, finance, or innovation and entrepreneurship. Queen's also offers a Science & Technology MBA.

Queen's University is a public institution. Established in 1960, its full-time MBA program is accredited by the Association to Advance Collegiate Schools of Business (AACSB), the Association of MBAs (AMBA), and the European Quality Improvement System (EQUIS). Queen's also offers a part-time accelerated MBA and an executive MBA. For details on the executive MBA program, see page 261.

Headlines

March 20, 2007: Queen's launches Centre for Governance

September 26, 2006: Bank of Nova Scotia gives $1 million for international exchange and disabled students

September 21, 2006: New MBA approach gives students custom experience

January 27, 2006: Research fellowship in accounting established

---

"I can't imagine doing an MBA any other way."

Famous MBA Alumni

Sam Gudewill, president and CEO of Innovex Equities Corp.
Mike Ball, president of Allergan Inc.
Jerry Del Missier, co-president of Barclay's Capital

Who Are My Classmates?

Full-time enrollment: 72
Women: 28%
International: 40%
Minority: N/A
Average age: 28
Accepted applicants enrolled: 42%

"The small-sized classes and access to faculty are unmatched."

The 411

Annual tuition and fees: $58,256 (resident), $63,283 (nonresident)*
Annual living expenses: $20,416*
Total program cost, including forgone salary: $139,694 (resident), $144,726 (nonresident)
Classes begin: May
Application deadline: March 15
Application fee: None
*Total for program.

Cliff Notes

Leading areas of study: Consulting, Entrepreneurship, Finance, Marketing
Average class size, core courses: 72
Average class size, electives: 18
Number of electives: 18
Teaching methods: Case studies (40%), lectures (35%), team projects (10%)

But What's It *Really* Like?

Graded by students:
Overall ranking: A+
Teaching quality: A+
Career services: A+

Graded by recruiters:
Overall ranking: B
Accounting: B
Analytical skills: A
Communication: C
Finance: C
General management: B
International business: B
Marketing: N/R
Operations/production: N/A
Teamwork skills: B

Bling

Average pre-MBA salary: $61,022
Average post-MBA salary: $87,700
Graduates with job offer by graduation: 52%
Companies recruiting on campus: 57
Top functional areas for graduates: Consulting, General Management, Marketing/Sales
Biggest recruiters: Canadian Imperial Bank of Commerce, Toronto Dominion Bank, PRTM, Deloitte, BCG

The Good, the Bad, and the Ugly: Students Speak Out

"The small-sized classes and access to faculty at a personal level were unmatched. In addition, the quality and backgrounds of the students added to the learning experience."

"Queen's School of Business is a hidden treasure in North America, but this is not the place to be if you are solely concerned with making it to Lehman Brothers or Goldman Sachs."

"In 11 months we did a full MBA. We sat in more hours of lecture than most two-year programs, and the quality of the students in our program was very, very high, with most being engineers and science majors, many with advanced degrees. There is no better school in Canada than Queen's."

"The one-year format is intense."

"I cannot overstate the value of the team-based model employed in this program. I learned far more about interacting with others under stressful conditions than I did in seven years of employment. The interpersonal skills I learned will greatly enhance my ability to manage teams through a perspective of equality that recognizes individuals for their strengths rather than faulting them for their weaknesses. This is not something that can be adequately taught via reading or lectures."

"The intensive 12-month program can be a little overwhelming some days, and it's not for everyone, but it teaches excellent time discipline, and overall I can't imagine doing an MBA any other way. Two years? Forget that."

"I can't speak highly enough of the overall experience. The small class size, outstanding access to administration and quality faculty, unbeatable alumni network, and prestigious name are tough to match."

"The one-year format is intense. There are definitely some trade-offs. Advantages are lower opportunity costs and short time back into the workforce. Disadvantages are that you can't go as in-depth into topics as you'd potentially like, and the at times overwhelming workload."

"Queen's model of putting you in teams that you retain throughout the year gives you hands-on experience on how to manage a team and lead it, and how to follow a leader. Since most of the courses had a team component in the grades, you had to make it work. In the process you learned how to develop a high-performance team."

 **Where to Stay**

Radisson Hotel Kingston Harbourfront
1 Johnson St.
Kingston, ON K7L 5H7
(613) 549-8100

Holiday Inn Kingston-Waterfront
2 Princess St.
Kingston, ON K7L 1A2
(613) 549-8400

The Queen's Inn
125 Brock St.
Kingston, ON K7L 1S1
(613) 546-0429

 Where to Eat

Kingston Brewing Company
34 Clarence St.
Kingston, ON K7L 1W9
(613) 542-4978

Chez Piggy
68-R Princess St.
Kingston, ON K7L 1A5
(613) 549-7673

Wooden Heads (gourmet pizza)
192 Ontario St.
Kingston, ON K7L 2Y8
(613) 549-1812

 Things to Do

Time to Laugh Comedy Club
394 Princess St.
Kingston, ON K7L 5N3
(613) 542-5233

Kingston 1000 Islands Cruises
263 Ontario St.
Kingston, ON K7K 2X5
(613) 549-5544

CHECK OUT BUSINESSWEEK.COM FOR MORE:

Admissions Q&A: Shannon Goodspeed discusses the Queen's MBA offering.

Expanded Profile: Everything you always wanted to know about Queen's, and then some.

Placement Q&A: Career Centre Director David Edwards on the need for lifelong career skills.

Search & Compare: See how Queen's stacks up against other top B-schools.

Access all the B-schools content on BusinessWeek.com by subscribing to MBA Insider.

Stanford University

Graduate School of Business
2006 Ranking: 6 (U.S.)
518 Memorial Way
Stanford, CA 94305
E-mail address: mba@gsb.stanford.edu
Web address: www.gsb.stanford.edu/
  mba/
For more info: Call the MBA admissions
  office at (650) 723-2766

✓ **B4UGO**

Applicants accepted: 7.9%
Average GMAT score: 721
Average years' work experience: 3.8
Average post-MBA salary increase:
  58.7%
**Average total first-year
  compensation:** $209,407

Why Stanford?

A highly selective program, Stanford's full-time MBA is a favorite among both students and recruiters, and has been a fixture among *BusinessWeek*'s Top 10 programs since the rankings were launched in 1988. Widely recognized for excellence in entrepreneurship and management, the school prides itself on its ability to "change lives, change organizations," and "change the world." GSB students benefit from a remodeled curriculum—which offers a more tailored learning experience—and can tap into the entrepreneurial fever of nearby Silicon Valley, which one student dubbed "the Holy Grail for B-schoolers." Near-perfect GMAT scores and classrooms packed with the next generation of corporate leaders are the norm. The professors are nothing to sneeze at, either. Intel's Andy Grove teaches here, and top executives such as Jack Welch, Herb Kelleher, and Steve Ballmer are regular visitors.

Stanford University is a private institution. Established in 1925, the GSB's full-time MBA program is accredited by the Association to Advance Collegiate Schools of Business (AACSB).

 Headlines

May 14, 2007: GSB students vie to be "Entrepreneur Idol"

April 22, 2007: GSB conference makes case for socially responsible and environmentally sustainable supply chains

June 26, 2006: Stanford agrees to accept GRE scores

June 5, 2006: GSB adopts more tailored curriculum model

"Unparalleled exposure to high-tech entrepreneurship."

Famous MBA Alumni

Henry McKinnell, chairman and former CEO of Pfizer

Phil Knight, founder and former CEO of Nike

Omid Koidestani, senior vice president at Google

Who Are My Classmates?

Full-time enrollment: 741
Women: 38%
International: 40%
Minority: 24%
Average age: N/A
Accepted applicants enrolled: 80%

"There's an overemphasis on the theoretical, esoteric, and ephemeral."

The 411

Annual tuition and fees: $45,921
Annual living expenses: $26,271
Total program cost, including forgone salary: $292,700
Classes begin: September
Application deadlines: October 22 to March 21
Application fee: $250

Cliff Notes

Leading areas of study: Entrepreneurship, Finance, Leadership, Organizational Behavior, Strategy
Average class size, core courses: 60
Average class size, electives: 34
Number of electives: 125
Teaching methods: Case studies (40%), team projects (15%), problem solving (15%)

But What's It *Really* Like?

Graded by students:
Overall ranking: A
Teaching quality: B
Career services: A+

Graded by recruiters:
Overall ranking: A
Accounting: B
Analytical skills: A+
Communication: A+
Finance: A
General management: A+
International business: A+
Marketing: A
Operations/production: C
Teamwork skills: B

Bling

Average pre-MBA salary: $74,158
Average post-MBA salary: $117,681
Graduates with job offer by graduation: 94%
Top functional areas for graduates: Finance/Accounting, Consulting, Marketing/Sales
Biggest recruiters: McKinsey, BCG, Morgan Stanley, Bain, Yahoo!

The Good, the Bad, and the Ugly: Students Speak Out

"Stanford's integration into the Silicon Valley network provides unparalleled exposure to high-tech entrepreneurship and access to CEOs of some of the world's most exciting companies, like Google, eBay, etc."

"The faculty members don't want to teach, and in many cases aren't prepared to teach, the basic business skills that ultimately make good managers. Instead, there's an overemphasis on the theoretical, esoteric, and ephemeral, all wrapped up in a cozy blanket of 'leadership' and 'teamwork' training."

"Our relatively small class size is a huge asset. Whether I need to find romantic restaurant recommendations in Carmel or get contacts at Brazilian cell-phone companies, everyone is always willing to help me out."

"The administration is pretty stifling here. It doesn't really allow MBAs to do out-of-the-box things while in school."

"Our small class size is a huge asset."

"At bigger business schools, there is a lot of competition for interview slots. At Stanford, if you really want to interview with a company that comes to campus, you can always get one because we are a smaller school. Interviews with consulting firms are also pretty much guaranteed."

"The school is too small to have the teaching resources to cater to the vastly different backgrounds (from nonprofit to private equity) of the students it accepts. I believe that this inability to teach people with little analytical experience has been hidden by grade nondisclosure."

"Alumni usually refer to their two years at the GSB as the two best years of their life. I'm not going to do that, because that implies that everything else is downhill. For me, Stanford is like Disneyland—too surreal to attend forever, but a great place to spend a limited period of time."

"I was surprisingly pleased with the teaching quality, and I really felt that I learned a lot in the classrooms. GSB professors care about students and are genuinely interested in getting to know us."

"Stanford is truly a transformational place—both professionally and personally. The academic content and quality of teaching are top notch, and the program inspires intense introspection. There is a strong focus on leadership, interpersonal dynamics, and generally 'knowing oneself,' which helps to distinguish Stanford alumni as thoughtful, genuine, and principled leaders."

Where to Stay

Stanford Terrace Inn
531 Stanford Ave.
Palo Alto, CA 94306
(650) 857-0333

Sheraton Palo Alto
625 El Camino Real
Palo Alto, CA 94301
(650) 328-2800

The Westin Palo Alto
675 El Camino Real
Palo Alto, CA 94301
(650) 321-4422

 Where to Eat

Evvia Estiatorio
420 Emerson St.
Palo Alto, CA 94301
(650) 326-0983

Empire Tap Room
651 Emerson St.
Palo Alto, CA 94301
(650) 321-3030

Hobee's
4224 El Camino Real
Palo Alto, CA 94306
(650) 856-6124

 Things to Do

**Rodin Sculpture Garden
(at the Cantor Arts Center)**
Lomita Dr. & Museum Way
Stanford, CA 94305
(650) 723-4177

**Hoover Institution on War,
Revolution and Peace**
434 Galvez Mall
Stanford, CA 94305
(650) 723-1754

CHECK OUT BUSINESSWEEK.COM FOR MORE:

Admissions Q&A: Derrick Bolton, director of MBA admissions, describes the ideal Stanford applicant.

Sample Application Essays and Interview Tips: Get the lowdown on what it takes to get in.

Video View: Listen to Dean Robert Joss discuss the importance of a B-school degree.

School Tour: Check out the campus before visiting.

Expanded Profile: Analyze all the admissions, academic, and career services statistics.

Access all the B-schools content on BusinessWeek.com by subscribing to MBA Insider.

Thunderbird

Thunderbird School of Global
Management
2006 Ranking: Second tier (U.S.)
15249 N. 59th Ave.
Glendale, AZ 85306-6000
E-mail address:
admissions@thunderbird.edu
Web address: www.thunderbird.edu
For more info: Call the admissions
office at (602) 978-7100

☑ B4UGO

Applicants accepted: 71%
Average GMAT score: 597
Average years' work experience: 4.8
Average post-MBA salary increase:
92.5%
**Average total first-year
compensation:** $107,889

Why Thunderbird?

The name says it all: "MBA—Global Management." At Thunderbird, *global* isn't a buzzword to attract students; it's in the school's DNA. To produce high-functioning international business leaders, Thunderbird packs students from dozens of countries into every class and requires MBA students to achieve proficiency in a second language before completing their degrees—one of the few U.S. B-schools to do so. While MBA students study in Glendale, the school's reach extends well past the Southwest. Through study-abroad opportunities and exchange programs, Thunderbird MBAs spend anywhere from a few weeks to an entire term in a country of their own choosing. A career management seminar—covering cross-cultural teams and global business etiquette—is mandatory.

Thunderbird is a private institution. Established in 1946, Thunderbird's full-time MBA program is accredited by the Association to Advance Collegiate Schools of Business (AACSB). Thunderbird also offers part-time and executive MBA programs. For details on Thunderbird's executive MBA program, see page 269.

 Headlines

April 16, 2007: Thunderbird announces joint degree with university in Taipei

May 8, 2006: Alumnus gives $1 million to support global entrepreneurship center

January 23, 2006: Thunderbird announces language proficiency requirement for MBAs

September 15, 2005: The Dalai Lama visits Thunderbird

*"Exactly what I
was looking for."*

Famous MBA Alumni

Jim Alling, president of Starbucks Coffee U.S.

William D. Perez, president and CEO of Wrigley Co.

Frances Aldrich Sevilla-Sacasa, president and CEO of U.S. Trust

 Who Are My Classmates?

Full-time enrollment: 548
Women: 32%
International: 47%
Minority: 17%
Average age: 28
Accepted applicants enrolled: 77%

"Hands down the leading MBA institution for international business."

The 411

Annual tuition and fees: $36,630
Annual living expenses: $6,335
Total program cost, including forgone salary: $155,930
Classes begin: September
Application deadline: June 30
Application fee: $125

Cliff Notes

Leading area of study: International Business
Average class size, core courses: 55
Average class size, electives: 45
Number of electives: 49
Teaching methods: Lectures (36%), case studies (24%), experiential learning (15%)

But What's It *Really* Like?

Graded by students:
Overall ranking: **B**
Teaching quality: **B**
Career services: **C**

Graded by recruiters:
Overall ranking: **B**
Accounting: **B**
Analytical skills: **C**
Communication: **B**
Finance: **B**
General management: **B**
International business: **A**
Marketing: **B**
Operations/production: **B**
Teamwork skills: **B**

$ Bling

Average pre-MBA salary: $42,000
Average post-MBA salary: $80,833
Graduates with job offer by graduation: 48%
Top functional areas for graduates: Marketing/Sales, Management Information Systems, Consulting, Finance/Accounting
Biggest recruiters: Cisco Systems, Johnson & Johnson, Sunguard, Capital One, Deloitte

The Good, the Bad, and the Ugly: Students Speak Out

"I defy anyone to identify a school that has such a unique focus, [and a] student body and alumni network as strong as Thunderbird's."

"Anyone interested in international business should seriously consider attending Thunderbird."

"Some professors were not good, I feel. [Also, the] cost is too expensive compared to the quality of the classes."

"It's hard to measure the international focus given at Thunderbird. I don't think it will help as much in landing the first job, but over a long time, the extra international focus will be crucial to [success in] upper-level management."

> *"Students interested in Wall Street should go to Wharton or Kellogg."*

"While there is a handful of so-so faculty, choosing the right classes means that you have access to those who are at the top of their game."

"I would recommend Thunderbird for international development, an international leadership track, maybe international marketing. I would not recommend it for entrepreneurship, finance, or anything accounting related."

"Thunderbird heightened my appreciation of diversity, and how to manage [it] and benefit from it in the workplace. In addition, my network has been expanded into corners of the globe that I had never been familiar with before."

"[Students who] are interested in becoming investment bankers to make a lot of money and work on Wall Street should go to Wharton or Kellogg. If they are interested in overseas management, marketing across borders, or international HR, they should go to Thunderbird."

"Thunderbird is hands down the leading MBA institution for international business. The diversity in the classroom between not only the students, but also the professors, creates business professionals with an understanding of other cultures and business practices. While other schools may try to emulate the atmosphere at Thunderbird, few are able to do so."

"Thunderbird has been exactly what I was looking for. Thunderbird has a student body of about 40% U.S. students and the rest foreigners. It's a great thing. Classes are great when you have a student from China telling you why China is growing so fast and giving you a Chinese perspective."

 **Where to Stay**

Thunderbird Executive Inn
15249 N. 59th Ave.
Glendale, AZ 85306
(602) 978-7987

Quality Inn & Suites at Talavi
5511 W. Bell Rd.
Glendale, AZ 85308
(602) 896-8900

Ramada Limited Glendale
7885 W. Arrowhead Towne Ctr. Dr.
Glendale, AZ 85308
(623) 412-2000

 Where to Eat

Caramba Fresh Mexican Food
6661 W. Bell Rd. #104,
Glendale, AZ 85308
(623) 487-1111

Chevy's Fresh Mex
7700 W. Arrowhead Towne Ctr. Dr.
Glendale, AZ 85308
(623) 979-0055

Mythos Greek Restaurant
2515 N. Scottsdale Rd.
Scottsdale, AZ 85257
(408) 947-6896

 Things to Do

Sahuaro Ranch Park Historical Area
9802 N. 59th Ave.
Glendale, AZ 85302
(623) 930-4200

Cerreta Candy Company
5345 W. Glendale Ave.
Glendale, AZ 85301
(623) 930-9000

CHECK OUT BUSINESSWEEK.COM FOR MORE:

Career Q&A: Vice President Kip Harrell talks about the job opportunities available to Thunderbird graduates.

Video View: Thunderbird's dean discusses the school's international focus.

School Tour: Take a tour of Thunderbird's Southwest campus, without ever getting on a plane.

Admissions Q&A: Judy Johnson, associate vice president for admissions, talks about Thunderbird's class profile.

Expanded Profile: Dig deeper with a more in-depth profile on the Thunderbird MBA.

Access all the B-schools content on BusinessWeek.com by subscribing to MBA Insider.

Università Bocconi

SDA Bocconi School of Management
2006 Ranking: Second tier (non-U.S.)
Via Balilla 18
Milano, Italy 20136
E-mail address: mbainfo@sdabocconi.it
Web address: www.sdabocconi.it/mba
For more info: Call general information
at 39-02-5836-3125

 B4UGO

Applicants accepted: 37%
Average GMAT score: 640
Average years' work experience: 4.8
Average post-MBA salary increase:
55.6%
Average total first-year
compensation: $118,100

Why SDA Bocconi?

Located in Italy's fashion and finance capital, SDA Bocconi is a low-cost alternative for a high-quality international B-school experience. At just $45,000 for the entire 14-month program, both tuition and forgone income are essentially cut in half compared to top two-year U.S. programs. But Bocconi doesn't skimp. The program unfolds in five phases, which include a thorough grounding in management basics and soft skills, from decision making to leadership, and an action learning project with selected companies that may include a group consulting assignment, research, or an entrepreneurial project. There are only three concentrations—strategy, finance, and marketing—and electives are quite limited. But 90% of graduates have jobs within three months of graduation, and starting salaries (about $80,000) are better than at many higher-ranked schools.

Università Bocconi is a private institution. Established in 1975, SDA Bocconi's full-time MBA program is accredited by the Association of MBAs (AMBA), the Associazione Italiana per la Formazione Manageriale (ASFOR), and the European Quality Improvement System (EQUIS). It also offers part-time and executive MBA programs.

 Headlines

May 2007: Bocconi names Gianemilio Osculati new chief executive

January 2007: MBA students attend "power dressing" workshop

January 2007: Bain, BCG seek internship candidates

September 2006: J&J and Nike recruiting at School of Management

"What sets it apart is the team spirit."

Famous MBA Alumni

Marco Saltalamacchia, senior vice president of BMW Group (Europe)
Andrea Barbier, president and CEO of YSL Beauté
Alessandro Lamanna, vice president of Nokia (Latin America)

 Who Are My Classmates?

Full-time enrollment: 107
Women: 40%
International: 54%
Minority: N/A
Average age: 28
Accepted applicants enrolled: 71%

"U.S. students may find it hard to market themselves back in the U.S. job market."

The 411

Annual tuition and fees: $44,820*
Annual living expenses: $22,140*
Total program cost, including forgone salary: $129,960
Classes begin: October
Application deadline: April 30
Application fee: $135
*Total for program.

Cliff Notes

Leading areas of study: Entrepreneurship, Finance, General Management, Marketing, Strategy
Average class size, core courses: 110
Average class size, electives: 36
Number of electives: 21
Teaching methods: Lectures (47%), team projects (15%) case studies (15%)

But What's It *Really* Like?

Graded by students:
Overall ranking: C
Teaching quality: C
Career services: C

Graded by recruiters:
Overall ranking: A
Accounting: A
Analytical skills: A
Communication: A
Finance: A
General management: A
International business: A
Marketing: A+
Operations/production: A+
Teamwork skills: A+

 Bling

Average pre-MBA salary: $54,000
Average post-MBA salary: $84,000
Graduates with job offer by graduation: 34%
Companies recruiting on campus: 103
Top functional areas for graduates: Consulting, Finance/Accounting, Marketing/Sales
Biggest recruiters: Bain, BCG, Fiat, Johnson & Johnson, Roland Berger, Wolters Kluwer

The Good, the Bad, and the Ugly: Students Speak Out

"SDA Bocconi provides a great atmosphere, and what sets it apart from other schools—I have plenty of friends attending other top-ranked schools—is the team spirit and collaboration among students."

"SDA Bocconi has the huge plus of having two different 60-person classes—an Italian one and an international one—that get to mingle with each other. It's like a big family."

"SDA Bocconi's MBA program is not good for Asian students because of its zero reputation in Asia."

"I had an excellent MBA experience, both personally and academically. I have also had more robust exposure to international business than I would have had if I had stayed in North America."

> *"The diversity of the class added a truly international perspective."*

"I was able to interact with colleagues from diverse professional and ethnic backgrounds—over 30 nationalities were represented. This gave me invaluable soft skills and knowledge of business practices around the world."

"Great professors. Great environment. Great quality/cost ratio."

"Career Services does not provide enough job opportunities for the students, and the alumni network is not helpful to many of the graduates."

"Not only did SDA Bocconi offer a great academic program, but, given the intimate size of the classes compared to most other schools, lectures were also extremely engaging, and everyone actively participated."

"I would strongly promote SDA Bocconi to any friend interested in an MBA program. The only outstanding issue is whether or not she or he would like to study in Italy. U.S. students may find it hard to market themselves back in the U.S. job market, but the international experience speaks for itself."

"The diversity of the class, both in nationality and in prior career experience, added a truly international perspective. It also undoubtedly contributed to the development of management and leadership skills."

"The Bocconi MBA is an MBA that people are doing *together*. Everyone knows everyone."

"The international program at SDA Bocconi is intense, stressful, and extremely rewarding."

 **Where to Stay**

NHOW Milan
Via Tortona 35
Milan, IT 20144
39-02-489-8861

Foresteria Monforte
Piazza Tricolore
Milan, IT 20129
39-02-7631-8516

Straf Hotel
Via San Raffaele 3
Milan, IT 20121
1-800-337-4685

 Where to Eat

Trattoria Milanese
Via Santa Marta 11
Milan, IT 20123
39-02-8645-1991

Giulio pane e ojo
Via L. Muratori 10
Milan, IT 20135
39-02-545-6189

10 Corso Como
Corso Como 10
Milan, IT 20154
39-02-654-831

 Things to Do

Duomo (cathedral)
Piazza del Duomo
Milan, IT 20121
39-02-864-63456

Teatro alla Scala (La Scala opera)
Piazza della Scala
Milan, IT 20121
39-02-7200-3744

CHECK OUT BUSINESSWEEK.COM FOR MORE:

Sample Application Essays: See what it takes to score a spot at SDA Bocconi.

Search & Compare: Find out how SDA Bocconi stacks up against other B-schools.

MBA Forums: Connect with other SDA Bocconi hopefuls.

Interview Tips: Hone your people skills with this how-to guide.

Expanded Profile: Everything you ever wanted to know about SDA Bocconi, and more.

Access all the B-schools content on BusinessWeek.com by subscribing to MBA Insider.

U. of British Columbia

Sauder School of Business
2006 Ranking: Second tier (non-U.S.)
2053 Main Mall
Vancouver, BC (Canada) V6T 1Z2
E-mail address: mba@sauder.ubc.ca
Web address: www.sauder.ubc.ca/mba
For more info: Call general information
at (604) 822-8500

 B4UGO

Applicants accepted: 54%
Average GMAT score: 617
Average years' work experience: 5.5
Average post-MBA salary increase:
105.9%
**Average total first-year
compensation:** $100,800

Why Sauder?

UBC's full-time MBA program prides itself on four I's: innovation, intensity, internationality, and incomparability. For 15 months, UBC students develop global business skills, choosing from eight areas of specialization and four subspecializations (which include Business Intelligence Systems and Sustainability and Business). A 13-week core incorporates seven key business disciplines and develops cross-functional skills needed to tackle complex problems. For those looking to become better leaders, Sauder offers a professional development program. The one-week program includes training in nonacademic skills, including personal productivity and handling the media. With exchange programs at more than 20 business schools around the world, UBC gives students ample opportunity to study outside idyllic Vancouver—though many insist they'd never leave.

UBC is a public institution. Established in 1955, Sauder's full-time MBA program is accredited by the Association to Advance Collegiate Schools of Business (AACSB) and the European Quality Improvement System (EQUIS). Sauder also offers a part-time MBA and an executive MBA in healthcare.

 Headlines

February 15, 2007: $1 million gift will fund new career center

January 8, 2007: Sauder alumni dominate "40 under 40" list of top young businesspeople

November 7, 2006: Sauder launches MBA specialization in sustainability and business

February 6, 2006: Centre for Health Care Management created

"The selection of courses was vast."

Famous MBA Alumni

Martin Glynn, former president and CEO of HSBC America

Joe Houssian, president and CEO of Intrawest

Pedro Man, former president of Starbucks Coffee Asia Pacific

 ## Who Are My Classmates?

Full-time enrollment: 228
Women: 33%
International: 58%
Minority: N/A
Average age: 29
Accepted applicants enrolled: 63%

"The faculty is what makes this program special."

The 411

Annual tuition and fees: $38,204*
Annual living expenses: $22,000*
Total program cost, including forgone salary: $108,766
Classes begin: August
Application deadlines: February 29 (international), April 30 (U.S.)
Application fee: $130
*Total for program.

Cliff Notes

Leading areas of study: Finance, General Management, Marketing, Strategy, Supply Chain Management
Average class size, core courses: 60
Average class size, electives: 24
Number of electives: 90
Teaching methods: Case sudies (35%), lectures (35%), team projects (20%)

But What's It *Really* Like?

Graded by students:
Overall ranking: C
Teaching quality: C
Career services: C

Graded by recruiters:
Overall ranking: B
Accounting: N/A
Analytical skills: B
Communication: B
Finance: B
General management: B
International business: B
Marketing: B
Operations/production: A
Teamwork skills: C

$ Bling

Average pre-MBA salary: $38,850
Average post-MBA salary: $80,000
Graduates with job offer by graduation: 76%
Top functional areas for graduates: Finance/Accounting, General Management, Marketing/Sales
Biggest recruiters: Best Buy Canada, Vancouver Coastal Health, RBC Financial, BC Hydro, General Motors, Telus

"The quality of the faculty and staff was superb, the selection of courses was vast, and class sizes were small. Also, we made lifelong bonds with peers from all over the world."

"UBC has potential, but it really needs to increase awareness of its MBA program and bring potential recruiters to the school."

"Vancouver is a great place to study if your priority is to have a good quality of life. If you want to work in one of the top investment banking firms or consulting firms in the United States, it's not the best one to choose."

"The companies that recruited were more interested in undergraduates."

"Sauder has an excellent mix of theory and practice."

"It seemed like the admissions [office] was willing to take anyone who was able to pay, even if they didn't have the necessary background or social skills required to work effectively on teams."

"The faculty is truly what makes this program special. They do not just stand in front of the classroom and lecture. They put challenging problems in front of you and really go that extra mile to support you, not only in your studies but in what you choose to do with your career."

"The companies that recruited at UBC were more interested in undergraduates, and very few seemed to value the additional education and experience that an MBA could deliver."

"Studying at UBC was a very good opportunity to meet different people from all over the world. With increasing globalization in business today, the program should really help me in my future career."

"The school's career services department is not good at keeping in contact with companies and alumni, both in Canada and abroad."

"UBC is a good value for the money, and has excellent teaching from famous professors who make themselves available to students. It's got a straightforward, no-gimmicks approach."

"Sauder gets many experienced and even high-powered applicants interested in the quality of life that Vancouver offers. Many people actually find Vancouver and other Canadian cities perferable to most cities in the United States as places to study, work, and bring up children."

Where to Stay

West Coast Suites at the University of British Columbia
5959 Student Union Blvd.
Vancouver, BC V6T 1K2
(604) 822-1000

Fairmont Hotel Vancouver (downtown Vancouver)
900 W. Georgia St.
Vancouver, BC V6C 2W6
(604) 684-3131

Delta Vancouver Suites (downtown Vancouver)
550 W. Hastings St.
Vancouver, BC V6B 1L6
(604) 689-8188

 Where to Eat

One More Sushi
5728 University Blvd.
Vancouver, BC V6T 1K6
(604) 222-0138

Burgoo
4434 W. 10th Ave.
Vancouver, BC V6H 1L1
(604) 221-7839

Vij's
1480 W. 11th Ave.
Vancouver, BC V6H 1L1
(604) 736-6664

 Things to Do

Museum of Anthropology at the University of British Columbia
6393 N.W. Marine Dr.
Vancouver, BC V6T 1Z2
(604) 822-5087

Granville Island Market
1661 Duranleau St., 2nd Floor
Vancouver, BC V6H 3S3
(604) 666-5784

CHECK OUT BUSINESSWEEK.COM FOR MORE:

MBA Forums: Connect with other Sauder hopefuls.

School Tour: Check out Sauder's scenic Vancouver campus via this photo essay.

Search & Compare: See how Sauder fares among other top international B-schools.

Expanded Profile: More stats and info about Sauder's full-time MBA program.

Access all the B-schools content on BusinessWeek.com by subscribing to MBA Insider.

U. of California at Berkeley

Haas School of Business
2006 Ranking: 8 (U.S.)
430 Student Services Building #1902
Berkeley, CA 94720-1902
E-mail address: N/A
Web address: www.haas.berkeley.edu
For more info: Call MBA admissions at
(510) 642-1405

☑ B4UGO

Applicants accepted: 14%
Average GMAT score: 710
Average years' work experience: 5.4
Average post-MBA salary increase:
57.3%
**Average total first-year
compensation:** $153,200

Why Berkeley?

Berkeley's MBA program might not be No. 1, but its students are having a blast—and learning a lot along the way. Widely recognized for excellence in finance, general management, marketing, and strategy, the school prides itself on a down-to-earth student body. While Berkeley is the least expensive Top 10 school, its graduates are eagerly sought-after by recruiters, who give the program straight A's in communication, teamwork, and analytical skills. Located just a short distance from Silicon Valley, Haas is a favorite of tech giants Yahoo!, Google, and Microsoft, as well as consultants McKinsey, BCG, and Bain. Nobody's complaining about the California weather, either.

Berkeley is a public institution. Established in 1943, Haas's full-time MBA program is accredited by the Association to Advance Collegiate Schools of Business (AACSB). Haas also offers part-time and executive MBA programs.

 Headlines

February 21, 2007: Young Entrepreneurs at Haas hosts program for youth

October 26, 2006: Haas offers new leadership course for first-year students

April 24, 2006: Haas alumnus Richard Blum pledges $15 million for poverty center

September 19, 2005: Job placement and salaries soar for Haas graduates

"The student body here truly pairs modesty with confidence."

Famous MBA Alumni

Donald Fisher, chairman and founder of Gap Inc.
Paul Otellini, president and CEO of Intel
Arun Sarin, CEO of Vodafone

 **Who Are My Classmates?**

Full-time enrollment: 486
Women: 31%
International: 39%
Minority: 38%
Average age: 29
Accepted applicants enrolled: 53%

"Berkeley provides a platform to let you do whatever you want."

The 411

Annual tuition and fees: $26,886 (resident), $37,950 (nonresident)
Annual living expenses: $22,497
Total program cost, including forgone salary: $228,236 (resident), $250,364 (nonresident)
Classes begin: August
Application deadlines: November 5 to March 12
Application fee: $175

Cliff Notes

Leading areas of study: Finance, General Management, Innovation, Marketing, Strategy
Average class size, core courses: 59
Average class size, electives: 40
Number of electives: 99
Teaching methods: Case studies (50%), lecures (25%), team projects (15%)

But What's It *Really* Like?

Graded by students:
Overall ranking: **A+**
Teaching quality: **B**
Career services: **A**

Graded by recruiters:
Overall ranking: **A**
Accounting: **B**
Analytical skills: **A**
Communication: **A**
Finance: **B**
General management: **A**
International business: **A**
Marketing: **A+**
Operations/production: **B**
Teamwork skills: **A**

💲 Bling

Average pre-MBA salary: $64,735
Average post-MBA salary: $101,859
Graduates with job offer by graduation: 86%
Top functional areas for graduates: Finance/Accounting, Marketing/Sales, Consulting, General Management
Biggest recruiters: Google, Deloitte, Bain, Bank of America, Abbott, Citigroup, McKinsey, Yahoo!

The Good, the Bad, and the Ugly: Students Speak Out

"Not only are my classmates brilliant, motivated, and experienced, but they are also fun to work with and don't mind getting their hands dirty. The student body here truly pairs modesty with confidence."

"I think the grade nondisclosure policies detract from learning. They make students lazy, and, because nobody cares about their grades, there isn't the back-and-forth and give-and-take discussion that we will encounter in the real world."

> *"There wasn't enough focus on leadership development."*

"My small yet diverse class (240 students) gave me exactly what I wanted—a chance to know each of my classmates personally; a truly collaborative, open, and constructive classroom environment; and a multitude of opportunities and possibilities."

"There was a huge spread in quality from one professor to the next. Some core professors were great, while I would have been surprised if others could get a job at a high school."

"I feel that its location gives Berkeley a major advantage over other schools for students who are interested in pursuing careers in digital media, entrepreneurship, or social ventures. The Bay Area is the heart of innovation, talent, and funding for these types of ventures, and the Haas School is intimately connected with all of the above."

"Though the career office does a good job with on-campus recruiting, it is not particularly helpful to students with less traditional job searches."

"Berkeley provides a platform to let you do whatever you want. I put together a sports management class and invited a host of guest speakers. One of them helped me get my dream job."

"There wasn't enough focus on leadership development. This was sorely lacking in the program."

"Besides the quality of the professors, the facilities, and having the Bay Area at your feet, what was most appealing for me was the quality of my classmates and the flexibility I had in shaping the exact MBA experience I wanted."

"Haas offers such a variety of courses and extracurricular activities that no matter what you are interestsed in, there is a way to pursue your career goals and make contacts through Haas alumni."

 **Where to Stay**

Berkeley City Club
2315 Durant Ave.
Berkeley, CA 94704
(510) 848-7800

Hotel Durant
2600 Durant Ave.
Berkeley, CA 94704
(510) 845-8981

Rodeway Inn
1461 University Ave.
Berkeley, CA 94702
(510) 848-3840

 Where to Eat

Chez Panisse
1517 Shattuck Ave.
Berkeley, CA 94709
(510) 548-5525

Plearn Thai
2050 University Ave.
Berkeley, CA 94704
(510) 841-2148

Smart Alec's
2355 Telegraph Ave.
Berkeley, CA 94704
(510) 704-4000

 Things to Do

Berkeley Art Museum and Pacific Film Archive
2625 Durant Ave.
Berkeley, CA 94720
(510) 642-0808

UC Botanical Garden
200 Centennial Dr.
Berkeley, CA 94720
(510) 643-2755

CHECK OUT BUSINESSWEEK.COM FOR MORE:

Chat: Admissions Directors Jett Pihakis and Peter Johnson field questions about the ideal Berkeley applicant.

Sample Application Essays and Interview Tips: Get the lowdown on what it takes to land a spot at Berkeley.

School Tour: Check out the campus before visiting.

Careers Q&A: Career Services Director Abby Scott explains why one-size-fits-all placement services just don't cut it.

Expanded Profile: All the statistics on Berkeley's full-time MBA.

Access all the B-schools content on BusinessWeek.com by subscribing to MBA Insider.

U. of California at Los Angeles

John E. Anderson Graduate School of
  Management
2006 Ranking: 12 (U.S.)
110 Westwood Plaza
Gold Hall, Suite B201
Los Angeles, CA 90095-1481
E-mail address:
  mba.admissions@anderson.ucla.edu
Web address: www.anderson.ucla.edu
For more info: Call the admissions
  office at (310) 825-6944

☑ B4UGO

Applicants accepted: 23%
Average GMAT score: 704
Average years' work experience: 4.8
Average post-MBA salary increase:
  79.4%
**Average total first-year
  compensation:** $142,928

Why UCLA?

Consistently ranked among the Top 20
programs, Anderson's full-time MBA is
the degree of choice for West Coast B-
schoolers looking for a top-notch program in finance, marketing, or
entrepreneurship. A highly selective
program, Anderson boasts an award-
winning faculty and wins high marks
from recruiters, especially in the areas
of accounting and communication
skills. The school prides itself on what
it calls "excellence without attitude," a
term coined to describe Anderson students' easygoing way, despite their considerable achievements. There's a lot to
be said for year-round temperatures in
the 70s, too. As one student noted:
"Where else can you wear flip-flops
year-round and take a surfing class
between finance and operations?"

UCLA is a public institution. Established in 1935, Anderson's full-time
MBA program is accredited by the Association to Advance Collegiate Schools of
Business (AACSB). Anderson also offers
part-time and executive MBA programs.
For details on UCLA's part-time MBA
program, see page 373. For details on its
executive MBA program, see page 273.

 Headlines

September 21, 2006: Anderson helps
launch training program for minority
entrepreneurs

September 12, 2006: Anderson hires
nine new faculty members for finance,
accounting, and marketing

January 3, 2006: Judy D. Olian
replaces Bruce Willison as dean

August 17, 2004: Anderson launches
new entertainment and media management institute

*"The faculty was
top notch."*

Famous MBA Alumni

Jeff Henley, chairman of Oracle Corp.
Mitch Kupchak, general manager of
the Los Angeles Lakers
William Gross, founder and CIO of
PIMCO

Who Are My Classmates?

Full-time enrollment: 740
Women: 35%
International: 33%
Minority: 30%
Average age: 28
Accepted applicants enrolled: 49%

"I found UCLA Anderson to be a real door-opener."

The 411

Annual tuition and fees: $28,446
(resident), $37,287 (nonresident)
Annual living expenses: $23,789
Total program cost, including forgone
salary: $215,110 (resident),
$232,792 (nonresident)
Classes begin: September
Application deadlines: October 24 to
April 23
Application fee: $175

Cliff Notes

Leading areas of study: Entrepreneur-
ship, Finance, General Management,
Marketing, Operations Management
Average class size, core courses: 71
Average class size, electives: 32
Number of electives: 73
Teaching methods: Lectures (70%),
case studies (16%), team projects
(10%)

But What's It *Really* Like?

Graded by students:
Overall ranking: **A**
Teaching quality: **B**
Career services: **B**

Graded by recruiters:
Overall ranking: **B**
Accounting: **A**
Analytical skills: **A**
Communication: **A**
Finance: **A**
General management: **B**
International business: **A**
Marketing: **A**
Operations/production: **A**
Teamwork skills: **A**

Bling

Average pre-MBA salary: $55,320
Average post-MBA salary: $99,237
Graduates with job offer by graduation:
85%
Top functional areas for graduates:
Finance/Accounting, Marketing/
Sales, Consulting
Biggest recruiters: Yahoo!, Deloitte
Consulting, Google, Citigroup,
Merrill Lynch

The Good, the Bad, and the Ugly: Students Speak Out

"While my undergraduate degree helped me discover who I was as a person, Anderson helped me discover who I was and what I wanted to be in my career. I now have a direction, and finally I feel like I have the tools necessary to be successful."

"Anderson offered the best combination of entrepreneurship, finance, and real estate, with strong research centers in each of these areas."

"Anderson helped me discover who I was."

"The career services office does not do much for students who do not follow traditional Anderson paths or, for that matter, who want to return east."

"The size of the program allows individuals to succeed and stand out, while the quality of the student body truly embodies the (sometimes overused) Anderson mantra of 'excellence without attitude,' enhancing the educational and social aspects of my time at Anderson."

"The faculty was top notch, the learning environment promoted a healthy balance of leadership and teamwork, and the return on investment was fantastic. Most importantly, though, the experience was unbeatable."

"I found UCLA Anderson to be a real door-opener. Companies here in LA seem to regard the school as the gold standard, and I found it very easy to gain access to companies and positions to which I previously would never have had access."

"With the access to a major metropolitan area, top-level faculty, and incredible classmates, I think this is the best school on the West Coast and deserving of recognition when compared to the top East Coast schools."

"Anderson provided me with a top-notch education in a collaborative environment that focused on the entire group's success. In addition, for anyone looking to move into the sports or entertainment arenas, Los Angeles is the place to be."

"Anderson provides a curriculum geared to entrepreneurship, which can serve anyone no matter what career path they pursue. The professors are second to none, and the environment is extremely collegial."

"I had literally never opened a spread sheet before business school. Now I understand the concepts of valuation and can build integrated models with all sorts of bells and whistles. I got up the learning curve faster [at Anderson] than I would have at a different school."

 **Where to Stay**

UCLA Guest House
330 Charles E. Young Dr. E.
Los Angeles, CA 90095
(310) 825-2923

Luxe Hotel Sunset Boulevard
11461 Sunset Blvd.
Los Angeles, CA 90049
(310) 476-6571

W Hotel Los Angeles—Westwood
930 Hilgard Ave.
Los Angeles, CA 90024
(310) 208-8765

 Where to Eat

Westwood Brewing Co.
1097 Glendon Ave.
Los Angeles, CA 90024
(310) 209-2739

Napa Valley Grille
1100 Glendon Ave.
Los Angeles, CA 90024
(310) 824-3322

In-N-Out Burger
922 Gayley Ave.
Los Angeles, CA 90024
(800) 786-1000

 Things to Do

Mildred E. Mathias Botanical Garden
777 Tiverton Ave.
Los Angeles, CA 90095
(310) 206-6707

Geffen Playhouse
10886 Le Conte Ave.
Los Angeles, CA 90024
(310) 208-5454

CHECK OUT BUSINESSWEEK.COM FOR MORE:

Admissions Q&A: Linda Baldwin, director of admissions, talks about what UCLA is looking for in an applicant.

Sample Application Essays and Interview Tips: Get the lowdown on what it takes to get in.

Video View: Listen to Dean Judy Olian explain how she prepares students for life after UCLA.

Recruiter Spotlight: Why UCLA is on the short list for companies like Yahoo! when they're looking for MBA talent.

MBA Journal: Learn about the B-school experience and beyond from a UCLA alumnus.

Access all the B-schools content on BusinessWeek.com by subscribing to MBA Insider.

University of Cambridge

Judge Business School
2006 Ranking: Second tier (non-U.S.)
Trumpington St.
Cambridge, United Kingdom CB2 1AG
E-mail address:
  mba-enquiries@jbs.cam.ac.uk
Web address: www.jbs.cam.ac.uk
For more info: Call general information
  at 44-1223-339-700

 B4UGO

Applicants accepted: 30%
Average GMAT score: 690
Average years' work experience: 7
Average post-MBA salary increase:
  67.2%
**Average total first-year
  compensation:** $128,165

Why Cambridge?

Customization is the name of the game at Judge, where students get to choose from three different consulting projects during the course of the program: two team-based assignments and one individual project. The one-year format means that students are limited to five electives, from 20 offered. But with only about 100 students, the program makes up for its limited course catalog with plenty of face time with professors. While more than 90% of students receive job offers and the average starting salary exceeds $100,000, recruiters are not big fans of the program. Part of the reason may be unfamiliarity. The program is young, and until recently only about 50 recruiters visited the campus each year—a fraction of the number that recruit at some top-ranked programs. The number is now up to 150.

The University of Cambridge is a public institution. Established in 1990, Judge's full-time MBA program is accredited by the Association of MBAs (AMBA) and the European Quality Improvement System (EQUIS).

 Headlines

February 13, 2007: Accenture, Fidelity, and IBM are among firms attending Cambridge-Oxford B-school recruiting event

October 13, 2006: Judge and Indian School of Business sign three-year student exchange agreement

July 19, 2006: Judge and Osaka U. create new joint biotech program

January 18, 2006: Cambridge appoints new Judge Business School director

*"An experience that
has changed my
worldview."*

Famous MBA Alumni

Tom Kao, president of BBDO China and Hong Kong

Fadi Boustany, CEO of Metropole Group in Monaco

Min Liao, deputy director-general of China Banking Regulatory Commission

 ## Who Are My Classmates?

Full-time enrollment: 150
Women: 33%
International: 90%
Minority: N/A
Average age: 30
Accepted applicants enrolled: 78.1%

> *"Not the best school if you are planning a career in investment banking."*

The 411

Annual tuition and fees: $62,000*
Annual living expenses: $20,000*
Total program cost, including forgone salary: $142,000
Classes begin: September
Application deadlines: December 7 to May 2
Application fee: None
*Total for program.

Cliff Notes

Leading areas of study: Entrepreneurship, Finance, International Business, Organizational Behavior, Technology
Average class size, core courses: 70
Average class size, electives: 20
Number of electives: 20
Teaching methods: Case studies (25%), lectures (25%), team projects (25%), experiential learning (25%)

But What's It *Really* Like?

Graded by students:
Overall ranking: **B**
Teaching quality: **B**
Career services: **A**

Graded by recruiters:
Overall ranking: **C**
Accounting: **C**
Analytical skills: **C**
Communication: **C**
Finance: **C**
International business: **C**
Marketing: **C**
Teamwork skills: **C**

Bling

Average pre-MBA salary: $60,000
Average post-MBA salary: $100,341
Graduates with job offer by graduation: 92%
Companies recruiting on campus: 150
Top functional areas for graduates: Finance/Accounting, Consulting, General Management
Biggest recruiters: Citigroup, Accenture, A.T. Kearney, Barclays, McKinsey, Cisco, Johnson & Johnson

⟨⟨⟩⟩ The Good, the Bad, and the Ugly: Students Speak Out

"The Cambridge MBA was certainly an experience that has changed my worldview. The international experience and exposure, plus the networking and leadership seminars from top CEOs and chairmen, have provided me with a lens that is both wide-screen and far-watching."

"Cambridge itself can't be undervalued in the selection and performance process of Judge Business School. Life at the college and meeting with academics, entrepreneurs, and employers from all spheres is incredible. Cambridge is a real community, and Judge is an integral part of it."

"The school definitely needs to grow in size in order to achieve the critical 'clout' for things like inviting recruiters to campus."

"An excellent program with great diversity and teamwork spirit."

"The Cambridge MBA is a really diverse and flexible program that can be tailored to fit your career aspirations."

"Cambridge's advisory board is amazingly involved in the business world. I have personally contacted three of its members for career advice, networking tips, etc. They are global leaders, and their school involvement is not just symbolic. They are actively engaged."

"Cambridge is not the best school if you are planning a career in investment banking. The school's strengths are consulting and entrepreneurship."

"The Cambridge MBA provides access not only to the MBA alumni, but also to the larger Cambridge alumni community, which is highly powerful in both Europe and Asia. This provides lifelong assistance that could open up future business opportunities wherever I choose to work."

"The Cambridge MBA is an excellent program with great diversity and teamwork spirit."

"The vast diversity we had in the class—scientists, teachers, engineers, consultants, marketers, lawyers, doctors, people from 45 different countries—and the opportunity to work in teams with these individuals gave me a much more rounded vision and learning experience."

"The range and quality of consulting projects, leadership seminars, and company visits (recruiting) was very strong throughout the program. Softer skills like management practice, teamwork, and marketing were also emphasized."

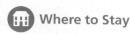 **Where to Stay**

Arundel House Hotel
Chesterton Rd.
Cambridge, UK CB4 3AN
44-1223-367-701

Royal Cambridge Hotel
Trumpington St.
Cambridge, UK CB2 1PY
44-1223-351-631

Hamilton Hotel
156 Chesterton Rd.
Cambridge, UK CB4 1DA
44-1223-365-664

 Where to Eat

La Margherita
15 Magdalene St.
Cambridge, UK CB3 0AF
44-1223-315-232

Chez Gérard
27-28 Bridge St.
Cambridge, UK CB2 IUJ
44-1223-448-620

The Coach & Horses
18 High St.
Cambridge, UK CB2 2LP
44-1223-506-248

 Things to Do

The Fitzwilliam Museum
Trumpington St.
Cambridge, UK CB2 1RB
44-1223-332-900

Cambridge Museum of Technology
Old Pumping Station, Cheddars Ln.
Cambridge, UK CB5 8LD
44-1223-386-650

CHECK OUT BUSINESSWEEK.COM FOR MORE:

Admissions Q&A: MBA Program Deputy Director Simon Learmount looks for ambition, career success, and "that something extra" in applicants.

Sample Application Essays and Interview Tips: Find out how you can make the cut at Judge.

School Tour: Before you buy a ticket, check out the Cambridge campus using this online photo essay.

Search & Compare: Use this interactive tool to conduct a side-by-side comparison and see how Judge stacks up against other top B-schools.

MBA Forums: Connect with other Cambridge hopefuls.

Access all the B-schools content on BusinessWeek.com by subscribing to MBA Insider.

University of Chicago

Graduate School of Business
2006 Ranking: 1 (U.S.)
5807 S. Woodlawn Ave.
Chicago, IL 60637
E-mail address:
admissions@ChicagoGSB.edu
Web address: www.chicagogsb.edu
For more info: Call the general
switchboard at (773) 702-7743

☑ B4UGO

Applicants accepted: N/A
Average GMAT score: 709
Average years' work experience: 4.7
Average post-MBA salary increase:
44.3%*
**Average total first-year
compensation:** $164,968

*Based in part on *BusinessWeek* survey data.

Why Chicago?

One of the oldest business schools in the United States, Chicago's GSB is also, officially, the best. Its star-studded faculty includes a MacArthur "genius" grant winner, while its alumni include the former CEOs of Goldman Sachs, Morgan Stanley, and Merrill Lynch. Under Dean Edward "Ted" Snyder since 2001, the school has taken steps to reduce its image as a quant jock haven—a new Italian-style piazza encourages student-faculty mingling, and Snyder's weekly breakfasts with students keep his finger on the program's pulse. Unlike many programs, Chicago permits first-year students to take advanced courses, leaving introductory courses for students who need them. With few required courses, students essentially design their own programs—a unique curriculum model among top B-schools.

The University of Chicago is a private institution. Established in 1898, GSB's full-time MBA program is accredited by the Association to Advance Collegiate

Schools of Business (AACSB). GSB also offers part-time and executive MBA programs. For details on Chicago's part-time MBA program, see page 377. For details on its executive MBA program, see page 277.

 ## Headlines

January 23, 2007: GSB wins $2.2 million grant for decision research center

April 14, 2006: GSB students host Greater China Conference

August 30, 2005: New GSB scholarships for women announced

August 2, 2005: Classes begin on new GSB campus in London

_____

*"The Career Services
staff is great."*

_____

Famous MBA Alumni

Jon Corzine, governor of New Jersey
Brady Dougan, CEO of Credit Suisse
  Group
Joe Mansueto, founder and CEO of
  Morningstar

 **Who Are My Classmates?**

Full-time enrollment: 1,125
Women: 35%
International: 40%
Minority: 41%
Average age: 28
Accepted applicants enrolled: N/A

"You can tailor your coursework to suit your own needs."

The 411

Annual tuition and fees: $45,500
Annual living expenses: $30,348
Total program cost, including forgone
  salary: $294,788*
Classes begin: September
Application deadlines: October 17,
  January 9, March 12
Application fee: $200

*Based in part on *BusinessWeek* survey data.

Cliff Notes

Leading areas of study: Entrepreneur-
  ship, Finance, General Manage-
  ment, Marketing, Strategy
Average class size, core courses: 59
Average class size, electives: 53
Number of electives: 77
Teaching methods: Case studies,
  lectures, team projects

But What's It *Really* Like?

Graded by students:
Overall ranking: A+
Teaching quality: A+
Career services: A+

Graded by recruiters:
Overall ranking: A+
Accounting: A+
Analytical skills: A+
Communication: A
Finance: A+
General management: A
International business: A+
Marketing: A
Operations/production: A+
Teamwork skills: A

$ Bling

Average pre-MBA salary: $71,546*
Average post-MBA salary: $103,219
Graduates with job offer by graduation:
  94%
Top functional areas for graduates:
  Finance/Accounting, Consulting,
  General Management
Biggest recruiters: McKinsey, Lehman
  Brothers, Merrill Lynch, Deutsche
  Bank, BCG

*Estimate based on *BusinessWeek* survey data.

The Good, the Bad, and the Ugly: Students Speak Out

"The best thing about Chicago GSB is that you can tailor your coursework to suit your own needs and take advanced courses in the area of your choice. That way, you're well prepared before interviews and summer internships in your particular career area."

"Chicago's reputation is limited outside of the United States, which weakens the recruitment in foreign countries. After deciding I wanted to get a job in Mexico, I had a hard time using school connections and had to rely more on my own personal network."

"Chicago GSB students are real people, not pretentious individuals. We learn to completely understand the business environment, which allows us to be prepared for almost any situation."

"A great time in a great city."

"I wish I were able to meet more people in my MBA class. I think that a core program where the same cohort of students attends, say, three or four basic courses, would help build a stronger network at Chicago."

"Dean Edward Snyder is great. He's responsive, even if the answer isn't always exactly what you want to hear. He's extremely bullish about Chicago GSB, and he has a clear vision for where he wants the school to go. I think he will continue to do great things for the school."

"The Career Services staff is great and very helpful. But if you're doing something a little more off-track, like entertainment, they aren't quite as much help as when you're doing something more traditional (banking, consulting, marketing, etc.)."

"City life in Chicago has to be taken into account before making a decision. Going to Chicago GSB meant not only a great education, but a great time in a great city as well."

"I had heard rumors that the school would be somewhat more focused on individual achievement than on community. I saw this type of behavior very little, no more than I would expect to see at any other top school."

"Chicago is lacking the camaraderie of some other schools. By the end of the two years, you recognize a lot of your 550 classmates, but you leave the school with only a handful of people you really call friends."

Where to Stay

Hotel Sax Chicago
333 Dearborn St.
Chicago, IL 60610
(312) 245-0333

Hard Rock Hotel
230 N. Michigan Ave.
Chicago, IL 60601
(312) 345-1000

International House
1414 E. 59th St.
Chicago, IL 60637
(773) 753-2270

 Where to Eat

La Petite Folie
1504 E. 55th St.
Chicago, IL 60615
(773) 493-1394

Opera
1301 S. Wabash
Chicago, IL 60605
(312) 461-0161

Medici on 57th
1327 E. 57th St.
Chicago, IL 60637
(773) 667-7394

 Things to Do

Museum of Science and Industry
57th St. and Lake Shore Dr.
Chicago, IL 60637
(773) 684-1414

Art Institute of Chicago
111 S. Michigan Ave.
Chicago, IL 60603
(312) 443-3600

CHECK OUT BUSINESSWEEK.COM FOR MORE:

Admissions Q&A: Stacey Kole, the B-school's deputy dean, describes the ideal Chicago applicant.

Sample Application Essays and Interview Tips: Get the lowdown on what it takes to get in.

Video View: Listen to B-school Dean Ted Snyder explain how Chicago regained students' confidence after administration conflicts.

School Tour: Check out the Hyde Park campus, seven miles south of downtown Chicago, before visiting.

Careers Q&A: Associate Dean Julie Morton on why recruiters still beat a path to Chicago's door.

Search & Compare: Find out how Chicago GSB stacks up against other top B-schools.

Access all the B-schools content on BusinessWeek.com by subscribing to MBA Insider.

University of Illinois

College of Business
2006 Ranking: Second tier (U.S.)
405 David Kinley Hall
1407 W. Gregory Dr.
Urbana, IL 61801
E-mail address: mba@uiuc.edu
Web address: www.mba.uiuc.edu/m/
For more info: Call MBA admissions at
(217) 244-7602

☑ B4UGO

Applicants accepted: 42%
Average GMAT score: 652
Average years' work experience: 4.5
Average post-MBA salary increase:
75.9%
**Average total first-year
compensation:** $108,556

Why Illinois?

Like many MBA programs, the Illinois MBA consists of first-year core courses in eight-week modules followed by an elective-heavy second year where students home in on their concentrations. Finance is the most popular, but marketing, information technology, operations management, general management, and a custom concentration are also available. For the ambitious, Illinois also offers numerous joint degree programs, including labor and industrial relations, law, computer science, and architecture. (Illinois boasts a new Center for Business and Public Policy as well.) In one course, students travel to India and develop a business plan aimed at tackling issues relating to the country's poverty. The school broke ground on new facilities in 2006 and expects to occupy them in the fall of 2008.

The University of Illinois at Urbana-Champaign is a public institution. Established in 1938, Illinois' full-time MBA program is accredited by the Association to Advance Collegiate Schools of Business (AACSB). Illinois also offers part-time and executive MBA programs.

 Headlines

June 1, 2007: Tech innovator Thomas Siebel pledges $100 million for science and engineering

October 26, 2006: College of Business hires an associate dean of e-learning

April 28, 2006: B-school breaks ground for new $60 million instructional building

March 31, 2006: $4 million Deloitte grant funds new Center for Professional Responsibilities in Business and Society

*"Great preparation at
a great value."*

Famous MBA Alumni

Alan Feldman, president, chairman, and CEO of Midas Inc.
Thomas Siebel, founder and former CEO of Siebel Systems
Mike Tokarz, chairman of MVC Capital

Who Are My Classmates?

Full-time enrollment: 208
Women: 28%
International: 45%
Minority: 17%
Average age: 27
Accepted applicants enrolled: 46%

"The overall quality of the students is very poor."

The 411

Annual tuition and fees: $19,500 (resident), $28,700 (nonresident)
Annual living expenses: $21,500 (resident), $21,900 (nonresident)
Total program cost, including forgone salary: $176,010 (resident), $195,210 (nonresident)
Classes begin: August
Application deadline: None
Application fee: $60 (U.S.), $75 (international)

Cliff Notes

Leading areas of study: Finance, General Management, Information Technology, Marketing, Operations Management
Average class size, core courses: 51
Average class size, electives: 30
Number of electives: 60
Teaching methods: Lectures (35%), team projects (30%), case studies (25%)

But What's It *Really* Like?

Graded by students:
Overall ranking: C
Teaching quality: C
Career services: C

Graded by recruiters:
Overall ranking: C
Accounting: A
Analytical skills: C
Communication: B
Finance: B
General management: B
International business: C
Marketing: B
Operations/production: A
Teamwork skills: B

Bling

Average pre-MBA salary: $47,005
Average post-MBA salary: $82,693
Graduates with job offer by graduation: 76%
Companies recruiting on campus: 29
Top functional areas for graduates: Finance/Accounting, Consulting, Marketing/Sales
Biggest recruiters: AT&T, General Electric, Deutsche Post World Net, IBM, Sears, Ford Motor Co.

The Good, the Bad, and the Ugly: Students Speak Out

"In my opinion, it is the second-best finance MBA in the state of Illinois. It's better than Kellogg and second only to the University of Chicago. The faculty, research, and instruction are really top notch. This program, with a bit more time, could become a serious alternative to Kellogg and Chicago for in-state students looking for great preparation at a great value."

"The best decision I have made in my life."

"Illinois is an outstanding value and an outstanding technical preparatory business school. What it lacks in career services, leadership development, and 'soft skills' it certainly makes up for in hard skills like finance and accounting."

"The Illinois MBA has great professors, especially in finance. In addition, Illinois business consulting has provided real-life consulting experience to students that is very similar to how a professional consulting firm is run."

"A great experience that I'll never ever regret."

"The program is culturally diverse, but perhaps errs on the side of being too diverse. Many classmates agree that students who enroll from abroad, only to return to their home countries immediately after graduation, are not willing to give back to the school in terms of network building, recruiting future graduates, donating time or money to the program, and so on."

"It has been an awesome experience. The best decision I have made in my life."

"The overall quality of the students is very poor and detracts from the overall experience."

"One thing I loved about the MBA experience was that, while I was able to focus on my particular area of interest, the studies, program, and experience broadened my approach and opened many new doors for me."

"If you want to learn new things, this is the right place. If you want to get several job offers and work for top-10 companies . . . maybe not."

"I believe the Illinois MBA program has a great faculty and does not lack anything other schools have. However, I admit that the Career Services office and the administration staff are incompetent."

"The University of Illinois MBA program offers an excellent business curriculum at a very reasonable price."

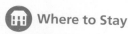 Where to Stay

Illini Union Guest Rooms
1401 W. Green St.
Champaign, IL 61821
(217) 333-3030

Hilton Garden Inn
1501 S. Neil St.
Champaign, IL 61820
(217) 352-9970

**Eastland Suites Hotel &
Conference Center**
1907 N. Cunningham Ave.
Urbana, IL 61802
(217) 367-8331

 Where to Eat

Radio Maria
119 N. Walnut St.
Champaign, IL 61820
(217) 398-7729

Papa Del's Pizza
206 E. Green St.
Champaign, IL 61820
(217) 359-7700

Crane Alley
115 W. Main St.
Urbana, IL 61801
(217) 384-7526

 Things to Do

**Krannert Art Museum and
Kinkead Pavilion**
500 E. Peabody Dr.
Champaign, IL 61820
(217) 333-1861

Alto Vineyards
4210 N. Duncan Rd.
Champaign, IL 61822
(217) 356-4784

CHECK OUT BUSINESSWEEK.COM FOR MORE:

Search & Compare: Use this interactive tool to directly compare Illinois with other schools on your short list.

School Tour: Never been? Take a virtual tour of the Illinois campus.

Expanded Profile: Delve deeper into the Illinois MBA with this extended online profile.

MBA Forums: Connect with other prospective Illinois applicants.

Access all the B-schools content on BusinessWeek.com by subscribing to MBA Insider.

University of London

London Business School
2006 Ranking: 5 (non-U.S.)
Regents Park
London, United Kingdom NW1 4SA
E-mail address: mbainfo@london.edu
Web address: www.london.edu
For more info: Call general information
at 44-207-000-7000

 **B4UGO**

Applicants accepted: N/A
Average GMAT score: 690
Average years' work experience: 5.6
Average post-MBA salary increase:
82.8%
**Average total first-year
compensation:** $203,425

Why LBS?

A top international option with an American flair, London Business School's full-time MBA, which emphasizes teamwork and projects, constantly changes to reflect student and recruiter feedback. Students live in London, one of the world's premier business capitals, and the school's program's flexible 15- to 21-month format gives students ample time to form networks with a diverse group of colleagues from more than 70 countries. LBS also draws first-rate recruiters from all over Europe—including top consulting and financial services companies—who rate it highly in accounting, finance, and analytical skills. An added bonus? Though program costs are a bit lofty ($90,000), the median starting salary for LBS graduates is among the highest for *BusinessWeek's* top-ranked international B-schools.

The University of London is a public institution. Established in 1965, LBS's full-time MBA program is accredited by the Association to Advance Collegiate Schools of Business

(AACSB), the Association of MBAs (AMBA), and the European Quality Improvement System (EQUIS). LBS also offers an executive MBA program. For details on LBS's executive MBA program, see page 281.

 Headlines

May 16, 2007: LBS announces new scholarship for "socially responsible" full-time MBAs

November 27, 2006: 96% of MBAs at LBS land jobs within three months of graduation

November 7, 2006: LBS names Robin Buchanan new dean

October 24, 2006: LBS launches innovative Institute for Technology

---

"LBS widened my field of vision dramatically."

Famous MBA Alumni

Sir John Sunderland, chairman of
Cadbury Schwepps
Julian Day, chairman and CEO of
RadioShack
Huw Jenkins, chairman and CEO of
UBS Investment Bank

Who Are My Classmates?

Full-time enrollment: 625
Women: 25%
International: 95%
Minority: N/A
Average age: 28
Accepted applicants enrolled: N/A

"Great teaching, great people, great location."

The 411

Annual tuition and fees: $44,490
Annual living expenses: $41,142
Total program cost, including forgone
salary: $307,508
Classes begin: September
Application deadlines: October 19 to
May 2
Application fee: $290

Cliff Notes

Leading areas of study: Entrepreneur-
ship, Finance, International
Business, Marketing, Strategy
Average class size, core courses: 79
Average class size, electives: 60
Number of electives: 72
Teaching methods: Case studies (33%),
lectures (33%), team projects (14%)

But What's It *Really* Like?

Graded by students:
Overall ranking: A
Teaching quality: A
Career services: A

Graded by recruiters:
Overall ranking: A+
Accounting: A+
Analytical skills: A+
Communication: A
Finance: A+
General management: A
International business: A
Marketing: A
Operations/production: B
Teamwork skills: A

$ Bling

Average pre-MBA salary: $68,122
Average post-MBA salary: $124,512
Graduates with job offer by graduation:
89%
Top functional areas for graduates:
Finance/Accounting, Consulting,
General Management
Biggest recruiters: Barclays, Booz
Allen Hamilton, McKinsey,
Lehman Brothers, Deutsche Bank

The Good, the Bad, and the Ugly: Students Speak Out

"Because of its relatively small size and youth, the university is large enough to have an impact internationally, yet small enough to be nimble and respond efficiently to issues and concerns from both sets of clients: the students and potential employers."

"I am quite concerned by the relatively little emphasis put on ethics. Ethics should be taught throughout the program, with possible visits to former or actual white-collar convicts who could really demonstrate the risk and consequences of unethical behavior."

"Too focused on investment banking and management consulting."

"London Business School has provided me with not only a global view of business but a global view of the world itself. London Business School professors and, more importantly, its student body have widened my field of vision dramatically."

"Career Services are too focused on the investment banking and management consulting career paths. They could be more helpful to those who are not seeking employment in these categories."

"Apart from the opportunities that this MBA has offered me (move to an international career, change of field and function, development of a diverse network, and so on), LBS has been a great experience that has broadened my mind as well as my prospects."

"Great teaching, great people, great location. If London were cheaper, the setting would be ideal."

"I am convinced that the MBA at London Business School has helped me become the best possible 'me' I could have been. This is in terms of hard knowledge, business skills, personal rediscovery, meeting great people, and doing fantastic events—all in a non-competitive and always-fun atmosphere."

"The student body is very collaborative and generates a positive vibe on the campus."

"LBS's professors are great. They are not only good teachers of specific faculties, but also they are really friendly and really motivating in general."

"LBS is an excellent school and getting better. It is the most international of all top schools, and the location is a great advantage, especially if one is looking for a career in finance. It helped me greatly as a career switcher."

 **Where to Stay**

Great Eastern Hotel
40 Liverpool St.
London, UK EC2M 7QN
44-207-618-5000

Landmark Hotel
222 Marylebone Rd.
London, UK NW1 6JQ
44-207-631-8000

Wigmore Court Hotel
23 Gloucester Pl.
London, UK W1U 8HS
44-207-935-0928

 Where to Eat

Giraffe
6-8 Blandford St.
London, UK W1U 4AV
44-207-935-2333

Le Pain Quotidien
72-75 Marylebone High St.
London, UK W1U 5JW
44-207-486-6154

Leon
3 Crispin Pl.
London, UK E1 6DW
44-207-247-4369

 Things to Do

Tate Modern Museum
Bankside
London, UK SE1 9TG
44-207-887-8888

The National Gallery
Trafalgar Square
London, UK WC2N 5DN
44-207-747-2885

CHECK OUT BUSINESSWEEK.COM FOR MORE:

Admissions Q&A: Admissions Director Julia Tyler explains how the program's global, multicultural approach reflects its home city.

School Tour: Look before you leap—see what it's like to attend LBS with *Business Week*'s exclusive photo essay.

Search & Compare: See how LBS fares among other top international B-schools.

Sample Application Essays: Peruse winning essays to find out what it takes to get in.

Expanded Profile: Want more? Find additional facts and figures on LBS in its extended online profile.

Access all the B-schools content on BusinessWeek.com by subscribing to MBA Insider.

University of Maryland

Robert H. Smith School of Business
2006 Ranking: 25 (U.S.)
Master's Program Office
2308 Van Munching Hall
College Park, MD 20742
E-mail address:
  Mba_info@rhsmith.umd.edu
Web address: www.rhsmith.umd.edu
For more info: Call general information
  at (301) 405-2189

B4UGO

Applicants accepted: 32%
Average GMAT score: 650
Average years' work experience: 5.1
Average post-MBA salary increase:
  53.3%
Average total first-year
  compensation: $96,914*
*Base salary and signing bonus only.

Why Maryland?

To create "leaders for the digital economy," Smith has created a program with two distinct aims: to teach the foundational theories at the heart of modern business and of-the-moment "best practices" emerging from global markets. Core courses such as strategic information systems and data models and decisions allow students to explore how information technology is changing business practices and creating opportunities. A wide assortment of electives includes what Smith claims is the largest offering of e-business courses anywhere. A wealth of opportunities for hands-on learning—including an MBA consulting program, a student-run investment fund, and a chance to work with an area venture capital group or study abroad—round out the program.

Maryland is a public institution. Established in 1947, Smith's full-time MBA program is accredited by the Association to Advance Collegiate Schools of Business (AACSB). Smith also offers part-time and executive MBA programs.

 Headlines

March 14, 2007: Smith to launch global MBA in 2008

June 21, 2006: Smith launches weekly video and audio podcasts

May 16, 2006: Smith receives $1.4 million for global business education

October 6, 2005: Smith announces major expansion and renovation plan

"The quality of the education is excellent."

Famous MBA Alumni

Carleton "Carly" Fiorina, former chairman and CEO of Hewlett-Packard

David Trone, senior vice president and senior analyst for Fox-Pitt, Kelton Inc.

Paul Norris, chairman and former CEO of W.R. Grace & Co.

Who Are My Classmates?

Full-time enrollment: 236
Women: 37%
International: 34%
Minority: 46%
Average age: 28
Accepted applicants enrolled: 40%

"Most professors were genuinely interested in me. They wanted me to succeed."

The 411

Annual tuition and fees: $28,157 (resident), $37,517 (nonresident)
Annual living expenses: $9,392
Total program cost, including forgone salary: $183,596 (resident), $202,316 (nonresident)
Classes begin: August
Application deadlines: November 1 to March 1
Application fee: $60

Cliff Notes

Leading areas of study: Consulting, Entrepreneurship, Finance, Marketing, Strategy
Average class size, core courses: 63
Average class size, electives: 31
Number of electives: 50
Teaching methods: Lectures (50%), case studies (25%), team projects (20%)

But What's It *Really* Like?

Graded by students:
Overall ranking: B
Teaching quality: C
Career services: C

Graded by recruiters:
Overall ranking: C
Accounting: B
Analytical skills: B
Communication: C
Finance: C
General management: B
International business: B
Marketing: B
Operations/production: B
Teamwork skills: C

Bling

Average pre-MBA salary: $54,249
Average post-MBA salary: $83,165
Graduates with job offers by graduation: 84%
Companies recruiting on campus: 91
Top functional areas for graduates: Finance/Accounting, Marketing/Sales, Consulting
Biggest recruiters: IBM, Citigroup, W.R. Grace, Black & Decker, Accenture, Fedex, Fannie Mae, Intel

The Good, the Bad, and the Ugly: Students Speak Out

"Smith gives students the opportunity to be extremely active in the future of Smith. They like feedback, and they are willing to change to make the school the best it can be."

"I found most of the professors to be genuinely interested in me. They constantly showed a sincere interest in my background and my future endeavors, and of course in sharing their expertise with me. I really felt that they enjoyed teaching and that they wanted me to succeed."

"If you are a cookie-cutter student, then you will be fine. But if you are the least bit different from the norm, the school doesn't know what to do with you. I do not recommend that marketing students even consider Smith—the few good marketing classes are scheduled for maximum difficulty, and there is no real support. Faculty members never show up for office hours, and if you run into any trouble of any sort, there is no help available—you are 100 percent on your own."

> ## *"Faculty members never show up for office hours."*

"The school administration does a poor job of listening to students; however, the faculty and staff are excellent and often make up for administration difficulties."

"While I am satisfied with the MBA program, I am not happy with the career opportunities for international students. Very few consulting and technology companies came for campus recruitment, and the Career Center does not seem to be doing anything to improve this."

"I loved my school and was president of my class. I feel confident that good relationships between the student body and administration can minimize any issues that arise, and I found that the administration would bend over backward when possible."

"The quality of the education is excellent, and the opportunities for professional development were exactly what I had desired for my investment. I simply cannot say enough positive things about my experience there."

"Smith offers a great program that delivers a solid value. The faculty members almost always possess an Ivy League background, and the curriculum can be compared to that of any top-ten school. The school offers a great opportunity for career switchers by putting them in touch with relevant employers. Living areas close to campus are very affordable, and the school offers scholarships or graduate assistantships to almost 60% of each incoming class."

 **Where to Stay**

Best Western Inn
8691 Baltimore Blvd.
College Park, MD 20740
(301) 474-2800

UMUC Marriott
Adelphi Rd. at University Blvd.
College Park, MD 20740
(301) 985-7300

Comfort Inn and Suites
9020 Baltimore Blvd.
College Park, MD 20740
(301) 441-8110

 Where to Eat

The Calvert House (American)
6211 Baltimore Ave.
College Park, MD 20740
(301) 864-5220

King's Park Café (Mediterranean)
7409 Baltimore Ave.
College Park, MD 20740
(301) 864-7900

Terrapin Taco House (Mexican)
4427 Lehigh Rd.
College Park, MD 20740
(301) 699-8595

 Things to Do

College Park Aviation Museum
1985 Corporal Frank Scott Dr.
College Park, MD 20740
(301) 864-6029

National Museum of Language
7100 Baltimore Ave.
College Park, MD 20740
(301) 864-7071

CHECK OUT BUSINESSWEEK.COM FOR MORE:

Admissions Q&A: MBA Admissions Director Sabrina White explains why the perfect Smith candidate is an "aggressive team player."

Sample Application Essays and Interview Tips: Learn what it takes to make it through the Smith application process.

School Tour: Want to know before you go? Use this photo essay to explore the Smith campus online.

A Day in the Life: Learn how Dana Lande, a class of 2004 grad, turned her passion for jewelry into a start-up business.

Search & Compare: See how Smith stacks up against other top B-schools.

Expanded Profile: Find more facts, more statistics, and more insights on the Smith MBA in its bigger, better online profile.

Access all the B-schools content on BusinessWeek.com by subscribing to MBA Insider.

University of Michigan

Stephen M. Ross School of Business
2006 Ranking: 5 (U.S.)
710 E. University Ave., E2540
Ann Arbor, MI 48109-1234
E-mail address: rossmba@umich.edu
Web address: www.bus.umich.edu
For more info: Call Academic Services at
(734) 647-4933

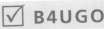

☑ B4UGO

Applicants accepted: 20%
Average GMAT score: 700
Average years' work experience: 5.1
Average post-MBA salary increase:
62.7%
Average total first-year
compensation: $142,304

Why Michigan?

A staple in *BusinessWeek*'s Top 10, Ross's full-time MBA is one of the most selective programs in the Midwest. Renowned for strong performance in consulting, finance, and general management, the school recently launched a large-scale remodeling effort, which should supply future students with state-of-the-art facilities. Interested B-schoolers can also take advantage of Ross's dual-degree program (which integrates a nonbusiness concentration into the MBA curriculum) or kick back in Ann Arbor, Michigan, which one student dubbed "the perfect college town." And there's always the "Go Blue!" factor: As one attendee observed, "We are probably the only Top 10 university where the school fight song is taught on the first day of class."

The University of Michigan is a public institution. Established in 1924, the Ross full-time MBA program is accredited by the Association to Advance Collegiate Schools of Business (AACSB). Ross also offers part-time and executive MBA programs. For details on Ross's executive MBA program, see page 285.

 Headlines

May 9, 2007: Erb Institute of Global Sustainable Enterprise unveils new student internship to bridge business and environment

April 23, 2007: Ross offers new master's degree in supply chain management

January 22, 2007: Faculty members win grants for international initiatives

June 13, 2006: Ross content goes public on iTunes U

"I learned a great deal about managing people."

Famous MBA Alumni

John V. Faraci, chairman and CEO of International Paper Co.

John DeLorean, founder of DeLorean Motor Co.

Sam Wyly, billionaire investor

Who Are My Classmates?

Full-time enrollment: 876
Women: 34%
International: 30%
Minority: 29%
Average age: 28
Accepted applicants enrolled: 70%

"The vibe here really makes everything crackle with possibility."

The 411

Annual tuition and fees: $38,289 (resident), $43,289 (nonresident)

Annual living expenses: $13,054 (resident), $19,054 (nonresident)

Total program cost, including forgone salary: $224,686 (resident), $246,686 (nonresident)

Classes begin: September

Application deadlines: November 1, January 3, March 1

Application fee: $180

Cliff Notes

Leading areas of study: Consulting, Finance, General Management, Marketing, Strategy

Average class size, core courses: 65

Average class size, electives: 40

Number of electives: 148

Teaching methods: Case studies (25%), simulations (25%), lectures (20%)

But What's It *Really* Like?

Graded by students:
Overall ranking: **A**
Teaching quality: **B**
Career services: **A**

Graded by recruiters:
Overall ranking: **A+**
Accounting: **A+**
Analytical skills: **A+**
Communication: **A+**
Finance: **A+**
General management: **A+**
International business: **A+**
Marketing: **A+**
Operations/production: **A+**
Teamwork skills: **A+**

$ Bling

Average pre-MBA salary: $61,000

Average post-MBA salary: $99,265

Graduates with job offer by graduation: 95%

Companies recruiting on campus: 606

Top functional areas for graduates: Consulting, Marketing/Sales, Finance/Accounting

Biggest recruiters: Microsoft, McKinsey, BCG, Deloitte Consulting, Amazon.com

((,)) The Good, the Bad, and the Ugly: Students Speak Out

"Michigan's seven-week Multidisciplinary Action Program (MAP) was by far the greatest learning experience I had during my MBA career. I was able to get real-life experience at arguably the top company within my desired field of study. And I learned a great deal about managing people."

"U of M's Office of Career Development needs an overhaul."

"For both education and career search, there are so many opportunities that students can feel lost about how best to prepare for their futures (e.g., which classes, professors, and extracurricular opportunities will best position them for a desired career). Likewise, there is little opportunity for individual assistance from professionals with career search preparation and assistance."

"I was really surprised at how big people's hearts are at the University of Michigan. The vibe here really makes everything crackle with possibility, whether you're trying to start a company or you're marketing an anti-malarial mosquito net. Or both."

"If Ross doesn't have exactly what you want, you'll have the opportunity to change the situation yourself. I convinced the administration to add a class in the spring (which was originally offered only in the fall). And there are other business students who have created additional classes based on their desired career focuses, including real estate and sports marketing."

"I believe the U of M's Office of Career Development (OCD) needs an overhaul. Quite frankly, there isn't enough attention paid to developing a more diverse set of opportunities for students. It could also be more aware of students' diverse career interests, particularly in disciplines where they must recruit off campus."

"The students at Ross have phenomenally diverse work backgrounds and career ambitions. Some are part of the Erb Institute for Global Sustainable Enterprise, while others focus on public policy, brand management, Wall Street finance, and/or manufacturing."

"I learned a lot, both fundamentals and practical applications, from my classes, colleagues, and extracurricular activities. Even though I was a television producer before getting my MBA, I am well prepared for a career in capital markets."

"My greatest disappointment is that academics seem to take a back seat to getting the dream job. I was rarely pushed to excel in my coursework. There are few negative consequences to slacking off in class and as a result many students perform at a substandard level."

Where to Stay

Campus Inn
615 E. Huron St.
Ann Arbor, MI 48104
(800) 666-8693

Bell Tower Hotel
300 S. Thayer St.
Ann Arbor, MI 48104
(800) 562-3559

Ann Arbor Bed & Breakfast
921 E. Huron St.
Ann Arbor, MI 48104
(734) 994-9100

 Where to Eat

Cottage Inn
512 E. William St.
Ann Arbor, MI 48104
(734) 663-3379

Gandy Dancer
401 Depot St.
Ann Arbor, MI 48104
(734) 769-0592

Zingerman's Deli
422 Detroit St.
Ann Arbor, MI 48104
(734) 663-3354

 Things to Do

Nichols Arboretum
1610 Washington Heights
Ann Arbor, MI 48104
(734) 998-9540

Ann Arbor Hands-On Museum
220 E. Ann St.
Ann Arbor, MI 48104
(734) 995-5439

CHECK OUT BUSINESSWEEK.COM FOR MORE:

Admissions Q&A: Jim Hayes, director of admissions and financial aid, describes the ideal Michigan applicant.

Sample Application Essays and Interview Tips: Advice on how to ace two key parts of the application process.

Video View: Listen to Professor Thomas Gladwin discuss the role of today's B-schools.

Alumni Insights: Learn what Michigan graduates have to say about their alma mater.

School Tour: Check out the campus before visiting.

Access all the B-schools content on BusinessWeek.com by subscribing to MBA Insider.

University of Minnesota

Carlson School of Management
2006 Ranking: Second tier (U.S.)
321 19th Ave. S, Suite 4-300
Minneapolis, MN 55455-9940
E-mail address: fulltimembainfo@
carlsonschool.umn.edu
Web address: www.csom.umn.edu
For more info: Call MBA information at
(612) 625-5555

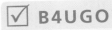 **B4UGO**

Applicants accepted: 41%
Average GMAT score: 661
Average years' work experience: 4.5
Average post-MBA salary increase:
81.6%
**Average total first-year
compensation:** $115,891

Why Minnesota?

The Carlson MBA offers many of the features found in higher-ranked programs. Most core courses are taken in the first semester, freeing up the second for electives designed to make students competitive internship candidates. Students design their own "professional portfolios," courses and activities designed to give them a leg up in their careers. In the second year, students choose from four programs—venture capital, brand management, funds management, and consulting—that give them a chance to work on real company problems. While the program is inexpensive for Minnesota residents, costs for nonresidents are on a par with those at higher-ranked schools. Post-MBA salaries are decent, but be prepared to stick around after graduation: 90% of students end up working in the Midwest.

The University of Minnesota is a public institution. Established in 1936,

Carlson's full-time MBA program is accredited by the Association to Advance Collegiate Schools of Business (AACSB). Carlson also offers part-time and executive MBA programs.

 Headlines

June 18, 2007: Economics department adds 10 to faculty

May 3, 2007: Carlson opens Center for Integrative Leadership

March 23, 2007: Carlson hosts Women's Leadership Conference

July 5, 2005: Alison Davis-Blake named dean, effective July 2006

"One of the best values for the money."

Famous MBA Alumni

Bill Van Dyke, former CEO of
Donaldson Co. Inc.
Bob Buuck, co-founder of American
Medical Systems
Robert Keppel, co-founder of
Rosemount Engineering Co.

Who Are My Classmates?

Full-time enrollment: 217
Women: 27%
International: 29%
Minority: 11%
Average age: 28
Accepted applicants enrolled: 44%

---

*"I couldn't have asked
for much more."*

The 411

Annual tuition and fees: $28,072
(resident), $38,161 (nonresident)
Annual living expenses: $14,400
Total program cost, including forgone
salary: $180,944 (resident),
$201,122 (nonresident)
Classes begin: August
Application deadlines: December 1,
February 15 (international),
December 15, February 15, April
15 (U.S.)
Application fee: $60 (U.S.), $90
(international)

Cliff Notes

Leading areas of study: Consulting,
Finance, Management Information
Systems, Marketing, Strategy
Average class size, core courses: 46
Average class size, electives: 30
Number of electives: 98
Teaching methods: Case studies (33%),
lectures (25%), experiential learning
(25%)

But What's It *Really* Like?

Graded by students:
Overall ranking: C
Teaching quality: C
Career services: B

Graded by recruiters:
Overall ranking: B
Accounting: A
Analytical skills: A
Communication: B
Finance: A
General management: B
International business: B
Marketing: B
Operations/production: A
Teamwork skills: B

Bling

Average pre-MBA salary: $48,000
Average post-MBA salary: $87,188
Graduates with job offer by graduation:
81%
Top functional areas for graduates:
Finance/Accounting, Marketing/
Sales, Consulting
Biggest recruiters: Medtronic, Cum-
mins, General Mills, Northwest
Airlines, 3M, Ameriprise, Target

The Good, the Bad, and the Ugly: Students Speak Out

"I consider the Carlson MBA to be one of the best values for the money on the market because it has the resources of a large university, the collegiality of a small school, the business resources of the Twin Cities, and the cost of living in the Midwest; it can't be beat."

"If [you] seek a job outside the Twin Cities, Carlson would not be your school."

"Carlson is a highly underrated program mainly because the students love the Twin Cities so much that they don't move to the coasts to pursue other opportunities. The career office is constantly frustrated when large national firms come in and few offers are accepted by students."

"Carlson School of Management provided me with access to a thriving business community in the Twin Cities. The program focused not only on academic development but also on developing the soft skills needed to be successful in the corporate world."

"If [you] seek a job outside the Twin Cities, such as on Wall Street or the West Coast, Carlson would not be your school."

"Because of its small size, the program is very integrated. It's a very networking-friendly environment, not only with classmates, but with the business community, alumni, faculty, and staff."

"The Carlson School of Management has such a big job market in Minnesota that it may be failing to try to expand its network to other countries and to the U.S. coasts."

"The Carlson School of Management is a strong full-time MBA program, as it offers an excellent mix of academic business theory mixed in with the actual practice of various business techniques. The academics are top notch, and almost all of my professors were very well informed and helpful. I couldn't have asked for much more in terms of the academics."

"I think Minnesota does a great job of combining the social/networking aspects of school with the classroom. The school is quick to change when students bring concerns to the MBA office."

"Not the caliber of students I expected. Administration seemed uninterested in the needs of students. Academic dishonesty was apparent."

 **Where to Stay**

Holiday Inn Metrodome
1500 Washington Ave. S.
Minneapolis, MN 55454
(612) 333-4646

Radisson University Hotel
615 Washington Ave. S.E.
Minneapolis, MN 55414
(612) 379-8888

Days Inn Minneapolis/University of Minnesota
2407 University Ave. S.E.
Minneapolis, MN 55414
(612) 623-3999

 Where to Eat

Minneapolis Town Hall Brewery
1430 Washington Ave. S.
Minneapolis, MN 55454
(612) 339-8696

Jewel of India
1427 Washington Ave. S.
Minneapolis, MN 55454
(612) 339-0002

Grandma's Saloon & Grill
1810 Washington Ave. S.
Minneapolis, MN 55454
(612) 340-0516

 Things to Do

Minneapolis Institute of Arts
2400 Third Ave. S.
Minneapolis, MN 55404
(612) 870-3131

Mall of America
60 E. Broadway
Bloomington, MN 55425
(952) 883-8800

CHECK OUT BUSINESSWEEK.COM FOR MORE:

Admissions Q&A: Get tips on making the cut from Carlson's Admissions Director Dustin Cornwell.

Search & Compare: See how Carlson stacks up against other B-schools on your short list.

Placement Q&A: Career Center chief Clare Foley discusses which employers recruit on campus and what they're looking for.

Expanded Profile: More facts, statistics, and insights on the Carlson full-time MBA.

Interview Tips: How to ace the interview at Carlson.

Access all the B-schools content on BusinessWeek.com by subscribing to MBA Insider.

University of Navarra

IESE Business School
2006 Ranking: 8 (non-U.S.)
Avda. Pearson, 21
Barcelona, Spain 08034
E-mail address: mbainfo@iese.edu
Web address: www.iese.edu
For more info: Call general information
at 34-93-253-42-00

B4UGO

Applicants accepted: 24%
Average GMAT score: 672
Average years' work experience: 4.3
Average post-MBA salary increase:
174.2%
Average total first-year
compensation: $155,560

Why IESE?

Located in a thriving European business hub, IESE gives students a unique and global learning experience. Drawing attendees from more than 50 countries, the school's 19-month, full-time MBA program offers electives ranging from social corporate responsibility to sports business management and uses a case-method-based curriculum to mirror real-life business situations and prepare students for fast-paced careers. IESE attendees also gain access to the school's vast alumni network, which includes roughly 26,000 people in 90-plus countries. Even better? Recruiters consider IESE's full-time program among the best in the world. About 98% of IESE students receive job offers within three months of graduation—many from well-known companies like Citigroup, Deutsche Bank, and BCG—and the average starting salary is close to $120,000.

The University of Navarra is a private institution. Established in 1964, IESE's full-time MBA program is accredited by the Association of MBAs (AMBA) and the European Quality Improvement System (EQUIS). IESE also offers an executive MBA program. For details on IESE's executive MBA program, see page 289.

 ## Headlines

October 17, 2006: IESE establishes new chair of strategic management

March 2, 2006: New chair of corporate social responsibility appointed at IESE

August 2, 2005: IESE graduates command higher salaries

April 18, 2005: Barcelona and Madrid campuses expanded

"An unbelievable learning experience."

Famous MBA Alumni

Alois Linder, executive vice president of Henkel KGAA
Alan Pace, managing director of Lehman Brothers
Amparo Moraleda, general manager of IBM Spain

Who Are My Classmates?

Full-time enrollment: 462
Women: 28%
International: 77%
Minority: N/A
Average age: 27
Accepted applicants enrolled: 70%

"Professors use case studies that are way too outdated."

The 411

Annual tuition and fees: $45,430
Annual living expenses: $7,000
Total program cost, including forgone salary: $173,102
Classes begin: September
Application deadline: June 17
Application fee: $130

Cliff Notes

Leading areas of study: Entrepreneurship, Ethics, General Management, Leadership, Strategy
Average class size, core courses: 70
Average class size, electives: 50
Number of electives: 86
Teaching methods: Case studies (75%), team projects (11%), lectures (7%)

But What's It *Really* Like?

Graded by students:
Overall ranking: **A**
Teaching quality: **A**
Career services: **A**

Graded by recruiters:
Overall ranking: **A+**
Accounting: **A+**
Analytical skills: **A+**
Communication: **A+**
Finance: **A+**
General management: **A+**
International business: **A+**
Marketing: **A+**
Operations/production: **A+**
Teamwork skills: **A+**

Bling

Average pre-MBA salary: $43,100
Average post-MBA salary: $118,160
Graduates with job offer by graduation: 83%
Companies recruiting on campus: 200
Top functional areas for graduates: Finance/Accounting, Consulting, Marketing/Sales
Biggest recruiters: Santander, BCG, Citigroup, Europraxis, Deutsche Bank

The Good, the Bad, and the Ugly: Students Speak Out

"I was a nontraditional student (with a background in nonprofit organizations) paired with engineers, CFAs, British military officers, brokers, toymakers, teachers, bankers, and motorcycle riders—and I thrived. Also, Barcelona rocks."

"IESE has an exceptionally strong, supportive, and open-minded student community. This creates an unbelievable learning experience and class dynamic during discussions and projects. Students are extremely enthusiastic, and social life is extraordinary."

"I was disappointed by the emphasis on soft skills and networking rather than on academic skills and real techniques."

"Attending IESE was the best decision I ever made."

"I found in IESE a challenging environment and a life-changing experience. I am sure it will turn out to be a wise investment."

"In terms of academics and job opportunities, IESE is very similar to other top-ranked schools in Europe, such as INSEAD or LBS. All major investment banks and consulting firms recruit actively at IESE, and it has amazing positioning in Spain."

"IESE stands out in terms of academic rigor, students' sense of responsibility, and team spirit. Also, I have acquired a second language (Spanish), which will be of tremendous value for me."

"While most schools take four days of light classes (attendance optional) with Fridays off, IESE dedicates itself to real education, real development, and real leadership advancement. The environment itself is designed to create teams of people who are results-oriented— but not at the expense of friendships and personal integrity."

"IESE professors sometimes use case studies from 1970, which are way too outdated."

"IESE is strong academically, but what stands out most is the people and their yearning to accept everybody into the community. Competition is never construed in a negative way."

"Most extracurricular activities are student-run and managed. The professors were challenging, yet approachable. Attending IESE was the best decision, both personally and professionally, I have ever made."

"Having only 210 students per class is definitely a strength that allows stronger bonding among students and closer contact with faculty."

 **Where to Stay**

Hotel Rialto
Ferran 40-42
Barcelona, ES 08002
34-93-318-52-12

Hotel Continental Palacete
Rambla de Catalunya, 30
Barcelona, ES 08007
34-93-445-76-57

Hotel Arts
Marina, 19-21
Barcelona, ES 08005
34-93-221-10-00

 Where to Eat

Carmelitas
Carme, 42
Barcelona, ES 08001
34-93-412-46-84

Vinotinto
Aribau, 27
Barcelona, ES 08011
34-93-451-10-27

Inopia
Carrer de Tamarit, 104
Barcelona, ES 08015
34-93-424-52-31

 Things to Do

Museu Picasso (Picasso Museum)
Montcada, 15-23
Barcelona, ES 08003
34-93-356-30-00

**Museu de la Xocolata
(Chocolate Museum)**
Comerç, 36
Barcelona, ES 08003
34-93-268-78-78

CHECK OUT BUSINESSWEEK.COM FOR MORE:

Placement Q&A: Career Director Alex Herrera talks about how IESE readies students for the job search.

School Tour: Never been to Barcelona? Get a taste with *Business Week's* IESE photo essay.

Admissions Q&A: Admissions Director Mireia Rius describes the ideal IESE applicant.

Search & Compare: See how IESE stacks up against other top B-schools.

Video View: IESE Professor Julia Prats discusses a research collaboration to study family businesses.

MBA Forums: Connect with other IESE hopefuls.

Access all the B-schools content on BusinessWeek.com by subscribing to MBA Insider.

U. of North Carolina

Kenan-Flagler Business School
University of North Carolina
   at Chapel Hill
2006 Ranking: 17 (U.S.)
Campus Box 3490
McColl Building
Chapel Hill, NC 27599
E-mail address: Mba_info@unc.edu
Web address: www.kenan-flagler.unc.edu
For more info: Call general information
   at (919) 962-8301

Why North Carolina?

As Dean Steve Jones is fond of saying, "A successful career depends on what you can do, not just on what you know." With that in mind, Kenan-Flagler has created a curriculum designed to produce graduates who can hit the ground running at graduation. The first year is built around two "integrative exercises" that require students to use all the skills they learned in earlier courses. Students may begin taking electives in the spring semester of their first year, giving them a leg up in the competition for summer internships. Every year, 20% of all electives are new to ensure that emerging topics in business and research are quickly reflected in the curriculum. Students may choose from eight concentrations, including customer and product management, entrepreneurship, global supply chain management, and sustainable enterprise.

✅ B4UGO

Applicants accepted: 39%
Average GMAT score: 682
Average years' work experience: 5.6
Average post-MBA salary increase: 95.9%
Average total first-year compensation: $128,602

The University of North Carolina at Chapel Hill is a public institution. Established in 1919, Kenan-Flagler's full-time MBA program is accredited by the Association to Advance Collegiate Schools of Business (AACSB). Kenan-Flagler also offers an executive MBA program. For details on the executive MBA program, see page 293.

 Headlines

March 20, 2007: Students compete in sustainable venture competition

March 20, 2007: David A. Hofmann named MBA associate dean

October 4, 2006: $1 million gift will support leadership initiative

August 31, 2005: Susan Amey named director of MBA career services

"I learned a ton."

Famous MBA Alumni

Claire Babrowski, former president and COO of RadioShack
Paul Clayton, CEO of Jamba Juice
Brent Callinicos, vice president and CFO, platforms and services division, for Microsoft

 Who Are My Classmates?

Full-time enrollment: 571
Women: 28%
International: 28%
Minority: 18.4%
Average age: 29
Accepted applicants enrolled: 42%

"The faculty is great, and the core classes were very strong."

The 411

Annual tuition and fees: $21,508 (resident), $39,882 (nonresident)
Annual living expenses: $20,840
Total program cost, including forgone salary: $177,356 (resident), $213,104 (nonresident)
Classes begin: August
Application deadlines: October 26 to March 7
Application fee: $135

Cliff Notes

Leading areas of study: Consulting, Finance, Leadership, Marketing, Real Estate
Average class size, core courses: 70
Average class size, electives: 45
Number of electives: 94
Teaching methods: Lectures (50%), case studies (25%), team projects (25%)

But What's It *Really* Like?

Graded by students:
Overall ranking: A
Teaching quality: A+
Career services: B

Graded by recruiters:
Overall ranking: A
Accounting: C
Analytical skills: A
Communication: A
Finance: A
General management: A
International business: A
Marketing: A
Operations/production: B
Teamwork skills: A

Bling

Average pre-MBA salary: $47,218
Average post-MBA salary: $92,505
Graduates with job offer by graduation: 86%
Top functional areas for graduates: Finanace/Accounting, Marketing/Sales, Consulting
Biggest recruiters: Bank of America, Citigroup, Deloitte Consulting, Lehman Brothers, Dell, IBM, Johnson & Johnson

"I chose Kenan-Flagler among four top business schools, and if I were given a [choice] again, I would definitely and immediately choose Kenan-Flagler."

"One aspect of my program that constantly impresses me is access to the faculty. Every professor I have had has been extremely open and accessible to meeting with students and has been encouraging of ongoing contact outside the classroom. This aspect of the program has truly enriched my experience."

"I am very glad that I was not accepted to HBS or Darden because I would probably have chosen them because of the higher rankings. In retrospect, my UNC MBA has been everything I hoped. I learned a ton."

"Leadership training is nearly nonexistent."

"The school has a very weak career services team. The career management personnel are extremely inexperienced, unresponsive, discouraging, and unenthusiastic. The school is good in teamwork training but very weak in leadership training. Leadership training is nearly nonexistent in the school's regular and nonregular curriculum."

"Earning an MBA at UNC was a great experience. I looked [at] and visited many other schools, but I found the students at UNC to be much more social and collegial. The faculty is great, and the core classes were very strong, which surprised me given my previous class work in my undergraduate business school's core classes."

"The school is great, and it will move up in the rankings because of the efforts of the dean. However, some aspects that need a lot of improvement are the financial aid distribution procedure and support for international students in their career search."

"The opportunities at Kenan-Flagler are boundless, and the learning environment is beyond compare. The student body radiates passion about business and UNC. That enthusiasm carries over into the business world to create an active and supportive alumni network of colleagues and friends. I am proud to be a part of the Kenan-Flagler community."

"While we do not have the strongest alumni network, every alumnus whom I encountered has been more than willing to assist in any way possible. I was able to get my internship early with the company that I wanted (IBM) and at the time of getting the ultimate offer from IBM I had multiple offers from other leading international companies. How could I complain?"

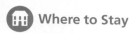 **Where to Stay**

The Carolina Inn
211 Pittsboro St.
Chapel Hill, NC 27516
(919) 933-2001

The Franklin Hotel
311 W. Franklin St.
Chapel Hill, NC 27516
(919) 442-9000

The Siena Hotel
1505 E. Franklin St.
Chapel Hill, NC 27514
(919) 929-4000

 Where to Eat

Lantern Restaurant (Asian, Pacific Rim)
423 Franklin St.
Chapel Hill, NC 27516
(919) 969-8846

Crook's Corner (Cajun, Creole)
610 Franklin St.
Chapel Hill, NC 27516
(919) 929-7643

Pepper's Pizza (Italian)
127 Franklin St.
Chapel Hill, NC 27514
(919) 967-7766

 Things to Do

Morehead Planetarium and Science Center
250 E. Franklin St.
Chapel Hill, NC 27514
(919) 962-1236

North Carolina Botanical Gardens
The University of North Carolina at Chapel Hill
College Box 3375, Totten Center
Chapel Hill, NC 27599
(919) 962-0522

CHECK OUT BUSINESSWEEK.COM FOR MORE:

Admissions Q&A: Admissions Director Sherrylyn Wallace describes the application process at UNC.

Sample Application Essays and Interview Tips: Discover what it takes to become a Tarheel.

School Tour: Before booking a flight, check out the UNC campus in beautiful Chapel Hill, a corner of the historic Research Triangle.

Video View: Dean Steve Jones discusses his vision of UNC as the leader in corporate sustainable development education.

Expanded Profile: Everything you ever wanted to know about Kenan-Flagler, and then some.

Access all the B-schools content on BusinessWeek.com by subscribing to MBA Insider.

University of Notre Dame

Mendoza College of Business
2006 Ranking: 26 (U.S.)
Notre Dame, IN 46556
E-mail address: mba.1@nd.edu
Web address: www.nd.edu/~mba
For more info: Call general information
at (574) 631-8488

☑ **B4UGO**

Applicants accepted: 44%
Average GMAT score: 673
Average years' work experience: 4.4
Average post-MBA salary increase:
117.1%
**Average total first-year
compensation:** $116,869

Why Notre Dame?

Mendoza has carved a niche for itself in the B-school world as a religious institution, with ethics playing a fundamental role in the MBA program. Opportunities to delve into social entrepreneurship and a focus on giving back to the community add context to the core curriculum. The new curriculum, introduced in 2005, stresses ideas that have since become commonplace, including an integrative course structure and personal assessments of individual strengths and weaknesses. Unique curriculum opportunities include an accelerated one-year MBA, as well as weeklong between-term "intensives" that give students hands-on experience. With nearly half of the 2006 class accepting offers in the Midwest, Mendoza's regional reputation makes it a strong choice for those who appreciate the region's charms, but others may have a more difficult time with recruitment.

Notre Dame is a private institution. Established in 1921, Mendoza's full-time MBA program is accredited by the Association to Advance Colle-giate Schools of Business (AACSB). Mendoza also offers an executive MBA program.

 Headlines

February 7, 2007: Accounting students help low-income residents prepare tax returns

January 29, 2007: Mendoza MBA program scores high in ethics survey

January 18, 2005: Karen Dowd appointed senior director of MBA Career Development

September 1, 2003: $3 million facility opened to encourage collaborative learning

"I grew as a leader, motivator, and manager."

Famous MBA Alumni

Richard J. Shields, CFO of Oakley, Inc.

Donald M. Casey, Jr., chairman of Johnson & Johnson Vision Care Group

Jim Corgel, general manager, independent software vendors and developer relations, at IBM

Who Are My Classmates?

Full-time enrollment: 330
Women: 26%
International: 22%
Minority: 17%
Average age: 27
Accepted applicants enrolled: 44%

"Cooperation and teamwork were the norm, not the exception."

The 411

Annual tuition and fees: $37,145
Annual living expenses: $14,595
Total program cost, including forgone salary: $182,456
Classes begin: August
Application deadlines: November 15 to May 1
Application fee: $100

Cliff Notes

Leading areas of study: Consulting, Entrepreneurship, Finance, General Management, Marketing
Average class size, core courses: 66
Average class size, electives: 37
Number of electives: 106
Teaching methods: Lectures (25%), case studies (23%), experiential learning (15%), team projects (15%)

But What's It *Really* Like?

Graded by students:
Overall ranking: **B**
Teaching quality: **C**
Career services: **B**

Graded by recruiters:
Overall ranking: **C**
Accounting: **B**
Analytical skills: **C**
Communication: **B**
Finance: **B**
General management: **B**
International business: **C**
Marketing: **B**
Operations/production: **B**
Teamwork skills: **B**

Bling

Average pre-MBA salary: $39,488
Average post-MBA salary: $85,746
Graduates with job offer by graduation: 80%
Top functional areas for graduates: Finance/Accouning, Consulting, Marketing/Sales
Biggest recruiters: IBM, United Airlines, Huron Consulting, OfficeMax, Whirlpool

The Good, the Bad, and the Ugly: Students Speak Out

"The MBA program and the school as a whole have a very deep sense of community and purpose. The quality of the education and classes is very good, and the program's focus on problem solving and social responsibility is a great mix. Finally, the alumni are incredibly supportive."

"Often overlooked by companies seeking MBA graduates."

"Notre Dame excels in certain areas, but if your career goals deviate from marketing or finance, it may be better to look for more specialized programs."

"The class work was challenging and definitely honed my business skills. I grew as a leader, motivator, and manager. The professors were excellent and really cared about the progress of their students."

"Because of its small size, Notre Dame is often overlooked by companies seeking to hire MBA graduates."

"Notre Dame's small class sizes created a very communal environment where ideas were freely shared and cooperation and teamwork were the norm, not the exception. Everyone helped everyone along."

"The spiritual nature of the institution, the focus on the common good, and the commitment to service are wonderful aspects of the program—but are not for everyone. South Bend is not for everyone. Although the ND network is phenomenal, if companies that interest you are not coming to campus, then you will need to be much more proactive in finding a position."

"Notre Dame is undervalued. The small class sizes gave me incredible exposure to my professors and to special venture projects. I learned strategic finance from the ex-CFO of McDonald's, and I learned strategy from the youngest partner in McKinsey's history. To top it off, the career center helped me find a fast-track high-exposure job where I was able to triple my before-school salary."

"The marketing program was not up to par in terms of the courses offered, teaching staff, and the amount of help given to students looking for jobs."

"When I compare my experience at Notre Dame to that of my friends at other MBA schools, it sounds to me like I'm enjoying the experience more."

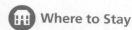 **Where to Stay**

South Bend Marriott
123 N. St. Joseph St.
South Bend, IN 46601
(574) 234-2000

Morris Inn
Notre Dame Ave.
Notre Dame, IN 46556
(574) 631-2000

Comfort Suites South Bend
52939 U.S. 933 N.
South Bend, IN 46637
(574) 272-1500

 Where to Eat

Noma (Asian fusion)
119 N. Michigan St.
South Bend, IN 46601
(574) 233-4959

Sean O'Casey's (pub)
123 N. St. Joseph St.
South Bend, IN 46601
(574) 234-2000

Sunny Italy Café (Italian)
601 N. Niles Ave.
South Bend, IN 46617
(219) 232-9620

 Things to Do

College Football Hall of Fame
111 S. St. Joseph St.
South Bend, IN 46601
(574) 235-9999

South Bend Chocolate Company Factory & Museum
3300 W. Sample St.
South Bend, IN 49964
(574) 233-2577

CHECK OUT BUSINESSWEEK.COM FOR MORE:

Video View: Dean Carol Woo talks about integrating ethics into the MBA program.

Sample Application Essay: Improve your essay writing by reading this example from a successful application.

Admissions Q&A: Admissions Director Mary Goss recommends personalized applications with an emphasis on community service.

Admissions Interview Tips: Find out what kind of questions to expect when interviewing at Mendoza.

School Tour: Get a feel for Mendoza's campus and student community through a picture slideshow.

Access all the B-schools content on BusinessWeek.com by subscribing to MBA Insider.

University of Pennsylvania

The Wharton School
2006 Ranking: 2 (U.S.)
420 Jon M. Huntsman Hall
3720 Walnut St.
Philadelphia, PA 19104
E-mail address:
mba.admissions@wharton.upenn.edu
Web address:
www.wharton.upenn.edu
For more info: Call MBA admissions at
(215) 898-6183

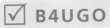 **B4UGO**

Applicants accepted: 18%
Average GMAT score: 712
Average years' work experience: 5.8
Average post-MBA salary increase:
29.2%*
**Average total first-year
compensation:** $136,343†

*Based in part on *BusinessWeek* survey data.
†Base salary and signing bonus only.

Why Wharton?

A fixture at the top of *BusinessWeek*'s biennial B-school rankings, Wharton's top-flight faculty and innovative curriculum place its full-time MBA program among the best in the nation. At nearly $50,000 a year, it's also one of the most expensive. A favorite among students, the program nevertheless has a reputation as being intensely competitive. Graduates are highly sought after by recruiters for jobs in finance and consulting, and are among the highest paid in the world. Founded in 1881, Wharton is the world's oldest business school, but it is far from stagnant—with more than 170 electives in its 11 academic departments, there is truly something for everyone. In June 2007, former Emory B-school dean Thomas Robertson was chosen to replace Patrick Harker at the helm.

The University of Pennsylvania is a private institution. Established in 1921,

Wharton's full-time MBA program is accredited by the Association to Advance Collegiate Schools of Business (AACSB). Wharton also offers an executive MBA program. For details on Wharton's executive MBA program, see page 297.

 ## Headlines

June 21, 2007: Thomas Robertson replaces Pat Harker as dean

May 9, 2007: Student entrepreneurs receive $10,000 awards

January 10, 2007: Wharton alumni give $6 million for scholarships

May 10, 2006: Wharton launches research partnership with European B-schools

---

"I was pushed like never before."

Famous MBA Alumni

Arthur Collins, CEO of Medtronic Inc.
Peter Lynch, vice chairman of Fidelity Management & Research Company
James D. Power III, founder and chairman of J. D. Power & Associates

Who Are My Classmates?

Full-time enrollment: 1,640
Women: 37%
International: 45%
Minority: 26%
Average age: 29
Accepted applicants enrolled: 67%

"The caliber of the students is mind-blowing."

The 411

Annual tuition and fees: $49,722
Annual living expenses: $22,226
Total program cost, including forgone salary: $315,060*
Classes begin: September
Application deadlines: October 11, January 3, February 28
Application fee: $225

*Based in part on *Business Week* survey data.

Cliff Notes

Leading areas of study: Entrepreneurship, Finance, Healthcare Administration, Marketing, Strategy
Average class size, core courses: 57
Average class size, electives: 39
Number of electives: 71
Teaching methods: Case studies (35%), team projects (25%), lectures (20%)

But What's It *Really* Like?

Graded by students:
Overall ranking: A
Teaching quality: B
Career services: A+

Graded by recruiters:
Overall ranking: A+
Accounting: A+
Analytical skills: A+
Communication: A+
Finance: A+
General management: A+
International business: A+
Marketing: A+
Operations/production: A
Teamwork skills: A

$ Bling

Average pre-MBA salary: $85,582*
Average post-MBA salary: $110,550
Graduates with job offer by graduation: 92%
Top functional areas for graduates: Finance/Accounting, Consulting, Marketing/Sales
Biggest recruiters: McKinsey, BCG, Bain, Goldman Sachs, Morgan Stanley

*Estimate based on *Business Week* survey data.

The Good, the Bad, and the Ugly: Students Speak Out

"Some have complained that too many companies come to campus too often and want too much contact with prospective applicants. This is a good problem to have—may it last forever."

"Over the past year, certain administration decisions, however valid and well thought out, have been communicated extremely poorly. This has led to widespread dissatisfaction with the administration and its decisions."

"The caliber of the students whom I have encountered at Wharton has been mind-blowing. The diversity of the student body, from nationality to experience, has enhanced my MBA experience tenfold."

"There's no one at the wheel of this ship."

"Did I learn anything new? Yes, but I could have learned it cheaper from books."

"One great thing about Wharton is the connectedness to the larger Penn campus. Although the school is self-sufficient, it is very easy to cross-register for courses and mingle with nonbusiness students. It is a very open and welcoming environment."

"Wharton's administration is completely disconnected from the student body. No one in the administration would know me if I bit them. Wharton is able to maintain its current status only because of the quality of the students and professors. There's no one at the wheel of this ship."

"Wharton is not just a finance school. The marketing, operations, and strategy departments were superb, and the professors distinguished themselves in the classroom."

"A much less highlighted aspect of the Wharton MBA is experiential leadership. Through Wharton's coproduction model, students are involved in key aspects of Wharton administration and student life. From admissions to international cultural and dance shows, Wharton students are able to hone their leadership skills while also having fun!"

"Wharton has made all my personal and professional dreams possible. I'm not saying it was easy. I was pushed like never before to give the best I could. But you know what? It's changed my life—and I've had fun all the way through it."

"Wharton has some weaknesses in preparing students for interviews, and the admissions office is painful to deal with, but other than that, it was a fantastic experience."

"If someone is passionate about finance or real estate, Wharton is the only place to go."

Where to Stay

The Inn at Penn
3600 Sansom St.
Philadelphia, PA 19104
(215) 222-0200

Sheraton University City
36th St. & Chestnut St.
Philadelphia, PA 19104
(215) 387-8000

Courtyard by Marriott: Philadelphia Downtown
21 N. Juniper St.
Philadelphia, PA 19107
(215) 496-3200

Where to Eat

Penne Restaurant & Wine Bar
3611 Walnut St.
Philadelphia, PA 19104
(215) 823-6222

New Deck Tavern
3408 Sansom St.
Philadelphia, PA 19104
(215) 386-4600

Pizza Allegros
3200 Chestnut St.
Philadelphia, PA 19104
(215) 222-3226

Things to Do

The Esther M. Klein Art Gallery
3701 Market St.
Philadelphia, PA 19104
(215) 966-6188

International House
3701 Chestnut St.
Philadelphia, PA 19104
(215) 387-5125

CHECK OUT BUSINESSWEEK.COM FOR MORE:

Admissions Q&A: Admissions Director Thomas Caleel describes the ideal Wharton applicant.

Sample Application Essays and Interview Tips: Get the lowdown on what it takes to get in.

Video View: Vice Dean Anjani Jain talks about the ever-evolving academic environment at Wharton.

School Tour: Check out the campus before visiting using this photo slide show.

Expanded Profile: More statistics, more facts, more insights on Wharton.

Access all the B-schools content on BusinessWeek.com by subscribing to MBA Insider.

University of Rochester

William E. Simon Graduate School of
  Business Administration
2006 Ranking: 28 (U.S.)
305 Schlegel Hall
Rochester, NY 14627
E-mail address:
  admissions@simon.rochester.edu
Web address:
  www.simon.rochester.edu/mba
For more info: Call general information
  at (585) 275-3533

☑ B4UGO

Applicants accepted: 37%
Average GMAT score: 673
Average years' work experience: 4.3
Average post-MBA salary increase:
  75.9%
**Average total first-year
  compensation:** $117,522

Why Rochester?

The new FACt (Frame, Analyze, Communicate) curriculum, launched in 2005, brings some of the crucial soft-skill elements into Simon's traditionally quant-heavy MBA program. Still, Simon's strengths lie in its finance program and its economics-based approach to learning; more than 40% of graduates accept finance positions postgraduation. Simon has recently reversed B-school convention by targeting younger students with no work experience—a practice that some say diminishes classroom give-and-take. (The 4-2 program accepts students fresh out of college, while the 3-2 program allows Rochester undergraduates to substitute the first-year MBA program for their last year.) Students praise the faculty but recognize that the school's undervalued reputation makes job search activities more challenging.

Rochester is a private institution. Established in 1962, Simon's full-time

MBA program is accredited by the Association to Advance Collegiate Schools of Business (AACSB). Simon also offers part-time and executive MBA programs.

 Headlines

April 20, 2007: Alumnus pledges $1.5 million for professorship

November 15, 2006: Simon's entrepreneurship program gets new leader

October 25, 2006: New staff hired for Career Management Center

April 2, 2004: Mark Zupan takes over as Simon's new dean

---

*"Strong alumni
network in the
finance area."*

Famous MBA Alumni

Arunas A. Chesonis, chairman and CEO of PAETEC Holding Corp.

Gino Santini, senior vice president of corporate policy and strategy at Eli Lilly and Co.

Mark S. Ain, founder and executive chairman of Kronus, Inc.

 **Who Are My Classmates?**

Full-time enrollment: 285
Women: 27%
International: 53%
Minority: 25%
Average age: 26
Accepted applicants enrolled: 43%

"Interaction with the professors is top notch."

The 411

Annual tuition and fees: $37,755
Annual living expenses: $18,965
Total program cost, including forgone salary: $209,106
Classes begin: September
Application deadlines: November 1 to June 1
Application fee: $125

Cliff Notes

Leading areas of study: Accounting, Economics, Finance, Marketing, Strategy
Average class size, core courses: 60
Average class size, electives: 42
Number of electives: 62
Teaching methods: Lectures (35%), case studies (30%), team projects (20%)

But What's It *Really* Like?

Graded by students:
Overall ranking: **C**
Teaching quality: **A**
Career services: **B**

Graded by recruiters:
Overall ranking: **B**
Accounting: **A+**
Analytical skills: **A**
Communication: **A**
Finance: **A**
General management: **A**
International business: **A**
Marketing: **A**
Operations/production: **A+**
Teamwork skills: **A**

$ **Bling**

Average pre-MBA salary: $47,833
Average post-MBA salary: $84,137
Graduates with job offer by graduation: 80%
Top functional areas for graduates: Finance/Accounting, General Management, Marketing
Biggest recruiters: Citigroup, Deloitte, Barclays, Procter & Gamble, Johnson & Johnson

The Good, the Bad, and the Ugly: Students Speak Out

"It's a top-10 school in terms of tuition, but not ranking. Outside of the northeast, it is an unknown program."

"When choosing a business school, I did not consider the impact a dean can have. Dean Mark Zupan's involvement and excitement toward the MBA program was fantastic."

"The school's network is too focused on finance. Students with other industry backgrounds and from foreign countries [find it] difficult to find their niches with the school's assistance. They just have to work it out by themselves."

"Simon is an excellent place for people who are interested in finance/accounting. A strong alumni network in the finance area helps a lot, and companies in the finance field know our school. I got my job offer through an alumnus. Finance, economics, and accounting are the three strongest areas at Simon."

> *"It was lacking in soft skill and communication training."*

"Top MBA jobs are still well within the grasp of Simon graduates, as evidenced by me and many of my classmates going to companies such as Citigroup, P&G, JPMorgan, etc., but you have to be proactive and grab those opportunities for yourself. The positive side of this is that the Simon name is well enough known to get your foot in the door; the rest is up to you."

"Unsurpassed education; but my school is focusing on the 3-2 students (still seniors in the undergraduate program when entering the MBA program), which I do not agree with."

"Simon has a superior quantitative curriculum second to no other MBA program. Those with analytical strengths and natural communication skills will benefit the most from the program. This was an extremely comprehensive finance- and economics-based curriculum, but it was lacking in soft skill and communication training."

"Simon is a smaller business school, so the interaction with the professors is top notch. They really try to make that connection with each student, to not just teach material, but to help each individual grow."

"The quality and quantity of companies that visit campus needs to increase. Also 90% of the elective courses are offered only in the evening combining both part-time and full-time students."

 **Where to Stay**

Hyatt Regency Rochester
125 E. Main St.
Rochester, NY 14604
(585) 546-1234

The Inn on Broadway
26 Broadway
Rochester, NY 14607
(585) 232-3595

Courtyard by Marriott
33 Corporate Woods
Rochester, NY 14623
(585) 292-1000

 Where to Eat

**Aladdin's Natural Eatery
(Mediterranean)**
646 Monroe Ave.
Rochester, NY 14607
(585) 442-5000

Beale Street Café (Cajun)
689 South Ave.
Rochester, NY 14620
(585) 271-4650

**Golden Port Dim Sum Restaurant
(Chinese)**
105 East Ave.
Rochester, NY 14604
(585) 256-1780

 Things to Do

George Eastman House
900 East Ave.
Rochester, NY 14607
(585) 271-3361

Seneca Park Zoo
2222 St. Paul St.
Rochester, NY 14621
(585) 336-7200

CHECK OUT BUSINESSWEEK.COM FOR MORE:

Video View: Dean Mark Zupan discusses the value of drawing in young talent and creating an internationally diverse student body.

Careers Q&A: Director of Career Management Patricia Phillips tells students how to make their focus and passion stand out in an interview.

Admissions Q&A: The director of admissions recommends which qualities to emphasize on a Simon application.

School Tour: Get an inside look at Rochester's campus and student activity.

Sample Application Essay: Browse four Simon essays to understand the questions and how to answer them.

Access all the B-schools content on BusinessWeek.com by subscribing to MBA Insider.

U. of Southern California

Marshall School of Business
2006 Ranking: 21 (U.S.)
611 Exposition Blvd.
Popovich Hall 200
Los Angeles, CA 90089
E-mail address:
   marshallmba@marshall.usc.edu
Web address: www.marshall.usc.edu
For more info: Call general information
   at (213) 740-7846

✓ B4UGO

Applicants accepted: 29%
Average GMAT score: 689
Average years' work experience: 5.1
Average post-MBA salary increase:
   36.7%
Average total first-year
   compensation: $107,872

Why USC?

Beautiful weather and Hollywood glitz aren't the only reasons to attend Marshall. Far from it. After a drop in the rankings led to a program overhaul in 2005, Marshall is well on the road to recovery with a new dean, James Ellis, at the helm. Students here are exposed to a cutting-edge curriculum. After a first-year grounding in business fundamentals that includes nine days of study abroad, students are expected to take a required course in innovation and to organize the remainder of their second-year studies around a functional concentration and an industry "vertical." The concentrations are fairly standard, but the verticals offer students intense exposure to a single industry—everything from high tech to consumer goods to nonprofits—across academic departments and disciplines.

USC is a private institution. Established in 1920, Marshall's full-time MBA is accredited by the Association to Advance Collegiate Schools of Business (AACSB). Marshall also offers part-time and executive MBA programs. For details on Marshall's part-time MBA program, see page 401. For details on Marshall's executive MBA program, see page 301.

Headlines

April 4, 2007: James G. Ellis named Marshall dean

January 11, 2007: Marshall students meet with Warren Buffett

February 13, 2006: Interim Dean Thomas Gilligan: innovation and global education are hallmarks of new curriculum

October 17, 2005: Marshall establishes sports business institute

---

"An intense learning environment."

Famous MBA Alumni

Terrence Lanni, founder and CEO of MGM Mirage
Chris DeWolfe, co-founder and CEO of MySpace
Paul Orfalea, founder of Kinko's

Who Are My Classmates?

Full-time enrollment: 532
Women: 34%
International: 26%
Minority: 44%
Average age: 28
Accepted applicants enrolled: 57%

"I did not learn as much about business as I wanted."

The 411

Annual tuition and fees: $40,500
Annual living expenses: $13,000
Total program cost, including forgone salary: $237,000
Classes begin: August
Application deadlines: November 1 to April 1
Application fee: $150

Cliff Notes

Leading areas of study: Entrepreneurship, Finance, Marketing, Portfolio Management, Real Estate
Average class size, core classes: 70
Average class size, electives: 36
Number of electives: 83
Teaching methods: Case studies (30%), team projects (30%), lectures (25%)

But What's It *Really* Like?

Graded by students:
Overall ranking: B
Teaching quality: C
Career services: A

Graded by recruiters:
Overall ranking: B
Accounting: A
Analytical skills: B
Communication: B
Finance: C
General management: B
International business: B
Marketing: B
Operations/production: B
Teamwork skills: B

Bling

Average pre-MBA salary: $65,000
Average post-MBA salary: $88,841
Graduates with job offer by graduation: 86%
Companies recruiting on campus: 273
Top functional areas for graduates: Finance/Accounting, Marketing/Sales, Consulting
Biggest recruiters: Amgen, General Electric, Mattel, Bank of America, Credit Suisse, Walt Disney, Procter & Gamble

The Good, the Bad, and the Ugly: Students Speak Out

"USC's program, while offering an intense learning environment, is balanced by a healthy approach to life that is the fabric of southern California living. Professors, professionals, and alumni are always accessible, regardless of position, and one is never left without an event to attend on the weekend."

"The curriculum is undergoing a complete overhaul for the better."

"I was somewhat disappointed with the quality of my MBA experience. I did not learn as much about business as I wanted. My teachers were sometimes fabulous, sometimes OK, and sometimes terrible. I feel that at the MBA level, they should all be outstanding."

"The warmth and grace of the folks at Marshall is unparalleled. From admissions to the program office, from the students to the alumni, the Marshall community cultivates allegiance founded on real behavior and feelings rather than on the school's brand name."

"Like all schools, USC has some things that it needs to improve upon, such as the quality of the teachers and the career placement center. But overall, I know that USC is headed in the right direction. The social activities, such as the football games, mixers, school parties, and school-sponsored trips, are all top rate and make the whole experience a lot of fun."

"The greatest strength at Marshall is the students. They are an incredible and diverse mix of intelligent, dedicated, motivated, and interesting people from all over the world."

"Marshall is in the midst of a fantastic improvement. The career resources have performed a 180 from the previous downslide. The curriculum is undergoing a complete overhaul for the better. And the student life continues to improve."

"The Marshall program office is not very well run. I feel there is a lack of quality from the dean on down. The saving grace is that the students know this and thus are very supportive of one another."

"The classroom environment and the Marshall culture both center around teamwork. The challenging course work is also supplemented by real-world projects. In 2 of 5 classes this semester I am working on projects for real companies. The learning opportunities from business leaders such as Jack Welch have increased. I have met top HR executives from Sun, The Limited, Google, Starbucks, UPS, and SAS Institute."

 **Where to Stay**

Los Angeles Radisson Hotel
3540 S. Figueroa St.
Los Angeles, CA 90007
(213) 748-4141

Omni Los Angeles Hotel
251 S. Olive St.
Los Angeles, CA 90012
(213) 617-3300

Westin Bonaventure
404 S. Figueroa St.
Los Angeles, CA 90071
(213) 624-1000

 Where to Eat

Philippe The Original
1001 N. Alameda St.
Los Angeles, CA 90012
(213) 628-3781

Water Grill
544 S. Grand St.
Los Angeles, CA 90071
(213) 891-0900

El Cholo Restaurant
1121 S. Western Ave.
Los Angeles, CA 90006
(323) 734-2773

 Things to Do

Getty Museum
1200 Getty Center Dr.
Los Angeles, CA 90265
(310) 440-7300

Venice Boardwalk
Pacific Ave. and Windward Ave.
Venice, CA 90291

CHECK OUT BUSINESSWEEK.COM FOR MORE:

Admissions Q&A: Keith Vaughn, director of full-time MBA admissions, describes the perfect Marshall applicant.

Interview Tips: What it takes to get a foot in the door at Marshall.

Sample Application Essays: Tips on how to write a solid essay for Marshall.

School Tour: Look before you leap—with this slide-show tour of the Marshall campus.

Search & Compare: See how Marshall stacks up against other top B-schools.

Access all the B-schools content on BusinessWeek.com by subscribing to MBA Insider.

U. of Texas at Austin

McCombs School of Business
2006 Ranking: 20 (U.S.)
MBA Program Office
1 University Station, B6004
Austin, TX 78712
E-mail address:
    McCombsMBA@mccombs.utexas.edu
Web address: www.mba.mccombs
    .utexas.edu
For more info: Call the admissions
    office at (512) 471-7617

☑ B4UGO

Applicants accepted: 34%
Average GMAT score: 673
Average years' work experience: 5.2
Average post-MBA salary increase:
    65.2%
Average total first-year
    compensation: $131,438

Why Texas-Austin?

Located in one of the most popular college towns in the country, McCombs is a Top 20 program that truly shines. Half the core is crammed into the first semester (freeing up the second for electives to prepare students for summer internships), while most of the second year is given over to electives, of which there are more than 100. With 5 concentrations, 13 specializations, and 16 dual-degree programs (including 7 offered with overseas partners), there really is something for everyone. The Plus Program exposes MBAs to industry leaders through communication workshops and consulting projects. For longhorns, the Texas MBA can be had for about $20,000 a year—half the out-of-state rate, and a bargain compared to top private schools.

The University of Texas at Austin is a public institution. Founded in 1922, McCombs's full-time MBA program is accredited by the Association to Advance Collegiate Schools of Business (AACSB). McCombs also offers part-time and executive MBA programs. For details on McCombs's part-time MBA program, see page 405.

Headlines

February 21, 2007: McCombs wins international case competition

October 23, 2006: McCombs makes *BusinessWeek*'s Top 20 for sixth time

October 19, 2006: 16 faculty members recognized for teaching excellence

September 8, 2006: 14 new professors join the McCombs faculty

"One of the best things about Texas is the access to faculty."

Famous MBA Alumni

William Johnson, chairman, president, and CEO of H.J. Heinz Co.
Donald Evans, former U.S. secretary of commerce
Gerard Arpey, chairman, president, and CEO of AMR Corp.

Who Are My Classmates?

Total enrollment: 517
Women: 27%
International: 25%
Minority: 21%
Average age: 28
Accepted applicants enrolled: 50%

"I am better prepared to reenter the business world."

The 411

Annual tuition and fees: $21,218 (resident), $38,022 (nonresident)
Annual living expenses: $15,322
Total program cost, including forgone salary: $186,424 (resident), $220,032 (nonresident)
Classes begin: August
Application deadlines: February 1 (international), April 1 (U.S.)
Application fee: $125

Cliff Notes

Leading areas of study: Consulting, Entrepreneurship, Finance, Marketing, Strategy
Average class size, core classes: 65
Average class size, electives: 29
Number of electives: 102
Teaching methods: Lectures (40%), case studies (35%), team projects (10%), experiential learning (10%)

But What's It *Really* Like?

Graded by students:
Overall ranking: B
Teaching quality: C
Career services: B

Graded by recruiters:
Overall ranking: A
Accounting: A+
Analytical skills: A
Communication: A+
Finance: A+
General management: A+
International business: A
Marketing: A+
Operations/production: A
Teamwork skills: A+

Bling

Average pre-MBA salary: $56,672
Average post-MBA salary: $93,649
Graduates with job offer by graduation: 90%
Top functional areas for graduates: Finance/Accounting, Marketing/Sales, Consulting
Biggest recruiters: Dell, Deloitte Consulting, Citigroup, Chevron, Microsoft, Merrill Lynch

The Good, the Bad, and the Ugly: Students Speak Out

"The collaborative environment challenged me to think about concepts in a new way, and I feel that I am better prepared to reenter the business world with a more strategic focus."

"The global trips at McCombs are outstanding. My trip to India was the single greatest part of my two years here. The faculty and administration's commitment to these global trips is paramount to their success."

"There is a huge amount of turnover in the program office, which makes it difficult [to maintain] consistent leadership."

"McCombs has helped me be so much more confident about my own skills and has provided opportunities with many, many top companies. It has also been one of the most fun and collegial environments I have ever been a part of."

"The program really needs an upgrade in terms of facilities."

"Career Services at McCombs is really bad. It brings in companies that are recruiting for positions requiring 0

years of experience and just a bachelor's degree as a minimum."

"I think the biggest help and hindrance the University of Texas faces is its location. Being in the heart of Austin, and part of a great larger institution, gives MBA students countless avenues for academic and social pursuits. However, the two years here cause students to fall in love with the area, making them hesitant to go to other locations across the country for employment, which hurts the school both in rankings and with recruiters."

"Overall the core program and professors are excellent, but the program really needs an upgrade in terms of facilities and needs more freedom from the university as a whole to better address the needs of its customers."

"I think one of the best things about Texas is the access to faculty. Our professors regularly host dinners at their homes for their classes or through student organizations. Additionally, they're very involved in school programs."

"McCombs is a great value. The academic offering is challenging and comprehensive. McCombs also has unique programs like the Global Plus [leadership] program and the Venture Capital Fellows [offering MBA students internships with V.C. firms]. Finally, you can't beat the ROI. There simply is not another program as prestigious and affordable as U.T."

 **Where to Stay**

DoubleTree Guest Suites
303 W. 15th St.
Austin, TX 78701
(512) 478-7000

Hilton Austin
500 E. 4th St.
Austin, TX 78701
(512) 482-8000

Hotel San Jose
1316 Congress Ave.
Austin, TX 78704
(512) 444-7322

 Where to Eat

Güero's Taco Bar
1412 S. Congress Ave.
Austin, TX 78704
(512) 447-7688

Trudy's Texas Star
409 W. 30th St.
Austin, TX 78705
(512) 477-2935

Shady Grove Restaurant
1624 Barton Springs Rd.
Austin, TX 78704
(512) 474-9991

 Things to Do

Bob Bullock Texas State History Museum
1800 N. Congress Ave.
Austin, TX 78711
(512) 936-8746

Blanton Museum of Art
The University of Texas at Austin
Martin Luther King Jr. Blvd. at Congress Ave.
Austin, TX 78701
(512) 471-5482

CHECK OUT BUSINESSWEEK.COM FOR MORE:

Admissions Q&A: Christina Mabley, director of admissions, discusses the application process and the McCombs student profile.

Interview Tips: See what admissions directors at McCombs are looking for when they meet prospective students.

Video View: McCombs Dean George Gau talks about curriculum changes at the school.

Search & Compare: See how McCombs compares to other top schools.

Expanded Profile: Dig deeper into the McCombs full-time MBA.

Access all the B-schools content on BusinessWeek.com by subscribing to MBA Insider.

University of Toronto

Joseph L. Rotman School of Management
2006 Ranking: 3 (non-U.S.)
105 St. George St.
Toronto, ON (Canada) M5S 3E6
E-mail address:
   mba@rotman.utoronto.ca
Web address: www.rotman.utoronto.ca
For more info: Call MBA admissions at
   (416) 978-3499

 B4UGO

Applicants accepted: 42%
Average GMAT score: 660
Average years' work experience: 4.7
Average post-MBA salary increase:
   47.4%
Average total first-year
   compensation: $106,230

Why Toronto?

Among Canadian B-schools, Rotman's focus on "integrative thinking" is unique. The goal: to give students the tools they need to solve modern business problems that don't fall into neat, functional categories. Through a group of courses, including a new integrative thinking practicum, and a lecture series featuring top CEOs—including Jack Welch and Michael Dell—the Rotman curriculum teaches students how to make tough decisions with incomplete information by drawing on insights from economics, strategy, marketing, finance, and other disciplines. Recruiters give the program straight A's—even awarding it higher marks on general management than higher-ranked Canadian schools. Still, despite its location in a financial capital, students complain about limited recruiting opportunities and lackluster career services.

   Toronto is a public institution. Established in 1960, Rotman's full-time MBA program is accredited by the Association to Advance Collegiate Schools of Business (AACSB). Rotman also offers part-time and executive MBA programs.

 Headlines

March 23, 2007: Rotman receives $50 million from Province of Ontario for new building

December 18, 2006: MBA students visit China to study business and economy

August 17, 2006: Five new professors join faculty

January 5, 2006: Student-run consulting agency formed to help nonprofits

"The school far exceeded my expectations."

Famous MBA Alumni

Peter Hickman, president and CEO of Merrill Lynch HSBC Canada
Solbyung Yoon Coveley, president and CEO of cStar Technologies Inc.
Rick Blickstead, president and CEO of Wellesley Central Health Corp.

 **Who Are My Classmates?**

Full-time enrollment: 546
Women: 28%
International: 37%
Minority: N/A
Average age: 28
Accepted applicants enrolled: 60%

"The school needs to revamp its placement department."

The 411

Annual tuition and fees: $31,539 (resident), $43,277 (nonresident)
Annual living expenses: $20,461 (resident), $24,723 (nonresident)
Total program cost, including forgone salary: $216,674 (resident), $248,674 (nonresident)
Classes begin: September
Application deadline: April 30
Application fee: $150

Cliff Notes

Leading areas of study: Business Design, Consulting, Finance, Integrative Thinking, Strategy
Average class size, core courses: 68
Average class size, electives: 40
Number of electives: 78
Teaching methods: Lectures (40%), case studies (25%), simulations (15%), team projects (15%)

But What's It *Really* Like?

Graded by students:
Overall ranking: B
Teaching quality: B
Career services: B

Graded by recruiters:
Overall ranking: A
Accounting: A
Analytical skills: A
Communication: A
Finance: A
General management: A
International business: A
Marketing: A
Operations/production: A
Teamwork skills: A

$ Bling

Average pre-MBA salary: $56,337
Average post-MBA salary: $83,067
Graduates with job offer by graduation: 62%
Companies recruiting on campus: 62
Top functional areas for graduates: Finance/Accounting, Consulting, General Management
Biggest recruiters: CIBC, RBC Financial Group, Deloitte, BMO Financial Group, ScotiaBank

The Good, the Bad, and the Ugly: Students Speak Out

"There is a very positive energy among staff and students at Rotman that the school is creating something special. It has the right approach, excellent leadership, and a strong vision of the future of business and management training. Overall, though the program was expensive and more work than I expected, the school far exceeded my expectations of what an MBA program could be."

"The school needs to revamp its placement department. Other than that, the school has some of the best faculty members in the world and is extremely responsive to student needs."

"Great faculty. Great overall academic experience."

"My experience at Rotman was outstanding. The school has a long way to go to improve the career placement services, but I truly believe that it's on the right path."

"Rotman is a great school overall. I am very happy with the quality of my business education, and I feel that I can compete successfully with graduates from any other school."

"Rotman needs to try a lot harder to look beyond Toronto. This being said, the school's teaching capacity and abilities are excellent and the caliber of students outstanding."

"I felt really wanted at Rotman. I was not just another source of revenue."

"Great faculty. Great overall academic experience. Performance of the placement office and recruiting opportunities left a lot to be desired."

"The integrative thinking aspect of the program was key, I believe, to differentiating it from traditional B-schools. Classes were small enough that I could participate, but large enough that there was diversity of thought. The proportion of international students was just right; I learned a lot working with my colleagues from abroad."

"One drawback is our career center; I believe that as our school grows, we need a bigger department that is more aggressive in finding job opportunities abroad, not just in Canada, to help raise our school's profile."

"Rotman gave us an opportunity to build our financial skills with top-notch finance professors such as John Hall, meet finance professionals from all the top Canadian banks and security brokers, and interview with the top Canadian financial institutions."

 **Where to Stay**

Holiday Inn
280 Bloor St. W.
Toronto, ON M5S 3B9
(416) 968-0010

Park Hyatt Toronto
4 Avenue Rd.
Toronto, ON M5R 2E8
(416) 925-1234

Courtyard by Marriott
475 Yonge St.
Toronto, ON M4Y 1X7
(416) 924-0611

 Where to Eat

Hal Burgers
244 Adelaide St. W.
Toronto, ON M5H 1X6
(416) 979-8787

Alize Restaurant
2459 Yonge St.
Toronto, ON M4P 2H6
(416) 487-2771

Five Doors North
2088 Yonge St.
Toronto, ON M4S 2A3
(416) 480-6234

 Things to Do

Casa Loma
1 Austin Ter.
Toronto, ON M5R 1X8
(416) 923-1171

CN Tower
301 Front St. W.
Toronto, ON M5V 2T6
(416) 868-6937

CHECK OUT BUSINESSWEEK.COM FOR MORE:

Interview Tips: Learn how to ace your Rotman interview.

School Tour: Check out what's happening on the Rotman campus with this photo slide show.

Search & Compare: See how Rotman stacks up in a side-by-side comparison with other top programs.

A Day in the Life: A Rotman MBA graduate describes working for a green electricity start-up.

Expanded Profile: More facts and figures on Rotman.

Access all the B-schools content on BusinessWeek.com by subscribing to MBA Insider.

University of Virginia

Darden School of Business
2006 Ranking: 15 (U.S.)
100 Darden Blvd.
Charlottesville, VA 22906
E-mail address: darden@virginia.edu
Web address: www.darden.virginia.edu
For more info: Call the admissions
    office at (434) 924-7281

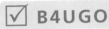 **B4UGO**

Applicants accepted: 29%
Average GMAT score: 688
Average years' work experience: 4.4
Average post-MBA salary increase:
  49.4%*
Average total first-year
  compensation: $145,585

*Based in part on *BusinessWeek* survey data.

Why Virginia?

Virginia's distinguished full-time MBA program is the choice of those who want the benefits of a big-name school with small-class attention. Darden is popular among students concentrating in consulting, entrepreneurship, finance, general management, and marketing. The "Darden difference" at this highly selective school is its challenging case method of instruction in a collaborative environment. Since 2005, Dean Robert Bruner has worked to build on the program's strengths, hiring more than a dozen new faculty members—many from outside the United States—to maintain the school's tradition of high-quality teaching without the aid of teaching assistants. The university, founded by Thomas Jefferson, is located in Charlottesville, a small city where, as one student says, the people "exude that wonderful southern charm and friendliness."

The University of Virginia is a public institution. Established in 1954, Darden's full-time MBA program is accredited by the Association to Advance Collegiate Schools of Business (AACSB). Darden also offers an executive MBA program.

 Headlines

March 12, 2007: Darden team wins venture capital competition

August 25, 2006: Darden welcomes record first-year MBA class

July 26, 2006: Alumnus pledges $1 million for scholarship fund

August 1, 2005: Robert Bruner named dean at Darden

"I wouldn't trade these two years for a million dollars."

Famous MBA Alumni

George David, chairman and CEO of United Technologies Corp.
U. Bertram Ellis Jr., chairman and CEO of iXL Enterprises
Steve Reinemund, former chairman and CEO of PepsiCo

 ## Who Are My Classmates?

Full-time enrollment: 654
Women: 31%
International: 34%
Minority: 12%
Average age: 28
Accepted applicants enrolled: 45%

"The top teachers found ways to truly challenge my thinking."

The 411

Annual tuition and fees: $37,500 (resident), $42,500 (nonresident)
Annual living expenses: $19,500
Total program cost, including forgone salary: $248,632 (resident), $258,632 (nonresident)*
Classes begin: August
Application deadlines: November 1, January 3, February 28
Application fee: $190

*Based in part on *BusinessWeek* survey data.

Cliff Notes

Leading areas of study: Consulting, Entrepreneurship, Finance, General Management, Marketing
Average class size, core courses: 62
Average class size, electives: 40
Number of electives: 100
Teaching methods: Case studies (70%), experiential learning (10%)

But What's It *Really* Like?

Graded by students:
Overall ranking: **A+**
Teaching quality: **A+**
Career services: **A+**

Graded by recruiters:
Overall ranking: **A+**
Accounting: **A**
Analytical skills: **A**
Communication: **A+**
Finance: **A**
General management: **A+**
International business: **A+**
Marketing: **A+**
Operations/production: **A+**
Teamwork skills: **A+**

$ Bling

Average pre-MBA salary: $67,316*
Average post-MBA salary: $100,575
Graduates with job offer by graduation: 91%
Top functional areas for graduates: Finance/Accounting, General Management, Consulting
Biggest recruiters: Danaher, Bank of America, Booz Allen Hamilton, Goldman Sachs, JPMorgan

*Estimate based on *BusinessWeek* survey data.

"The strength of the Darden network and the access to a vast array of companies have greatly exceeded my expectations and have made the decision to attend Darden one of the best decisions I have made."

"The opportunity to spend a significant amount of time with the faculty outside of the classroom was very meaningful to me, as was being involved in organizations in the school."

"The current emphasis on obtaining a summer internship and a postgraduation job take away from the learning that should be taking place while in school. Though this may be helpful for consultants and investment bankers, it is extremely detrimental to others who are in business school to get an education."

"It was not a cutthroat, in-your-face MBA program."

"The case method and high expectations in the classroom have provided me with the skills and confidence to excel in my new job, as evidenced by my success over the summer."

"If Darden were a company and I were in private equity, I would buy it in a heartbeat. Of all the top business schools, I think it is the most undervalued in the marketplace. I wouldn't trade these two years for a million dollars."

"It takes a special person to want to come to learn at business school for two years, and not being in a major city takes away some of Darden's appeal. We just didn't have people here from top-flight consulting firms or investment banks/hedge funds/private equity for these reasons."

"The top teachers at Darden have found ways to truly challenge my thinking as it applies not only to business, but to how I view the world."

"I was very surprised when I got to Darden and found that it was not a cutthroat, in-your-face MBA program. My learning team and class sections were very helpful and greatly aided my learning experience—almost as greatly as the professors and the classes themselves."

"I felt like I matured beyond my expectations and was exposed to great minds and great thinking. However, the challenging workload, case method curriculum, isolated location, and smaller student body is not the ideal situation for everybody."

 **Where to Stay**

Sponsor's Executive Residence Center
The Darden School
100 Darden Blvd.
Charlottesville, VA 22906
(434) 243-5000

Best Western Cavalier Inn
105 N. Emmet St.
Charlottesville, VA 22903
(434) 296-8111

Residence Inn by Marriott
1111 Milmont St.
Charlottesville, VA 22903
(434) 923-0300

 Where to Eat

Abbott Center Dining
The Darden School
100 Darden Blvd.
Charlottesville, VA 22906
(434) 924-7270

Starr Hill
709 W. Main St.
Charlottesville, VA 22903
(434) 977-0017

The College Inn
1511 University Ave.
Charlottesville, VA 22903
(434) 977-2710

 Things to Do

Monticello
931 Thomas Jefferson Pkwy.
Charlottesville, VA 22902
(434) 984-9822

The Paramount Theater
215 E. Main St.
Charlottesville, VA 22902
(434) 979-1922

CHECK OUT BUSINESSWEEK.COM FOR MORE:

Video View: Listen to Dean Robert Bruner discuss the case study method, the Darden honor code, and academic rigor.

Placement Q&A: Everette Fortner, director of Darden's Career Development Center, talks about adjusting to the global market, companies that typically hire Darden students, and the school's career-oriented curriculum.

Sample Application Essays and Interview Tips: Find the tricks of the trade used by successful Darden applicants.

Admissions Q&A: Sara Neher, director of admissions, talks about what qualities Darden seeks in an applicant.

MBA Journal: Read about a Darden student's experience, from admissions to the job hunt.

Access all the B-schools content on BusinessWeek.com by subscribing to MBA Insider.

U. of Western Ontario

Richard Ivey School of Business
2006 Ranking: 2 (non-U.S.)
1151 Richmond St. N.
London, ON (Canada) N6A 3K7
E-mail address: mba@ivey.uwo.ca
Web address: www.ivey.uwo.ca
For more info: Call the main
switchboard at (519) 661-3212

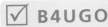

B4UGO

Applicants accepted: N/A
Average GMAT score: 650
Average years' work experience: 5
Average post-MBA salary increase:
48.4%
**Average total first-year
compensation:** $113,050

Why Western Ontario?

The thing that sets Ivey apart from the rest of the MBA pack, besides its 12-month format and its reliance on case studies, is its "cross-enterprise leadership" approach. By teaching students to look beyond organizational silos and giving them the skills to effect enterprisewide change, the Ivey approach produces graduates who can continuously adapt to the forces of globalization and technological change that are sweeping the business world. One of the hallmarks of the Ivey MBA is a consulting project that student teams conduct for a real client. With a dozen electives and specializations in finance, entrepreneurship, and healthcare, students can tailor their MBA to match their career goals. Ivey is second only to Queen's in *Business Week*'s 2006 ranking.

Western Ontario is a private institution. Established in 1948, Ivey's full-time MBA program is accredited by the Association to Advance Collegiate Schools of Business (AACSB) and the European Quality Improvement Sys-

tem (EQUIS). Ivey also offers an executive MBA program.

 Headlines

April 26, 2007: $1 million gift to fund scholarships for women

November 29, 2006: Ivey receives $2.5 million gift for entrepreneurship institute

November 23, 2006: Ivey students offer free consulting to nonprofit groups

May 30, 2006: Ivey welcomes first 12-month MBA class

"The school exceeded my expectations in every aspect."

Famous MBA Alumni

Thomas Bailey, founder of Janus Capital
E. Scott Beattie, president, chairman, and CEO of Elizabeth Arden
Arkadi Kuhlmann, chairman and CEO of ING Direct Bancorp

Who Are My Classmates?

Full-time enrollment: 173
Women: 34%
International: 27%
Minority: N/A
Average age: 29
Accepted applicants enrolled: N/A

"The school needs more diversity in its student base."

The 411

Annual tuition and fees: $64,315 (resident), $74,480 (nonresident)*
Annual living expenses: $17,955*
Total program cost, including forgone salary: $136,040 (resident), $146,205 (nonresident)
Classes begin: September
Application deadline: None
Application fee: $143
*Total for program.

Cliff Notes

Leading areas of study: Consulting, Entrepreneurship, Finance, Marketing, Strategy
Average class size, core courses: 70
Average class size, electives: 28
Number of electives: 12
Teaching methods: Case studies (70%), lectures (10%), simulations (10%), team projects (10%)

But What's It *Really* Like?

Graded by students:
Overall ranking: A+
Teaching quality: A+
Career services: A+

Graded by recruiters:
Overall ranking: B
Accounting: A
Analytical skills: B
Communication: B
Finance: B
General management: B
International business: B
Marketing: B
Operations/production: C
Teamwork skills: A

Bling

Average pre-MBA salary: $53,770
Average post-MBA salary: $79,800
Graduates with job offer by graduation: 61%
Top functional areas for graduates: Consulting, Finance/Accounting, Marketing/Sales
Biggest recruiters: Deloitte, Royal Bank of Canada, TD Bank, Bank of Montréal, Accenture

The Good, the Bad, and the Ugly: Students Speak Out

"The difference between the Ivey MBA and those of other schools is the people. Both faculty and students are top of class. I learned more from my peers than I would have at another school."

"Ivey is an outstanding school. Under the old two-year program, international students had time to adapt. However, with the new one-year program, this will be challenging. Also, the school needs more diversity in its student base."

"The Richard Ivey School of Business greatly surpassed my expectations of graduate education."

"The academic activities outside of daily classes bring real life to the program."

"Despite not having access to bottom-less pits of money like many of its U.S. competitors, Ivey has built a top-rated business program on the backs of professors who genuinely care about the learning and success of their students. The academic activities that exist outside of daily classes, like the case competitions and interactive group challenges in other disciplines, are outstanding and bring real life to the program."

"Success at Ivey comes, to a large extent, from the student's engagement in school activities. This isn't an institution for mere academics."

"I think the Richard Ivey School of Business is an undiscovered gem for the opportunities I have in front of me today for my chosen field of work in finance."

"If Ivey was located in the United States instead of Canada, it would definitely have ranked in the top five programs in the world. I am proud to be an Ivey graduate, and I feel capable of competing with and even doing better than graduates from other top business schools of the world."

"My two years at Ivey were absolutely the best experience of my life. The school exceeded my expectations in every aspect. Career management did an amazing job at helping students with résumés, preparing for interviews, job searches, and placements. Without its help and the amazing program at Ivey, I would not be heading down the path I am today."

"Ivey's reputation isn't as strong in the U.S. or globally as a few of its peers. Ivey alumni are predominantly in Canada. If Americans want to work in the U.S. I'd suggest they study in the U.S. I don't think the Ivey name will carry well in the U.S."

 **Where to Stay**

Residence Inn by Marriott
383 Colborne St.
London, ON N6B 3P5
(519) 433-7222

Lamplighter Inn
591 Wellington Rd. S.
London, ON N6C 4R3
(519) 433-7222

London Executive Suites
362 Dundas St.
London, ON N6B 1V8
(800) 265-5955

 Where to Eat

Canuck Pizza
120 York St.
London, ON N6A 1A9
(519) 672-2222

Elephant & Castle
355 Wellington St.
London, ON N6A 3N7
(519) 434-4554

Scallions
219 Queens Ave.
London, ON N6A 1J8
(519) 432-1333

 Things to Do

Bellamere Winery
1260 Gainsborough Rd.
London, ON N6H 5K8
(519) 473-2273

Honest Lawyer
228 Dundas St.
London, ON N6A 1H3
(519) 433-4913

CHECK OUT BUSINESSWEEK.COM FOR MORE:

Admissions Q&A: Get the inside scoop from an Ivey admissions officer.

School Tour: Save travel expenses—tour the Ivey campus online first.

Sample Application Essays: See how successful applicants responded to Ivey's question.

Search & Compare: Do a side-by-side comparison to find out how Ivey stacks up against other top international schools.

Expanded Profile: More facts and figures on Ivey.

Access all the B-schools content on BusinessWeek.com by subscribing to MBA Insider.

U. of Wisconsin at Madison

School of Business
2006 Ranking: Second tier (U.S.)
Room 3150 Grainger Hall
975 University Ave.
Madison, WI 53706
E-mail address: MBA@bus.wisc.edu
Web address: www.bus.wisc.edu/mba/
For more info: Call MBA information at
(608) 262-4000

B4UGO

Applicants accepted: 33%
Average GMAT score: 656
Average years' work experience: 4
Average post-MBA salary increase:
56.5%
Average total first-year
compensation: $113,554

Why Wisconsin?

When Wisconsin overhauled its MBA curriculum recently, it scrapped its general MBA and replaced it with 13 specializations, allowing students to get more granular—focusing, for example, on brand management or marketing research instead of marketing. Unlike most programs, where the first year is largely devoted to core courses, the Wisconsin program has students focusing on their concentrations almost literally from the first day of classes. That early focus, along with hands-on learning and connections to top executives in each student's specialty, provides for more rapid career advancement. Under the new configuration, more than 95% of Wisconsin's students land jobs within three months of graduation, many of them with top consumer products companies such as Procter & Gamble, General Mills, and Kraft Foods.

Wisconsin is a public institution. Established in 1945, its full-time MBA program is accredited by the Associa-

tion to Advance Collegiate Schools of Business (AACSB). Wisconsin also offers part-time and executive MBA programs.

 ## Headlines

Fall 2008: New $40 million addition to MBA facilities set to open

May 18, 2007: First class graduates under new specialized MBA curriculum

July 30, 2006: Bloomberg: Wisconsin ties Harvard for most S&P 500 CEOs

April 11, 2006: Wisconsin MBAs win international case competition

------

"Students are smart yet friendly, down-to-earth, and helpful."

Famous MBA Alumni

Tadashi Okamura, chairman and former CEO of Toshiba Corp.

Jeffrey J. Rotsch, executive vice president of General Mills

John P. Morgridge, chairman emeritus and former CEO of Cisco Systems

Who Are My Classmates?

Full-time enrollment: 224
Women: 29%
International: 20%
Minority: 16%
Average age: 28
Accepted applicants enrolled: 71%

"The intense course load easily leads to burnout."

The 411

Annual tuition and fees: $11,099 (resident), $26,537 (nonresident)

Annual living expenses: $16,586

Total program cost, including forgone salary: $160,184 (resident), $191,060 (nonresident)

Classes begin: September

Application deadlines: November 1 to May 15

Application fee: $45

Cliff Notes

Leading areas of study: Finance, Marketing, Portfolio Management, Real Estate, Supply Chain Management

Average class size, core courses: 54

Average class size, electives: 19

Number of electives: 125

Teaching methods: Lectures (30%), case studies (25%), team projects (18%)

But What's It *Really* Like?

Graded by students:
Overall ranking: C
Teaching quality: B
Career services: B

Graded by recruiters:
Overall ranking: C
Accounting: C
Analytical skills: C
Communication: C
Finance: C
General management: C
International business: C
Marketing: B
Operations/production: B
Teamwork skills: C

Bling

Average pre-MBA salary: $52,407

Average post-MBA salary: $82,000

Graduates with job offer by graduation: 83%

Top functional areas for graduates: Finance/Accounting, Marketing/Sales, Consulting

Biggest recruiters: General Electric, Abbott, General Mills, Kraft, Bristol-Myers Squibb, IBM, Procter & Gamble, UBS

The Good, the Bad, and the Ugly: Students Speak Out

"I enjoyed University of Wisconsin-Madison for its team-oriented atmosphere. It did not feel cutthroat at all. Students are smart yet friendly, down-to-earth, and helpful."

"A large number of the MBA students are offered scholarships."

"The University of Wisconsin-Madison is second to none for people who know what they want to do once they graduate. I specifically was in the Brand and Product Management Program, which along with other specializations has an executive advisory board that meets once a semester with roughly 15 senior VPs from many of the top companies. The board's dedication to the students is remarkable, and the insight I got from interacting with board members is invaluable."

"The University of Wisconsin-Madison is a very well-organized program that exceeded all of my expectations. Everyone involved in the program, from the students to the faculty to the support staff, were first-rate."

"The professors' teaching abilities have been uneven—some were fantastic, some very poor."

"The Center for Brand and Product Management is a hidden gem of brand management programs. You will be hearing more about our program in coming years."

"The Applied Security Analysis Program used to provide excellent training for security analysis. Now that it is part of the MBA program, the curriculum has been watered down sufficiently that students no longer can compete as effectively for top positions."

"The intense course load and amount of time necessary to complete team projects easily leads to burnout and hurts morale."

"I'm in the A.C. Nielsen Center for Marketing Research. This is a phenomenal program. I believe that if people are interested in a marketing research career, then they need to be at the Nielsen Center and the University of Wisconsin."

"A large number of the MBA students are offered scholarships or project/teaching assistantships. I did not have to incur a student loan for my MBA, and I still received a great education."

"UW has some of the best specialized programs in the nation."

 Where to Stay

Sheraton Madison Hotel
760 John Nolen Dr.
Madison, WI 53713
(608) 251-2300

Radisson Hotel Madison
517 Grand Canyon Dr.
Madison, WI 53719
(608) 833-0100

Crowne Plaza
4402 E. Washington Ave.
Madison, WI 53704
(608) 244-4703

 Where to Eat

Great Dane Pub & Brewing Co.
123 E. Doty St.
Madison, WI 53703
(608) 284-0000

Café Montmarte
127 E. Mifflin St.
Madison, WI 55454
(608) 255-5900

State Street Brats
603 State St.
Madison, WI 53703
(608) 255-5544

 Things to Do

Madison Museum of Contemporary Art
227 State St.
Madison, WI 53703
(608) 257-0158

Olbrich Botanical Gardens
3330 Atwood Ave.
Madison, WI 53704
(608) 246-4550

CHECK OUT BUSINESSWEEK.COM FOR MORE:

Interview Tips: Don't get taken by surprise—find out what to expect during an interview.

Expanded Profile: Dig deeper into the Madison full-time program with more facts, statistics, and insights.

Search & Compare: See how Wisconsin stacks up against your other prospective schools.

School Tour: Use this photo slide show to get a feel for the Madison campus before you visit.

Admissions Q&A: MBA Admissions Director Betsy Kacizak on how applications are evaluated at Wisconsin.

Access all the B-schools content on BusinessWeek.com by subscribing to MBA Insider.

Vanderbilt University

Owen Graduate School of Management
2006 Ranking: 30 (U.S.)
410 21st Ave. S.
Nashville, TN 37203
E-mail address:
   admissions@owen.vanderbilt.edu
Web address: www.owen.vanderbilt.
   edu/vanderbilt/
For more info: Call the main
   switchboard at (615) 322-2534

☑ B4UGO

Applicants accepted: 47%
Average GMAT score: 644
Average years' work experience: 4.7
Average post-MBA salary increase:
   77.1%
**Average total first-year
   compensation:** $131,604

Why Vanderbilt?

Vanderbilt B-schoolers graduate with a solid education and a solid sense of camaraderie. While many don't associate Nashville with Wall Street, finance is one of Owen's many strengths. An emphasis on teamwork and a small-school atmosphere result in close ties among students and a high degree of school loyalty, so it's not surprising that alumni are willing to help new graduates in their search for jobs. That's a good thing, since the school's location—far from the nation's centers of commerce and industry—can make on-campus recruiting a challenge. To capitalize on Vanderbilt's academic medical center, Owen offers a healthcare MBA. The students who choose this option complete the same MBA core classes with an additional emphasis on the business of healthcare. The location also draws MBA students looking for careers in the entertainment industry.

Vanderbilt is a private institution. Established in 1969, Owen's full-time MBA program is accredited by the Association to Advance Collegiate Schools of Business (AACSB). Owen also offers an executive MBA program.

 Headlines

May 23, 2007: Owen hires six new faculty members and announces five endowed chairs

November 18, 2005: Leadership development program launched

July 21, 2005: Owen creates new healthcare MBA

March 3, 2005: Jim Bradford takes helm after nine months as acting dean

"Vanderbilt has an excellent finance curriculum."

Famous MBA Alumni

Doug Parker, chairman and CEO of
US Airways
David N. Farr, president, chairman,
and CEO of Emerson Electric Co.
Sara Gates, vice president of Sun
Microsystems

 Who Are My Classmates?

Full-time enrollment: 371
Women: 28%
International: 26%
Minority: 13%
Average age: 28
Accepted applicants enrolled: 60%

"Overemphasis on research has taken a toll."

The 411

Annual tuition and fees: $40,323
Annual living expenses: $20,635
Total program cost, including forgone
salary: $222,712
Classes begin: August
Application deadlines: November 15
to March 3
Application fee: $100

Cliff Notes

Leading areas of study: Entrepreneur-
ship, Finance, Healthcare, Market-
ing, Strategy
Average class size, core courses: 40
Average class size, electives: 30
Number of electives: 110
Teaching methods: Lectures (40%), case
studies (30%), team projects (20%)

But What's It *Really* Like?

Graded by students:
Overall ranking: **B**
Teaching quality: **B**
Career services **B**

Graded by recruiters:
Overall ranking: **B**
Accounting: **B**
Analytical skills: **B**
Communication: **B**
Finance: **A**
General management: **B**
International business: **B**
Marketing: **A**
Operations/production: **B**
Teamwork skills: **A**

 Bling

Average pre-MBA salary: $50,398
Average post-MBA salary: $89,268
Graduates with job offer by graduation:
77%
Top functional areas for graduates:
Finance/Accounting, Consulting,
Marketing/Sales
Biggest recruiters: Bank of America,
Citigroup, Deloitte, Cap Gemini,
General Electric, Harrah's
Entertainment

The Good, the Bad, and the Ugly: Students Speak Out

"Owen focuses very much on how what we learn applies in the 'real world,' so that when we graduate, we hit the ground running."

"What this school needs is an individual who will walk in and shake things up a bit, reach out to alumni in powerful places, and begin to recruit students who are focused and motivated and are going places."

"The yearly class sizes are large enough to allow for diversity of backgrounds and experiences, but small enough to keep someone from getting lost. Plus, the types of students the school recruits are intelligent and ambitious, but not 'stuck-up' or detrimentally competitive."

"I got to know everyone in my program."

"The new dean needs time to improve on the stagnation that has occurred over the past few years. He's making progress, but years of neglect and an overemphasis on research have taken a toll."

"I cannot emphasize enough how strong the relationships are between the students at Owen. The informal interactions have helped create a strong network of friends that, I pray, will continue to be strong when we graduate."

"I think Owen needs to work on developing a better overall curriculum. For a school that touts its general management education, I think it needs to improve certain core areas."

"I feel I got to know everyone in my program very well, which is exactly what I wanted out of my MBA experience."

"Owen has an identity crisis. Efforts to innovate the program are half-hearted. The few excellent opportunities outside of doing very well in finance and getting a corporate finance position are in the fields of entrepreneurship and healthcare."

"Vanderbilt has an excellent finance curriculum. There are many top-notch professors who are well known, and the small class size makes them accessible. Alumni are more accessible because they have fewer current students calling on them during the job search process."

"The Owen community allows students to bond and network in ways I don't feel would be possible in many other shcools."

 **Where to Stay**

Nashville Marriott at Vanderbilt
2555 West End Ave.
Nashville, TN 37203
(615) 321-1300

Loews Vanderbilt Hotel
2100 West End Ave.
Nashville, TN 37203
(615) 320-1700

Courtyard-Vanderbilt/West End
1901 West End Ave.
Nashville, TN 37203
(615) 327-9900

 Where to Eat

F. Scott's Restaurant and Jazz Bar
2210 Crestmoor Rd.
Nashville, TN 37215
(615) 269-5861

Boscos Nashville Brewing
1805 21st Ave. S.
Nashville, TN 37212
(615) 385-0050

Acorn Restaurant
114 28th Ave. N.
Nashville, TN 37203
(615) 320-4399

 Things to Do

Robert's Western World
416 Broadway
Nashville, TN 37203
(615) 244-9552

Country Music Hall of Fame and Museum
222 Fifth Ave.
Nashville, TN 37203
(615) 416-2001

CHECK OUT BUSINESSWEEK.COM FOR MORE:

Admissions Q&A: John Roeder, director of admissions, discusses the Owen's application process.

Video View: Dean Jim Bradford on keeping the offerings at Owen fresh.

School Tour: Planning an Owen visit? Check out the campus before you go using this photo slide show.

Expanded Profile: Everything you ever wanted to know about Owen.

Search & Compare: See how Owen stacks up against other top schools.

Access all the B-schools content on BusinessWeek.com by subscribing to MBA Insider.

Wake Forest University

Babcock Graduate School of
Management
2006 Ranking: Second tier (U.S.)
Worrell Professional Center
1834 Wake Forest Rd.
Winston-Salem, NC 27106
E-mail address:
admissions@mba.wfu.edu
Web address: www.mba.wfu.edu/
For more info: Call general information
at (866) 925-3622

☑ B4UGO

Applicants accepted: 50%
Average GMAT score: 632
Average years' work experience: 4.5
Average post-MBA salary increase:
56.8%
**Average total first-year
compensation:** $110,761

Why Wake Forest?

Prospective students be forewarned:
Babcock's full-time MBA program is the
B-school equivalent of boot camp.
Intense workloads and tight schedules
take their toll, especially in the first year,
when MBA students take 14 required
courses before moving on to their career
concentrations. Throughout, the focus
is on hands-on learning: a first-year integrative exercise and a second-year consulting practicum challenge students to
solve complex problems using all their
newly acquired skills. Babcock's
approach to entrepreneurship focuses on
skills that will serve students well
throughout their careers—whether starting their own ventures or working for an
established company.

Wake Forest University is a private
institution. Established in 1969, Babcock's full-time MBA program is
accredited by the Association to
Advance Collegiate Schools of Business

(AACSB). Babcock also offers part-
time and executive MBA programs. For
details on Wake Forest's part-time
MBA program, see page 421.

 Headlines

May 30, 2007: Babcock expands student diversity initiatives

May 9, 2007: B-schoolers to help
develop sustainable commerce in
Nicaragua

January 3, 2007: Part-time MBA programs get new home in Charlotte

March 6, 2006: $1 million alumni gift
for teaching social responsibility

---

*"The access that I had
to professors was
priceless."*

Famous MBA Alumni

Ken Thompson, president, chairman, and CEO of Wachovia

Susan Alt, CEO of Volvo Logistics North America

Charles Ergen, chairman and CEO of EchoStar Communications

 Who Are My Classmates?

Full-time enrollment: 160
Women: 30%
International: 21%
Minority: 14%
Average age: 28
Accepted applicants enrolled: 50%

"I would rate the Career Management Center as a real weak point."

The 411

Annual tuition and fees: $33,500
Annual living expenses: $15,380
Total program cost, including forgone salary: $201,180
Classes begin: August
Application deadlines: November 1 to May 1
Application fee: $75

Cliff Notes

Leading areas of study: Consulting, Entrepreneurship, Finance, Marketing, Operations Management
Average class size, core courses: 45
Average class size, electives: 25
Number of electives: 50
Teaching methods: Case studies (40%), experiential learning (20%), lectures (20%)

But What's It *Really* Like?

Graded by students:
Overall ranking: C
Teaching quality: C
Career services: C

Graded by recruiters:
Overall ranking: C
Accounting: A
Analytical skills: B
Communication: B
Finance: B
General management: A
International business: B
Marketing: B
Operations/production: B
Teamwork skills: B

Bling

Average pre-MBA salary: $51,660
Average post-MBA salary: $81,013
Graduates with job offer by graduation: 73%
Companies recruiting on campus: 32
Top functional areas for graduates: Finance/Accounting, Marketing/Sales, Consulting
Biggest recruiters: Bank of America, Scotia Capital, Alltel, Booz Allen Hamilton, Fedex

The Good, the Bad, and the Ugly: Students Speak Out

"Wake Forest is an extremely underrated school. I have studied under some outstanding professors who may have been tough at times, but who have taught me a tremendous amount. I have also enjoyed the size of the classes. There are lots of student/student and student/professor debates that contribute to the learning environment."

"The school's singular focus on graduate management programs enhances the individual attention that each student receives. The faculty members are always available to discuss coursework, to chat about job prospects, or to talk about how to proceed on a consulting project. The administration holds regular town hall meetings to ensure that ideas from the student body are carefully considered. Many suggestions contributed by members of our graduating class significantly affected the program content for incoming MBA classes."

"The workload was a shocker."

"I hope the Wake Forest program gets it together because the program seems to be suffering from a lack of identity. I would rate the Career Management Center as a real weak point."

"I feel that the access that I had to professors was priceless. My conversations with them brought richness to the classroom discussion and made the learning more concrete."

"I had a great experience at Wake Forest. Wake Forest provides an excellent opportunity for participating in a wide variety of leadership positions in the clubs and school events, the students are friendly/hard working/team players, the professors are very accessible and helpful, and the alumni are very supportive. The only downside might be that its reputation isn't as well known internationally as that of a Top 10 school."

"Like any school, Wake Forest has its pluses and minuses, but I feel that the quality of the experience here more than makes up for any pitfalls. A word to the wise, however: they don't call it 'Work Forest' for nothing. I had amazing teachers, terrific classmates, and incredible intellectual stimulation and made great career connections, but I would not characterize it as fun. The workload was a shocker."

"Going to school at Wake Forest has its benefits but there are challenges to overcome in job hunting."

"I am getting my concentration in marketing, and I am not pleased with the teaching, the alumni, and the career management center's efforts. The program is too inflexible, and the career connections are just not there."

 **Where to Stay**

Holiday Inn Select
5790 University Pkwy.
Winston-Salem, NC 27105
(336) 767-9595

Courtyard by Marriott
3111 University Pkwy.
Winston-Salem, NC 27105
(336) 727-1277

Hampton Inn
5719 University Pkwy.
Winston-Salem, NC 27105
(336) 767-9009

 **Where to Eat**

Ryan's Restaurant
719 Coliseum Dr.
Winston-Salem, NC 27106
(336) 724-6132

Twin City Chop House
115 S. Main St.
Winston-Salem, NC 27101
(336) 748-8600

La Carreta
725 Coliseum Dr.
Winston-Salem, NC 27106
(336) 722-3709

 Things to Do

Germanton Art Gallery & Winery
3530 Hwy. 8 & 65
Germanton, NC 27019
(800) 322-2894

Winston Cup Museum
1355 N. Martin Luther King Jr. Dr.
Winston-Salem, NC 27101
(336) 724-4557

CHECK OUT BUSINESSWEEK.COM FOR MORE:

Admissions Q&A: Admissions Director Stacy Poindexter Owen on why Babcock is putting more emphasis on work experience.

School Tour: Planning a campus visit? Check out this photo essay first.

Search & Compare: See how Babcock compares with other top B-schools around the world.

Placement Q&A: Career Services Director Andy Dreyfuss describes what Babcock graduates have to offer top employers.

Expanded Profile: Have more questions? Check out Babcock's bigger, better online profile.

Access all the B-schools content on BusinessWeek.com by subscribing to MBA Insider.

Washington University

Olin School of Business
2006 Ranking: 27 (U.S.)
Campus Box 1133
1 Brookings Dr.
St. Louis, MO 63130
E-mail address: mba@olin.wustl.edu
Web address: www.olin.wustl.edu/mba/
For more info: Call general information
   at (314) 935-7301

☑ B4UGO

Applicants accepted: 33%
Average GMAT score: 674
Average years' work experience: 3.8
Average post-MBA salary increase:
  60.7%
Average total first-year
  compensation: $119,357

Why Wash U?

With a class size of roughly 140 students, a tight-knit community and personalized attention are strong selling points for Olin. But applied learning is what makes the program special. Olin's Center for Experiential Learning connects students with companies seeking help in devising new strategies, faculty members enliven lectures with their latest research, and top executives are brought into the classroom to impart corner-office wisdom. A pass/fail grading system, unusual among U.S. B-schools, fosters an environment of collaboration instead of competition. Flexibility is another plus, with dual-degree programs available in architecture, biomedical engineering, East Asian studies, law, and social work. Olin is among the least selective Top 30 programs, and post-MBA salaries are among the group's lowest.

Washington University is a private institution. Established in 1917, Olin's full-time MBA program is accredited by the Association to Advance Colle-giate Schools of Business (AACSB). Olin also offers part-time and executive MBA programs. For details on Olin's part-time MBA program, see page 425. For details on Olin's executive MBA program, see page 309.

Headlines

February 27, 2006: New assistant dean and MBA admissions director selected

April 28, 2005: Mahendra Gupta named new dean of Olin

February 14, 2005: Alumnus Robert Frick endows new professorship at Olin

March 28, 2003: MBA curriculum gets major overhaul

"One receives a very well-rounded learning experience."

Famous MBA Alumni

David McCalpin, CMO of General Electric's Consumer & Industrial unit

William J. Shaw, president and COO of Marriott International

W. Patrick McGinnis, president and CEO of Nestle Purina PetCare Co.

Who Are My Classmates?

Full-time enrollment: 288
Women: 26%
International: 34%
Minority: 18%
Average age: 27
Accepted applicants enrolled: 47%

"Innovative, challenging, and real-world applicable courses."

The 411

Annual tuition and fees: $38,729
Annual living expenses: $26,675
Total program cost, including forgone salary: $237,340
Classes begin: August
Application deadlines: November 5 to May 1
Application fee: $100

Cliff Notes

Leading areas of study: Consulting, Finance, General Management, Marketing, Strategy
Average class size, core courses: 64
Average class size, electives: 38
Number of electives: 81
Teaching methods: Case studies (40%), team projects (25%), lectures (20%)

But What's It *Really* Like?

Graded by students:
Overall ranking: C
Teaching quality: A
Career services: C

Graded by recruiters:
Overall ranking: C
Accounting: B
Analytical skills: B
Communication: C
Finance: B
General management: C
International business: B
Marketing: N/A
Operations/production: C
Teamwork skills: B

Bling

Average pre-MBA salary: $53,266
Average post-MBA salary: $85,583
Graduates with job offer by graduation: 85%
Top functional areas for graduates: Finance/Accounting, Marketing/Sales, General Management
Biggest recruiters: Citigroup, Emerson, Johnson & Johnson, Nestle Purina PetCare, First National Bank of Omaha

The Good, the Bad, and the Ugly: Students Speak Out

"Washington University is a school that allows a person, through experiential learning, active involvement in the pursuit of his or her MBA. Through global management studies, a sound and very intense core program, and extracurricular activities, one receives a very well-rounded learning experience."

"The caliber of students was not as high as I would have expected. Involvement in class discussions was weak to moderate, and that disappointed me."

"Because of the smaller class size, there are fewer recruiters."

"The top-notch faculty combined with the small class size made this a tremendous learning experience."

"The school is amazing, but students will struggle with its reputation for a long time to come when it comes to their job search. Olin is extremely well known by Midwest employers, but the school has a long way to go with other geographic regions."

"Not only is the environment an inviting one, but the school prides itself on creating innovative, challenging, and real-world applicable courses for its curriculum, including courses and consultancies working for external companies in real-life situations."

"I feel that Wash U is out of touch with MBA students—although it makes an effort to obtain feedback every year, it is not able to make progress. . . . In my eyes, the problem is complacency in admissions and lack of involvement by the faculty."

"We had a leadership speaker series led by the ex-CEO of Emerson, Chuck Knight, to teach us how Emerson had had consistent positive earnings throughout his 27 years [as CEO], how he cultivated the leaders, and how he enforced the execution culture. He invited five other CEOs from IBM, GE, Anheuser-Busch, Honeywell, and Emerson. I dare you to find any other business school in the world that can offer a class taught by six world-class CEOs."

"The biggest negative is that because of the smaller class size, there are far fewer recruiters that come onto campus for hiring."

"Olin is a unique experience due to its relatively small size. You know all of your classmates, faculty, and staff and they know you. It is a very close-knit environment."

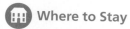 **Where to Stay**

Clayton on the Park
8025 Bonhomme Ave.
St. Louis, MO 63105
(314) 721-8588

Seven Gables Inn
26 N. Meramec St.
Clayton, MO 63135
(314) 863-8400

**Crowne Plaza Hotel
St. Louis—Clayton**
7750 Carondelet Ave.
Clayton, MO 63105
(314) 726-5400

 Where to Eat

J Bucks (American)
101 S. Hanley Rd.
Clayton, MO 63105
(314) 725-4700

Miss Saigon (Vietnamese)
6101 Delmar in the Loop
St. Louis, MO 63112
(314) 863-4949

BARcelona (Spanish tapas)
34 N. Central Ave.
Clayton, MO 63105
(314) 863-9909

 Things to Do

Anheuser-Busch Brewery
12th and Lynch Sts.
St. Louis, MO 63118
(314) 577-2626

St. Louis Art Museum
One Fine Arts Dr., Forest Park
St. Louis, MO 63110-1380
(314) 721-0072

CHECK OUT BUSINESSWEEK.COM FOR MORE:

Expanded Profile: Get the program basics and student body statistics from Olin's online MBA profile.

Admissions Q&A: Admissions Director Brad Pearson talks about looking for candidates with strong leadership abilities.

Admissions Interview Tips: Students talk about using preparation and personality to impress the admissions office at Olin.

Application Essays: Figure out how to master Olin's application essays.

Careers Q&A: Head of Career Services discusses the importance of teaching lifelong job search skills.

Access all the B-schools content on BusinessWeek.com by subscribing to MBA Insider.

Yale University

School of Management
2006 Ranking: 19 (U.S.)
135 Prospect St.
New Haven, CT 06520
E-mail address:
mba.admissions@yale.edu
Web address: www.mba.yale.edu
For more info: Call admissions at (203) 432-5635

☑ **B4UGO**

Applicants accepted: 15%
Average GMAT score: 700
Average years' work experience: 4.7
Average post-MBA salary increase: 98%
Average total first-year compensation: $152,795

Why Yale?

With its innovative new curriculum, Yale's School of Management has scrapped an array of courses in finance, marketing, and other mainstays of management education and replaced them with a series of eight new multidisciplinary courses. Instead of studying functional disciplines in a vacuum, the new courses challenge students to tackle complex business problems, using all the skills in the managerial toolkit. With only about 200 students in the class of 2008, small classes are the norm, and a high degree of faculty-student interaction is a given. The program's grading policies—it doesn't calculate student GPAs or class rank—encourage cooperation among students, avoiding the competitive atmosphere that pervades some top B-schools and creating a tight-knit alumni network. It shows, too. Nearly half of all MBA alumni participate in Yale's fund-raising efforts.

Yale University is a private institution. Established in 1976, Yale SOM's full-time MBA program is accredited by the Association to Advance Collegiate Schools of Business (AACSB). Yale SOM also offers an executive MBA for professionals in the healthcare industry.

 Headlines

October 13, 2006: Report: Yale ranks first in female MBA enrollment

September 5, 2006: Stressing innovation, Yale SOM introduces new MBA curriculum

November 7, 2005: Yale one of first institutions to offer joint MBA/Ph.D. degree

April 26, 2005: Joel M. Podolny named new dean of the Yale SOM

"The 'thinking person's MBA.'"

Famous MBA Alumni

Wendi (Deng) Murdoch, former vice president of NewsCorp and wife of Rupert Murdoch

Indra Nooyi, president and CEO of PepsiCo

John D. Howard, CEO of Bear Stearns Merchant Banking Group

 Who Are My Classmates?

Full-time enrollment: 395
Women: 34%
International: 21%
Minority: 26%
Average age: 28
Accepted applicants enrolled: 44%

"The career office needs improvement."

The 411

Annual tuition and fees: $43,932
Annual living expenses: $21,920
Total program cost, including forgone salary: $235,242
Classes begin: August
Application deadlines: October 24, January 9, March 12
Application fee: $200

Cliff Notes

Leading areas of study: Finance, Investment Management, Leadership, Marketing, Strategy
Average class size, core classes: 59
Average class size, electives: 21
Number of electives: 118
Teaching methods: Lectures (40%), case studies (30%), experiential learning (10%), simulations (10%), team projects (10%)

But What's It *Really* Like?

Graded by students:
Overall ranking: **A**
Teaching quality: **A**
Career services: **A**

Graded by recruiters:
Overall ranking: **B**
Accounting: **B**
Analytical skills: **B**
Communication: **A**
Finance: **A**
General management: **A**
International business: **A**
Marketing: **B**
Operations/production: **C**
Teamwork skills: **A**

 Bling

Average pre-MBA salary: $50,144
Average post-MBA salary: $99,307
Graduates with job offer by graduation: 89%
Top functional areas for graduates: Finance/Accounting, Consulting, Marketing/Sales
Biggest recruiters: Citigroup, Standard & Poor's, IBM, JP Morgan, Lehman Brothers

The Good, the Bad, and the Ugly: Students Speak Out

"My time at SOM has been a formative experience. I see the world in a very different way now, and I believe that I am a much better all-around person. A year ago I was telling my younger brother that I did not think he needed business school; now I tell him that he should attend Yale SOM with no reservations whatsoever."

"Before I came into the Yale MBA, I was 100% certain of my career path after school—a rise into museum management. I now find that I am achieving a 180-degree career switch, moving into a leadership development program in the renewable energy sector. I still find it an amazing compliment to Yale, to my peers, and my MBA education that I have achieved something I would have thought unthinkable only two years ago."

"It's been a really exciting time to be at Yale SOM."

"SOM is in the midst of a major fundraising campaign, and the school should have an entirely new campus built by 2008. It's been a really exciting time to be at Yale SOM."

"The class choices will always be a problem for a small school. I am not sure whether I would like to trade this for a larger and much more impersonal program, but this is definitely a problem."

"Our new dean, Joel Podolny (affectionately called J-Pod by us students), is a truly inspiring leader who will guide the school to new heights in the future."

"The career office needs improvement. It does pretty well for students in mainstream jobs like investment banking, consulting, and marketing. The staff seems to struggle, however, with those of us in more narrowly defined fields. It can be frustrating."

"I tend to think of Yale as the 'thinking person's MBA.' We are the obvious leader in the behavioral fields, both finance and economics, and while we cover the traditional fields through case study as well, we have pushed into new ground."

"The Yale SOM program is not for every candidate, in particular one looking to 'get his ticket punched' to go directly to Wall St. or McKinsey. Conversely, if prospective students are seeking to fundamentally challenge how they regard themselves as a manager in a global environment, this is the ideal learning environment. I entered SOM as a former consultant thinking I already had all the answers. I am graduating with an appreciation for how naive I really was."

Where to Stay

Omni New Haven Hotel at Yale
155 Temple St.
New Haven, CT 06510
(203) 772-6664

The Marriott Courtyard at Yale
30 Whalley Ave.
New Haven, CT 06511
(203) 777-6221

New Haven Hotel
229 George St.
New Haven, CT 06510
(203) 498-3100

 Where to Eat

Barcelona
155 Temple St.
New Haven, CT 06510
(203) 848-3000

Union League Café
1032 Chapel St.
New Haven, CT 06510
(203) 562-4299

Zinc
964 Chapel St.
New Haven, CT 06510
(203) 624-0507

 Things to Do

Yale University Art Gallery
1111 Chapel St.
New Haven, CT 06520
(203) 432-0600

Yale Repertory Theatre
1120 Chapel St.
New Haven, CT 06520
(203) 432-1234

CHECK OUT BUSINESSWEEK.COM FOR MORE:

Admissions Q&A: Admissions Director Anne Coyle discusses the networking and social advantages that Yale offers.

Interview Tips: Get the lowdown on how to win over Yale's admissions office.

Search & Compare: Find out how Yale SOM stacks up against other top schools.

Expanded Profile: For more facts and figures, check out Yale's extended online profile.

MBA Forums: Connect with other prospective Yale SOM students.

Access all the B-schools content on BusinessWeek.com by subscribing to MBA Insider.

York University

Schulich School of Business
2006 Ranking: 9 (non-U.S.)
4700 Keele St.
Toronto, ON (Canada) M3J 1P3
E-mail address:
    intladmissions@schulich.yorku.ca
Web address: www.schulich.yorku.ca
For more info: Call MBA admissions at
    (416) 736-5060

☑ B4UGO

Applicants accepted: 29%
Average GMAT score: 662
Average years' work experience: 6.1
Average post-MBA salary increase:
    94.5%
Average total first-year
    compensation: $91,580*
*Base salary and signing bonus only.

Why York?

Calling itself "Canada's Global Business School," Schulich touts one of the most diverse full-time MBA programs in North America: nearly 60% of students hold passports from countries outside of Canada. Additionally, over the past few years, the school has opened satellite centers in Beijing, Mumbai, and Seoul. (More locations should follow in the near future.) With core courses kept to a minimum, 27 credit hours are available for electives—there are more than 100—allowing students to choose two specializations from 19 available. Though starting salaries aren't high compared to top-ranked U.S. schools, 90% of graduates have jobs within 3 months of graduation, and the school earns high marks from recruiters in finance and accounting.

York University is a public institution. Established in 1965, the Schulich full-time MBA program is accredited by the Ontario Council of Graduate Studies (OCGS). Schulich also offers accelerated, part-time, and executive MBA programs.

 Headlines

June 25, 2007: National survey ranks Schulich No. 1 in corporate social responsibility

May 16, 2007: Webcam tool allows Schulich students to brush up on interviewing skills

October 6, 2006: Career forum encourages B-schoolers to work in developing nations

March 17, 2006: Schulich establishes chair in global business history

"An excellent education for affordable tuition."

Famous MBA Alumni

Robert McEwen, chairman and CEO of U.S. Gold Corp.
Richard Waugh, president and CEO of Scotiabank
Paul Tsaparis, president and CEO of Hewlett-Packard (Canada) Ltd.

Who Are My Classmates?

Full-time enrollment: 528
Women: 32%
International: 57%
Minority: N/A
Average age: 29
Accepted applicants enrolled: 86%

"Too many part-time instructors."

The 411

Annual tuition and fees: $20,188 (resident), $28,500 (nonresident)
Annual living expenses: $15,000 (resident), $16,000 (nonresident)
Total program cost, including forgone salary: $157,296 (resident), $175,920 (nonresident)
Classes begin: September
Application deadlines: February 1 (international), May 1 (domestic)
Application fee: $150

Cliff Notes

Leading areas of study: Finance, International Business, Marketing, Strategy
Average class size, core courses: 45
Average class size, electives: 30
Number of electives: 120
Teaching methods: Lectures (40%), case studies (30%), team projects (15%)

But What's It *Really* Like?

Graded by students:
Overall ranking: B
Teaching quality: C
Career services: C

Graded by recruiters:
Overall ranking: A
Accounting: A
Analytical skills: B
Communication: B
Finance: A
General management: A
International business: A
Marketing: C
Operations/production: B
Teamwork skills: B

Bling

Average pre-MBA salary: $43,460
Average post-MBA salary: $84,550
Graduates with job offer by graduation: 56%
Companies recruiting on campus: 157
Top functional areas for graduates: Finance/Accounting, Marketing/Sales, Consulting
Biggest recruiters: Canadian Imperial Bank of Commerce, Toronto-Dominion Bank, Deloitte, Royal Bank of Canada, Scotiabank

The Good, the Bad, and the Ugly: Students Speak Out

"My Schulich experience was a great mix of quantitative/qualitative/leadership/teamwork skills, with high relevance to the real world."

"The job placement [rate] and the school's ability to assist in job placement are extremely low. The people at the career center are too lax, never reply to e-mails, and are not proactive at all."

"Schulich has a great mix of students. It's also unique for attracting a large number of women and a very diverse class, which is really great."

"Professors are friendly, helpful, and encouraging."

"Too many part-time instructors, and the career development center does not help much."

"Schulich is a good school. However, it would be better if it concentrated more on learning than on academic requirements."

"The administration is utterly unconcerned with student complaints regarding major issues with professors and other students. Most of the professors are amazing, as are most of the students, but anybody who does have a problem is pretty much on his or her own."

"Schulich helped me out during my most difficult time—when I was raising my newborn baby—and I was able to get my MBA while starting a family."

"My learning curve was not as high as expected; a lot of the material was overlapping and not value added."

"At Schulich, I received an excellent education for affordable tuition."

"Schulich deserves its excellent and continuously improving reputation. It continues to draw top students and faculty who contribute to the quality of the learning experience. It is riding this upward spiral of strength to the top."

"I expected the studies would be more intensive and difficult. I graduated with honors, and it was not hard."

"Schulich offers numerous scholarships and part-time jobs to students, and professors are friendly, helpful, and encouraging."

"My MBA experience at Schulich surpassed anything I was expecting from this program. It prepared me to continue on my career path."

"I loved every minute that I was at Schulich."

Where to Stay

Holiday Inn Yorkdale
3450 Dufferin St.
Toronto, ON M6A 2V1
(877) 477-5817

Le Royal Meridien King Edward Hotel
37 King St. E.
Toronto, ON M5C 1E9
(416) 863-9700

Novotel
3 Park Home Ave.
North York, ON M2N 6L3
(416) 733-2929

 Where to Eat

Bamboo Hut
2150 Steeles Ave. W.
Concord, ON L4K2Y7
(905) 761-7598

The Duke of Devon
66 Wellington St. W.
Toronto, ON M5K 1A2
(416) 642-DUKE

La Risata Restaurant
2777 Steeles Ave.
North York, ON M3J 3K5
(416) 665-4372

 Things to Do

CN Tower
301 Front St. W.
Toronto, ON M5V 2T6
(416) 868-6937

Royal Ontario Museum
100 Queen's Park
Toronto, ON M5S 2C6
(416) 586-8000

CHECK OUT BUSINESSWEEK.COM FOR MORE:

Admissions Q&A: Charmaine Courtis, head of student services, describes the ideal Schulich applicant.

Sample Application Essays: Find out how you can make the cut at Schulich.

School Tour: Explore York's campus before visiting using this photo slide show.

Search & Compare: Is Schulich on your short list? See how it stacks up against other top B-schools.

Expanded Profile: More Schulich facts, statistics, and insights.

Access all the B-schools content on BusinessWeek.com by subscribing to MBA Insider.

Columbia University

Columbia Business School
2007 Ranking: 6
The Executive MBA Programs
Warren Hall
1125 Amsterdam Ave., Room 404
New York, NY 10025-1717
E-mail address:
embainfo@columbia.edu
Web address: www2.gsb.columbia.edu/
emba/
For more info: Call the EMBA office at
(212) 854-2211

Why Columbia?

Having dropped out of the *Business-Week* ranking in 2005 amid widespread student dissatisfaction, Columbia staged an almost unprecedented comeback two years later, catapulting to No. 6. And it's easy to see why. The limited course offerings, fluff classes, and poorly prepared classmates that generated the criticism three years ago are, for the most part, gone.

Under the modified cohort system used by Columbia, clusters of about 65 students take all their courses together for the first two terms. The first three terms are given over to core courses, while the final two terms focus on electives and a semester-long international seminar that allows students to delve into business, political, and cultural issues in five international locations. Classes are offered every other weekend, and one-week residencies start each of the first two terms.

☑ B4UGO

Applicants accepted: N/A
Average GMAT score: N/A
Average years' work experience: 9
Average base salary: $112,000

Nearly half of all students work in finance, accounting, or investment banking, as befits a program located in the financial capital of the world.

Columbia University is a private institution. Established in 1968, Columbia's executive MBA program is accredited by the Association to Advance Collegiate Schools of Business (AACSB). Columbia also offers a full-time MBA program. For details on Columbia's full-time MBA, see page 9.

◉ Who Are My Classmates?

Executive MBA enrollment: 606
Women: 29%
International: 22%
Minority: 37%
Average age: 32

"The perfect blend of academic rigor and practical skills."

Where Do They Come From?

Work background: 2% have the title of president, chairman, or CEO; 5% work in the nonprofit sector
Percentage with advanced degrees: 20
Percentage who live within 45 miles of school: 84
Top functional areas: Finance/Accounting (32%), Consulting (17%), Marketing/Sales (17%)
Top employers: Ernst & Young, IBM, JPMorgan Chase, General Electric, Morgan Stanley

---

"The professional connections I made are already proving valuable."

The 411

Program length: 20 months
Workload: 17 hours per week in class; 20 hours per week outside of class
Total program cost: $133,200
Housing provided for EMBA students: No
Distance from major airport: 7 miles
Access to health club for EMBA students: Yes
Classes begin: September
Application deadline: June 1
Application fee: $160

Cliff Notes

Leading areas of study: Finance, General Management, Leadership, Marketing, Strategy
Concentrations/specializations: None
Joint-degree programs: None
Average class size, core courses: 64
Average class size, electives: 35
Number of electives: 58
Teaching methods: Case studies (30%), lectures (30%), team projects (25%)

But What's It *Really* Like?

Graded by EMBA directors:
Overall: A+

Program quality, graded by students:
Overall: A+
Teaching quality: A+
Caliber of classmates: A+
Housing: A+
Logistics: A
Support: A+

Curriculum, graded by students:
Overall: A+
E-business: A+
Entrepreneurship: A+
Ethics: A+
Finance: A+
International business: A+
Marketing: A+
Strategy: A
Teamwork: A+

Prominent Faculty

Paul Ingram: Business Management
Bernd Schmitt: International Business
and Marketing
Julian Yeo: Accounting

 The Good, the Bad, and the Ugly: Students Speak Out

"Columbia offered the perfect blend of academic rigor and development of practical managerial decision-making skills. These skills will prove invaluable in enhancing our business careers."

"It is a fantastic program, and the professional connections I made are already proving to be very valuable."

"The choice of electives was very poor."

"The academic work was not very challenging—some of this most likely on account of the fact that most of what was available in terms of course offerings I had seen or done before."

"The Columbia EMBA program is the best in the world. It is rigorous yet flexible. The students are the most intelligent and hardest working I have encountered. The faculty members are world class and on the cutting edge of their fields."

"As part of my Columbia experience, I was able to participate in courses held in partner universities sponsored and taught by Columbia faculty in London, Munich, and Shanghai (some taught by Nobel prize winners!). Learning and experiencing the intricacies of commerce in our global environment doesn't get any better than at Columbia Business School!"

"Columbia has given me a completely new outlook."

"Starting in the fourth and fifth terms, the choice of electives was very poor. I understand that we cannot get all the courses we want, but the best courses were all taken. Good finance courses were offered under the daytime MBA schedule, during weekdays, which is inconvenient for the majority of the class, as we work during the weekdays."

"Columbia Business School has given me a completely new outlook on business and life. The quality of the professors is extremely high. The professors make you feel like there is no better place to be than in class on a Saturday afternoon."

 **Where to Stay**

The Lucerne Hotel
76th St. and Amsterdam Ave.
New York, NY 10024
(212) 875-1000

On the Ave Hotel
2178 Broadway
New York, NY 10016
(212) 362-1100

The Belleclaire Hotel
250 W. 75th St.
New York, NY 10024
(212) 362-7700

 Where to Eat

Dinosaur Bar-B-Q
646 W. 131st St.
New York, NY 10027
(212) 694-1777

Le Monde
2885 Broadway
New York, NY 10025
(212) 531-3939

Meridiana
2756 Broadway
New York, NY 10025
(212) 222-4453

 Things to Do

Madame Tussauds Wax Museum
234 W. 42nd St.
New York, NY 10036
(800) 246-8872

Top of the Rock
30 Rockefeller Center
New York, NY 10020
(212) 698-2000

CHECK OUT BUSINESSWEEK.COM FOR MORE:

Expanded Profile: For more details on Columbia's EMBA program, check out its expanded online profile.

Search & Compare: Find out how Columbia's executive MBA stacks up against other top EMBA programs.

Sample Application Essay and Interview Tips: Ace the Columbia admissions process using these helpful tips.

Best Schools by Specialty: Find out why Columbia is tops for marketing and finance.

School Tour: Planning a visit? Check out Columbia's New York City campus before you go.

Access all the B-schools content on BusinessWeek.com by subscribing to MBA Insider.

Cornell University

Johnson Graduate School of
  Management
2007 Ranking: 13
Cornell Executive MBA Program
221 Sage Hall
Ithaca, NY 14853-6201
E-mail address: emba@cornell.edu
Web address: www.cornellemba.com
For more info: Call the EMBA office at
  (607) 255-4251

☑ B4UGO

Applicants accepted: 63%
Average GMAT score: N/A
Average years' work experience: 13
Average base salary: $156,500

Why Cornell?

The Cornell executive MBA supplies the management tool kit for busy mid-career executives who are seeking to advance their careers. With a curriculum designed to impart the kind of cross-functional knowledge required of senior managers, and integrated courses that teach theory in the context of practical application, the Cornell EMBA delivers a solid understanding of business fundamentals.

First-year courses focus on the basics, including marketing, management, accounting, and leadership. During the second year, students move on to courses in strategy, managerial decision making, and corporate governance. A global business project, allowing students to use their newly acquired strategy tools to analyze a product or service in an international setting, is also part of the second year. During the course of the program, students spend a week on Cornell's Ithaca campus before each of the four terms, with the remaining classes taking place on alternating weekends at a conference center in Palisades, New York, 15 miles from Manhattan.

Cornell University is a private institution. Established in 1999, Johnson's executive MBA program is accredited by the Association to Advance Collegiate Schools of Business (AACSB). Johnson also offers a full-time MBA program. For details on Johnson's full-time MBA program, see page 13.

 Who Are My Classmates?

Executive MBA enrollment: 113
Women: 40%
International: N/A
Minority: 38%
Average age: 35

"The experience at Cornell was invaluable."

Where Do They Come From?

Work background: 3% have the title of president, chairman, or CEO; 12% work at organizations with 100 or fewer employees; 5% work in the nonprofit sector
Percentage with advanced degrees: 27
Percentage who live within 45 miles of school: 59
Top functional areas: Human Resources (23%), Consulting (15%), Finance/Accounting (14%)
Top employers: General Electric, IBM, Johnson & Johnson, Merrill Lynch, Bloomberg

---

"Head and shoulders above Wharton, NYU, and Columbia."

The 411

Program length: 22 months
Workload: 6 hours per week in class; 20 hours per week outside of class
Total program cost: $122,400
Housing provided for EMBA students: Yes
Distance from major airport: 15 miles
Access to health club for EMBA students: Yes
Classes begin: July
Application deadlines: None
Application fee: $150

Cliff Notes

Leading area of study: General Management
Concentrations/specializations: None
Joint-degree programs: None
Average class size, core courses: 65
Average class size, electives: N/A
Number of electives: None
Teaching methods: Case studies (30%), lectures (30%), team projects (15%)

But What's It *Really* Like?

Graded by EMBA directors:
Overall: A

Program quality, graded by students:
Overall: A
Teaching quality: A+
Caliber of classmates: A+
Housing: A
Logistics: A+
Support: A+

Curriculum, graded by students:
Overall: A
E-business: A
Entrepreneurship: A
Ethics: A+
Finance: A
International business: A
Marketing: A
Strategy: C
Teamwork: A+

Prominent Faculty

David J. BenDaniel: Entrepreneurship
and Personal Enterprise
Elizabeth A. Mannix: Management
Vithala Rao: Marketing

 ### The Good, the Bad, and the Ugly: Students Speak Out

"The experience at Cornell was invaluable. The peers, the professors, the staff, and the overall experience were once in a lifetime. I met great people and had a great learning experience that is helping me confront the world's most difficult problems as I run my organization."

"Career services should be improved."

"Because the Cornell EMBA is an off-campus program, I believe we did not get access to the same variety of courses and professors as the full-time students. It was helpful to have a course on leadership behavior at the beginning of the program. It would have been helpful to do an evaluation to see how our behaviors had changed at the end. Also, a good portion of the EMBA program was based on group work, so it would have been helpful to facilitate analysis/feedback from my classmates as well."

"The Cornell EMBA program provided world-class professors and a very challenging curriculum. The program attracted high-performing students who challenged one another on a daily basis. Head and shoulders above Wharton, NYU, Columbia, and all the rest."

"Career services should be improved. Cornell should provide more interaction with corporate recruiters and arrange career fairs."

"Cornell provided an incredibly rich learning environment with an interesting and diverse student body, excellent professors, great facilities, and challenging courses. The professors are at the top of their fields, and all gave their time and energy to enable our learning."

"The coursework was challenging to the point of sadism, but the professors were extremely good at reconfiguring the delivery of the material to suit the EMBA environment. I never felt as though I were attending a 'lite' version of a full-time class."

"I continued to find that the faculty members were leaders in their respective fields, while at the same time, easily accessible to students. I also found my classmates to be dynamic leaders with very diverse backgrounds and experiences that led to robust discussion both inside and outside the classroom."

 **Where to Stay**

The Statler Hotel
130 Statler Dr.
Ithaca, NY 14853
(800) 541-2501

A Comfort Woods Guesthouse
971 Comfort Rd.
Danby, NY 14883
(607) 277-1620

Annie's Garden Bed & Breakfast
220 Pearl St.
Ithaca, NY 14850
(607) 273-0888

 Where to Eat

Blue Stone Bar & Grill
110 N. Aurora St.
Ithaca, NY 14850
(607) 272-2371

Asian Noodle House
204 Dryden Rd.
Ithaca, NY 14850
(607) 272-9106

Sangam Indian Curry
Downtown Ithaca Commons
Ithaca, NY 14850
(607) 272-6716

 Things to Do

Taughannock Falls State Park
Rte. 89
Trumansburg, NY 14886
(800) 456-CAMP

King Ferry Winery
Cayuga Wine Trail
King Ferry, NY 13081
(315) 364-5100

CHECK OUT BUSINESSWEEK.COM FOR MORE:

Video View: Listen to Dean Bob Swieringa discuss the integration of science and business.

Expanded Profile: Check out Cornell's online EMBA profile for more statistics and more quotes from recent graduates.

Search & Compare: See how Cornell compares to other top-tier EMBA programs.

School Tour: Check out the Ithaca campus before you apply.

Classroom Voices: Cornell Professors Stuart Hart and Robert Frank talk about their latest books.

Access all the B-schools content on BusinessWeek.com by subscribing to MBA Insider.

Duke University

Fuqua School of Business
2007 Ranking: 9
One Towerview Dr.
Box 90127
Durham, NC 27708
E-mail address: executive-mba-info@
fuqua.duke.edu
Web address: www.fuqua.duke.edu/
mba/executive
For more info: Call the EMBA office of
admissions at (919) 660-7804

Why Duke?

Fuqua's global EMBA program caters to those extremely busy executives who would prefer to be able to learn from home through the online distance learning component that makes up 60% of the program. The rest of the course is completed in two-week terms: two terms are completed on Duke's North Carolina campus, and one term each is spent exploring Europe, Asia, and South America. Unlike most other global programs, Fuqua does not work with partner institutions, but instead picks different destinations where students can interact with government and business representatives and witness a variety of cultural experiences.

While the curriculum is primarily management-focused, a specialized Health Sector Management concentration is also available. According to Duke, about half of all students get promoted before they graduate, while many take on strategic roles or additional P&L respon-

✓ B4UGO

Applicants accepted: N/A
GMAT: Not required
Average years' work experience: 15.6
Average base salary: $113,081*
*Estimate based on *BusinessWeek* survey data.

sibilities. And then there's the return on investment: most alumni report double-digit annual salary increases—for every year after they obtain their degrees.

Duke University is a private institution. Established in 1984, Fuqua's executive MBA program is accredited by the Association to Advance Collegiate Schools of Business (AACSB). Fuqua also offers a full-time MBA program. For details on Fuqua's full-time MBA program, see page 21.

 Who Are My Classmates?

Executive MBA enrollment: 171
Women: 17%
International: 20%
Minority: 45%
Average age: 40

"The Duke global EMBA was perfect: rigorous yet flexible."

Where Do They Come From?

Percentage with advanced degrees: N/A

Percentage who live within 45 miles of school: 11

Top functional areas: Marketing/Sales (20%), General Management (19%), Operations/Logistics (17%)

Top employers: IBM, Capital One, Bank of America, Cisco, Wachovia

"The student body was senior executives—not first-time managers."

The 411

Program length: 19 months

Workload: 36 hours per week in class (residency weeks); 15–20 hours per week outside of class

Total program cost: $123,500

Housing provided for EMBA students: Yes

Distance from major airport: 15 miles

Access to health club for EMBA students: Yes

Classes begin: May

Application deadlines: July to March

Application fee: $175

Cliff Notes

Leading area of study: General Management

Concentrations/specializations: Health Sector Management

Joint-degree programs: None

Average class size, core courses: 67

Average class size, electives: N/A

Number of electives: None

Teaching methods: Lectures (40%), case studies (40%)

But What's It *Really* Like?

Graded by EMBA directors:
Overall: **A+**

Program quality, graded by students:
Overall: **A**
Teaching quality: **A+**
Caliber of classmates: **A+**
Housing: **A**
Logistics: **B**
Support: **A+**

Curriculum, graded by students:
Overall: **A**
E-business: **A**
Entrepreneurship: **C**
Ethics: **B**
Finance: **B**
International business: **A+**
Marketing: **B**
Strategy: **A**
Teamwork: **A+**

Prominent Faculty

John Graham: Finance
Rick Staelin: Marketing
Will Mitchell: Strategy

 ### The Good, the Bad, and the Ugly: Students Speak Out

"Fuqua's long experience in working with executives is a huge asset. The combination of classroom-style residencies and distance learning through Duke's proprietary software is excellent. No other program could offer this combination of proven success and schedule flexibility. In addition, the student body was composed of senior executives—not first-time managers. Duke should be even more rigorous in selecting candidates for the global EMBA program. The program is excellent and built on teamwork. [But] about 10% to 15% of executives did not have the skills/stamina/attitude needed to fully contribute to their teams."

"The Duke global EMBA was perfect: rigorous yet flexible."

"Fuqua needs to enhance its career guidance for executives—even people with 25 years of professional experience can use assistance. The macroeconomics course needs updating, and this being a global program, it might have been nice to have an introduction to South Asian and Middle Eastern economies."

"The Duke experience, specifically the global EMBA program, is unmatched. Most [instructors] were excellent because they had experience with teaching the program previously, which has a demographic much different from that of a full-time or weekend program. The Fuqua operations staff was fantastic. If there were any issues, they swarmed on them and resolved them quickly. Combine taking courses while having to function at your job plus an older, more experienced demographic, and the students end up becoming as much of the learning experience as the instructors."

> *"Fuqua needs to enhance its career guidance for executives."*

"The format of Duke's global EMBA program makes managing school and work responsibilities much easier."

"Additional leadership training through role-playing case projects, more active involvement by program staff regarding logistical matters at on-site residences, increased leadership focus, and additional human resource management training [would have improved the program]."

 **Where to Stay**

Washington Duke Inn & Golf Club
3001 Cameron Blvd.
Durham, NC 27705
(919) 490-0999

Millennium Hotel Durham
2800 Campus Walk Ave.
Durham, NC 27705
(919) 383-8575

Brookwood Inn at Duke University
2306 Elba St.
Durham, NC 27705
(919) 286-3111

 Where to Eat

Blue Corn Café
716 Ninth St.
Durham, NC 27705
(919) 286-9600

Metro 8 Steakhouse
746 Ninth St.
Durham, NC 27705
(919) 416-1700

Magnolia Grill
1002 Ninth St.
Durham, NC 27705
(919) 286-3609

 Things to Do

Nasher Museum of Art
2001 Campus Dr.
Durham, NC 27705
(919) 684-5135

Sarah P. Duke Gardens
426 Anderson St.
Durham, NC 27705
(919) 684-3698

CHECK OUT BUSINESSWEEK.COM FOR MORE:

B-School News: Find out why Dean Blair Sheppard was selected to take over in 2007 and how he will use his business savvy to create a distinct Fuqua image.

Best Schools by Specialty: Discover what makes Fuqua tops for management and marketing.

Sample Application Essays and Interview Tips: Fourteen sample essays present effective ways to handle Fuqua's questions. Plus, tips for tackling the interview.

Expanded Profile: More facts, statistics, and insights on the Fuqua executive MBA program.

Search & Compare: Put Fuqua to the test with a side-by-side comparison between Duke and other top EMBA programs.

Access all the B-schools content on BusinessWeek.com by subscribing to MBA Insider.

Emory University

Goizueta Business School
2007 Ranking: 7
Office of Admissions
1300 Clifton Rd., Suite W288
Atlanta, GA 30322
E-mail address:
admissions@bus.emory.edu
Web address: www.goizueta.emory.edu/
degree/emba
For more info: Call the admissions
office at (404) 727-6311

Why Emory?

Goizueta is known for a strong general management focus that develops leadership capabilities, regardless of the experience that individual students bring to the program. Leadership skills are taught through courses on leadership styles and leading organizational change, while global business know-how is developed during a 10-day International Colloquium. Goizueta students benefit from personal interaction with the renowned faculty, who get high marks for teaching quality. The school claims that students graduate with the equivalent of an additional 7 to 10 years of managerial experience.

Executives can choose between two EMBA programs: an alternating weekend course that runs for 16 months or a modular EMBA that offers a more global experience. The modular format will suit those who need greater flexibility—it includes eight weeklong modules

☑ B4UGO

Applicants accepted: 85%
Average GMAT score: N/A
Average years' work experience: 11.8
Average base salary: $123,932

completed at Emory (in addition to the International Colloquium) and an online distance learning component.

Emory is a private institution. Established in 1978, Goizueta's executive MBA program is accredited by the Association to Advance Collegiate Schools of Business (AACSB). Goizueta also offers full-time and part-time MBA programs. For details on Goizueta's full-time MBA program, see page 25. For details on its part-time MBA program, see page 333.

 Who Are My Classmates?

Executive MBA enrollment: 121
Women: 16%
International: 7%
Minority: 27%
Average age: 35

"Solid program with academically rigorous coursework."

Where Do They Come From?

Work background: 9% have the title of president, chairman, or CEO; 23% work at organizations with 100 or fewer employees; 14% work in the nonprofit sector

Percentage with advanced degrees: 29

Percentage who live within 45 miles of school: 19

Top functional areas: Finance/Accounting (19%), Marketing/Sales (18%), General Management (12%), Management Information Systems (12%)

Top employers: General Electric, Coca-Cola, Delta Airlines, UPS, AT&T

"Instructors are truly best in class."

The 411

Program length: 16 months

Workload: 7 hours per week in class; 25 hours per week outside of class

Total program cost: $88,000

Housing provided for EMBA students: No

Distance from major airport: 12 miles

Access to health club for EMBA students: Yes

Classes begin: January

Application deadlines: None

Application fee: $140

Cliff Notes

Leading areas of study: Finance, General Management, Leadership, Marketing, Strategy

Concentrations/specializations: None

Joint-degree programs: None

Average class size, core courses: 50

Average class size, electives: 50

Number of electives: 29

Teaching methods: Case studies (40%), lectures (30%), team projects (10%), distance learning (10%)

But What's It *Really* Like?

Graded by EMBA directors:
Overall: **A**

Program quality, graded by students:
Overall: **A+**
Teaching quality: **A+**
Caliber of classmates: **A+**
Housing: **B**
Logistics: **A**
Support: **A+**

Curriculum, graded by students:
Overall: **A+**
E-business: **A+**
Entrepreneurship: **A**
Ethics: **A**
Finance: **A**
International business: **A**
Marketing: **C**
Strategy: **A+**
Teamwork: **A**

Prominent Faculty

Rick Gilkey: Organization and
   Management
Robert Kazanjian: Organization and
   Management
Rajendra Srivastava: Marketing

 **The Good, the Bad,
and the Ugly: Students
Speak Out**

"EMBA instructors are truly best in class. Their strengths certainly included their vast research, consulting, and prior real-world experience, and their passion for teaching. Nearly all of the professors had the ability and desire to connect with their students in both a learning and a social environment. Most important, I believe that virtually all of the professors did an excellent job of leveraging the experience of their students."

"Too focused on theory and research."

"It would have been helpful to tape some of the classes in order for us to refer back to those classes and use more wikis in order to improve the off-campus discussions."

"I felt that the analytical skills instruction in the program was far above that of other programs some of my colleagues have attended."

"The school is very influential in the Atlanta business market, and I would have liked to see more leaders from the community speak to the classes."

"More wikis [would] improve the off-campus discussions."

"The program office was extremely attentive to the details and unique requirements of every student's situation—travel, family balance, illness, etc. With the nurture and care provided by both faculty and the program office, it was difficult not to feel spoiled in a good way."

"Some of the instructors were a bit too focused on theory and research, and this sometimes made really cementing the lessons that were taught difficult. Some of the professors also tended to get stuck on older cases, which, although they teach great core business lessons, were quite a bit dated."

"Emory provided a solid program with academically rigorous coursework, team-based projects, and an outstanding group of talented classmates who were very supportive and collaborative throughout the program."

 Where to Stay

Emory Conference Center Hotel/ Emory Inn
1615 Clifton Rd.
Atlanta, GA 30322
(800) 933-6679

Wyndham Midtown Atlanta
125 10th St. N.E.
Atlanta, GA 30309
(404) 873-4900

Four Seasons Atlanta
75 14th St.
Atlanta, GA 30309
(404) 253-3853

 Where to Eat

Sotto Sotto
313 N. Highland Ave.
Atlanta, GA 30307
(404) 523-6678

Watershed
406 W. Ponce de Leon Ave.
Decatur, GA 30030
(404) 378-4900

The Flying Biscuit Café
1655 McLendon Ave.
Atlanta, GA 30307
(404) 687-8888

 Things to Do

Carter Presidential Center
One Copenhill Ave.
Atlanta, GA 30307
(404) 331-0296

The World of Coca-Cola
55 Martin Luther King Jr. Dr. S.W.
Atlanta, GA 30303
(404) 676-5151

CHECK OUT BUSINESSWEEK.COM FOR MORE:

Sample Application Essays and Interview Tips: Learn how to ace Emory's questions about work experience and teamwork.

Admissions Q&A: Admissions Director Julie Barefoot comments on what kind of student fits into the Emory's culture.

Expanded Profile: Dig deeper into the Emory EMBA program with this online profile.

Search & Compare: See how Emory's EMBA program stacks up against other top choices in categories such as faculty, electives, and costs.

Access all the B-schools content on BusinessWeek.com by subscribing to MBA Insider.

ESADE Business School

Escuela Superior de Administración y
  Dirección de Empresas
2007 Ranking: 21
Av. Esplugues, 92-96
Barcelona, Spain E-08034
E-mail address: exedBCN@esade.edu
Web address: www.esade.edu
For more info: Call general information
  at 34-93-280-40-08

☑ B4UGO

Applicants accepted: 65%
Average GMAT score: 650
Average years' work experience: 9.3
Average base salary: $79,011

Why ESADE?

While other executive MBA programs teach academic disciplines in isolation, ESADE's favors a more integrated approach structured around five broad themes: general management, integrating resources, designing the strategy, the global economy, and leading the future. Each theme includes a series of courses, but the program goes well beyond classroom and online work. A weeklong outdoor immersion experience involves self-evaluation, teamwork training, and decision-making exercises, while weeklong international study tours to U.K. and U.S. business schools include lectures by business leaders and company visits. As part of the program, EMBA students also tackle problems confronting their own organizations.

During the 18-month program, students attend classes on Fridays and Saturdays with the choice of either a weekly program in Barcelona or a biweekly schedule in Madrid. ESADE also offers, with Georgetown, a dual-degree global EMBA, as well as an executive masters in marketing and sales with a separate, highly specialized curriculum.

ESADE is a private institution. Established in 2001 in Barcelona and 2002 in Madrid, ESADE's executive MBA program is accredited by the Association to Advance Collegiate Schools of Business (AACSB). ESADE also offers full-time and part-time MBA programs. For details on ESADE's full-time MBA program, see page 29.

👤 Who Are My Classmates?

Executive MBA enrollment: 172
Women: 15%
International: 9%
Minority: N/A
Average age: 34

"A good balance of theory and practice."

Where Do They Come From?

Work background: 11% have the title of president, chairman, or CEO; 42% work at organizations with 100 or fewer employees; 1% work in the nonprofit sector

Percentage with advanced degrees: 7

Percentage who live within 45 miles of school: 65

Top functional areas: Human Resources (21%), Management Information Systems (20%), General Management (18%)

Top employers: Hewlett-Packard, Morgan Stanley, Amgen, Sony

"There should be fewer exams."

The 411

Program length: 18 months

Workload: 15 hours per week in class; 15 hours per week outside of class

Total program cost: $66,690

Housing provided for EMBA students: No

Distance from major airport: 15 miles

Access to health club for EMBA students: Yes

Classes begin: January (Barcelona), February (Madrid)

Application deadlines: December (Barcelona), November (Madrid)

Application fee: $105

Cliff Notes

Leading areas of study: Entrepreneurship, Finance, General Management, Leadership, Marketing

Concentrations/specializations: None

Joint-degree programs: Yes

Average class size, core courses: 40

Average class size, electives: N/A

Number of electives: None

Teaching methods: Case studies (30%), lectures (25%), team projects (20%)

But What's It *Really* Like?

Graded by EMBA directors:
Overall: C

Program quality, graded by students:
Overall: A
Teaching quality: B
Caliber of classmates: A
Housing: C
Logistics: A
Support: B

Curriculum, graded by students:
Overall: C
E-business: A+
Entrepreneurship: A
Ethics: A+
Finance: A+
International business: A+
Marketing: A
Strategy: B
Teamwork: A

Prominent Faculty

Eugènia Bieto: Business Policy
Richard Boyatzis: Human Resource Management
Luis de Sebastián Carazo: Economics

 The Good, the Bad, and the Ugly: Students Speak Out

"I find ESADE's program structure ideal, having a good balance of theory and practice, as well as a number of intensive weeks out of the business school's campus (including outdoor leadership training and three international exchange programs: Europe, Asia, and the United States). The variety of professors, with a good mix of local and international/foreign professors, gives ESADE a very interesting approach and vision of management."

"There should be fewer exams and more hands-on training, especially on presentation skills."

"There was too much work to do in each subject."

"Although it seems a long time, the program is really too dense to be completed in 18 months. It could be optimized to have enough time for every subject. I think it is quite complicated to cover all the EMBA program requirements in such a short period of time for individuals having managing roles in their companies."

"There was too much work to do in each one of the subjects, and sometimes all professors wanted to have feedback in the same week."

"My global perspective has opened, and the program broadened my way of seeing the company itself and the globalization of the markets. An outstanding EMBA program!"

"In order not to lose focus when you are overburdened with your job, your family, and the EMBA work, it would have helped to have a wrap-up session at the end of each quarter, summarizing the most important concepts."

"The school's philosophy of promoting cooperation among participants, and not competition, fit very well with my way of thinking."

"ESADE not only has a very good level of professors but also an important and useful networking system, and people sharing the program are valuable persons you can learn from."

"ESADE is an excellent school and very well organized. The human touch in the curriculum is appreciated, such as the LEAD coaching program and other personal development assignments."

Where to Stay

Hotel Arts
Marina 19-21
Barcelona, ES 08005
34-93-221-10-00

Design Hotels: Casa Camper
Carrer Elisabets 11
Barcelona, ES 08001
(800) 337-4685

Design Hotels: Grand Hotel Central
Via Laietana 30
Barcelona, ES 08003
(800) 337-4685

 Where to Eat

Inopia
Carrer de Tamarit 104
Barcelona, ES 08015
34-93-424-52-31

Ca L'Isidre
Carrer Les Flors 12
Barcelona, ES 08001
34-93-441-11-39

La Clara
Gran Via de les Corts Catalanes 442
Barcelona, ES 08015
34-93-289-34-60

 Things to Do

Museu Picasso (Picasso Museum)
Montcada 15-23
Barcelona, ES 08003
34-93-356-30-00

**Museu de la Xocolata
(Chocolate Museum)**
Comerç 36
Barcelona, ES 08003
34-93-268-78-78

CHECK OUT BUSINESSWEEK.COM FOR MORE:

Expanded Profile: For more details on ESADE's EMBA program, check out its expanded online profile.

Search & Compare: Find out how ESADE's executive MBA stacks up against other top EMBA programs.

School Tour: Check out the ESADE campus before planning your visit, using this online photo essay.

Access all the B-schools content on BusinessWeek.com by subscribing to MBA Insider.

Georgetown University

Robert Emmett McDonough School of
Business
2007 Ranking: 12
3520 Prospect St. N.W., Suite 214
Washington, DC 20057-1221
E-mail address: msb-iemba@msb.edu
Web address: www.msb.georgetown.
edu/prospective/executive/iemba
For more info: Call the EMBA office at
(202) 687-2704

 **B4UGO**

Applicants accepted: 50%
Average GMAT score: 620
Average years' work experience: 13
Average base salary: $119,321

Why Georgetown?

In recent years, McDonough has redefined itself as a B-school that provides a global business education with world-class faculty and resources. The international executive MBA combines biweekly classroom experience, in which students study business basics, with the centerpiece of the program: a series of four weeklong residencies that involve months of preparation and give students a chance to apply their newfound skills. Two of the residencies are international and call on teams of students to act as consultants to both established and start-up companies in emerging markets.

During the course of the program, students study international business management, strategic analysis, management communications, and business-government relations. A number of research centers at the school, such as the Capital Markets Research Center, keep McDonough at the forefront of knowledge creation. In addition, the Georgetown University Women's Leadership Initiative hosts conferences and networking events for aspiring women business leaders.

Georgetown University is a private institution. Established in 1994, McDonough's executive MBA program is accredited by the Association to Advance Collegiate Schools of Business (AACSB). McDonough also offers a joint executive MBA with ESADE, plus full-time and part-time MBA programs. For details on McDonough's full-time MBA program, see page 33.

 ## Who Are My Classmates?

Executive MBA enrollment: 104
Women: 19%
International: 31%
Minority: N/A
Average age: 37

"Most professors were excellent communicators."

Where Do They Come From?

Work background: 8% have the title of president, chairman, or CEO: 25% work at organizations with 100 or fewer employees: 8% work in the nonprofit sector

Percentage with advanced degrees: 42

Percentage who live within 45 miles of school: 94

Top industries: Technology (33%), Government (19%), Consulting (15%)

Top employers: AOL, U.S. government, Booz Allen Hamilton, Ernst & Young, PricewaterhouseCoopers

> ## *"The overall IT experience was abysmal."*

The 411

Program length: 18 months

Workload: 8 hours per week in class; 18 hours per week outside of class

Total program cost: $93,935

Housing provided for EMBA students: No

Distance from major airport: 5 miles

Access to health club for EMBA students: Yes

Classes begin: September

Application deadlines: January 31, March 31, May 31

Application fee: $175

Cliff Notes

Leading areas of study: Finance, International Business, Leadership, Operations Management, Strategy

Concentrations/specializations: None

Joint-degree programs: Yes

Average class size, core courses: 52

Average class size, electives: 52

Number of electives: 4

Teaching methods: Case studies (30%), lectures (30%), experiential learning (15%), team projects (15%)

But What's It *Really* Like?

Graded by EMBA directors:
Overall: C

Program quality, graded by students:
Overall: A
Teaching quality: A
Caliber of classmates: A
Housing: B
Logistics: B
Support: B

Curriculum, graded by students:
Overall: B
E-business: A+
Entrepreneurship: A+
Ethics: A
Finance: C
International business: A+
Marketing: A+
Strategy: A+
Teamwork: A+

Prominent Faculty

Paul Almeida: International Business Strategy
Robert Bies: Leadership
Ricardo Ernst: Global Logistics and Operations Management

 ## The Good, the Bad, and the Ugly: Students Speak Out

"Most professors had a strong combination of thought leadership and industry consulting experience, so they were very current. The vast majority were also excellent communicators and true 'teachers.'"

"Excellent foreign residencies."

"Instead of the whole class having to choose electives, the option of different electives in multiple groups would have helped more."

"It is one of the few international EMBA programs that offers electives for four months, excellent foreign residencies, and superb faculty. It utilizes the exceptional resources available through Georgetown's programs in foreign service, public policy, and law and ties them to international business. Overall an exceptional value."

"The few speakers that we did have provided great insight and exposure to the real world. I wish we had more of these speakers."

"The finance side of things was weak, but that came mostly from teaching styles. However, all of the professors are very strong in their knowledge of the subject matter, and it is obvious that an engaging classroom is a serious priority."

"The new dean, George Daly, has given a huge uplift and character to the McDonough business school. He's really taken the time to talk to all students, faculty, and staff and started to give progress reports on all the improvements at the business school."

"The overall IT experience was abysmal—from printers that didn't work, to WiFi that was spotty, to having to install software that didn't play nice with other programs. A real mess."

"The teaching was excellent and was exceeded only by the quality of the students. The international residencies were very rich and provided us with opportunities to directly apply newly learned skills, models, and frameworks in a global business context."

"Georgetown provided a unique combination of exceptional faculty, motivated and diverse students, and fabulous courses. That combination is simply not available at other schools."

Where to Stay

The Georgetown Inn
1310 Wisconsin Ave.
Washington, DC 20007
(202) 333-8900

The Fairmont Washington, DC
2401 M St.
Washington, DC 20037
(202) 429-2400

Key Bridge Marriott
1401 Lee Hwy.
Rosslyn, VA 22209
(703) 524-6400

 Where to Eat

Leopold's Kafe & Konditorei
3318 M St.
Washington, DC 20007
(202) 965-6005

Ching Ching Cha
1063 Wisconsin Ave.
Washington, DC 20007
(202) 333-8288

Pizzeria Paradiso—Georgetown
3282 M St.
Washington, DC 20007
(202) 337-1245

 Things to Do

Blues Alley (jazz club)
1073 Wisconsin Ave.
Washington, DC 20007
(202) 337-4141

Dumbarton Oaks Gardens
1703 32nd St. N.W.
Washington, DC 20007
(202) 339-6401

CHECK OUT BUSINESSWEEK.COM FOR MORE:

Admissions Q&A: Admissions Director Monica Gray talks about the collaborative culture at Georgetown and the importance of active participation.

Expanded Profile: Read McDonough's online EMBA profile to find out what makes it stand out from the pack.

Search & Compare: Use this interactive tool to do a side-by-side comparison of McDonough and other EMBA programs on your short list.

School Tour: Before you apply, give the Georgetown campus the once-over using this online photo essay.

Access all the B-schools content on BusinessWeek.com by subscribing to MBA Insider.

INSEAD

The European Institute of Business
  Administration
2007 Ranking: 18
Boulevard de Constance
Fontainebleau, France 77305
E-mail address: mba.info@insead.edu
Web address: www.insead.edu
For more info: Call general information
  at 33-1-60-72-40-00

Why INSEAD?

If you're looking for an executive MBA that will broaden your horizons—as a manager, a leader, and an actor on the global stage—then look no further. That, in a nutshell, is what the INSEAD EMBA promises. Students begin with five modules of core courses and then choose from electives such as private equity, strategies for Asia Pacific, and the psychology of leadership. Along the way, they are matched with professional coaches to help draft their own personal leadership development plans. Finally, they wrap up the program with a computer-based business simulation that allows them to analyze the potential long-term effects of their business decisions.

During the 14-month program, students spend eight weeks on the Fontainebleau campus and four weeks in Singapore. In between the on-campus sessions, they apply what they've learned at work. EMBA students hail from more than 20 different countries

☑ B4UGO

Applicants accepted: N/A
Average GMAT score: 640
Average years' work experience: 11
Average base salary: $164,000

and have an average of 11 years of work experience.

INSEAD is a private institution. Established in 2003, INSEAD's executive MBA program is accredited by the Association to Advance Collegiate Schools of Business (AACSB). INSEAD also offers a full-time program. For details on INSEAD's full-time MBA program, see page 53.

 Who Are My Classmates?

Executive MBA enrollment: 59
Women: 24%
International: 75%
Minority: N/A
Average age: 36

"Thanks to this degree, I got the position I was aiming for."

Where Do They Come From?

Work background: 7% have the title of president, chairman, or CEO; 12% work at organizations with 100 or fewer employees

Percentage with advanced degrees: 5

Percentage who live within 45 miles of school: 5

Top functional areas: General Management (27%), Finance/Accounting (25%), Marketing/Sales (14%)

Top employers: Electricité de France, Shell, Deutsche Bank, UBS, SAP

"The rhythm was very intense."

The 411

Program length: 14 months

Workload: 40 hours per week in class (12 weeks); 15 hours per week outside of class

Total program cost: $110,000

Housing provided for EMBA students: Yes

Distance from major airport: 60 miles

Access to health club for EMBA students: Yes

Classes begin: November

Application deadlines: March 24 to September 15

Application fee: $260

Cliff Notes

Leading areas of study: Entrepreneurship, General Management, International Business, Leadership, Strategy

Concentrations/specializations: None

Joint-degree programs: None

Average class size, core courses: 59

Average class size, electives: 30

Number of electives: 17

Teaching methods: Case studies (33%), lectures (33%), team projects (20%)

But What's It *Really* Like?

Graded by EMBA directors:
Overall: A

Program quality, graded by students:
Overall: A
Teaching quality: A
Caliber of classmates: A+
Housing: B
Logistics: B
Support: B

Curriculum, graded by students:
Overall: A
E-business: B
Entrepreneurship: A
Ethics: C
Finance: A+
International business: A+
Marketing: A+
Strategy: C
Teamwork: A+

Prominent Faculty

Charles Galuni: Organizational Behavior
Herminia Ibarra: Organizational Behavior
Pascal Maenhout: Finance

 ## The Good, the Bad, and the Ugly: Students Speak Out

"The INSEAD EMBA provided me with the right balance of high-level courses I was looking for in a very international environment. During the INSEAD EMBA, I was also able to reflect on myself and fine-tune my career choice. At the end of this experience and thanks to this degree, I got the exact position I was aiming for."

"Time is always an issue in such a program. I would have loved to have more time to discuss some of the issues within my class, or within the groups I was in. As the rhythm was very intense, this was rarely possible."

"With 26 nationalities, communication is a real issue."

"The program allows you to apply the theoretical knowledge [from class] in your company environment and provides you with highly experienced feedback from the faculty as well as from your peers. On top of that, it has a unique leadership development program. I also believe that the diversity one finds at INSEAD provides easier access to the global business world."

"The program provides you with highly experienced feedback."

"With 26 nationalities represented in the class, communication is a real issue. Higher-level [requirements] in English should help."

"The '1 week per month on campus' formula is, in my opinion, much better than the typical 1/2 day per week offered by other programs. This allows the program to draw participants from more distant locations and facilitates work/EMBA balance."

"One of the best features of the program is the relationship that the program maintains with alumni. For example, alumni are invited to return to campus and join elective courses with current students. This is a unique way to foster interaction between classes and fulfill the promise of 'lifelong learning.'"

 **Where to Stay**

L'Aigle Noir
27 Place Napoléon Bonaparte
Fontainebleau 77300, FR
33-1-60-74-60-00

Hôtel Napoléon
9 rue Grande
Fontainebleau 77300, FR
33-1-64-22-20-39

Londres
1 Place du Général de Gaulle
Fontainebleau 77300, FR
33-1-64-22-20-21

 Where to Eat

Au Bureau
12 rue Grande
Fontainebleau 77300, FR
33-1-60-39-00-01

Pizza Pazza
1 rue Bouchers
Fontainebleau 77300, FR
33-1-60-72-05-61

Chez Bernard
3 rue Royale
Fontainebleau 77300, FR
33-1-64-22-24-68

 Things to Do

Château de Fontainebleau
Place du Général de Gaulle
Fontainebleau 77300, FR
33-1-60-71-50-70

Forest of Fontainebleau
4 rue Royale
Fontainebleau 77300, FR
33-1-60-74-80-22

CHECK OUT BUSINESSWEEK.COM FOR MORE:

Expanded Profile: For more details on INSEAD's EMBA program, check out its expanded online profile.

Sample Application Essay and Interview Tips: Learn what it takes to ace the admissions process at INSEAD.

Search & Compare: Find out how INSEAD's executive MBA stacks up against other top EMBA programs.

School Tour: Planning a visit? Check out INSEAD's Fontainebleau campus before you go.

Access all the B-schools content on BusinessWeek.com by subscribing to MBA Insider.

Instituto de Empresa

IG Business School
2007 Ranking: 15
María de Molina, 13
28006 Madrid, Spain
E-mail address: admissions@ie.edu
Web address: www.ie.edu
For more info: Call EMBA admissions at
  34-91-568-96-10

 **B4UGO**

Applicants accepted: 41%
Average GMAT score: 680
Average years' work experience: 11
Average base salary: $91,800

Why Instituto de Empresa?

If extensive travel is not an option, this online executive MBA may be just the solution. IE's program comprises two weeklong sessions in Madrid, a weeklong session in Shanghai, and two six-month online learning periods. IE says that the online classes, with discussions that may last for several days, allow for more thoughtful debate than is possible in a physical classroom. With a comprehensive global focus, IE tackles subjects such as change management, motivation, conflict resolution, quality service, redesigning processes, organizational design, and knowledge management. Would-be entrepreneurs are particularly well served: they have access to more than 200 tutors who mentor them in business plan development.

The typical IE student has 11 years of work experience and holds an executive or senior management position. Real estate, consumer products, and high-tech industries are all well represented. While the main campus is located in Madrid, about 80% of students are not Spanish, representing approximately 65 nationalities.

Instituto de Empresa is a private institution. Established in 1973, IE's executive MBA program is accredited by the Association to Advance Collegiate Schools of Business (AACSB). IE also offers full-time and part-time MBA programs.

 ## Who Are My Classmates?

Executive MBA enrollment: 63
Women: 22%
International: 81%
Minority: N/A
Average age: 36

"The perfect fit for people who need a quality program with flexibility."

Where Do They Come From?

Work background: 10% have the title of president, chairman, or CEO; 15% work at organizations with 100 or fewer employees
Percentage with advanced degrees: 10
Percentage who live within 45 miles of school: 5
Top functional areas: Finance/Accounting (21%), General Management (18%), Marketing/Sales (18%)
Top employers: Ericsson, Ford, SAT, DHL, Pepsi

"A truly great international experience."

The 411

Program length: 13 months
Workload: 12 hours per week in class; 20 hours per week outside of class
Total program cost: $63,500
Housing provided for EMBA students: No
Distance from major airport: 7 miles
Access to health club for EMBA students: Yes
Classes begin: November
Application deadline: None
Application fee: $162

Cliff Notes

Leading areas of study: Corporate Social Responsibility, Entrepreneurship, General Management, International Business, Strategy
Concentrations/specializations: None
Joint-degree programs: None
Average class size, core courses: 35
Average class size, electives: N/A
Number of electives: None
Teaching methods: Case studies (80%), team projects (10%), lectures (8%)

But What's It *Really* Like?

Graded by EMBA directors:
Overall: C

Program quality, graded by students:
Overall: A+
Teaching quality: B
Caliber of classmates: A
Housing: C
Logistics: A+
Support: B

Curriculum, graded by students:
Overall: C
E-business: A+
Entrepreneurship: B
Ethics: A
Finance: A
International business: A
Marketing: B
Strategy: A
Teamwork: B

Prominent Faculty

David Allen: Strategy
Monika Hamori: Human Resources
Gayle Allard: Economic
    Environment

 The Good, the Bad,
and the Ugly: Students
Speak Out

"This program is the perfect fit for people who need a quality program, but with the flexibility that their jobs require. I have been able to travel internationally, move internationally, and even change careers during the program. IE has been everything I needed and then some."

"Staff did not treat students as customers."

"I am 200% satisfied with the international executive MBA at the Instituto de Empresa. The program has exceeded my expectations in different ways. It is especially suited for students who are looking for a really intensive, steep learning curve, like I was searching for. Further, it is truly a great international experience, which was a main criterion on my list. In addition, it has a European flavor, although the curriculum is American business school based."

"IE administration is not as good as it could be. Staff did not treat students as customers. It is inefficient and slow, and staff members frequently made promises they could not keep. That said, the problems were solved eventually, and IE did come through with the solutions. But it really needs to focus on getting better management in IT and in administration."

"A very intense and stimulating experience."

"The international executive MBA at Instituto de Empresa is a very intense and stimulating experience. The workload is extreme, but the amount of valuable new information assimilated is very high. The depth of experience of the classmates and professors is the real value proposition. Anyone can pick up theory from a book—it's learning how best to apply that theory in any situation that really makes you an effective manager."

"The professors were excellent, and the teaching outstanding. IE just lets itself down with the support functions. If it gets those things right, it could present serious competition to the world leaders in this field."

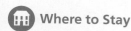 **Where to Stay**

Hostal La Macarena
Cava De San Miguel, 8
Madrid, ES 28005
34-91-365-92-21

InterContinental Hotel
Paseo de la Castellana, 49
Madrid, ES 28046
34-91-700-73-00

ME Madrid Reina Victoria
Plaza de Santa Ana, 14
Madrid, ES 28012
34-91-701-60-00

 Where to Eat

Balear
Calle Sagunto, 18
Madrid, ES 28010
34-91-447-91-15

Los Cedros
Calle de Allendesalazar, 4
Madrid, ES 28043
34-91-415-44-60

Indochina
Calle del Barquillo, 10
Madrid, ES 28004
34-91-524-03-18

 Things to Do

Museo Nacional del Prad
Calle Ruiz de Alarcón, 23
Madrid, ES 28014
34-91-330-28-00

Plaza Puerta del Sol
Downtown
Madrid, ES 28013

CHECK OUT BUSINESSWEEK.COM FOR MORE:

Expanded Profile: For more details on Instituto de Empresa's EMBA program, check out its expanded online profile.

Search & Compare: Find out how Instituto de Empresa's executive MBA stacks up against other top EMBA programs.

School Tour: Check out the Instituto de Empresa's Barcelona campus.

Video View: Dean Santiago Iniguez discusses the Americanization of European higher education.

Access all the B-schools content on BusinessWeek.com by subscribing to MBA Insider.

IMD

International Institute for Management
  Development (IMD)
2007 Ranking: 16
Ch. de Bellerive 23
1001 Lausanne, Switzerland
E-mail address: info@imd.ch
Web address: www.imd.ch/programs/
  emba
For more info: Call an EMBA program
  adviser at 41-0-21 618 0700

Why IMD?

At IMD, globalization is more than just a catch phrase. It's a complete experience. Over the course of the 16-month program, EMBA students spend weeks in Silicon Valley, Shanghai, Dublin, and Bucharest, meeting with government officials and corporate leaders. In the classroom, they work closely with a diverse group of executives and faculty—each group includes individuals from more than 20 nationalities. Students typically come to IMD after working in two countries, and most speak three languages. On average, they have a decade of management experience; one out of eight is a president, chairman, or CEO.

The program includes 13 weeks at the IMD campus in Switzerland and more than 40 weeks of distance learning that involves completing assignments tailored to students' individual companies. In addition to giving students a global business outlook, IMD

☑ B4UGO

Applicants accepted: N/A
Average GMAT score: 585
Average years' work experience: 13.9
Average base salary: $193,500

says that the program allows students to develop strategies for profiting from good ideas and sharpens leadership, problem-solving, and execution skills.

IMD is a private institution. Established in 1999, IMD's executive MBA program is accredited by the Association to Advance Collegiate Schools of Business (AACSB). IMD also offers a full-time MBA. For details on IMD's full-time MBA program, see page 57.

 Who Are My Classmates?

Executive MBA enrollment: 60
Women: 19%
International: 92%
Minority: N/A
Average age: 38

"It's pragmatic and focuses on real-life issues."

Where Do They Come From?

Work background: 13% have the title of president, chairman, or CEO; 7% work at organizations with 100 or fewer employees

Percentage with advanced degrees: 49

Percentage who live within 45 miles of school: 8

Top functional areas: General Management (45%), Finance/Accounting (20%), Marketing/Sales (10%)

Top employers: Novartis, A.P. Moeller Maersk, UBS, ABB, Deutsche Post, DHL

"Would have liked more theoretical teaching."

The 411

Program length: 16 months

Workload: 43 hours per week in class (on-campus weeks); 15 hours per week outside of class

Total program cost: $101,000

Housing provided for EMBA students: Yes

Distance from major airport: 40 miles

Access to health club for EMBA students: Yes

Classes begin: July, October

Application deadline: None

Application fee: $165

Cliff Notes

Leading areas of study: Entrepreneurship, General Management, International Business, Leadership, Strategy

Concentrations/specializations: None

Joint-degree programs: None

Average class size, core courses: 60

Average class size, electives: 30

Number of electives: 6

Teaching methods: Experiential learning (30%), case studies (25%), distance learning (20%)

But What's It *Really* Like?

Graded by EMBA directors:
Overall: A

Program quality, graded by students:
Overall: B
Teaching quality: B
Caliber of classmates: A
Housing: B
Logistics: A
Support: A

Curriculum, graded by students:
Overall: B
E-business: B
Entrepreneurship: B
Ethics: C
Finance: C
International business: A
Marketing: B
Strategy: A+
Teamwork: B

Prominent Faculty

William Fischer: Technology
    Management
Philip Rosenzweig: Strategy and
    International Management
Paul Strebel: Strategic Change
    Management

 ## The Good, the Bad, and the Ugly: Students Speak Out

"The IMD EMBA is an excellent program because it's pragmatic and focuses on real-life issues. Teachers are world-class. Classmates are very senior. Moreover, the modules are all over, which changed my perspective on the world."

"Although IMD has a very practical approach to business education, I would have liked more (and more thorough) theoretical teaching, notably in such areas as supply chain management and finance. This was a weak point at IMD."

"IMD directly affected my company's perception of me."

"IMD takes very good care of its participants. Each participant is made to feel like a guest, and each participant's views are taken extremely seriously."

"After the first 10 weeks in the classroom, most of the rest of the program is done through virtual teams and a few weeks of being physically together at IMD or on field trips, so there was actually too little classroom time."

"Too little classroom time."

"It is a great program; the venue is terrific, the premises fantastic. The attempt to make it very practical and useful has the downside that it all becomes very subjective; nothing is right or wrong. The program should be spiced up with a test or two on more rigorous subjects to keep the academic balance."

"IMD focused on how to identify opportunities across different sectors and different regions using standard frameworks. It also focused on how to build a strategy and how to structure and successfully manage an organization. Finally, the projects that I worked on for the EMBA focused on issues internal to my company. All of these directly affected my company's perception of me and the value that I add to the company."

"The discovery expeditions to Ireland, Romania, China, and Silicon Valley gave participants an excellent overview of global economics, business, and cultures. It's truly a global program."

Where to Stay

Mövenpick Radisson Hotel
Avenue de Rhodanie 4
1007 Lausanne, CH
41-21-612-76-12

Hôtel au Lac
Place de la Navigation 4
1006 Lausanne, CH
41-21-617-14-51

Hotel du Port
Place du Port 5
1006 Lausanne, CH
41-21-612-04-44

Where to Eat

Chalet Suisse
Rte. du Signal 40
1018 Lausanne, CH
41-21-312-23-12

Le Pinocchio
Avenue de la Harpe 16
1007 Lausanne, CH
41-21-616-40-37

Le Bistrot Louis
Place de l'Europe 9
1003 Lausanne, CH
41-21-213-03-00

Things to Do

Olympic Museum
Quai d'Ouchy 1
1001 Lausanne, CH
41-21-621-65-11

Boat trip to France (30 minutes)
Compagnie Générale de Navigation sur le lac Léman
Avenue de Rhodanie 17
1007 Lausanne, CH
41-84-881-18-48

CHECK OUT BUSINESSWEEK.COM FOR MORE:

Admissions Q&A: Admission Director Katty Ooms Suter on why IMD's application process requires 17 essays, and how applicants can stand out from the crowd.

Q&A: IMD Director Sean Meehan explains IMD's approach to using cultural diversity as a learning experience.

Expanded Profile: Discover all there is to know about IMD's executive MBA program with this online EMBA profile.

Search & Compare: Do a side-by-side comparison between IMD and other EMBA programs on your short list.

School Tour: Take a virtual tour of the IMD campus on the shores of Lake Geneva with this photo essay.

Access all the B-schools content on BusinessWeek.com by subscribing to MBA Insider.

New York University

Leonard N. Stern School of Business
2007 Ranking: 19
Henry Kaufman Management Center
44 W. 4th St., Suite 4-100
New York, NY 10012
E-mail address:
   executive@stern.nyu.edu
Web address: www.w4.stern.nyu.edu/
   emba/
For more info: Call the EMBA office at
   (800) NYU-EMBA

☑ B4UGO

Applicants accepted: N/A
Average GMAT score: N/A
Average years' work experience: 13
Average base salary: $192,802

Why NYU?

The NYU EMBA emphasizes global strategy, leadership, and career development. Students can begin the 22-month program in January or August, and classes meet on Fridays and Saturdays on alternating weeks. Before the second year, the class votes on which elective classes will be offered the following year. Among the most popular: Bankruptcy and Managing High Performance Teams. Students may choose a concentration from among the electives. Stern also offers a nine-credit finance specialization for EMBA students.

As part of NYU's focus on global business strategy, students are required to take two one-week global study tours. The locations have included Budapest, São Paolo, Beijing, and Tokyo. While abroad, students meet with industry leaders, financial institutions, and government organizations. EMBA students don't participate in on-campus recruiting events, but they have access to career planning services, including one-on-one career counseling. Self-sponsored students also have access to hundreds of job postings.

NYU is a private institution. Established in 1982, Stern's executive MBA program is accredited by the Association to Advance Collegiate Schools of Business (AACSB). Stern also offers full-time and part-time MBA programs. For details on Stern's full-time MBA program, see page 73. For details on its part-time MBA program, see page 357.

 Who Are My Classmates?

Executive MBA enrollment: 208
Women: 20%
International: 28%
Minority: N/A
Average age: 37

"The student body and curriculum were well rounded."

Where Do They Come From?

Percentage with advanced degrees: 43
Percentage who live within 45 miles of school: 61
Top industries: Financial services (34%), Technology (17%), Pharmaceuticals/Healthcare (13%)
Top functional areas: General Management (39%), Finance/Accounting (13%), Marketing/Sales (13%)
Top employers: JPMorgan Chase, Johnson & Johnson, Citigroup, IBM, Federal Reserve Bank of New York

---

"Access to Career Services could be improved."

The 411

Program length: 22 months
Workload: 12 hours per week in class (every other week); 15–30 hours per week outside of class
Total program cost: $128,000
Housing provided for EMBA students: Yes
Distance from major airport: 10 miles
Access to health club for EMBA students: Yes
Classes begin: January, August
Application deadline: May 30
Application fee: $150

Cliff Notes

Leading areas of study: Finance, General Management, International Business, Marketing, Strategy
Concentrations/specializations: Finance, Leadership
Joint-degree programs: None
Average class size, core courses: 60
Average class size, electives: 21
Number of electives: 200+
Teaching methods: Case studies (30%), lectures (30%), team projects (25%)

But What's It *Really* Like?

Graded by EMBA directors:
Overall: A+

Program quality, graded by students:
Overall: A
Teaching quality: B
Caliber of classmates: A
Housing: A+
Logistics: B
Support: B

Curriculum, graded by students:
Overall: A+
E-business: B
Entrepreneurship: A
Ethics: A+
Finance: B
International business: A
Marketing: B
Strategy: C
Teamwork: A+

Prominent Faculty

Aswath Damodaran: Finance
Douglas Guthrie: Management
Ingo Walter: Finance

 The Good, the Bad, and the Ugly: Students Speak Out

"NYU created a very diverse group of students for my class. This was critical to my learning process. Other schools are known for very focused areas, such as finance, etc. With NYU, the student body and curriculum were well rounded."

"The access to Career Services could be improved. I felt that as executive MBAs, we didn't have access to any of those facilities and, quite frankly, were turned away, often hastily."

> ## "The right balance of financial and managerial focus."

"It was a phenomenal program, with the right balance of financial and managerial focus. The faculty was phenomenal, and the staff was exceptional at handling administrative activities to allow students to focus on learning. [The program was] very global and team-focused, aligning well with today's environment. Each of the two years involved a weeklong international study tour. Most B-schools have only one."

> ## "I began using what I had learned from day one."

"Some [instructors] didn't have enough real-world experience, and that became obvious rather quickly. Others were at the top of their field, and we knew it—and we learned!"

"Superb faculty, understanding and accommodating of our professional lives, without sacrificing academic rigor and high expectations. They were highly knowledgeable, respectful, and thought-provoking. My experience gave me all that I wanted and more— I began using what I had learned from day one."

"There was a high level of respect from the faculty for the experience that the executive class brings to the classroom, and there was no busywork. The relevance of assignments and coursework was clear and therefore meaningful. Over the 22 months, my class became like a family and will be part of my personal and professional network forever. My hat goes off to NYU Stern for providing such a wonderful learning and networking experience."

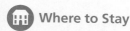 **Where to Stay**

W New York—Union Square
201 Park Ave. S.
New York, NY 10003
(212) 979-5052

Holiday Inn Manhattan Downtown
138 Lafayette St.
New York, NY 10013
(212) 966-8898

Washington Square Hotel
103 Waverly Pl.
New York, NY 10011
(212) 777-9515

 Where to Eat

Mamoun's Falafel
119 MacDougal St.
New York, NY 10012
(212) 674-8685

Patsy's Pizzeria
67 University Pl.
New York, NY 10003
(212) 533-3500

Spice
60 University Pl.
New York, NY 10003
(212) 982-3758

 Things to Do

Sing Sing Karaoke
9 St. Mark's Pl.
New York, NY 10003
(212) 387-7800

Washington Square Park
Fifth Ave. at Waverly Pl.
New York, NY 10003

CHECK OUT BUSINESSWEEK.COM FOR MORE:

Expanded Profile: Take a look at Stern's expanded online profile for more details about its EMBA program.

Search & Compare: See how NYU compares to other top-tier EMBA programs.

School Tour: Get a feel for Stern's Greenwich Village location through this photo essay.

Best Schools by Specialty: Find out why Stern gets top marks for finance and marketing.

Access all the B-schools content on BusinessWeek.com by subscribing to MBA Insider.

Northwestern University

Kellogg School of Management
2007 Ranking: 1
James L. Allen Center
2169 Campus Dr.
Evanston, IL 60208-2800
E-mail address:
    emba@kellogg.northwestern.edu
Web address: www.kellogg.
    northwestern.edu/emba
For more info: Call the EMBA office at
    (847) 467-7020

Why Northwestern?

Kellogg's EMBA program has made a habit of coming out on top in *Business-Week*'s rankings, earning the No. 1 designation four times since 2001. A highly engaged student body and a faculty with a flair for its members bringing their research interests and consulting work into the classroom make for a program in which the real world is front and center. Opportunities for students include the option to conduct an independent study project at their own company.

The first year begins with an intense Live-in Week that provides a foundation for initiating classmate relationships and developing study groups for the remainder of the program; the second year repeats this by bringing together all Kellogg EMBAs, including those in partner institutions in Israel, Germany, Canada, and Hong Kong. In addition to these global programs and

B4UGO

Applicants accepted: N/A
Average GMAT score: N/A
Average years' work experience: 14
Average base salary: $206,739

the regional program near Chicago, a Kellogg-Miami program provides another North American alternative.

Northwestern is a private institution. Established in 1976, Kellogg's executive MBA program is accredited by the Association to Advance Collegiate Schools of Business (AACSB). Kellogg also offers full-time and part-time MBA programs. For details on Kellogg's full-time MBA program, see page 77.

 Who Are My Classmates?

Executive MBA enrollment: 526
Women: 17%
International: 20%
Minority: 35%
Average age: 38

"Everything it's advertised to be and then some."

Where Do They Come From?

Work background: 6% have the title of president, chairman, or CEO; 9% work at organizations with 100 or fewer employees; 3% work in the nonprofit sector

Percentage with advanced degrees: 34

Percentage who live within 45 miles of school: 43

Top functional areas: Finance/Accounting (20%), Marketing/Sales (20%), General Management (19%)

Top employers: Motorola, Baxter Healthcare, General Electric, IBM, John Deere

---

"Adjunct professors were weak on the whole."

The 411

Program length: 22 months

Workload: 9 hours per week in class; 25 hours per week outside of class

Total program cost: $135,000

Housing provided for EMBA students: Yes

Distance from major airport: 19 miles

Access to health club for EMBA students: Yes

Classes begin: September

Application deadline: June 15

Application fee: $150

Cliff Notes

Leading areas of study: Finance, General Management, International Business, Marketing, Strategy

Concentrations/specializations: None

Joint-degree programs: None

Average class size, core courses: 57

Average class size, electives: 29

Number of electives: 27

Teaching methods: Case studies (30%), team projects (30%), lectures (25%)

But What's It *Really* Like?

Graded by EMBA directors:
Overall: **A+**

Program quality, graded by students:
Overall: **A**
Teaching quality: **A**
Caliber of classmates: **B**
Housing: **A**
Logistics: **A**
Support: **A**

Curriculum, graded by students:
Overall: **A+**
E-business: **B**
Entrepreneurship: **A**
Ethics: **A**
Finance: **B**
International business: **B**
Marketing: **A**
Strategy: **C**
Teamwork: **A**

Prominent Faculty

Janice C. Eberly: Finance
Lakshman Krishnamurthi: Marketing
Sergio Rebelo: Finance

 The Good, the Bad, and the Ugly: Students Speak Out

"This was a life-changing experience. In almost every class there were 'aha moments'—even in subjects that I was very knowledgeable about."

"In almost every class there were 'aha moments.'"

"Kellogg's EMBA program is everything it's advertised to be and then some. I couldn't be happier with the caliber of classmates and faculty in the program, and there has never been a moment when I questioned whether I had selected the correct program to attend. It was a huge personal sacrifice to pursue an executive MBA, but I would do it all over again if I could go to Kellogg."

"Instructors were excellent in terms of their knowledge, ability to engage the class, and focus upon the important topics. Adjunct professors were weak on the whole."

"The combination of excellent people and a well-rounded curriculum gave me the knowledge I needed to move to the next level in my career. . . . The Kellogg program makes you work in your study group a lot, which mirrors the real world. It takes a lot to coordinate and make your team work to the best of its ability, just like in the real world. Priceless."

"We did not have enough time in the classroom to fully develop many analytical frameworks and apply them to our work-life situations. Better management of class time as a whole could really help to create a more in-depth dive down instead of what felt like a 'for dummies' blow through on many subjects. Overall, as a business undergraduate and someone who has been running a company for 15 years, I felt that a few classes were simply retreads of undergraduate intro classes that I had when I was 23. Having paid $120,000 of my own money, I expected better."

"Excellent people and a well-rounded curriculum."

 **Where to Stay**

Omni Orrington
1710 Orrington Ave.
Evanston, IL 60201
(847) 866-1248

Hilton Garden Inn
1818 Maple Ave.
Evanston, IL 60201
(847) 475-6400

Best Western University Plaza
1501 Sherman Ave.
Evanston, IL 60201
(800) 381-2830

 Where to Eat

Tommy Nevins Pub
1450-1458 Sherman Ave.
Evanston, IL 60201
(847) 869-0450

Koi
624 Davis St.
Evanston, IL 60201
(847) 866-6969

Prairie Moon
1502 Sherman Ave.
Evanston, IL 60201
(847) 864-8328

 Things to Do

Chicago Botanical Garden
1000 Lake Cook Rd.
Glencoe, IL 60022
(847) 835-5440

Architectural Tours (with the Chicago Architecture Foundation)
224 S. Michigan Ave.
Chicago, IL 60604
(312) 922-3432 x241

CHECK OUT BUSINESSWEEK.COM FOR MORE:

Expanded Profile: Still curious? Find out if Kellogg is right for you by checking out its expanded EMBA profile online.

Video View: Hear what Dean Dipak Jain has to say about the improving job market for MBAs.

Admissions Q&A: Admissions Director Beth Flye discusses Kellogg's holistic approach to education and the school's culture.

Placement Q&A: Those looking to change careers can find out how the career resources center prepares students for the future.

School Tour: Check out Northwestern's Evanston campus before applying.

Search & Compare: Conduct a side-by-side analysis of Kellogg's executive MBA and other top EMBA programs.

Access all the B-schools content on BusinessWeek.com by subscribing to MBA Insider.

Ohio State University

Max M. Fisher College of Business
2007 Ranking: 14
110 Pfahl Hall
280 W. Woodruff Ave.
Columbus, OH 43210
E-mail address: MBA@fisher.osu.edu
Web address: www.fisher.osu.edu/
  prospective/graduate/emba
For more info: Call the EMBA office at
  (614) 292-9300

✓ B4UGO

Applicants accepted: 88%
GMAT: Not required
Average years' work experience: 13.4
Average base salary: $115,000

Why Ohio State?

Ohio State is one of the least expensive top-ranked EMBA programs, making it especially attractive for students who are not sponsored by their companies. But it's far from a no-frills program. The integrative curriculum includes a series of team-taught courses designed to approach business problems from multiple perspectives. The class is divided into teams specifically designed to complete team projects as a cross-functional unit. A global integration course focusing on the international dimension of business problems and a required international experience in January of the second year round out the program.

The once-a-month format (Thursday through Saturday) combined with a distance learning component makes the program manageable for busy executives who might not have the time for the standard alternate weekend format of many EMBA programs. And the GMAT test is not required. The vast majority of students come from the Midwest, with nearly half living within 45 miles of the school.

Ohio State is a public institution. Established in 1999, Fisher's executive MBA program is accredited by the Association to Advance Collegiate Schools of Business (AACSB). Fisher also offers full-time and part-time MBA programs. For details on Fisher's full-time MBA program, see page 81. For details on its part-time MBA program, see page 361.

Who Are My Classmates?

Executive MBA enrollment: 99
Women: 22%
International: 4%
Minority: 9%
Average age: 36

"Brilliant and challenging professors."

Where Do They Come From?

Work background: 9% have the title of president, chairman, or CEO; 7% work at organizations with 100 or fewer employees; 13% work in the nonprofit sector
Percentage with advanced degrees: 9
Percentage who live within 45 miles of school: 43
Top functional areas: Finance/Accounting (26%), Marketing/Sales (20%), Consulting (18%)
Top employers: Ashland, Nationwide Insurance, Murray Energy, Cardinal Health, General Electric

---

"The program allows only three electives."

The 411

Program length: 18 months
Workload: 6 hours per week in class; 20 hours per week outside of class
Total program cost: $64,900
Housing provided for EMBA students: Yes
Distance from major airport: 15 miles
Access to health club for EMBA students: Yes
Classes begin: January
Application deadline: September 30
Application fee: $60 before June 30, $200 after

Cliff Notes

Leading areas of study: Accounting, Finance, Marketing, Strategy, Supply Chain
Concentrations/specializations: None
Joint-degree programs: None
Average class size, core courses: 54
Average class size, electives: 54
Number of electives: 132
Teaching methods: Case studies (25%), distance learning (25%), team projects (25%)

But What's It *Really* Like?

Graded by EMBA directors:
Overall: C

Program quality, graded by students:
Overall: A
Teaching quality: A
Caliber of classmates: B
Housing: B
Logistics: A+
Support: B

Curriculum, graded by students:
Overall: B
E-business: A
Entrepreneurship: A
Ethics: B
Finance: A
International business: B
Marketing: B
Strategy: A+
Teamwork: B

Prominent Faculty

Jay Barney: Entrepreneurship, Management, Agency Theory
Roy Lewicki: Executive Leadership, Ethics
Anil Makhija: Corporate Finance, Privatization Strategies

 ## The Good, the Bad, and the Ugly: Students Speak Out

"The faculty has an excellent ability to weave together the various disciplines during classroom discussion. Faculty members also have a great strength in bringing their real-world experience [into the classroom] and drawing out the experience of the class."

"The administrative staff supporting the program was weak. At times it felt like they weren't able to help, or were unwilling."

"A fantastic holistic experience."

"The work-life balance was important to me with a young child, and this program made it very easy for me to interact directly with colleagues fully when on campus, to travel to classes upon relocating midprogram, and to spend adequate time with my family."

"In statistics and accounting, the professors overemphasized calculations rather than analysis. Few EMBAs are going to crunch the numbers—their job will be more to understand and analyze them—so that was a mild disappointment to me."

"It was a business experience that gave me knowledge about all aspects of all types of companies. This was combined with the high experience level of my fellow students for a fantastic holistic experience."

"The classroom experience could be improved through more experiences and less instruction. Although discussion was welcomed, many times it was silenced before the real value was extracted."

"Highly motivated and successful classmates and brilliant and challenging professors combined with outstanding facilities far exceeded my expectations. My mind was expanded, my thought processes were challenged, and my overall knowledge of the business world was significantly increased on many fronts."

"More electives [would be an improvement]; the program allows only three electives."

"The quality of the professors and students at Ohio State exceeded even my wildest expectations."

 **Where to Stay**

The Blackwell
2110 Tuttle Park Pl.
Columbus, OH 43210
(614) 247-4000

University Plaza Hotel & Conference Center
3110 Olentangy River Rd.
Columbus, OH 43202
(614) 267-7461

Fairfield Inn and Suites
3031 Olentangy River Rd.
Columbus, OH 43202
(614) 267-1111

 Where to Eat

The Buckeye Hall of Fame Café
1421 Olentangy River Rd.
Columbus, OH 43212
(614) 291-2233

The Happy Greek
1554 N. High St.
Columbus, OH 43201
(614) 291-7777

Bistro 2110
2110 Tuttle Park Pl.
Columbus, OH 43210
(614) 247-4000

 Things to Do

Wexner Center for the Arts
1871 N. High St.
Columbus, OH 43201
(614) 292-3535

Union Station Video Café
630 N. High St.
Columbus, OH 43201
(614) 228-3546

CHECK OUT BUSINESSWEEK.COM FOR MORE:

Expanded Profile: Find more facts, statistics, and student comments in Ohio State's online EMBA profile.

Search & Compare: See how Ohio State stacks up against other EMBA programs you're considering.

Sample Application Essays: How to ace the essay portion of the Ohio State application.

Access all the B-schools content on BusinessWeek.com by subscribing to MBA Insider.

Queen's University

Queen's School of Business
2007 Ranking: 23
Goodes Hall
Kingston, ON (Canada) K7L 3N6
E-mail address:
    execmba@business.queensu.ca
Web address: www.execmba.com/
    national
For more info: Call the EMBA office at
    (613) 533-6811

Why Queen's?

Rejecting the one-size-fits-all approach, Queen's newly revised EMBA curriculum allows for more customization than most other programs provide, and a few other bells and whistles besides. To start, students may specialize in finance, strategic marketing, or global business. Using an innovative assessment tool, they may also create a customized package of coaching and development activities to bolster their strengths and mitigate their weaknesses as leaders. In the classroom, they get an integrated approach—learning how to use multiple tools to solve multidimensional problems. And they learn crucial teamwork and leadership skills as part of teams that last for the duration of the program.

The Queen's EMBA runs for 15 months, with campuses in Toronto, Calgary, Vancouver, Edmonton, and Montréal. While the program includes three on-campus sessions totaling just over five weeks, 60% of classes are conducted through videoconferencing. These remote classes are held every other week and take place all day Friday and Saturday morning.

Queen's School of Business is a private institution. Established in 1992, the Queen's executive MBA program is accredited by the Association to Advance Collegiate Schools of Business (AACSB). Queen's also offers a full-time program. For details on Queen's full-time MBA program, see page 93.

☑ B4UGO

Applicants accepted: N/A
Average GMAT score: 586
Average years' work experience: 14.3
Average base salary: $123,800

 Who Are My Classmates?

Executive MBA enrollment: 301
Women: 32%
International: 23%
Minority: N/A
Average age: 38

"Faculty, course material, and curriculum are fantastic."

Where Do They Come From?

Work background: 8% have the title of president, chairman, or CEO; 1% work in the nonprofit sector

Percentage with advanced degrees: 11

Percentage who live within 45 miles of school: 30

Top industries: Technology (26%), Financial services (19%), Government (18%), Manufacturing (17%), Pharmaceutical/Biotechnology (7%)

Top employers: Royal Bank of Canada, Bell Canada, Government of Canada, Nortel, Ballard Power Systems

___

"International exposure should be mandatory."

___

The 411

Program length: 15 months

Workload: 6 hours per week in class; 19 hours per week outside of class

Total program cost: $69,000

Housing provided for EMBA students: Yes

Distance from major airport: 10 miles

Access to health club for EMBA students: Yes

Classes begin: August

Application deadline: None

Application fee: None

Cliff Notes

Leading areas of study: Corporate Social Responsibility, Entrepreneurship, International Business, Leadership, Strategy

Concentrations/specializations: Finance, Strategic Marketing, Global Business

Joint-degree programs: None

Average class size, core courses: 120

Average class size, electives: 40

Number of electives: 8

Teaching methods: N/A

But What's It *Really* Like?

Graded by EMBA directors:
Overall: B

Program quality, graded by students:
Overall: B
Teaching quality: A
Caliber of classmates: B
Housing: A
Logistics: A
Support: A

Curriculum, graded by students:
Overall: A
E-business: B
Entrepreneurship: B
Ethics: B
Finance: B
International business: C
Marketing: B
Strategy: B
Teamwork: B

Prominent Faculty

Julian Barling: Human Resources
Elspeth Murray: Strategy and New Ventures
Ken Wong: Marketing Strategy

 The Good, the Bad, and the Ugly: Students Speak Out

"Everything about the Queen's program is outstanding. A great deal of thought is applied to building complete teams that can work together to achieve superior results. The faculty, the course material, and the overall curriculum are fantastic."

"Other schools might provide similar skills at much lower fees."

"I attended a voluntary international one-week conference for EMBA students. International exposure was invaluable and should be a mandatory part of the program."

"Queen's provided a unique learning environment that challenged students to work both independently and as part of a team. Although the workload was very demanding, I strongly believe that I am leaving this program with a toolkit of skills that will enable me to excel at future roles within my organization.

Top-quality professors and classmates with diverse backgrounds further added to this valuable experience."

"It was a great program, but if I hadn't wanted to complete the program in 15 months, other schools might have provided me with similar skills at much lower fees."

"I was consistently impressed with the quality of the professors in the program. Each of the professors had an active practice or current expertise in their area of instruction. The program managed all of the small stuff, allowing me to focus on the curriculum."

"Since my profession is in financial services, I would have liked a couple more advanced finance courses."

"The experiences shared by my classmates and professors were excellent, and the support from the coordinators made the MBA a great experience. The fact that the program was short and allowed full-time work was crucial in managing time to complete an MBA. My teammates were amazing— the projects we worked on, the contacts they brought in, and the experiences they shared."

"The Queen's EMBA program was invaluable. I was able to use work business issues as team projects and then implement the team recommendations back into our company. This brought value to the team work and provided immediate benefits to my organization."

 **Where to Stay**

Radisson Hotel Kingston Harbourfront
1 Johnson St.
Kingston, ON K7L 5H7
(613) 549-8100

Holiday Inn Kingston—Waterfront
2 Princess St.
Kingston, ON K7L 1A2
(613) 549-8400

The Queen's Inn
125 Brock St.
Kingston, ON K7L 1S1
(613) 546-0429

 Where to Eat

Kingston Brewing Company
34 Clarence St.
Kingston, ON K7L 1W9
(613) 542-4978

Chez Piggy
68-R Princess St.
Kingston, ON K7L 1A5
(613) 549-7673

Wooden Heads
192 Ontario St.
Kingston, ON K7L 2Y8
(613) 549-1812

 Things to Do

Time to Laugh Comedy Club
394 Princess St.
Kingston, ON K7L 5N3
(613) 542-5233

Kingston 1000 Islands Cruises
263 Ontario St.
Kingston, ON K7K 2X5
(613) 549-5544

CHECK OUT BUSINESSWEEK.COM FOR MORE:

Expanded Profile: For more details on the Queen's EMBA program, check out its expanded online profile.

Search & Compare: Find out how the Queen's executive MBA stacks up against other top EMBA programs.

Access all the B-schools content on BusinessWeek.com by subscribing to MBA Insider.

Southern Methodist University

Edwin L. Cox School of Business
2007 Ranking: 11
P.O. Box 750507
Dallas, TX 75275-0507
E-mail address:
mbainfo@mail.cox.smu.edu
Web address: www.cox.smu.edu/grad/
mba/emba
For more info: Call EMBA information
at (214) 768-3154

☑ B4UGO

Applicants accepted: 56%
Average GMAT score: N/A
Average years' work experience: 15
Average base salary: $118,412

Why SMU?

Consistently ranked in *BusinessWeek*'s top tier, the 21-month SMU Cox EMBA program is structured much like any EMBA program: the first half gives students some basic business tools, and the second half focuses on using them. But that's where the similarity ends. Cox uses a "cohort" system that requires students to move through the program as a group—a format more common among full-time MBA programs—creating a tight-knit class. The usual classes in management, finance, and strategy are supplemented by opportunities to present business plans to venture capitalists and two international trips to Latin America and Asia.

Cox prides itself on attracting students with diverse backgrounds. They average 10 years of management experience, among the most for *Business-Week*'s top 25, and include people with business backgrounds and also physicians, architects, and attorneys. Every-

thing, from carefully crafted study groups to the classrooms themselves, is designed to foster peer-to-peer learning.

SMU is a private institution. Established in 1976, Cox's executive MBA program is accredited by the Association to Advance Collegiate Schools of Business (AACSB). Cox also offers full-time and part-time MBA programs. For details on the Cox part-time MBA program, see page 369.

 Who Are My Classmates?

Executive MBA enrollment: 168
Women: 22%
International: 27%
Minority: 37%
Average age: 36

"Finance, marketing, and accounting are cornerstone strengths."

Where Do They Come From?

Work background: 2% have the title of president, chairman, or CEO; 10% work at organizations with 100 or fewer employees; 1% work in the nonprofit sector

Percentage with advanced degrees: 15

Percentage who live within 45 miles of school: 99

Top functional areas: General Management (21%), Operations/Logistics (21%), Marketing/Sales (16%)

Top employers: Texas Instruments, IBM, Fannie Mae, Verizon, Alcatel

---

"The administrative staff was excellent."

The 411

Program length: 21 months

Workload: 8 hours per week in class; 20 hours per week outside of class

Total program cost: $84,135

Housing provided for EMBA students: No

Distance from major airport: 5 miles

Access to health club for EMBA students: Yes

Classes begin: August

Application deadline: May 31

Application fee: $100

Cliff Notes

Leading areas of study: Entrepreneurship, Finance, Leadership, Marketing, Strategy

Concentrations/specializations: None

Joint-degree programs: None

Average class size, core courses: 95

Average class size, electives: 95

Number of electives: 1

Teaching methods: Lectures (50%), case studies (20%), experiential learning (10%), team projects (10%)

But What's It *Really* Like?

Graded by EMBA directors:
Overall: **A**

Program quality, graded by students:
Overall: **A+**
Teaching quality: **A**
Caliber of classmates: **B**
Housing: **B**
Logistics: **A+**
Support: **B**

Curriculum, graded by students:
Overall: **A+**
E-business: **A+**
Entrepreneurship: **A+**
Ethics: **A**
Finance: **A+**
International business: **A+**
Marketing: **A+**
Strategy: **B**
Teamwork: **A**

Prominent Faculty

Jeff Allen: Finance and M&A
Bill Dillon: Marketing Research
Tassu Shervani: Global Marketing

 The Good, the Bad, and the Ugly: Students Speak Out

"Seasoned and talented faculty, vast industrial experience of fellow students, brand-new teaching facility with latest technology, and a cohort-type system creating a good networking opportunity are some of the reasons why I would choose the same school again."

"Not everyone works for a Fortune 100 company. I think more time could have been spent on how to manage and grow a smaller company."

"More time could have been spent on how to manage a smaller company."

"Great program. I view finance, marketing, and accounting as cornerstone strengths of SMU. As a commuting student, IT technology adoption for extra review sessions would help me."

"SMU needs more leadership development and human resources classes. We had a fabulous professor for human resources, but with only one class allocated to this, we barely scratched the surface, and HR is applicable to everyone."

"I have developed a great relationship with many alumni in the community in addition to my classmates. Initially, I was shocked at the caliber of the people in my classes. I am very proud to have such close ties with my classmates. The administrative staff who facilitated all the logistical aspects of the program was excellent. They truly helped me focus on the important things."

"Improved career planning and assistance with exploring job opportunities [would help]. The EMBA program is very reluctant to offer any real help in this regard, since there is a concern that companies will stop sponsoring students into the program."

"Instructors leveraged a tremendous amount of real-world experience in their given specialties. The connection of theory and practical application accelerated my ability to leverage my new knowledge immediately within the workplace."

Where to Stay

Radisson Hotel
6060 N. Central Expy.
Dallas, TX 75206
(214) 750-6060

Doubletree—Campbell Center
8250 N. Central Expy.
Dallas, TX 75206
(214) 691-8700

Hilton Park Cities
5954 Luther Ln.
Dallas, TX 75225
(214) 368-0400

 Where to Eat

Peggy Sue BBQ
6600 Snider Plaza
Dallas, TX 75205
(214) 987-9188

Kuby's Sausage House
6601 Snider Plaza
Dallas, TX 75205
(214) 363-2231

Trinity Hall Irish Pub & Restaurant
5321 E. Mockingbird Ln.
Dallas, TX 75206
(214) 887-3600

 Things to Do

Dallas Museum of Art
1717 N. Hardwood St.
Dallas, TX 75201
(214) 922-1200

Addison Improv Comedy Club
4890 Belt Line Rd.
Dallas, TX 75254
(972) 404-8501

CHECK OUT BUSINESSWEEK.COM FOR MORE:

Admissions Q&A: Admissions Director Patti Cudney discusses why SMU looks for students who want to be part of a collaborative environment.

Sample Application Essays: Read these essays for pointers on how to ace the essay portion of the SMU application.

Video View: Dean Al Niemi explains why Dallas is a great place for executive education.

Expanded Profile: More facts and student comments on the SMU EMBA program.

Search & Compare: Directly compare SMU with your other top-choice schools.

School Tour: Considering Cox? Scroll through these photos of the SMU campus first.

Access all the B-schools content on BusinessWeek.com by subscribing to MBA Insider.

Thunderbird

Thunderbird School of Global
Management
2007 Ranking: 22
15249 N. 59th Ave.
Glendale, AZ 85306-6000
E-mail address: emba@t-bird.edu
Web address: www.thunderbird.edu/
For more info: Call the EMBA office at
(602) 978-7384

Why Thunderbird?

A lot of EMBA programs offer a one-week trip abroad and call themselves "global," but Thunderbird really is. The 16-month curriculum is punctuated by two global trips—five days in Mexico and ten days in Asia or Europe—but the international aspects of the program don't end there. The 51 credits required to complete the degree are split between world business and international studies, with business staples such as finance and marketing taught alongside politics and cross-cultural communications. And it's the only U.S.-based program that requires proficiency in a language other than English. Instruction in Chinese, French, Portuguese, and Spanish is offered.

Classes are taught on Fridays and Saturdays on alternating weekends, with two one-week residencies on the Glendale campus required. Students average about 12 years of work experience, including 6 in management. While most come from the Phoenix metro

✓ **B4UGO**

Applicants accepted: 78%
GMAT: Not required
Average years' work experience: 12
Average base salary: $115,000

area, non-U.S. citizens or dual citizens make up about 30% of each class.

Thunderbird is a private institution. Established in 1991, Thunderbird's executive MBA program is accredited by the Association to Advance Collegiate Schools of Business (AACSB), the European Quality Improvement System (EQUIS), and the North Central Association of Colleges and Schools (NCA). Thunderbird also offers a full-time MBA. For details on Thunderbird's full-time MBA program, see page 101.

 Who Are My Classmates?

Executive MBA enrollment: 83
Women: 25%
International: 25%
Minority: 47%
Average age: 37

"The biweekly weekend format was ideal."

Where Do They Come From?

Work background: 8% have the title of president, chairman, or CEO; 19% work at organizations with 100 or fewer employees; 4% work in the nonprofit sector

Percentage with advanced degrees: 19

Percentage who live within 45 miles of school: 68

Top functional areas: General Management (23%), Marketing/Sales (23%), Operations/Logistics (18%)

Top employers: Intel, Honeywell, American Express, Cox Communications, IBM

"There could have been more emphasis on leadership and ethics."

The 411

Program length: 16 months

Workload: 16 hours per week in class (every other week); 20 hours per week outside of class

Total program cost: $67,000

Housing provided for EMBA students: Yes

Distance from major airport: 25 miles

Access to health club for EMBA students: Yes

Classes begin: August

Application deadline: May 15

Application fee: $125

Cliff Notes

Leading areas of study: International Business, International Political Economy, Leadership, Marketing, Strategy

Concentrations/specializations: None

Joint-degree programs: None

Average class size, core courses: 49

Average class size, electives: N/A

Number of electives: None

Teaching methods: Case studies (50%), team projects (17%), lectures (13%)

But What's It *Really* Like?

Graded by EMBA directors:
Overall: B

Program quality, graded by students:
Overall: A+
Teaching quality: A
Caliber of classmates: A+
Housing: A+
Logistics: B
Support: A

Curriculum, graded by students:
Overall: B
E-business: A
Entrepreneurship: B
Ethics: A
Finance: B
International business: A+
Marketing: A+
Strategy: A
Teamwork: A

Prominent Faculty

Dale Davison: Accounting
Sundaresan Ram: International Marketing
Mary Teagarden: Global Strategy

 ### The Good, the Bad, and the Ugly: Students Speak Out

"The lockstep biweekly weekend format of the program was ideal, the experience/caliber of the professors was high, and the interactive and participative aspects allowed me to form close lifelong relationships with my student colleagues."

"I liked the international focus, excellent library facilities, administrative staff, and the quality of our faculty and the students."

"Although I am very satisfied with the experience, there could have been more multimedia, and more emphasis on leadership and ethics."

"Professors were knowledgeable and passionate."

"Thunderbird provides the same education as any other top-notch MBA program, but with a global twist.

Thunderbird has prepared me to conduct business with a cultural mindset."

"The professors were extremely knowledgeable and passionate about what they were teaching. The program was very challenging and was a good combination of real-world applications and theory."

"I would like to see more emphasis on language training. The language training during the first two trimesters was outstanding. I studied Mandarin Chinese and really learned a lot. However, after the second trimester, the language training stopped; it should have continued throughout the program. With languages, you 'use it or lose it.' One of the distinguishing features of the Thunderbird experience is the language aspect, and that should continue in all five trimesters."

"At my age and stage of my career, the next challenge is a world becoming 'flatter' by the day. The new challenges of communication, negotiation, and management across frontiers and cultures require leadership knowledge with a global perspective. Only a premier program such as Thunderbird could provide me with the experience and education relevant to this challenge. The quality and depth of teachers' knowledge is paramount in the success of this program."

 **Where to Stay**

Thunderbird Executive Inn
15249 N. 59th Ave.
Glendale, AZ 85306
(602) 978-7987

Quality Inn & Suites at Talavi
5511 W. Bell Rd.
Glendale, AZ 85308
(602) 896-8900

Ramada Limited Glendale
7885 W. Arrowhead Towne Ctr. Dr.
Glendale, AZ 85308
(623) 412-2000

 Where to Eat

Caramba Fresh Mexican Food
6661 W. Bell Rd. #104
Glendale, AZ 85308
(623) 487-1111

Chevy's Fresh Mex
7700 W. Arrowhead Towne Ctr. Dr.
Glendale, AZ 85308
(623) 979-0055

Mythos Greek Restaurant
2515 N. Scottsdale Rd.
Scottsdale, AZ 85257
(408) 947-6896

 Things to Do

Sahuaro Ranch Park Historical Area
9802 N. 59th Ave.
Glendale, AZ 85302
(623) 930-4200

Cerreta Candy Company
5345 W. Glendale Ave.
Glendale, AZ 85301
(623) 930-9000

CHECK OUT BUSINESSWEEK.COM FOR MORE:

Expanded Profile: For more details on Thunderbird's EMBA program, check out its expanded online profile.

Search & Compare: Find out how Thunderbird's executive MBA stacks up against other top EMBA programs.

School Tour: Thinking of visiting the Glendale campus? Take an advance look with this online photo essay.

Video View: President Angel Cabrera talks about his plans for Thunderbird.

Access all the B-schools content on BusinessWeek.com by subscribing to MBA Insider.

U. of California at Los Angeles

John E. Anderson Graduate School of
  Management
2007 Ranking: 8
110 Westwood Plaza, Suite A101F
Box 951481
Los Angeles, CA 90095
E-mail address:
  emba.admissions@anderson.ucla.edu
Web address: www.anderson.ucla.edu/
  x310.xml
For more info: Call the EMBA office at
  (310) 825-2032

Why UCLA?

UCLA has had a top-tier EMBA program since 2001 by offering students a
challenging curriculum and top-flight
faculty, most of whom also teach in
Anderson's top-ranked full-time program.
But what makes the EMBA program
unique is the quality of the students who
attend. With nearly 13 years' experience
and GMAT scores above 650, Anderson's
EMBA students are a highly qualified
group. The program itself focuses on
global business—year two concludes with
an international seminar at a location of
the student's own choosing—and leadership skills, which are taught through
courses, presentations, and lectures by distinguished CEOs.

The curriculum builds up to a six-
month field study in which teams of students use the skills they've learned to
develop a business strategy for a real company. Anderson also offers unique electives that include game theory, role of the

☑ B4UGO

Applicants accepted: N/A
Average GMAT score: 655
Average years' work experience: 12.9
Average base salary: $154,000

general manager, and thinking on your
feet. The program lasts 22 months, and
students take classes on an alternate
weekend schedule.

UCLA is a public institution. Established in 1981, Anderson's executive
MBA program is accredited by the
Association to Advance Collegiate
Schools of Business (AACSB). Anderson also offers full-time and part-time
MBA programs. For details on Anderson's full-time MBA program, see page
117. For details on its part-time MBA
program, see page 373.

Who Are My Classmates?

Executive MBA enrollment: 139
Women: 20%
International: 24%
Minority: 34%
Average age: 37

*"The quality of the
education was
exceptional."*

Where Do They Come From?

Work background: 4% have the title of president, chairman, or CEO; 13% work at organizations with 100 or fewer employees; 8% work in the nonprofit sector
Percentage with advanced degrees: 32
Percentage who live within 45 miles of school: 59
Top functional areas: Management Information Systems (19%), General Management (13%), Finance/Accounting (11%)
Top employers: Amgen, Johnson & Johnson, Nicholas Applegate, Qualcomm, Northrop Grumman

---

"Some instructors did not provide any formal instruction."

The 411

Program length: 22 months
Workload: 15 hours per week in class; 20 hours per week outside of class
Total program cost: $95,116
Housing provided for EMBA students: Yes
Distance from major airport: 10 miles
Access to health club for EMBA students: Yes
Classes begin: September
Application deadline: April 1
Application fee: $175

Cliff Notes

Leading areas of study: Entrepreneurship, Finance, General Management, Leadership, Media/Entertainment
Concentrations/specializations: General Management
Joint-degree programs: None
Average class size, core courses: 70
Average class size, electives: 30
Number of electives: 12
Teaching methods: Case studies (25%), experiential learning (25%), lectures (25%)

But What's It *Really* Like?

Graded by EMBA directors:
Overall: A

Program quality, graded by students:
Overall: A+
Teaching quality: A+
Caliber of classmates: A+
Housing: A+
Logistics: C
Support: A

Curriculum, graded by students:
Overall: A
E-business: A+
Entrepreneurship: A+
Ethics: B
Finance: A+
International business: A
Marketing: A+
Strategy: B
Teamwork: A

Prominent Faculty

Antonio Bernardo: Finance
Edward Leamer: Management
Carol Scott: Marketing

 ### The Good, the Bad, and the Ugly: Students Speak Out

"The quality of the education delivered by the faculty was exceptional. The program environment was intense and has been unmatched in both my work and my academic life. The instructors were very knowledgeable and cutting edge in their fields. The Anderson program has helped hone my leadership instincts and has better prepared me for executive-level positions. It has given me confidence in my ability to execute at all levels of my organization."

"The noncore elective courses could have had stronger professors, [and] the curriculum could be better integrated and laid out."

> ### *"I was blown away by the quality of the faculty."*

"The school did a great job in giving students with limited time, like me, the support we needed. Based on my new job responsibilities as an officer of a public company, it was very difficult for me to balance work and school, but this was one of the best experiences of my life."

> ### *"The program is very demanding."*

"Some instructors used a pure case-based approach to teaching and did not provide any formal instruction. This was not good. Cases are meant to supplement lecture material."

"I really liked the way the program was structured—the various skill sets were very well balanced, there were great elective choices, and the administrative staff was so on top of everything that we didn't have to worry about anything except our class work. I was blown away by the quality of the faculty. Each quarter I thought to myself, 'There's no way the next set of professors is going to be as good as this quarter', but in the end there wasn't a single professor who disappointed."

"The program is very demanding and requires a significant investment of time. Studying or team assignments often required 25 to 30 hours per week outside of the classroom."

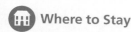 **Where to Stay**

UCLA Guest House
330 Charles E. Young Dr. E.
Los Angeles, CA 90095
(310) 825-2923

Luxe Hotel Sunset Boulevard
11461 Sunset Blvd.
Los Angeles, CA 90049
(310) 476-6571

W Hotel Los Angeles–Westwood
930 Hilgard Ave.
Los Angeles, CA 90024
(310) 208-8765

 Where to Eat

Westwood Brewing Co.
1097 Glendon Ave.
Los Angeles, CA 90024
(310) 209-2739

Napa Valley Grille
1100 Glendon Ave.
Los Angeles, CA 90024
(310) 824-3322

In-N-Out Burger
922 Gayley Ave.
Los Angeles, CA 90024
(800) 786-1000

 Things to Do

Mildred E. Mathias Botanical Garden
777 Tiverton Ave.
Los Angeles, CA 90095
(310) 206-6707

Geffen Playhouse
10886 Le Conte Ave.
Los Angeles, CA 90024
(310) 208-5454

CHECK OUT BUSINESSWEEK.COM FOR MORE:

Expanded Profile: Still undecided? Go to Anderson's expanded EMBA profile online for more facts, statistics, and insights.

Search & Compare: Use this interactive tool to see how Anderson stacks up against other top EMBA programs.

Best Schools by Specialty: Find out why Anderson is tops in marketing and entrepreneurship.

Sample Application Essays and Interview Tips: Get the lowdown on what it takes to get in.

Video View: Dean Judy Olian discusses trends in the MBA world and how they're playing out at UCLA.

Access all the B-schools content on BusinessWeek.com by subscribing to MBA Insider.

University of Chicago

Graduate School of Business
2007 Ranking: 3
450 N. Cityfront Plaza Dr.
Chicago, IL 60611
E-mail address: xp@chicagogsb.edu
Web address: www.chicagogsb.edu/
execmba
For more info: Call the EMBA office at
(312) 464-8750

☑ B4UGO

Applicants accepted: N/A
GMAT: Not required
Average years' work experience: 16
Average base salary: $127,545*
*Estimate based on *BusinessWeek* survey data.

Why Chicago?

Chicago's EMBA takes a deep approach that studies business fundamentals within the context of related academic disciplines such as sociology, economics, and statistics. GSB aims to produce students armed with strong analytical and problem-solving abilities by developing a range of perspectives that allows students to delve right into the heart of business issues. With more Nobel Prizes sprinkled among its faculty than any other business school, students can expect to receive a quant-heavy education in an intellectually stimulating environment.

GSB offers a global experience, with permanent campuses in Chicago, London, and Singapore, and students can expect to study at all three campuses during the course of the program regardless of their primary campus. Students in London and Singapore take classes in one-week periods, while those in Chicago have an alternate-weekend schedule with four weeklong sessions.

The University of Chicago is a private institution. Established in 1943, GSB's executive MBA program is accredited by the Association to Advance Collegiate Schools of Business (AACSB). GSB also offers full-time and part-time MBA programs. For details on GSB's full-time MBA program, see page 125. For details on its part-time MBA program, see page 377.

 Who Are My Classmates?

Executive MBA enrollment: 180
Women: 28%
International: 13%
Minority: 32%
Average age: 38

"The faculty was incredibly responsive and accessible."

Where Do They Come From?

Percentage with advanced degrees: 24
Percentage who work in the nonprofit sector: 5
Percentage who live within 45 miles of school: 60
Top functional areas: Marketing/Sales (18%), Finance (12%), Operations/Logistics (12%)
Top industries: Financial services (23%), Consulting (12%), Pharmaceuticals/Biotechnology (10%), Technology (8%), Manufacturing (8%)

> ### *"The international part of the program was fantastic."*

The 411

Program length: 21 months
Workload: 12 hours per week in class; 15–20 hours per week outside of class
Total program cost: $120,000
Housing provided for EMBA students: No
Distance from major airport: 20 miles
Access to health club for EMBA students: Yes
Classes begin: June
Application deadline: April
Application fee: $100

Cliff Notes

Leading area of study: General Management
Concentrations/specializations: None
Joint-degree programs: None
Average class size, core courses: 90
Average class size, electives: 50
Number of electives: 12
Teaching methods: Case studies, lectures, team projects

But What's It *Really* Like?

Graded by EMBA directors:
Overall: A+

Program quality, graded by students:
Overall: B
Teaching quality: A+
Caliber of classmates: A
Housing: C
Logistics: B
Support: C

Curriculum, graded by students:
Overall: B
E-business: A
Entrepreneurship: B
Ethics: C
Finance: A+
International business: A
Marketing: B
Strategy: B
Teamwork: B

Prominent Faculty

Marianne Bertrand: Competitive Strategy
Ronald Burt: Strategic Leadership
Mark Zmijewski: Financial Analysis and Strategy

 The Good, the Bad, and the Ugly: Students Speak Out

"Chicago GSB provided a true MBA, rather than a watered-down version [of a full-time MBA]. All the professors were leaders in their respective fields."

"I have a hard time believing that the quality of this program could be surpassed. This was a life-altering event for me. As a political science major in undergraduate school, I always felt I was missing a lot of the tools I needed to succeed further in business. The GSB gave me the tools I need, but just as importantly, it gave me a lot more confidence. It was just a great experience."

"The pace could have been slower."

"Twenty-one months of every other weekend causes the program to be very fast-paced. It would have been nice if the pace could have been slower."

"The academics and student community were as great as I expected. What I didn't expect was how accessible the faculty would be. I am meeting a professor this week to help me with a problem—this more than two months after leaving the program. They were phenomenal and incredibly responsive and accessible. I had no idea that University of Chicago professors would spend that much time on me, especially when I asked questions out of the mainstream of the class topics."

"All professors were leaders in their respective fields."

"Some professors whose backgrounds were only in academia were uneasy with many of the real-world situations the class injected into their lectures. . . . Administration was a bit disorganized in the beginning and not very 'customer focused.'"

"The professors for the EMBA program are experienced, well trained, terrifically motivated, and passionate instructors who also teach in the full-time program. We did not get third-string professors."

"It exceeded my expectations in every way. The international part of the program was fantastic."

 **Where to Stay**

Hotel Sax Chicago
333 Dearborn St.
Chicago, IL 60610
(312) 245-0333

Hard Rock Hotel
230 N. Michigan Ave.
Chicago, IL 60601
(312) 345-1000

International House
1414 E. 59th St.
Chicago, IL 60637
(773) 753-2270

 Where to Eat

La Petite Folie
1504 E. 55th St.
Chicago, IL 60615
(773) 493-1394

Opera
1301 S. Wabash
Chicago, IL 60605
(312) 461-0161

Medici on 57th
1327 E. 57th St.
Chicago, IL 60637
(773) 667-7394

 Things to Do

Museum of Science and Industry
57th St. and Lake Shore Dr.
Chicago, IL 60637
(773) 684-1414

Art Institute of Chicago
111 S. Michigan Ave.
Chicago, IL 60603
(312) 443-3600

CHECK OUT BUSINESSWEEK.COM FOR MORE:

Expanded Profile: For more details on GSB's EMBA program, check out its expanded online profile.

Sample Application Essay: Get an idea of what to expect and how to answer Chicago's questions.

Best Schools by Specialty: Find out why Chicago is tops for marketing, finance, and management.

Video Views: Dean Edward Snyder talks about setting a new course for GSB.

School Tour: Check out the Hyde Park campus, seven miles south of downtown Chicago, before visiting.

Search & Compare: Find out how GSB's executive MBA stacks up against other top EMBA programs.

Access all the B-schools content on BusinessWeek.com by subscribing to MBA Insider.

University of London

London Business School
2007 Ranking: 20
Regents Park
London, United Kingdom NW1 4SA
E-mail address: emba-office@london.edu
Web address: www.london.edu/
emba.html
For more info: Call general information
at 44-207-000-7000

☑ B4UGO

Applicants accepted: 54%
Average GMAT score: 665
Average years' work experience: 10
Average base salary: $122,828

Why LBS?

This 20-month EMBA program is packed with projects, including an international assignment, management report, and optional skills portfolio, in addition to its core courses and required six electives. Choices of elective courses are vast, with more than 70 classes in all, a third of which are scheduled in the evenings and on weekends. A management report completed in the second half of the program allows students to apply their newly acquired skills to solving a problem within their own company. A weeklong international assignment, where students work closely with a company abroad, is also required. Workshops on topics including writing, public speaking, and dealing with the media are also available.

To accommodate traveling students, EMBA core courses are held every other week on Fridays and Saturdays. Electives are offered in a block week, alternating weekend, and weekly daytime and evening formats. LBS also offers a global EMBA program with more of an international flavor.

London Business School is a private institution. Established in 1983, LBS's executive MBA program is accredited by the Association to Advance Collegiate Schools of Business (AACSB). LBS also offers a full-time MBA program. For details on LBS's full-time MBA, see page 133.

💬 Who Are My Classmates?

Executive MBA enrollment: 293
Women: 16%
International: 75%
Minority: N/A
Average age: 33

*"I could apply what
I learned immediately
in my day job."*

Where Do They Come From?

Work background: 2% have the title of president, chairman, or CEO; 6% work at organizations with 100 or fewer employees; 5% work in the nonprofit sector

Percentage with advanced degrees: 50

Percentage who live within 45 miles of school: 62

Top functional areas: General Management (18%), Finance/Accounting (17%), Consulting (14%)

Top employers: Shell, BAE Systems, ARM Holdings, Citigroup, JPMorgan

---

"The international assignments were a fantastic experience."

The 411

Program length: 20 months

Workload: 15 hours per week in class; 30 hours per week outside of class

Total program cost: $85,000

Housing provided for EMBA students: No

Distance from major airport: 17 miles

Access to health club for EMBA students: Yes

Classes begin: September

Application deadline: None

Application fee: $240

Cliff Notes

Leading areas of study: Finance, General Management, International Business, Leadership, Strategy

Concentrations/specializations: None

Joint-degree programs: None

Average class size, core courses: 75

Average class size, electives: 60

Number of electives: 72

Teaching methods: Lectures (40%), case studies (40%), simulations (5%), team projects (5%)

But What's It *Really* Like?

Graded by EMBA directors:
Overall: **A+**

Program quality, graded by students:
Overall: **B**
Teaching quality: **B**
Caliber of classmates: **B**
Housing: **B**
Logistics: **A**
Support: **B**

Curriculum, graded by students:
Overall: **A**
E-business: **B**
Entrepreneurship: **A+**
Ethics: **B**
Finance: **A**
International business: **B**
Marketing: **B**
Strategy: **B**
Teamwork: **B**

Prominent Faculty

Sir Andrew Likierman: Management
Joao Cocco: Finance
Catalina Stefanescu: Decision
Sciences

 The Good, the Bad, and the Ugly: Students Speak Out

"I traveled from Eastern Europe to London to attend, and it was worth it because each time I came back after a weekend of classes, I could apply what I learned immediately in my day job."

"For commuters, it is quite difficult to spend two days per week on campus while working. The choice of electives is very big, but more should be offered, especially for commuting students."

"A career service office focused on EMBAs is required."

"The international assignments were certainly one of the best moments and highest learning experiences of the program. Teams of four to six people were sent to a company for one week to analyze a particular issue that this company was facing. I participated in two assignments, in India and the Ukraine. It was a fantastic experience that allowed us to apply our newly learned skills within a completely new and challenging environment."

"The EMBA program at London Business School could benefit from a greater operations focus, concentrating more on the implementation issues facing organizations."

"It changed the way I think about business."

"A lot of executives—although currently employed, and some of them sponsored—are quite keen on making a career change. A career service office focused on EMBAs is required."

"Sometimes I was obliged to stay in Italy, and I missed the class. It would have been great to be allowed to follow it online. The learning would have been less (no class interaction), but better than nothing."

"Excellent program, really enjoyed it—it changed the way I think about business and gave me a lot more confidence in the business world."

"London Business School was the most expensive school in which to undertake the MBA program. However, the quality of the faculty and teaching format is worth paying the premium."

Where to Stay

Great Eastern Hotel
40 Liverpool St.
London, UK EC2M 7QN
44-207-618-5000

Landmark Hotel
222 Marylebone Rd.
London, UK NW1 6JQ
44-207-631-8000

Wigmore Court Hotel
23 Gloucester Pl.
London, UK W1U 8HS
44-207-935-0928

 Where to Eat

Giraffe
6-8 Blandford St.
London, UK W1U 4AV
44-207-935-2333

Le Pain Quotidien
72-75 Marylebone High St.
London, UK W1U 5JW
44-207-486-6154

Leon
3 Crispin Pl.
London, UK E1 6DW
44-207-247-4369

 Things to Do

Tate Modern Museum
Bankside
London, UK SE1 9TG
44-207-887-8888

The National Gallery
Trafalgar Square
London, UK WC2N 5DN
44-207-747-2885

CHECK OUT BUSINESSWEEK.COM FOR MORE:

Expanded Profile: For more details on the LBS EMBA program, check out its expanded online profile.

Search & Compare: Find out how the LBS executive MBA stacks up against other top EMBA programs.

Sample Application Essay and Interview Tips: Learn how to ace the LBS admissions process.

Best Schools by Specialty: Find out why LBS is tops for entrepreneurship.

School Tour: Planning a visit? Before you go, check out LBS's Regents Park campus with this online photo essay.

Access all the B-schools content on BusinessWeek.com by subscribing to MBA Insider.

University of Michigan

Stephen M. Ross School of Business
2007 Ranking: 4
1000 Oakbrook Dr., Suite 220
Ann Arbor, MI 48104-6794
E-mail address: emba@umich.edu
Web address: www.bus.umich.edu/
  Admissions/Emba
For more info: Call the EMBA office at
  (734) 615-9700

B4UGO

Applicants accepted: N/A
GMAT: Not required
Average years' work experience: 15.3
Average base salary: $178,000

Why Michigan?

If it's flexibility you want, Michigan is the place for you. Its executive MBA program combines a once-a-month weekend schedule with an advanced online-distance learning program—including streaming video, simulations, and case studies—that lets students study from home. Compared to those in other programs, students here are a bit older and a bit wiser, making for an engaging classroom experience. It also makes for a program that's more intensely focused on the concerns of senior executives, including leadership, strategy, and critical thinking skills. Courses include "Decision Making under Uncertainty" and "Leading Organizational Change."

The Professional Development Program prompts students to complete a self-assessment and personal growth plan in the first year and further develop crucial career skills in the second. As part of Ross's action-based curriculum, students take on a four-month summer assignment, the Executive Multidisciplinary Action Project, in which they apply knowledge by acting as consultants and designing business solutions for actual companies.

Michigan is a public institution. Established in 2001, Ross's executive MBA program is accredited by the Association to Advance Collegiate Schools of Business (AACSB). Ross also offers full-time and part-time MBA programs. For details on Ross's full-time MBA program, see page 141.

Who Are My Classmates?

Executive MBA enrollment: 174
Women: 17%
International: 17%
Minority: 24%
Average age: 39

"The faculty was engaged and truly wanted to be there."

Where Do They Come From?

Work background: 9% have the title of president, chairman, or CEO; 12% work at organizations with 100 or fewer employees; 14% work in the nonprofit sector

Percentage with advanced degrees: 47

Percentage who live within 45 miles of school: 33

Top functional areas: General Management (29%), Marketing/Sales (19%), Finance/Accounting (16%)

Top employers: DTE Energy, Eaton Corp., Ford Motor Co., General Motors, Pfizer

---

"The caliber of the students was outstanding."

The 411

Program length: 21 months

Workload: 20 hours per month in class; 20 hours per week outside of class (nonresidency weeks)

Total program cost: $115,000 (resident), $120,000 (nonresident)

Housing provided for EMBA students: Yes

Distance from major airport: 23 miles

Access to health club for EMBA students: Yes

Classes begin: August, January

Application deadlines: December 1 to May 1 (August admission), June 1 to November 1 (January admission)

Application fee: $125

Cliff Notes

Leading areas of study: General Management, Leadership, Marketing, Organizational Behavior, Strategy

Concentrations/specializations: None

Joint-degree programs: None

Average class size, core courses: 60

Average class size, electives: 60

Number of electives: 12

Teaching methods: Case studies (30%), distance learning (30%), lectures (20%), team projects (20%)

But What's It *Really* Like?

Graded by EMBA directors:
Overall: A+

Program quality, graded by students:
Overall: A
Teaching quality: A+
Caliber of classmates: A
Housing: A
Logistics: C
Support: A

Curriculum, graded by students:
Overall: A+
E-business: A
Entrepreneurship: B
Ethics: B
Finance: A
International business: A
Marketing: A+
Strategy: A
Teamwork: A

Prominent Faculty

Tom Kinnear: Marketing
M. P. Narayanan: Finance
Valerie Suslow: Economics and Public
  Policy

 The Good, the Bad, and the Ugly: Students Speak Out

"The curriculum, the project work, and the network I have built have all exceeded my expectations. [The professors have] practical experience; world renown, with papers and books published frequently; and a willingness to spend time outside of class with students. The caliber of the students was outstanding from an experience, skill set, and willingness to learn and share perspective. Couple that with outstanding levels of instruction, and we all came away very enriched."

"I would have liked more guidance about how to attain career objectives."

"The strength of the faculty was its ability to draw on the multitude of business experiences in the classroom and frame them educationally. The adjunct professors brought real-life experiences—leading-edge education—[to

the classroom]. . . . The time commitment [one must make] to the program is extensive. It is also a worthy investment."

"A worthy investment."

"The few times we had guest speakers come in made the coursework come alive. A bit more of that would have been great."

"I had high expectations for Michigan coming in, and it exceeded all of them. The classmates were smart and ambitious, with strong business acumen along with strong social acumen. The faculty was engaged, and you got the sense that they truly wanted to be there. Finally, the staff did whatever it took to deliver a strong customer experience."

"At times, I think the amount of reading and preparation for individual classes could be a little overwhelming, considering that we all had full-time professional careers during the program."

"Given the growing tendency for EMBA programs to be funded by participants, I would have liked to have had more guidance about how to attain our long-term career objectives and how to leverage the education to meet these goals."

 **Where to Stay**

Campus Inn
615 E. Huron St.
Ann Arbor, MI 48104
(800) 666-8693

Bell Tower Hotel
300 S. Thayer St.
Ann Arbor, MI 48104
(800) 562-3559

Ann Arbor Bed & Breakfast
921 E. Huron St.
Ann Arbor, MI 48104
(734) 994-9100

 Where to Eat

Cottage Inn
512 E. William St.
Ann Arbor, MI 48104
(734) 663-3379

Gandy Dancer
401 Depot St.
Ann Arbor, MI 48104
(734) 769-0592

Zingerman's Deli
422 Detroit St.
Ann Arbor, MI 48104
(734) 663-3354

 Things to Do

Nichols Arboretum
1610 Washington Heights
Ann Arbor, MI 48104
(734) 998-9540

Ann Arbor Hands-On Museum
220 E. Ann St.
Ann Arbor, MI 48104
(734) 995-5439

CHECK OUT BUSINESSWEEK.COM FOR MORE:

Expanded Profile: More facts, more statistics, and more insights on the Ross executive MBA program.

Search & Compare: See how Ross stacks up against other top EMBA programs.

Sample Application Essays: Learn how to impress admissions directors with essays on leadership and personal development.

B-school Roundtable: Watch Ross's dean discuss the future of management with other deans at top programs.

Dean Profile: Dean Richard Dolan discusses Ross's image, ethics, and the launching of the executive MBA program.

Best Schools by Specialty: Learn why Ross's management program is rated one of the best in the country.

Access all the B-schools content on BusinessWeek.com by subscribing to MBA Insider.

University of Navarra

IESE Business School
2007 Ranking: 17
Avda. Pearson 21
Barcelona, Spain 08034
E-mail address: embabcn@iese.edu
Web address: www.iese.edu
For more info: Call general information
    at 34-93-253-4200

Why IESE?

IESE is one of the more expensive top-ranked EMBA programs, but for mid-career executives looking for an international EMBA with a focus on general management and leadership, it's worth a look. The program itself is bilingual—Spanish and English—and students spend a week in Shanghai. The program relies heavily on case studies, which are analyzed individually, as part of a team, and finally in an instructor-led general discussion. With more than half of all students holding the title of president, chairman, or CEO, students learn as much from peers as from faculty.

Students may enroll in IESE's standard EMBA in Barcelona, which offers a weekly format, or in Madrid, where weekly and biweekly formats are available. Classes meet on Fridays and Saturdays, and students spend four to six weeks on the two campuses. The 16-month global EMBA described above has residential sessions in Barcelona, Madrid, Shanghai, and Silicon Valley.

☑ B4UGO

Applicants accepted: 68%
Average GMAT score: 600
Average years' work experience: 12
Average base salary: $169,300

The information that follows is on that program.

IESE is a private institution. Established in 1982, IESE's EMBA program is accredited by the Association of MBAs (AMBA) and the European Quality Improvement System (EQUIS). IESE also offers a full-time MBA program. For details on IESE's full-time MBA program, see page 149.

 Who Are My Classmates?

Executive MBA enrollment: 41
Women: 15%
International: 85%
Minority: N/A
Average age: 38

"A balanced combination of management skills, values, and ethics."

Where Do They Come From?

Work background: 52% have the title of president, chairman, or CEO; 25% work at organizations with 100 or fewer employees; 2% work in the nonprofit sector

Percentage with advanced degrees: 90

Percentage who live within 45 miles of school: 5

Top functional areas: General Management (30%), Finance/Accounting (23%), Operations/Logistics (14%)

Top employers: Porsche, Banco Santander Central Hispano, J.T.I. International, Novaris, Siemens

---

"One of the MBA world's best-kept secrets."

The 411

Program length: 16 months

Workload: 64 hours per week in class (residency weeks); 25 hours per week outside of class (nonresidency weeks)

Total program cost: $126,244

Housing provided for EMBA students: Yes

Distance from major airport: 15 miles

Access to health club for EMBA students: No

Classes begin: September

Application deadline: None

Application fee: $130

Cliff Notes

Leading area of study: General Management

Concentrations/specializations: None

Joint-degree programs: None

Average class size, core courses: 40

Average class size, electives: N/A

Number of electives: None

Teaching methods: Case studies (25%), distance learning (20%), experiential learning (20%)

But What's It *Really* Like?

Graded by EMBA directors:
Overall: **A**

Program quality, graded by students:
Overall: **A**
Teaching quality: **A+**
Caliber of classmates: **C**
Housing: **B**
Logistics: **B**
Support: **B**

Curriculum, graded by students:
Overall: **A**
E-business: **A**
Entrepreneurship: **A+**
Ethics: **A+**
Finance: **B**
International business: **B**
Marketing: **B**
Strategy: **C**
Teamwork: **B**

Prominent Faculty

Johanna Mair: Corporate Strategy and Entrepreneurial Strategies
Pedro Videla: Economics
Eric Weber: Accounting and Control

 ## The Good, the Bad, and the Ugly: Students Speak Out

"I believe that IESE's program is one of the MBA world's best-kept secrets. It is a balanced program that has a world-class faculty and an innovative modular approach, as well as a strong program for developing global virtual teamwork skills. IESE's global EMBA has helped me further my career as well as develop my personal work-life balance skills and leadership skills."

"I would add more coursework in the marketing/strategy area. The ambiguity of these topics is difficult to master."

"IESE has a balanced combination of management skills, values, ethics, and vision for a 'people-oriented' management career."

> ### "Not as good in Asian business nuances."

"One of the shortcomings was the lack of feedback on assignments— obviously you received a grade, but you did not always get the corrected and commented paper back from the professors."

"I found IESE a great place for three reasons: the faculty is outstanding, the school has a great touch to stimulate entrepreneurship, and the whole school is totally dedicated to students, from faculty to the last gatekeeper."

> ### "One shortcoming was the lack of feedback on assignments."

"Team activity was great, but it sometimes limits the opportunity to get closer to other teams."

"It helped structure my managerial style and gave me the tools and framework to address some of the most complex business issues and to share my views with top management."

"Professors were very well versed in a European setting, but not as good in Asian business nuances."

"One of the most impressive aspects was the ability of the professors to make all subjects interesting. As leading members in their field, they not only taught case studies but used their experience, mixed with the experience of class members, to provide a deeper insight into the issues being analyzed."

 **Where to Stay**

Hotel Rialto
Ferran 40-42
Barcelona, ES 08002
34-93-318-5212

Hotel Continental Palacete
Rambla de Catalunya 30
Barcelona, ES 08007
34-93-445-7657

Hotel Arts
Marina 19-21
Barcelona, ES 08005
34-93-221-1000

 Where to Eat

Carmelitas
Carme 42
Barcelona, ES 08001
34-93-412-4684

Vinotinto
Aribau 27
Barcelona, ES 08011
34-93-451-1027

Inopia
Carrer de Tamarit 104
Barcelona, ES 08015
34-93-424-5231

 Things to Do

Museu Picasso (Picasso Museum)
Montcada 15-23
Barcelona, ES 08003
34-93-356-3000

**Museu de la Xocolata
(Chocolate Museum)**
Comerç 36
Barcelona, ES 08003
34-93-268-7878

CHECK OUT BUSINESSWEEK.COM FOR MORE:

Admissions Q&A: Admissions Director Mireia Rius describes the application process.

Expanded Profile: More facts, statistics, and student comments on the IESE EMBA.

Search & Compare: Compare IESE's executive MBA with other top EMBA programs, both stateside and abroad.

Video View: Dean Jordi Canals discusses the appeal of foreign business school programs.

School Tour: Get a feel for IESE's Barcelona campus with this photo essay.

Access all the B-schools content on BusinessWeek.com by subscribing to MBA Insider.

University of North Carolina

Kenan-Flagler Business School
University of North Carolina
at Chapel Hill
2007 Ranking: 10
Campus Box 3490
McColl Building
Chapel Hill, NC 27599-3490
E-mail address: emba@unc.edu
Web address: www.kenan-lagler.unc.
edu/programs/emba
For more info: Call the EMBA office at
(919) 962-8863

✓ B4UGO

Applicants accepted: 73%
Average GMAT score: 600
Average years' work experience: 10.3
Average base salary: $107,500

Why UNC?

With one of the most affordable highly ranked EMBA programs around, Kenan-Flagler offers a great ROI for executives working their way up. Analysis, strategy, and leadership are the focus of the core curriculum, while 10 additional electives allow students to tailor the EMBA experience to their own needs. Important soft-skill development is addressed through seminars and simulations that hone leadership, networking, and communication skills. While student rate teaching quality only fair, they praise the faculty's ability to stimulate discussion and bring cutting-edge research into the classroom.

Career development is emphasized throughout the program, starting with the Professional Development Plan that students create in one of their first courses. Executives can opt for a weekend schedule or the OneMBA, a global program for more experienced executives. The global program meets Friday through Sunday once a month, with weeklong residencies in Hong Kong, the Netherlands, Mexico, Brazil, and Washington, D.C.

UNC is a public institution. Established in 1986, Kenan-Flagler's executive MBA program is accredited by the Association to Advance Collegiate Schools of Business (AACSB). It also offers full-time and part-time MBA programs. For details on the full-time MBA program, see page 153.

Who Are My Classmates?

Executive MBA enrollment: 114
Women: 28%
International: 9%
Minority: 22%
Average age: 35

"One of the best programs in the country."

Where Do They Come From?

Work background: 2% have the title of president, chairman, or CEO; 16% work at organizations with 100 or fewer employees; 9% work in the nonprofit sector

Percentage with advanced degrees: 29

Percentage who live within 45 miles of school: 45

Top functional areas: Consulting (16%), General Management (16%), Management Information Systems (16%)

Top employers: IBM, Capital One, Bank of America, Progress Energy, Cisco, John Deere, Wachovia

---

"A few faculty members were substandard."

The 411

Program length: 20 months

Workload: 13 hours per week in class; 20 hours per week outside of class

Total program cost: $67,200

Housing provided for EMBA students: Yes

Distance from major airport: 20 miles

Access to health club for EMBA students: Yes

Classes begin: January (weekend program)

Application deadlines: April 7, July 14, October 1

Application fee: $135

Cliff Notes

Leading areas of study: Finance, International Business, Leadership, Marketing, Strategy

Concentrations/specializations: Analysis, Strategy, Leadership

Joint-degree programs: None

Average class size, core courses: 58

Average class size, electives: 29

Number of electives: 38

Teaching methods: Case studies (50%), lectures (16%), experiential learning (10%), simulations (10%), team projects (10%)

But What's It *Really* Like?

Graded by EMBA directors:
Overall: A+

Program quality, graded by students:
Overall: B
Teaching quality: B
Caliber of classmates: B
Housing: A+
Logistics: A+
Support: A+

Curriculum, graded by students:
Overall: A
E-business: B
Entrepreneurship: A
Ethics: B
Finance: B
International business: B
Marketing: A
Strategy: B
Teamwork: A

Prominent Faculty

Sridhar Balasubramanian: Marketing
Peter Brews: Entrepreneurship and
  Global Strategy
Anil Shivdasani: Finance

 The Good, the Bad, and the Ugly: Students Speak Out

"UNC is, in my opinion, one of the best programs in the country. I've had the opportunity to speak with MBA graduates from various other top-ranked programs (Kellogg, Fuqua, Wharton, etc.). I believe the quality of the education I received from Kenan-Flagler can easily compare and compete with these well-known, highly visible institutions."

"Many [instructors] were very good. There were, however, a few faculty members who were substandard, did not really care, and needed to be replaced. A more tightly integrated curriculum would have helped reinforce the material better. Also, it seemed like they segregated the EMBAs from the MBAs—not really good for networking."

"The team formulation method at UNC is fabulous. My five-person team is the community that I leaned on when the work-school-life balance seemed unbearable. My classmates were extremely talented, accomplished professionals who contributed to my learning inside the classroom and out."

"The pace of the program was frenetic. I would have been willing to lengthen the program by two months if I could have gotten a couple of breaks within it. It was often difficult to digest information because of the pace."

> *"Classmates contributed to my learning inside the classroom and out."*

"[EMBAs need] better access to full-time recruiting. Not everyone is in an executive program to get a promotion in their current company. Some folks are truly looking for a career change. Once it has been proven that a student's company is not paying for any of the education, an EMBA student should be allowed to access all the on-campus recruiting and internship programs afforded a full-time MBA."

"Everything the school advertised was real. The program maintained an excellent balance between individual effort and collaborative teamwork, and the professors were of a very high caliber."

"This program focused a lot on skills I was weak in (teamwork, communication, and strategy). This was critical to me landing a job at McKinsey. Not sure I could have accomplished this in another program."

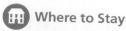 **Where to Stay**

The Carolina Inn
211 Pittsboro St.
Chapel Hill, NC 27516
(919) 933-2001

The Franklin Hotel
311 W. Franklin St.
Chapel Hill, NC 27516
(919) 442-9000

The Siena Hotel
1505 E. Franklin St.
Chapel Hill, NC 27514
(919) 929-4000

 Where to Eat

Lantern Restaurant
423 Franklin St.
Chapel Hill, NC 27516
(919) 969-8846

Crook's Corner
610 Franklin St.
Chapel Hill, NC 27516
(919) 929-7643

Pepper's Pizza
127 Franklin St.
Chapel Hill, NC 27514
(919) 967-7766

 Things to Do

Morehead Planetarium and Science Center
250 E. Franklin St.
Chapel Hill, NC 27514
(919) 962-1236

North Carolina Botanical Gardens
The University of North Carolina at Chapel Hill
College Box 3375, Totten Center
Chapel Hill, NC 27599
(919) 962-0522

CHECK OUT BUSINESSWEEK.COM FOR MORE:

Video View: Listen to Dean Steve Jones on Kenan-Flagler's focus on sustainable development.

Sample Application Essays and Interview Tips: Read up to seven essays to get a feel for what UNC is looking for in a potential applicant.

Expanded Profile: Need more information? Check out the Kenan-Flagler online EMBA profile for more statistics, facts, and student comments.

Search & Compare: See how UNC's executive MBA stacks up against other top EMBA programs.

School Tour: Planning a visit before you decide? Check out the UNC campus first, using this photo essay.

Access all the B-schools content on BusinessWeek.com by subscribing to MBA Insider.

University of Pennsylvania

The Wharton School
2007 Ranking: 2
G21 Jon M. Huntsman Hall
3730 Walnut St.
Philadelphia, PA 19104-2800
E-mail address: mbaexec-admissions@
wharton.upenn.edu
Web address: www.wharton.upenn.edu/
mbaexecutive
For more info: Call the EMBA office at
(215) 898-5887

☑ B4UGO

Applicants accepted: 32%
Average GMAT score: 696
Average years' work experience: 10
Average base salary: $212,700

Why Wharton?

Wharton's two-year EMBA stresses its academic equality with Wharton's highly acclaimed full-time MBA curriculum, requiring the same core courses and offering a similarly wide variety of electives. Wharton's learning lab provides an experimental laboratory that develops innovative technology-based teaching methods—including simulations and interactive programs—while leadership-learning teams used throughout the first year develop leadership and teamwork skills. The teams complete in a Field Application Project in which they tackle a real-life business problem confronted by one student's company and conduct a complete analysis.

A second campus in San Francisco offers a West Coast option for those who can't make it to Philadelphia. On both coasts, classes meet on Fridays and Saturdays every other week, with additional three-day sessions and a required week abroad. The program attracts a highly talented group of students. In Philadelphia, the Class of 2009 averages GMAT scores of nearly 700, 10 years' experience, and annual compensation well north of $200,000.

The University of Pennsylvania is a private institution. Established in 1971, Wharton's executive MBA program is accredited by the Association to Advance Collegiate Schools of Business (AACSB). Wharton also offers a full-time MBA. For details on Wharton's full-time MBA program, see page 161.

Who Are My Classmates?

Executive MBA enrollment: 234
Women: 20%
International: 20%
Minority: 32%
Average age: 33

"Academically challenging and stimulating."

Where Do They Come From?

Percentage with advanced degrees: 37
Percentage who work in the nonprofit
sector: 2
Percentage who live within 45 miles
of school: 20
Top functional areas: Finance/
Accounting (32%), Consulting
(20%), General Management
(13%)
Top industries: Financial services
(33%), Consulting (12%), Pharma-
ceuticals/Biotechnology (12%),
Technology (8%), Energy (7%)

> ## *"Wharton's student body cannot be matched."*

The 411

Program length: 24 months
Workload: 10 hours per week in class;
22 hours per week outside of class
Total program cost: $142,440
Housing provided for EMBA
students: Yes
Distance from major airport: 8 miles
Access to health club for EMBA
students: Yes
Classes begin: May
Application deadline: February 1
Application fee: $180

Cliff Notes

Leading areas of study: Entrepreneur-
ship, Finance, General Manage-
ment, International Business,
Strategy
Concentrations/specializations: None
Joint-degree programs: None
Average class size, core courses: 57
Average class size, electives: 52
Number of electives: 26
Teaching methods: Case studies
(35%), team projects (25%),
lectures (20%)

But What's It *Really* Like?

Graded by EMBA directors:
Overall: **A+**

Program quality, graded by students:
Overall: **B**
Teaching quality: **A**
Caliber of classmates: **A**
Housing: **A**
Logistics: **B**
Support: **A+**

Curriculum, graded by students:
Overall: **B**
E-business: **A**
Entrepreneurship: **A+**
Ethics: **B**
Finance: **A+**
International business: **B**
Marketing: **C**
Strategy: **B**
Teamwork: **B**

Prominent Faculty

Andrew Abel: Finance
Patricia Danzon: Healthcare
    Management
Michael Useem: Management

 The Good, the Bad, and the Ugly: Students Speak Out

"The quality of Wharton's student body, faculty, curriculum, and alumni network cannot be matched by other schools. The ability of the Wharton name to open doors and to establish immediate credibility in the business community is powerful. I wouldn't waste my time earning an MBA from anywhere else."

"The classroom experience was fantastic. The only thing that could improve it is if the classes were smaller. Smaller class size could make the experience more personal."

"Smaller class size could make the experience more personal."

"I had a tremendous experience at the school. Instructors were very competent in their fields and always willing to make time for students."

"Professors were top notch—although they didn't always have practical work experience. The more that Wharton could bring experienced executives into the classroom, the better the experience would be."

"I was very surprised by the consistent caliber and dedication of my classmates. Our professors over and over emphasized how well-prepared and motivated the executive students were relative to the full-time students despite working full time."

"The vast majority of the EMBA instructors were well organized, drew on real-world experience, and engaged the students' intellects and past work experience relative to the course content. A few professors seemed to have taught their course content so many times that they seemed a little stale."

"[The program would benefit from] fewer core requirements, a larger supply of available electives, more advanced electives, and increased opportunities for informal interaction with classmates in order to really leverage the experience of the class."

"The program was academically challenging and stimulating, and the caliber of the students, faculty, and administration was fantastic."

"Most EMBA programs are 'watered down' programs. This is not the case at Wharton. I wanted the detail and rigor. Wharton exceeded my expectations."

Where to Stay

The Inn at Penn
3600 Sansom St.
Philadelphia, PA 19104
(215) 222-0200

Sheraton University City
36th St. & Chestnut St.
Philadelphia, PA 19104
(215) 387-8000

Courtyard by Marriott:
Philadelphia Downtown
21 N. Juniper St.
Philadelphia, PA 19107
(215) 496-3200

 Where to Eat

Penne Restaurant & Wine Bar
3611 Walnut St.
Philadelphia, PA 19104
(215) 823-6222

New Deck Tavern
3408 Sansom St.
Philadelphia, PA 19104
(215) 386-4600

Pizza Allegros
3200 Chestnut St.
Philadelphia, PA 19104
(215) 222-3226

 Things to Do

The Esther M. Klein Art Gallery
3701 Market St.
Philadelphia, PA 19104
(215) 966-6188

International House
3701 Chestnut St.
Philadelphia, PA 19104
(215) 387-5125

CHECK OUT BUSINESSWEEK.COM FOR MORE:

Expanded Profile: Learn more about the Wharton EMBA by reading its in-depth online profile.

Best Schools by Specialty: Find out why Wharton's strengths include entrepreneurship, marketing, finance, and management.

Dean Profile: An inside look at Wharton's newest dean, Thomas Robertson, and his plans for the legendary institution.

Video View: Vice Dean Anjani Jain discusses the ever-evolving Wharton curriculum.

School Tour: Discover the charms of the Wharton campus before applying.

Access all the B-schools content on BusinessWeek.com by subscribing to MBA Insider.

U. of Southern California

Marshall School of Business
2007 Ranking: 5
611 Exposition Blvd.
Popovich Hall, Suite 308
Los Angeles, CA 90089-2633
E-mail address:
uscemba@marshall.usc.edu
Web address: www.marshall.usc.edu/
web/EMBA.cfm?doc_id=961
For more info: Call the EMBA office at
(213) 740-7846

☑ B4UGO

Applicants accepted: 65%
Average GMAT score: N/A
Average years' work experience: 14.2
Average base salary: $197,000

Why USC?

Executives who are looking for the tools to tackle complex business problems will appreciate Marshall's thematic curriculum. The Marshall approach stresses the interrelatedness of business disciplines such as marketing and finance rather than teaching each subject in isolation. Case studies and lectures are the main teaching methods, leaving some students wanting more class discussion. But with students averaging more than 10 years of management experience, few programs have higher-caliber students. The Marshall EMBA is offered on two campuses, in Los Angeles and San Diego, with a biweekly weekend schedule and an international residency.

Like a number of institutions, Marshall now offers a global EMBA (GEMBA) completed in 10 modules and based in a partner institution, Antai College of Economics and Management, in Shanghai. Students in the GEMBA program benefit from exposure to company visits and international travel during an Asia business field trip, as well as a more diverse classroom experience.

USC is a private institution. Established in 1985, Marshall's executive MBA program is accredited by the Association to Advance Collegiate Schools of Business (AACSB). Marshall also offers full-time and part-time MBA programs. For details on Marshall's full-time MBA program, see page 169. For details on its part-time MBA program, see page 401.

◓ Who Are My Classmates?

Executive MBA enrollment: 196
Women: 18%
International: 3%
Minority: 34%
Average age: 38

"The roster of professors is superb."

Where Do They Come From?

Work background: 5% have the title of president, chairman, or CEO; 1% work in the nonprofit sector

Percentage with advanced degrees: 13

Percentage who live within 45 miles of school: 94

Top functional areas: General Management, (27%), Accounting (15%), Management Information Systems (12%), Operations/ Logistics (12%)

Top employers: NBC Universal, Qualcomm, Boeing, Johnson & Johnson, Nestlé

"The network is unsurpassed."

The 411

Program length: 22 months

Workload: 12 hours per week in class; 20 hours per week outside of class

Total program cost: $84,500

Housing provided for EMBA students: No

Distance from major airport: 13 miles

Access to health club for EMBA students: Yes

Classes begin: August

Application deadline: June 1

Application fee: $150

Cliff Notes

Leading area of study: General Management

Concentrations/specializations: None

Joint-degree programs: None

Average class size, core courses: 70

Average class size, electives: N/A

Number of electives: None

Teaching methods: Case studies (25%), lectures (25%), team projects (20%)

But What's It *Really* Like?

Graded by EMBA directors:
Overall: A

Program quality, graded by students:
Overall: A+
Teaching quality: A+
Caliber of classmates: A
Housing: A
Logistics: A
Support: A

Curriculum, graded by students:
Overall: A+
E-business: A+
Entrepreneurship: A+
Ethics: A
Finance: A+
International business: A+
Marketing: A
Strategy: A+
Teamwork: A+

Prominent Faculty

Mark DeFond: Accounting
Sampath Rajagopalan: Information and Operations Management
Alan Shapiro: Finance

 The Good, the Bad, and the Ugly: Students Speak Out

"The roster of professors is superb (our finance professor was one of the five most-sought-after professors in the country). Both the depth and the breadth of the material are perfectly tailored to professional people who want to acquire the necessary skills on their way to becoming future corporate and/or entrepreneurial leaders."

"USC could improve the marketing portion of the program. The management portions of the program were very focused on CEO-level requirements, but not the needs of front-line managers."

"Focused on CEO-level requirements, not the needs of front-line managers."

"Both the quality of the program and the USC network were outstanding. It's a ton of work, but I'd do it again in an instant! Strengths include the professors' seniority and experience in dealing with executives and their collective desire to engage in discussion, debate, and dialogue, all the while encouraging the students to challenge the status quo of academic theory vs. real-life realities."

"We're in Los Angeles—I think we could have taken advantage of more opportunities to have speakers from Fortune 500 companies."

"USC's 'themed approach' is extremely helpful to tie concepts to other obviously related and not-so-obviously related coursework. The network is unsurpassed. This is great for helping to secure future opportunities, while the curriculum is designed to provide practical real-time application."

"The marketing portion of the program needs a little work, but other than that, the program is very strong top to bottom."

"The program stretched me beyond what I believed I was capable of doing and as a result made me a better leader and manager. At its core, the program created a way of viewing and thinking about the world that struck the right balance between analysis and action."

"USC provided an amazing, practical, global learning experience. Each student left with a sharpened set of business tools to successfully tackle the daily challenges of C-level international leadership."

Where to Stay

Los Angeles Radisson Hotel
3540 S. Figueroa St.
Los Angeles, CA 90007
(213) 748-4141

Omni Los Angeles Hotel
251 S. Olive St.
Los Angeles, CA 90012
(213) 617-3300

Westin Bonaventure
404 S. Figueroa St.
Los Angeles, CA 90071
(213) 624-1000

 Where to Eat

Philippe The Original
1001 N. Alameda St.
Los Angeles, CA 90012
(213) 628-3781

Water Grill
544 S. Grand St.
Los Angeles, CA 90071
(213) 891-0900

El Cholo Restaurant
1121 S. Western Ave.
Los Angeles, CA 90006
(323) 734-2773

 Things to Do

Getty Museum
1200 Getty Center Dr.
Los Angeles, CA 90265
(310) 440-7300

Venice Boardwalk
Pacific Ave. & Windward Ave.
Venice, CA 90291

CHECK OUT BUSINESSWEEK.COM FOR MORE:

Sample Application Essays and Interview Tips: Learn how to master USC's essay questions and make an impression during information sessions before the interview.

Admissions Q&A: Marshall admission directors contrast the application process for different MBA programs.

Expanded Profile: Everything you ever wanted to know about the Marshall executive MBA but were afraid to ask.

Search & Compare: Look before you leap—run the numbers for Marshall and other top EMBA programs on your short list.

Access all the B-schools content on BusinessWeek.com by subscribing to MBA Insider.

Villanova University

School of Business
2007 Ranking: 25
Executive MBA Program
601 County Line Rd.
Radnor, PA 19087-4523
E-mail address:
vemba_info@villanova.edu
Web address: www.villanova.edu/
business/execmba/
For more info: Call the EMBA office at
(610) 523-1793

☑ B4UGO

Applicants accepted: N/A
Average GMAT score: N/A
Average years' work experience: 13
Average base salary: $107,000

Why Villanova?

Villanova's EMBA program is organized around five content areas: strategy and positioning, leading change and managing people, measurement and performance systems, executive coaching, and "systems thinking," a way of examining problems from all angles that forms the cornerstone of the program. Following a one-week residency at the start of each year, students take courses in each content area every semester, ending with a major project on systems thinking in the second year. Several times each semester, senior executives visit for "fireside chats" with students on Friday nights.

Classes meet every other week, on Fridays and Saturdays, for 21 months. In the spring of the first year, students spend eight days abroad, studying an international business in an emerging economy. Five business research centers, including the Center for Entrepreneurship, call Villanova home. And the school has recently undergone a $26 million renovation, including a new 65,000-square-foot atrium and applied finance lab.

Villanova is a private institution. Established in 2000, Villanova's executive MBA program is accredited by the Association to Advance Collegiate Schools of Business (AACSB). Villanova also offers a part-time MBA. For details on its part-time MBA program, see page 417.

⬤ Who Are My Classmates?

Executive MBA enrollment: 62
Women: 26%
International: 10%
Minority: 29%
Average age: 38

"An unbelievable learning experience."

Where Do They Come From?

Work background:13% work at organizations with 100 or fewer employees; 3% work in the non-profit sector

Percentage with advanced degrees: 10

Percentage who live within 45 miles of school: 61

Top functional areas: Operations/ Logistics (39%), Marketing/ Sales (26%), Consulting (10%), General Management (10%)

Top employers: JPMorgan Chase, Rohm and Haas, sanofi-aventis, Sunoco, Boeing

---

"Living facilities could have been improved on."

The 411

Program length: 21 months

Workload: 8 hours per week in class; 20 hours per week outside of class

Total program cost: $85,000

Housing provided for EMBA students: Yes

Distance from major airport: 22 miles

Access to health club for EMBA students: Yes

Classes begin: August

Application deadline: None

Application fee: $75

Cliff Notes

Leading areas of study: General Management, Leadership, Strategy, Systems Thinking, Technology

Concentrations/specializations: None

Joint-degree programs: None

Average class size, core courses: 31

Average class size, electives: N/A

Number of electives: None

Teaching methods: Case studies (30%), team projects (30%), lectures (20%)

But What's It *Really* Like?

Graded by EMBA directors:
Overall: **B**

Program quality, graded by students:
Overall: **B**
Teaching quality: **B**
Caliber of classmates: **A**
Housing: **A+**
Logistics: **B**
Support: **A+**

Curriculum, graded by students:
Overall: **A+**
E-business: **A**
Entrepreneurship: **C**
Ethics: **A**
Finance: **C**
International business: **B**
Marketing: **B**
Strategy: **A+**
Teamwork: **A+**

Prominent Faculty

Jonathan P. Doh: Management and Operations

Thomas Monahan: Accounting and Information Systems

Michael Pagano: Finance

 The Good, the Bad, and the Ugly: Students Speak Out

"I think the Villanova EMBA is a tremendous program and offers an unbelievable learning experience. Its mission is to transform students, and it stays true to this mission in everything it does. It was a first-rate learning experience."

"The classroom facilities were fantastic, but the living facilities could have been improved on."

"I wish there were recruitment opportunities on campus."

"While not overlooking the financial, economic, and ethical disciplines, the systems thinking course actively engaged the class in learning a fascinating problem-solving process. We learned not only how to use what we already knew, but also how to realize what we did not know and how to learn what we needed to know. In addition, we acquired a strong awareness of how the activities of one part of a large, complex system affect and are affected by the other parts."

"I'm sorry it is over."

"I wish that there were recruitment opportunities on campus from major consulting and financial services firms. While I understand that the majority of EMBA students are currently employed, having the ability to interview for new opportunities with leading organizations would provide significant added value."

"I investigated three other well-respected programs in the Philadelphia area, and Villanova stood head and shoulders above the competition. The program was a wonderful experience, and I would absolutely do it again. Truth be known, I'm sorry it is over."

"We heard great guest speakers, but they were few and far between."

"The holistic approach to the curriculum really tied all the individual courses together quite well. Access to faculty was abundant [and] the weekend residency requirement really led to a culture of immersion and interaction with my fellow students; lifelong friendships were forged."

 **Where to Stay**

The Radnor Hotel
591 E. Lancaster Ave.
St. Davids, PA 19087
(610) 688-5800

Philadelphia Marriott West
111 Crawford Ave.
W. Conshohocken, PA 19428
(610) 941-5600

Radisson Hotel Valley Forge
1160 First Ave.
King of Prussia, PA 19406
(610) 337-2000

 Where to Eat

Wild Onion
900 Conestoga Rd.
Rosemont, PA 19010
(610) 527-4826

Blush
24 N. Merion Ave.
Bryn Mawr, PA 19010
(610) 527-7700

Fuji Mountain Restaurant
14 N. Merion Ave.
Bryn Mawr, PA 19010
(610) 527-7777

 Things to Do

Lights of Liberty Show
600 Chestnut St.
Philadelphia, PA 19106
(215) 925-8077

The Franklin Institute Science Museum
222 N. 20th St.
Philadelphia, PA 19103
(215) 448-1200

CHECK OUT BUSINESSWEEK.COM FOR MORE:

Expanded Profile: For more details on Villanova's EMBA program, check out its expanded online profile.

Search & Compare: Find out how Villanova's executive MBA stacks up against other top EMBA programs.

Access all the B-schools content on BusinessWeek.com by subscribing to MBA Insider.

Washington University

Olin School of Business
2007 Ranking: 24
Campus Box 1158
1 Brookings Dr.
St. Louis, MO 63130-4899
E-mail address: emba@wustl.edu
Web address: www.olin.wustl.edu/
execed/
For more info: Call the EMBA office at
(314) 935-9009

☑ **B4UGO**

Applicants accepted: N/A
GMAT: Not required
Average years' work experience: 15.2
Average base salary: $106,105*

*Estimate based on *BusinessWeek* survey data.

Why Wash U?

If you're looking for a program that will take you to the next level, Olin's executive MBA may be it. Students here average more than 15 years of experience and are typically mid- to upper-level managers seeking to break out of functional positions and take on a strategic role in their organizations. The program's focus is on how to apply disciplines such as finance and marketing to the kind of complex business problems faced by senior executives.

The 56-credit-hour program is cohort-based—you'll spend the entire 20 months as part of the same team. It's offered in two formats: every other weekend or one three-day weekend each month. Both include at least two extended residencies, including one in Shanghai. Both also include a heavy professional development component throughout the program: assessment and coaching as well as leadership and communication training. Classes are taught by the same professors who teach in Olin's highly ranked full-time MBA program.

Washington University is a private institution. Established in 1983, Olin's executive MBA program is accredited by the Association to Advance Collegiate Schools of Business (AACSB). Olin also offers full-time and part-time MBA programs. For details on Olin's full-time MBA program, see page 201. For details on its part-time MBA program, see page 425.

 Who Are My Classmates?

Executive MBA enrollment: 225
Women: 21%
International: 10%
Minority: 18.5%
Average age: 38

"The international trip was fantastic."

Where Do They Come From?

Work background: 8% have the title of president, chairman, or CEO; 12% work at organizations with 100 or fewer employees; 9% work in the nonprofit sector

Percentage with advanced degrees: 25

Percentage who live within 45 miles of school: 76

Top functional areas: General Management (20%), Marketing/Sales (17%), Operations/Logistics (16%)

Top employers: Anheuser-Busch, Edward Jones, Emerson, Monsanto, Boeing

---

"The school did not assist with employment searches."

The 411

Program length: 20 months

Workload: 20 to 30 hours per week

Total program cost: $83,900

Housing provided for EMBA students: Yes

Distance from major airport: 12 miles

Access to health club for EMBA students: Yes

Classes begin: September

Application deadline: None

Application fee: $100

Cliff Notes

Leading areas of study: General Management, Growth, Innovation and Creativity, International Business, Strategy

Concentrations/specializations: None

Joint-degree programs: None

Average class size, core courses: 40

Average class size, electives: N/A

Number of electives: None

Teaching methods: Case studies (35%), experiential learning (25%), team projects (15%)

But What's It *Really* Like?

Graded by EMBA directors:
Overall: **B**

Program quality, graded by students:
Overall: **B**
Teaching quality: **A**
Caliber of classmates: **B**
Housing: **A**
Logistics: **A**
Support: **A**

Curriculum, graded by students:
Overall: **A**
E-business: **C**
Entrepreneurship: **C**
Ethics: **C**
Finance: **B**
International business: **B**
Marketing: **A**
Strategy: **A+**
Teamwork: **C**

Prominent Faculty

James T. Little: Strategy and Economics
Panos Kouvelis: Operations and Manufacturing Management
Todd R. Zenger: Business Strategy

 The Good, the Bad, and the Ugly: Students Speak Out

"When [my wife and I] began the EMBA program, we had already been in business 15 years, and we thought we knew our business pretty well. As we progressed through the program, we studied and discussed other businesses to a degree and depth such that we knew certain things about them that we did not know about our own company."

"Organizational behavior classes were weak."

"In my class, a fairly high percentage of students were paying for the program themselves. However, the school did not really provide any assistance with employment searches. I feel that the school should make an effort to bring the students and the employment community together."

"The international trip was fantastic. I continue to apply what I learned on at least a weekly basis and probably more regularly than that."

"With one notable exception, our organizational behavior classes were a little weak. Functional classes were excellent (marketing, finance, operations), and the strategy and economics courses were better than I could have expected. But I would have liked to have seen a little better thought put into those 'soft' skill courses."

"I cannot say enough about the excellence of the faculty and how approachable and helpful they are. The same is true of the support staff. A very user-friendly program."

"The decision to attend Washington University's EMBA program was the best professional decision I have made thus far. My clinical background did not include business, so I originally hesitated to enter an executive program. Now, my professors, peers/friends, administrative staff, coworkers, and [my employer's] executive leadership will all agree that Washington University's EMBA program has enhanced my analytical and business skills beyond everyone's expectations."

"Only very few U.S. EMBA programs truly provide a strategically forward, leadership-oriented curriculum for experienced managers and executives. Olin is one of those very few schools."

Where to Stay

Clayton on the Park
8025 Bonhomme Ave.
St. Louis, MO 63105
(314) 721-8588

Seven Gables Inn
26 N. Meramec St.
Clayton, MO 63135
(314) 863-8400

Crowne Plaza Hotel St. Louis—Clayton
7750 Carondelet Ave.
Clayton, MO 63105
(314) 726-5400

 Where to Eat

J Bucks
101 S. Hanley Rd.
Clayton, MO 63105
(314) 725-4700

Miss Saigon
6101 Delmar in the Loop
St. Louis, MO 63112
(314) 863-4949

BARcelona
34 N. Central Ave.
Clayton, MO 63105
(314) 863-9909

 Things to Do

Anheuser-Busch Brewery
12th & Lynch Sts.
St. Louis, MO 63118
(314) 577-2626

St. Louis Art Museum
One Fine Arts Dr., Forest Park
St. Louis, MO 63110-1380
(314) 721-0072

CHECK OUT BUSINESSWEEK.COM FOR MORE:

Expanded Profile: Looking for more? Check out the expanded online profile for the Olin EMBA.

Search & Compare: Find out how Olin's executive MBA program stacks up against other top EMBA programs.

Sample Application Essays and Interview Tips: Ace the Olin admissions process using these pointers.

School Tour: Planning a visit? Check out Olin's St. Louis campus before you go.

Access all the B-schools content on BusinessWeek.com by subscribing to MBA Insider.

Boston College

Carroll School of Management
2007 Ranking: 4th in the Northeast
140 Commonwealth Ave.
Fulton Hall, Room 315
Chestnut Hill, MA 02467
E-mail address: bcmba@bc.edu
Web address: www.bc.edu/schools/
csom/mba/academics/eveningcore.
html
For more info: Call MBA general
admission at (617) 552-3920

☑ B4UGO

Applicants accepted: 62%
Average GMAT score: 603
Average years' work experience: 5.1
**Average time to complete the
program:** 36 months
Completion rate: 94%

○ Who Are My Classmates?

Part-time enrollment: 569
Women: 27%
International: 11%
Minority: 11%
Average age: 28
Average base salary at admission:
$62,340
Reason for getting an MBA: Career
advancement with current employer
(59.3%), career advancement with
new employer (14.8%), change
industries/functional areas
(25.9%)*

*Estimates based on *BusinessWeek* survey data.

Why BC?

Like their full-time MBA counterparts, evening students at BC have their choice of 10 specializations, including asset management, change leadership, and even a do-it-yourself custom option. As part of the program, which calls for 38 credits in core classes and 18 in electives, students take a series of four interactive courses called management practice modules, which sharpens analytical, teamwork, and management skills. The courses include a leadership project and venture planning experience. The international management experience, an elective that culminates in a 2½-week trip abroad, is the high point for many students.

Boston College is a private institution. Established in 1957, Carroll's part-time MBA program is accredited by the Association to Advance Collegiate Schools of Business (AACSB). Carroll also offers a full-time MBA.

"The professors, students, and environment were extremely enriching."

Where Do They Come From?

Top functional areas:
Finance/Accounting (38%), Operations/Production (17%), General Management (12%), Marketing/Sales (12%)

Top industries: Financial services (30%), Healthcare (16%), Technology (13%)

Top companies: Fidelity Investments, State Street Corp., Investors Bank & Trust, EMC Corp., PricewaterhouseCoopers

---

"The program has a strong focus on finance."

The 411

Maximum time to complete the program: 60 months

Can PT students switch to the FT MBA program: Yes

Tuition per credit hour: $1,126

Classes begin: September, January

Application deadlines: May 1, June 1, October 15

Application fee: $100

Getting In

Relative importance of:
GMAT scores: Important
Work experience: Very important
Application essay: Important
Interview: Not considered
Recommendations: Important
Transcripts: Very important

Getting Out

Number of credits required for degree: 56

Access to Career Services for part-timers: Yes

Access to alumni database for part-timers: Yes

Part-timers permitted to interview on campus for internships: Yes

Part-timers permitted to interview on campus for full-time jobs: Yes

Graduates reporting post-MBA salary increase: 51.7%*

Average increase: 39.6%*

*Estimate based on *Business Week* survey data.

Cliff Notes

Leading areas of study: Accounting, Finance, General Management, Marketing, Strategy

Average class size, core courses: 40

Average class size, electives: 35

Number of electives: 81

Teaching methods: Case studies (40%), lectures (25%), team projects (20%)

Faculty sharing with FT program: 100%

Classes meet: Days, weeknights, week-long sessions

Average workload per week: 18 hours

But What's It *Really* Like?

Program quality, graded by students:
Overall: **A**
Teaching quality: **A+**
Caliber of classmates: **A**
Facilities: **C**
Support: **B**

Curriculum, graded by students:
Overall: **A+**
E-business: **B**
Entrepreneurship: **C**
Ethics: **A**
Finance: **A+**
International business: **B**
Marketing: **A**
Strategy: **B**
Teamwork: **A**

 The Good, the Bad, and the Ugly: Students Speak Out

"The professors, students, and environment were extremely enriching. I felt as though I was part of a community. I could not have asked for a better experience."

"Some of the classes fell a little bit flat."

"It was fantastic that evening students were permitted to participate in the wonderful travel-learning programs like Tech Trek, International Management Experience Europe, and International Management Experience Asia."

"The program has a strong focus on finance, and many part-time students work in finance."

"Career services should be available for a longer period of time."

"I have been very pleased overall with my MBA experience at BC. Some of the classes were spectacular, and some of the classes fell a little bit flat. But overall, I feel that I received a quality education and learned a ton."

"The BC family is very close-knit, especially among the alumni. I received job interviews in industries where I never thought I would have a chance."

"Career services should be available to recent graduates for a longer period of time. Currently the maximum is three months. I will not be looking for another job (even within my company) for another year after graduating."

"I loved the BC Carroll School MBA program. The faculty, staff, and students had a true sense of community, which is extremely difficult to achieve in a part-time program."

Where to Stay

Courtyard by Marriott Brookline
40 Webster St.
Brookline, MA 02446
(617) 734-1393

Sheraton Newton Hotel
320 Washington St.
Newton, MA 02458
(617) 969-3010

Doubletree Guest Suites Boston
400 Soldiers Field Rd.
Allston, MA 02134
(617) 783-0090

 Where to Eat

Appetito's Restaurant
761 Beacon St.
Newton Centre, MA 02459
(617) 244-9881

Bangkok Bistro at Cleveland Circle
1952 Beacon St.
Brighton, MA 02135
(617) 739-7270

Pino's Pizza
1920 Beacon St.
Brighton, MA 02135
(617) 566-6468

 Things to Do

The Samuel Adams Brewery
30 Germania St.
Boston, MA 02130
(617) 368-5080

New England Aquarium
Central Wharf
Boston, MA 02110
(617) 973-5200

CHECK OUT BUSINESSWEEK.COM FOR MORE:

Making the Grade: Find out what it takes to get in with a look at sample application essays and interview tips for Carroll's MBA program.

School Tour: Walk the halls, glance into classrooms, and see where students interact with faculty on this photo tour of the BC campus.

Search & Compare: Find out how Carroll compares to other part-time programs based on specialties and other criteria.

Expanded Profile: Check out more details on the BC part-time program and all it has to offer with our in-depth online profile.

Access all the B-schools content on BusinessWeek.com by subscribing to MBA Insider.

Boston University

School of Management
2007 Ranking: 2nd in the Northeast
595 Commonwealth Ave.
Boston, MA 02215
E-mail address: MBA@bu.edu
Web address: www.management.bu.
edu/gpo/parttime/index.html
For more info: Call graduate admissions
at (617) 353-2670

Why BU?

Part-time MBA students at BU get the best of both worlds: they can be part of a cohort, much as in a full-time program, or go it alone. Cohort students take their first five core classes with the same 50 to 60 students, while self-paced students follow their own schedule. Courses are offered at the Boston campus and at a new satellite campus in Tyngsboro. The program offers students six concentrations: entrepreneurship, finance, international management, marketing, strategy and business analysis, and public and nonprofit management.

Boston University is a private institution. Established in 1925, BU's part-time MBA program is accredited by the Association to Advance Collegiate Schools of Business (AACSB). BU also offers full-time and executive MBA programs.

 **B4UGO**

Applicants accepted: 79%
Average GMAT score: 604
Average years' work experience: 5
Average time to complete the program: 41 months
Completion rate: 81%

 Who Are My Classmates?

Part-time enrollment: 547
Women: 34%
International: 14%
Minority: 33%
Average age: 28
Average base salary at admission: $51,468
Reason for getting an MBA: Career advancement with current employer (41.7%), career advancement with new employer (16.7%), change industries/functional areas (41.7%)*

*Estimates based on *BusinessWeek* survey data.

"The program broadened my knowledge of entrepreneurship."

Where Do They Come From?

Top functional areas:
Finance/Accounting (60%),
Marketing/Sales (20%), Operations/
Production (20%)
Top industries: Financial services
(60%), Healthcare (20%), Technology (20%)
Top companies: Fidelity Investments,
Bank of America, Investors Bank &
Trust, Boston University, EMC

---

*"I did not enjoy BU's
constant focus on
teamwork."*

The 411

Maximum time to complete the
program: 72 months
Can PT students switch to the FT
MBA program: No
Tuition per credit hour: $1,092
Classes begin: September, January
Application deadlines: November 15
to May 15 (fall), September 15
(spring)
Application fee: $100

Getting In

Relative importance of:
GMAT scores: Important
Work experience: Very important
Application essay: Important
Interview: Considered

Recommendations: Very important
Transcripts: Important

Getting Out

Number of credits required for degree:
64
Access to Career Services for part-
timers: Yes
Access to alumni database for part-
timers: Yes
Part-timers permitted to interview on
campus for internships: Yes
Part-timers permitted to interview on
campus for full-time jobs: Yes
Graduates reporting post-MBA salary
increase: 50%*
Average increase: 40%*
*Estimate based on *BusinessWeek* survey data.

Cliff Notes

Leading areas of study: Finance,
General Management, Healthcare
Administration, Management
Information Systems, Marketing
Average class size, core courses: 38
Average class size, electives: 22
Number of electives: 55
Teaching methods: Case studies
(50%), lectures (30%), team projects
(10%)
Faculty sharing with FT program:
53%
Classes meet: Days, weeknights
Average workload per week: 16 hours

But What's It *Really* Like?

Program quality, graded by students:
Overall: **A**
Teaching quality: **A**
Caliber of classmates: **A+**
Facilities: **A+**
Support: **B**

Curriculum, graded by students:
Overall: **C**
E-business: **B**
Entrepreneurship: **B**
Ethics: **C**
Finance: **A+**
International business: **B**
Marketing: **A**
Strategy: **A**
Teamwork: **A+**

 The Good, the Bad, and the Ugly: Students Speak Out

"This program enhanced my skills to enable me to become a great manager in the field that I chose. It has also broadened my knowledge of entrepreneurship and has taught me the fundamentals of venturing out on my own."

"Overall the cost/benefit was very favorable for me."

"I did not enjoy BU's constant focus on teamwork. I think that in some courses it undermined our ability to work on our own."

"The program provided me with an extensive set of tools, knowledge, and general business 'know-how' that has made me extremely confident in my ability to perform and lead."

"The program really opened my eyes about all the career possibilities open to someone with my skill sets. I feel empowered in my career in a way I definitely did not before. It cost me a lot personally. But overall the cost/benefit was very favorable for me."

"The program made me confident in my ability to lead."

"For the most part, professors were of a very high caliber, and I rarely, if ever, felt as though part-time students were getting a lower-quality education than full-time students."

"Some of the core courses had so many students that it was difficult to participate. This was sometimes frustrating, as a large percentage of the grade was dependent on class participation."

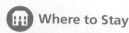 **Where to Stay**

Hotel Commonwealth
650 Beacon St.
Boston, MA 02215
(617) 933-5000

Copley Square Hotel
47 Huntington Ave.
Boston, MA 02116
(617) 536-9000

Hyatt Regency Cambridge
575 Memorial Dr.
Cambridge, MA 02139
(617) 492-1234

 Where to Eat

Dalias Bistro & Wine Bar
1657 Beacon St.
Brookline, MA 02445
(617) 730-8040

Eastern Standard
528 Commonwealth Ave.
Boston, MA 02215
(617) 532-9100

Beijing Café
728 Commonwealth Ave.
Boston, MA 02215
(617) 536-1616

 Things to Do

Boston Duck Tours
3 Copley Pl., Suite 310
Boston, MA 02116
(617) 267-3825

Boston Playwrights' Theatre
949 Commonwealth Ave.
Boston, MA 02215
(866) 811-4111

CHECK OUT BUSINESSWEEK.COM FOR MORE:

Expanded Profile: Itching for more? Check out our detailed online profile of BU's part-time MBA program for more in-depth information.

Search & Compare: See how BU's part-time program measures up against others in the region when it comes to tuition, course offerings, and other considerations.

Sample Application Essays and Interview Tips: Get the lowdown on what it takes to get in.

Access all the B-schools content on BusinessWeek.com by subscribing to MBA Insider.

Carnegie Mellon University

David A. Tepper School of Business
2007 Ranking: 5th in the Mid-Atlantic
5000 Forbes Ave.
Pittsburgh, PA 15213
E-mail address: mba-admissions
@andrew.cmu.edu
Web address: www.tepper.cmu.edu/
For more info: Call MBA admissions at
(412) 268-2272

Why Carnegie Mellon?

With a full-time MBA that has long garnered praise for its intensity and interdisciplinary approach, Tepper has adapted that model for working professionals. The FlexTime program is identical to its full-time counterpart, but courses take just 7½ weeks to complete instead of the standard 12. With only a third of the program devoted to core courses, students have nearly two years to pursue concentrations—most earn 3 or 4 from the 11 on offer. Many electives are project-based, allowing students to apply what they've learned to real company problems.

Carnegie Mellon is a private institution. Established in 1985, Tepper's part-time MBA program is accredited by the Association to Advance Collegiate Schools of Business (AACSB). Tepper also offers a full-time MBA. For details on Tepper's full-time MBA program, see page 5.

☑ B4UGO

Applicants accepted: 85%
Average GMAT score: 628
Average years' work experience: 4.8
**Average time to complete the
  program:** 33 months
Completion rate: 100%

💬 Who Are My Classmates?

Part-time enrollment: 193
Women: 31%
International: 0%
Minority: 33%
Average age: 29
Average base salary at admission:
  $66,147
Reason for getting an MBA: Career
  advancement with current employer
  (51%), career advancement with
  new employer (11.8%), change
  industries/functional areas
  (37.3%)*

*Estimates based on *BusinessWeek* survey data.

> *"A thread of social responsibility ties the program together."*

Where Do They Come From?

Top functional areas: Operations/ Production (33%), Management Information Systems (20%), Marketing/Sales (13%)
Top industries: Technology (21%), Manufacturing (18%), Healthcare (16%)
Top companies: Carnegie Mellon, Westinghouse Electric, Alcoa, Equitable Resources, Medrad

---

"Less diversified than the full-time class."

The 411

Maximum time to complete the program: 48 months
Can PT students switch to the FT MBA program: Yes
Tuition per credit hour: $1,485
Classes begin: August
Application deadlines: October 27, January 5, March 9, April 27
Application fee: $100

Getting In

Relative importance of:
GMAT scores: Very important
Work experience: Very important
Application essay: Very important
Interview: Very important
Recommendations: Very important
Transcripts: Very important

Getting Out

Number of credits required for degree: 64
Access to Career Services for part-timers: Yes
Access to alumni database for part-timers: Yes
Part-timers permitted to interview on campus for internships: Yes
Part-timers permitted to interview on campus for full-time jobs: Yes
Graduates reporting post-MBA salary increase: 62.5%*
Average increase: 38.8%*

*Estimate based on *BusinessWeek* survey data.

Cliff Notes

Leading areas of study: Entrepreneurship, Finance, Marketing, Product Operations Management, Strategy
Average class size, core courses: 67
Average class size, electives: 45
Number of electives: 142
Teaching methods: Lectures (50%), case studies (25%), simulations (15%)
Faculty sharing with FT program: 100%
Classes meet: Weeknights
Average workload per week: 17 hours

"Helped me achieve a different career trajectory."

But What's It *Really* Like?

Program quality, graded by students:
Overall: **C**
Teaching quality: **B**
Caliber of classmates: **B**
Facilities: **B**
Support: **C**

Curriculum, graded by students:
Overall: **C**
E-business: **A**
Entrepreneurship: **B**
Ethics: **C**
Finance: **B**
International business: **C**
Marketing: **B**
Strategy: **A**
Teamwork: **B**

 The Good, the Bad, and the Ugly: Students Speak Out

"The program is mislabeled as only churning out 'quant jocks.' In fact, a thread of humanity and social responsibility ties the program together."

"A very high percentage of the part-time students come from an engineering background—the part-time class is less diversified than the full-time class."

"The course availability in the evenings is marginal. Summer sessions, which are required in order to graduate in three years, have a stunningly limited selection."

"The MBA has definitely helped me in achieving a different career trajectory. I've already been offered a management role with an 80% raise in total compensation."

"Course availability in the evenings is marginal."

"I will give credit to CMU for really ensuring that the part-timers are getting the same education as the day students. I feel that when I walk out the door with my degree, I will have the same, if not a better, education as my full-time counterparts."

"Carnegie Mellon University's Distance Learning Program is phenomenal—cutting edge, innovative. I had never seen anything like it."

"I have discussed my education with those who have gone to the 'top tier' programs. If I could go to any school in the country for free and based my decision purely on the quality of education, I would still have decided upon the Tepper School of Business."

Where to Stay

Wyndham Garden Hotel
3454 Forbes Ave.
Pittsburgh, PA 15213
(412) 683-2040

Holiday Inn University Center
100 Lytton Ave.
Pittsburgh, PA 15213
(412) 682-6200

Residence Inn by Marriott
3896 Bigelow Blvd.
Pittsburgh, PA 15213
(412) 621-2200

 Where to Eat

Primanti Brothers Restaurant
3803 Forbes Ave.
Pittsburgh, PA 15213
(412) 621-4444

Mad Mex
370 Atwood St.
Pittsburgh, PA 15213
(412) 681-5656

Aladdin's Eatery
5878 Forbes Ave.
Pittsburgh, PA 15217
(412) 421-5100

 Things to Do

Pittsburgh Zoo & PPG Aquarium
One Wild Place
Pittsburgh, PA 15206
(412) 665-3640

The Andy Warhol Museum
117 Sandusky St.
Pittsburgh, PA 15212
(412) 237-8300

CHECK OUT BUSINESSWEEK.COM FOR MORE:

Admissions Q&A: Laurie Stewart, director of admissions, offers insight into common application blunders, how the program is evolving, and what it takes to get into Tepper.

Interview Tips: Suggestions on what to do when face-to-face with your admissions interviewer.

Video View: Listen to Dean Ken Dunn describe the various interdisciplinary tracks students can choose in designing their course of study.

Expanded Profile: Dig deeper into the Tepper part-time MBA program with this detailed online profile.

Search & Compare: Find out how Tepper stacks up against other top schools in the region.

Access all the B-schools content on BusinessWeek.com by subscribing to MBA Insider.

Drexel University

Bennett S. LeBow College of Business
2007 Ranking: 2nd in the Mid-Atlantic
105 Matheson Hall
32nd & Market Sts.
Philadelphia, PA 19104
E-mail address: mba@drexel.edu
Web address: www.lebow.drexel.edu/
For more info: Call the MBA program
at (215) 895-2115

☑ B4UGO

Applicants accepted: 25%
Average GMAT score: 600
Average years' work experience: 8.5
**Average time to complete the
program:** 32 months
Completion rate: 88%

◯ Who Are My Classmates?

Part-time enrollment: 552
Women: 43%
International: 6%
Minority: 33%
Average age: 29
Average base salary at admission:
$55,454*
Reason for getting an MBA: Career
advancement with current employer
(62.2%), career advancement with
new employer (16.2%), change
industries/functional areas
(21.6%)*

*Estimates based on *Business Week* survey data.

Why Drexel?

Part-time MBA students have two choices at Drexel—a traditional professional MBA with day, evening, and online classes and the LEAD MBA, a 24-month evening program where students progress in cohorts, much like a full-time MBA. The programs offer concentrations in entrepreneurship, marketing, and other subjects—10 and 5, respectively—and have a heavy focus on leadership and technology management. A third choice—a part-time accelerated online MBA that can be completed in two years—is also available.

Drexel is a private institution. Established in 1947, LeBow's part-time MBA program is accredited by the Association to Advance Collegiate Schools of Business (AACSB). LeBow also offers full-time and executive MBA programs.

"The caliber of students was outstanding."

Where Do They Come From?

Top functional areas:
Finance/Accounting (30%), Marketing/Sales (15%), Consulting (10%), General Management (10%), Human Resources (10%), Management Information Systems (10%)
Top industries: Financial services (30%), Manufacturing (30%), Healthcare (20%)
Top companies: Lockheed Martin, DuPont, Vanguard, Siemens, Susquehanna Investment Services

---

"A great collaborative atmosphere."

The 411

Maximum time to complete the program: 84 months
Can PT students switch to the FT MBA program: Yes
Tuition per credit hour: $835
Classes begin: September, January, March, June
Application deadlines: August 24, November 23, February 22, May 24
Application fee: $50

Getting In

Relative importance of:
GMAT scores: Very important
Work experience: Very important
Application essay: Important
Interview: Considered
Recommendations: Important
Transcripts: Very important

Getting Out

Number of credits required for degree: 60
Access to Career Services for part-timers: Yes
Access to alumni database for part-timers: Yes
Part-timers permitted to interview on campus for internships: Yes
Part-timers permitted to interview on campus for full-time jobs: Yes
Graduates reporting post-MBA salary increase: 51.2%*
Average increase: 32.2%*

*Estimate based on *Business Week* survey data.

Cliff Notes

Leading areas of study: Accounting, Entrepreneurship, Finance, International Business, Marketing
Average class size, core courses: 19
Average class size, electives: 25
Number of electives: 69
Teaching methods: Lectures (40%), case studies (25%), team projects (20%)
Faculty sharing with FT program: 100%
Classes meet: Weeknights, weeklong sessions, online
Average workload per week: 9 hours

But What's It *Really* Like?

Program quality, graded by students:
Overall: **A**
Teaching quality: **B**
Caliber of classmates: **B**
Facilities: **B**
Support: **B**

Curriculum, graded by students:
Overall: **A+**
E-business: **A**
Entrepreneurship: **A**
Ethics: **B**
Finance: **A**
International business: **C**
Marketing: **A**
Strategy: **B**
Teamwork: **A**

 ### The Good, the Bad, and the Ugly: Students Speak Out

"I attended the LEAD Cohort Program [a two-year part-time program taught in class and online]. The caliber of the students in my class was outstanding. The professors were top notch. The administration took care of just about every need I had during the length of the program."

"Nonexistent career services."

"I had a very rigorous and fulfilling undergraduate experience and expected the same from my MBA program. I was disappointed in the academic caliber of the program and of my fellow students and in the quality of instruction. I felt that the program was overpriced and that I did not learn as much as I could have."

"A lot of help and support from the entire faculty and a great collaborative atmosphere."

"I did not learn as much as I could have."

"Poor teachers, poor administrators, and nonexistent career services."

"The program was challenging and utilized current case studies that were relevant in today's business environment. The program focused on developing the student's analytical skills as well as the technical skills needed to succeed as a future leader."

"My undergraduate degree was more stringent and challenging."

"I'm actively recruiting my friends to apply. I tell them about the connections you can make with classmates who come from Coke, GE, IBM, Home Depot, Georgia-Pacific . . . and those are just the people in my small group."

Where to Stay

Club Quarters
1628 Chestnut St.
Philadelphia, PA 19103
(215) 282-5000

Hampton Inn Philadelphia Center City
1301 Race St.
Philadelphia, PA 19107
(215) 665-9100

Sheraton University City Hotel
3549 Chestnut St.
Philadelphia, PA 19104
(877) 459-1146

 Where to Eat

Le Bec Fin
1523 Walnut St.
Philadelphia, PA 19102
(215) 567-1000

Lombardi's Pizza
1809 Walnut St.
Philadelphia, PA 19103
(215) 564-5000

Pat's King of Steaks
1237 E. Passyunk Ave.
Philadelphia, PA 19147
(215) 468-1546

 Things to Do

Chestnut Hill
Chestnut Hill Visitor's Center
8426 Germantown Ave.
Philadelphia, PA 19118
(215) 247-6696

South Street
Philadelphia, PA 19147

CHECK OUT BUSINESSWEEK.COM FOR MORE:

Expanded Profile: Find more details on Drexel's part-time MBA program in its online profile.

Search & Compare: See how Drexel stacks up against other part-time MBA programs using this interactive tool.

School Tour: Planning a visit? Check out Drexel's Philadelphia campus before you go.

Forums: Connect with other Drexel hopefuls using our online forums.

Access all the B-schools content on BusinessWeek.com by subscribing to MBA Insider.

Elon University

Martha and Spencer Love School of
Business
2007 Ranking: 2nd in the South
2750 Campus Box
Elon, NC 27244
E-mail address: gradadm@elon.edu
Web address: www.elon.edu/e-web/
academics/graduate/mba/
For more info: Call the MBA program
at (800) 334-8448, ext. 3

Why Elon?

While most schools have distinct full-time and part-time programs, Elon combines both formats in a single program. All classes meet once a week from 6 to 9 p.m., so working students have full access to the range of resources the school has to offer. Among them: an integrated curriculum, executive speakers, and hands-on learning opportunities. Two-week study-abroad trips take students to Beijing, Shanghai, Hong Kong, London, Brussels, Buenos Aires, and Santiago. Spouses are invited to come along.

Elon is a private institution. Established in 1984, the Love School of Business's part-time MBA program is accredited by the Association to Advance Collegiate Schools of Business (AACSB).

☑ B4UGO

Applicants accepted: 79%
Average GMAT score: 550
Average years' work experience: 9.3
**Average time to complete the
program:** 27 months
Completion rate: 92%

● Who Are My Classmates?

Part-time enrollment: 131
Women: 38%
International: 4%
Minority: 23%
Average age: 32
Average base salary at admission:
$57,500
Reason for getting an MBA: Career
advancement with current employer
(64.5%), career advancement with
new employer (11.3%), change
industries/functional areas
(24.2%)*

*Estimates based on *BusinessWeek* survey data.

> *"I have personally
> recommended the
> program to my peers."*

Where Do They Come From?

Top functional areas: General Management (40%), Operations/Production (18%), Marketing/Sales (17%)

Top industries: Manufacturing (36%), Financial services (18%), Nonprofit (11%)

Top companies: Sony-Ericsson, Underwriters Labs, UNC Healthcare, LabCorp, Cisco Systems

---

"Not as rigorous as I had expected."

The 411

Maximum time to complete the program: 72 months

Can PT students switch to the FT MBA program: Separate FT MBA not offered

Tuition per credit hour: $440

Classes begin: August, February

Application deadlines: None

Application fee: $50

Getting In

Relative importance of:
GMAT scores: Very important
Work experience: Very important
Application essay: Considered
Interview: Not considered
Recommendations: Considered
Transcripts: Very important

Getting Out

Number of credits required for degree: 39

Access to Career Services for part-timers: Yes

Access to alumni database for part-timers: Yes

Part-timers permitted to interview on campus for internships: N/A

Part-timers permitted to interview on campus for full-time jobs: N/A

Graduates reporting post-MBA salary increase: 62.5%*

Average increase: 27.9%*

*Estimate based on *Business Week* survey data.

Cliff Notes

Leading areas of study: Entrepreneurship, General Management, Leadership

Average class size, core courses: 18

Average class size, electives: 18

Number of electives: 8

Teaching methods: Lectures (40%), team projects (20%), distance learning (20%)

Faculty sharing with FT program: N/A

Classes meet: Weeknights

Average workload per week: 18 hours

"Does not allow for specialization."

But What's It *Really* Like?

Program quality, graded by students:
Overall: **A+**
Teaching quality: **B**
Caliber of classmates: **A**
Facilities: **A+**
Support: **A+**

Curriculum, graded by students:
Overall: **B**
E-business: **C**
Entrepreneurship: **C**
Ethics: **A**
Finance: **C**
International business: **A**
Marketing: **C**
Strategy: **C**
Teamwork: **A+**

 The Good, the Bad, and the Ugly: Students Speak Out

"Elon has an excellent MBA program; it's very focused on making sure that students are learning the material. The professors bend over backwards to accommodate personal and professional conflicts and schedules. I have personally recommended the program to many of my peers."

"The program was not as rigorous as I had expected."

"The program I'm in does not allow for a lot of specialization. It's great for most people, but I would not recommend it for someone who wants to specialize."

"Elon is a hidden treasure. The experience was amazing, especially the global opportunities."

"Small class sizes and an engaging faculty."

"While the program is pretty solid, it is still in its infancy. It needs a better focus on individuals looking to switch careers, rather than those trying to climb the ladder at their present employers."

"The Elon MBA program provided an outstanding experiential learning environment, focusing on leadership in a global economy. It has relatively small class sizes, an engaging faculty, and a close-knit student/faculty/staff community."

"I have grown as an individual as well as a professional. The program is fast-paced if you want it to be, or you can take a slower route. The program cost is affordable. All in all, it's top notch."

"Elon is a hidden treasure."

 **Where to Stay**

The Acorn Inn
301 W. Haggard Ave.
Elon College, NC 27244
(336) 585-0167

Best Western Burlington
770 Huffman Mill Rd.
Burlington, NC 27215
(336) 584-0151

Burke Manor Inn Bed & Breakfast
303 Burke St.
Gibsonville, NC 27249
(336) 449-6266

 Where to Eat

O'Charley's
521 Huffman Mill Rd.
Burlington, NC 27215
(336) 584-5652

Sal's Italian Restaurant
402 Huffman Mill Rd.
Burlington, NC 27215
(336) 584-3726

Sidetrack Grill
110 W. Lebanon Ave.
Elon College, NC 27244
(336) 584-1769

 Things to Do

Four Seasons Town Center
410 Four Seasons Town Ctr.
Greensboro, NC 27407
(336) 292-0171

West End Station
138 W. Lebanon Ave.
Elon College, NC 27244
(336) 585-1227

CHECK OUT BUSINESSWEEK.COM FOR MORE:

Expanded Profile: Find more details on Elon's part-time MBA program in its online profile.

Search & Compare: See how Elon stacks up against other part-time MBA programs using this interactive tool.

Forums: Connect with other Elon hopefuls using our online forums.

Access all the B-schools content on BusinessWeek.com by subscribing to MBA Insider.

Emory University

Goizueta Business School
2007 Ranking: 1st in the South
Evening MBA
1300 Clifton Rd.
Atlanta, GA 30322
E-mail address:
eveningmba@bus.emory.edu
Web address: www.goizueta.emory.edu/
degree/eveningmba/index.asp
For more info: Call the Evening MBA
Program at **(404) 727-4477**

☑ B4UGO

Applicants accepted: 61%
Average GMAT score: 627
Average years' work experience: 6
**Average time to complete the
program:** 33 months
Completion rate: 97%

page 25. For details on its executive MBA program, see page 225.

Why Emory?

Looking for a blazingly fast part-time MBA? Look no further. While students can take up to five years to complete the nine core classes and nine electives needed for the degree, there's an alternative: Accelerated Course Electives— optional three-week intensive classes offered during semester breaks—that allow students to complete the program in as little as 24 months. Still, Goizueta doesn't skimp. More than a dozen concentrations are available, there's a leadership program for part-timers, and a six- to eight-day international trip caps off the experience.

Emory is a private institution. Established in 1992, Goizueta's part-time MBA program is accredited by the Association to Advance Collegiate Schools of Business (AACSB). Goizueta also offers full-time and executive MBA programs. For details on Goizueta's full-time MBA program, see

 Who Are My Classmates?

Part-time enrollment: 265
Women: 32%
International: 0%
Minority: 22%
Average age: 29
Average base salary at admission: $77,294
Reason for getting an MBA: Career advancement with current employer (25.7%), career advancement with new employer (34.3%), change industries/functional areas (40%)*

*Estimates based on *Business Week* survey data.

"I wouldn't have my job today without Goizueta."

Where Do They Come From?

Top functional areas: Finance/ Accounting (21%), Marketing/ Sales (18%), Operations/ Production (17%)

Top industries: Consumer products (22%), Financial services (13%), Technology (12%)

Top companies: General Electric, Emory University, Home Depot, McMaster Carr, Philip Morris

---

"Some classes were simply not offered to part-time students."

The 411

Maximum time to complete the program: 60 months

Can PT students switch to the FT MBA program: No

Tuition per credit hour: $1,250

Classes begin: September

Application deadlines: March 1, June 1

Application fee: $150

Getting In

Relative importance of:
GMAT scores: Very important
Work experience: Important
Application essay: Important
Interview: Important
Recommendations: Important
Transcripts: Very important

Getting Out

Number of credits required for degree: 54

Access to Career Services for part-timers: Yes

Access to alumni database for part-timers: Yes

Part-timers permitted to interview on campus for internships: No

Part-timers permitted to interview on campus for full-time jobs: Yes

Graduates reporting post-MBA salary increase: 76.3%*

Average increase: 39.8%*

*Estimate based on *BusinessWeek* survey data.

Cliff Notes

Leading areas of study: Decision Analysis, Finance/Capital Markets, Leadership, Management Consulting, Marketing

Average class size, core courses: 57

Average class size, electives: 36

Number of electives: 32

Teaching methods: Lectures (35%), case studies (35%), team projects (15%)

Faculty sharing with FT program: 100%

Classes meet: Weeknights

Average workload per week: 18 hours

"Emory catered to our special needs."

But What's It *Really* Like?

Program quality, graded by students:
Overall: **A+**
Teaching quality: **A**
Caliber of classmates: **A+**
Facilities: **A+**
Support: **A+**

Curriculum, graded by students:
Overall: **A+**
E-business: **A**
Entrepreneurship: **A+**
Ethics: **B**
Finance: **B**
International business: **A+**
Marketing: **A**
Strategy: **A**
Teamwork: **A**

 The Good, the Bad, and the Ugly: Students Speak Out

"I wouldn't have my job today without the education, confidence, and connections I gained at Goizueta. I use the education almost every day in my job to evaluate new markets, prioritize new features in my product, and build a business case to fund new projects."

> ## "The professors are excellent and challenging."

"Some instructors for the full-time program were not available to the part-time program. Thus, some classes that would be very useful were simply not offered to part-time students."

"Without question, Goizueta is a first-tier MBA program. The academic rigor, reputation for excellence, tight-knit community, and first-class staff were major contributors to my great experience here."

> ## "Without question, Goizueta is a first-tier MBA program."

"I think my Emory experience was fantastic. The professors are excellent and challenging. Every professor knows what you are learning in your other classes and paces the material accordingly. There was a good balance of group work, individual work, case studies, and articles. Class discussions and coursework were very current."

"Emory catered to our special needs as evening students. They often had food for us, evening office hours, evening meeting times, and so on. But sometimes professors did not want to stay late to teach the evening program—we lost out because of that."

"This is the best educational experience I've ever had. Lifelong friendships were just a bonus!"

Where to Stay

Emory Conference Center Hotel/ Emory Inn
1615 Clifton Rd.
Atlanta, GA 30322
(800) 933-6679

Wyndham Midtown Atlanta
125 10th St. N.E.
Atlanta, GA 30309
(404) 873-4900

Four Seasons Atlanta
75 14th St.
Atlanta, GA 30309
(404) 253-3853

 Where to Eat

Sotto Sotto
313 N. Highland Ave.
Atlanta, GA 30307
(404) 523-6678

Watershed
406 W. Ponce de Leon Ave.
Decatur, GA 30030
(404) 378-4900

The Flying Biscuit Café
1655 McLendon Ave.
Atlanta, GA 30307
(404) 687-8888

 Things to Do

Carter Presidential Center
One Copenhill Ave.
Atlanta, GA 30307
(404) 331-0296

The World of Coca-Cola
55 Martin Luther King Jr. Dr. S.W.
Atlanta, GA 30303
(404) 676-5151

CHECK OUT BUSINESSWEEK.COM FOR MORE:

Sample Application Essays and Interview Tips: Check out sample essays and interview advice geared toward Emory applicants.

Careers Q&A: Career Center Director Son Pham and his predecessor, Carol Asamoah, describe how Goizueta connects students with employers.

Search & Compare: Find out how Emory measures up to other top programs across the country.

Expanded Profile: Check out the online profile for Emory's evening MBA program for more info on the class profile, admissions, and program features.

Access all the B-schools content on BusinessWeek.com by subscribing to MBA Insider.

Georgia State University

J. Mack Robinson College of Business
2007 Ranking: 3rd in the South
35 Broad St. N.W.
Atlanta, GA 30302
E-mail address:
   mastersadmissions@gsu.edu
Web address: www.robinson.gsu.edu/
   academic/flexible.html
For more info: Call admissions at (404)
   413-7130

☑ B4UGO

Applicants accepted: 66%
Average GMAT score: 605
Average years' work experience: 6
**Average time to complete the
   program:** 36 months
Completion rate: 87%

Why Georgia State?

Georgia State's 42-credit core includes courses in strategic leadership, negotiations, and managing in a global economy, as well as a capstone course on global competitive strategy. A domestic or international residency is optional. Core courses are completed in cohorts to help classmates network, and the staff helps smooth the way—registering students, ordering books, even providing snacks. The program is offered in four locations and two formats—a two-year program in Alpharetta, downtown Atlanta, or Henry County with courses every other Thursday evening and Saturday, and a three-year program at the off-campus Brookhaven Center with courses every other Monday and Wednesday evening.

Georgia State is a public institution. Established in 1958, Robinson's part-time MBA program is accredited by the Association to Advance Collegiate Schools of Business (AACSB). Robinson

also offers full-time/part-time hybrid MBA and executive MBA programs.

 Who Are My Classmates?

Part-time enrollment: 1,320
Women: 39%
International: 9%
Minority: 27%
Average age: 30
Average base salary at admission:
   $67,500
Reason for getting an MBA: Career advancement with current employer (40%), career advancement with new employer (24.6%), change industries/functional areas (35.4%)*

*Estimates based on *BusinessWeek* survey data.

"This program gave me the confidence to start my own business."

Where Do They Come From?

Top functional areas: Finance/
Accounting (22%), Operations/
Production (18%), Marketing/Sales
(17%)
Top industries: Consulting (24%),
Nonprofit (18%), Technology
(13%)
Top companies: Georgia Pacific,
Georgia State University, Accenture,
BellSouth, Coca-Cola

---

*"There was a lot of
flexibility in choosing
courses."*

The 411

Maximum time to complete the
program: 60 months
Can PT students switch to the FT
MBA program: No
Tuition per credit hour: $214 (resi-
dent), $853 (nonresident)
Classes begin: August, January, May
Application deadlines: April 1,
September 15, February 1 (U.S.);
February 1, April 1, September 1
(international)
Application fee: $50

Getting In

Relative importance of:
GMAT scores: Very important
Work experience: Very important
Application essay: Important

Interview: Considered
Recommendations: Considered
Transcripts: Very important

Getting Out

Number of credits required for degree:
51
Access to Career Services for part-
timers: Yes
Access to alumni database for part-
timers: Yes
Part-timers permitted to interview on
campus for internships: Yes
Part-timers permitted to interview on
campus for full-time jobs: Yes
Graduates reporting post-MBA salary
increase: 53%*
Average increase: 41.8%*
*Estimate based on *BusinessWeek* survey data.

Cliff Notes

Leading areas of study: Accounting,
Computer Information Systems,
Finance, Managerial Sciences, Mar-
keting
Average class size, core courses: 28
Average class size, electives: 22
Number of electives: 163
Teaching methods: Case studies
(35%), lectures (30%), team projects
(15%)
Faculty sharing with FT program:
N/A
Classes meet: Weeknights, weekends,
weeklong sessions, online
Average workload per week: 20 hours

But What's It *Really* Like?

Program quality, graded by students:
Overall: **B**
Teaching quality: **A**
Caliber of classmates: **C**
Facilities: **C**
Support: **C**

Curriculum, graded by students:
Overall: **B**
E-business: **A**
Entrepreneurship: **A**
Ethics: **B**
Finance: **B**
International business: **A+**
Marketing: **B**
Strategy: **B**
Teamwork: **C**

 The Good, the Bad, and the Ugly: Students Speak Out

"This program enhanced my existing business knowledge, improved my project management skills, improved my teamwork skills, helped me to meet many other young professionals in Atlanta, and gave me the confidence and experience I needed to start my own business."

"GSU is a screaming deal. I'd recommend the program to anyone."

"The work was not as challenging as I had expected."

"There was a lot of flexibility in choosing the courses I was interested in. There were many professors offering many courses at the same time. I had the opportunity to take the courses of my interest with the professors of my choice."

"A surprising number of my classmates were of very poor caliber, and for the majority of my classes the work was not as challenging as I had expected."

"A well-run program with great professors who typically fall outside the 'ivory tower' academic mold and a surprisingly high-quality student body. Plus, GSU is a screaming deal. I'd highly recommend the program to anyone seeking an MBA, part-time or full-time!"

"Going to Georgia State University for an MBA was the dumbest mistake I have ever made. The faculty is unqualified and unprofessional and incompetent. The classes are not conveniently scheduled, and the school staff and faculty could not care less about students. . . . Georgia State University's MBA program is a joke."

 **Where to Stay**

Holiday Inn Atlanta Downtown
101 International Blvd. N.E.
Atlanta, GA 30303
(404) 524-5555

Travelodge Atlanta Downtown
311 Courtland St. N.E.
Atlanta, GA 30303
(404) 659-4545

Wyndham Garden Hotel Atlanta Downtown
175 Piedmont Ave. N.E.
Atlanta, GA 30303
(404) 659-2727

 Where to Eat

Afrodish Restaurant
209 Edgewood Ave. S.E.
Atlanta, GA 30303
(404) 522-1054

King & I
1510 Piedmont Ave. N.E., Suite F
Atlanta, GA 30324
(404) 892-7743

The Sundial Restaurant, Bar & View
210 Peachtree St. N.W.
Atlanta, GA 30303
(404) 589-7506

 Things to Do

Halo Lounge
817 W. Peachtree St.
Atlanta, GA 30308
(404) 962-7333

The World of Coca-Cola
55 Martin Luther King Jr. Dr. S.W.
Atlanta, GA 30303
(404) 676-5151

CHECK OUT BUSINESSWEEK.COM FOR MORE:

Expanded Profile: Hungry for more? Find more details on Georgia State's part-time MBA program in its online profile.

Search & Compare: Use our handy interactive tool to see how Georgia State stacks up against other part-time MBA programs in the region.

School Tour: Planning a visit? Check out Georgia State's Atlanta campus before you go.

Forums: Connect with other Georgia State hopefuls using our online forums.

Access all the B-schools content on BusinessWeek.com by subscribing to MBA Insider.

Indiana University Southeast

School of Business
2007 Ranking: 3rd in the Midwest
4201 Grant Line Rd.
New Albany, IN 47150
E-mail address: iusmba@ius.edu
Web address: www.ius.edu/Business
For more info: Call the main
switchboard at (812) 941-2364

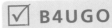 **B4UGO**

Applicants accepted: 60%
Average GMAT score: 561
Average years' work experience: 5.5
**Average time to complete the
program:** 36 months
Completion rate: 91%

Why Indiana University Southeast?

For students with a recent undergraduate business degree, the IUS MBA requires 36 credits—30 in required courses and 6 in electives—but those without a business degree may be required to complete as many as 20 more. Areas of focus include decision-making fundamentals, communication skills, and strategic management. Classes are available at the New Albany campus and the downtown Louisville Graduate Center. The least expensive ranked program in the Midwest, the IUS MBA is also one of the few part-time programs anywhere with a community service requirement.

Indiana University Southeast is a public institution. Established in 1991, its part-time MBA program is accredited by the Association to Advance Collegiate Schools of Business (AACSB).

 Who Are My Classmates?

Part-time enrollment: 220
Women: 37%
International: 1%
Minority: 16%
Average age: 29
Average base salary at admission: $34,000*
Reason for getting an MBA: Career advancement with current employer (52.6%), career advancement with new employer (36.8%), change industries/functional areas (10.5%)*

*Estimates based on *BusinessWeek* survey data.

"IUS has an awesome program."

Where Do They Come From?

Top functional areas:
Finance/Accounting (33%), Consulting (22%), Management Information Systems (10%), General Management (10%)

Top industries: Financial services (24%), Manufacturing (20%), Consumer products (15%)

Top companies: General Electric, Humana, Yum! Brands, UPS, Brown-Forman

---

"The MBA program could offer more electives."

The 411

Maximum time to complete the program: 84 months

Can PT students switch to the FT MBA program: FT MBA not offered

Tuition per credit hour: $270 (resident), $577 (nonresident)

Classes begin: August, January, May, June

Application deadlines: July 1 (fall), November 1 (spring), April 1 (summer)

Application fee: $35 (U.S.), $60 (international)

Getting In

Relative importance of:
GMAT scores: Very important
Work experience: Important
Application essay: Important
Interview: Considered
Recommendations: Considered
Transcripts: Very important

Getting Out

Number of credits required for degree: 36

Access to Career Services for part-timers: Yes

Access to alumni database for part-timers: No

Part-timers permitted to interview on campus for internships: N/A

Part-timers permitted to interview on campus for full-time jobs: N/A

Graduates reporting post-MBA salary increase: 29.4%*

Average increase: 44.1%*

*Estimate based on *Business Week* survey data.

Cliff Notes

Leading areas of study: Accounting, Finance, General Management, Leadership, Strategy

Average class size, core courses: 18

Average class size, electives: 15

Number of electives: 13

Teaching methods: Lectures (30%), case studies (25%), experiential learning (15%), simulations (15%), team projects (15%)

Faculty sharing with FT program: N/A

Classes meet: Weeknights

Average workload per week: 12 hours

But What's It *Really* Like?

Program quality, graded by students:
Overall: A+
Teaching quality: A+
Caliber of classmates: B
Facilities: B
Support: B

Curriculum, graded by students:
Overall: A+
E-business: C
Entrepreneurship: C
Ethics: A+
Finance: C
International business: C
Marketing: C
Strategy: A+
Teamwork: B

 ### The Good, the Bad, and the Ugly: Students Speak Out

"IUS has an awesome program. The campus is loaded with technology, and the classes are cutting edge. All the classes could be applied to what I was doing in my current job."

"The MBA program could offer more electives. Once you get to your last semester, there are few classes to choose from."

"The Career Services Department could be much more active."

"I was always a good employee, but the knowledge I have gained from school has helped me see my business from a different angle. I have strengthened my critical thinking skills, have a strong grasp of organizational systems, and understand the importance of operating nonprofits just like for-profit endeavors."

"I have strengthened my critical thinking skills."

"There should be less quantitative testing and more involved group work. The finance and economics classes were the worst classes in the entire program."

"The MBA instructors were excellent. They are all knowledgeable in their fields and were able to discuss topics in a way that students could understand. The only weakness I can think of is that some held office hours during the day when some students could not make it because of their work schedules."

"The Career Services Department could be much more active for the MBA program. We received e-mails regarding job postings only infrequently."

 Where to Stay

Holiday Inn Express Louisville—N.W.
411 W. Spring St.
New Albany, IN 47150
(812) 945-2771

Hampton Inn New Albany
506 W. Spring St.
New Albany, IN 47150
(812) 944-4600

Comfort Suites Jeffersonville
360 Eastern Blvd.
Jeffersonville, IN 47130
(812) 282-2100

Where to Eat

Hungry Pelican
2604 Charlestown Rd.
New Albany, IN 47150
(812) 948-1692

Kobe Japanese Steakhouse
301 Southern Indiana Ave.
Jeffersonville, IN 47130
(812) 280-8500

Onions Restaurant & Tea House
4211 Charlestown Rd.
New Albany, IN 47150
(812) 981-0188

Things to Do

Carnegie Center for Art & History
201 E. Spring St.
New Albany, IN 47150
(812) 944-7336

Culbertson Mansion State Historic Site
914 E. Main St.
New Albany, IN 47150
(812) 944-9600

CHECK OUT BUSINESSWEEK.COM FOR MORE:

Expanded Profile: Hungry for more? Find more details on Indiana's part-time MBA program in its online profile.

Search & Compare: See how Indiana stacks up against other part-time MBA programs using this interactive tool.

Forums: Connect with other Indiana hopefuls using our online forums.

Access all the B-schools content on BusinessWeek.com by subscribing to MBA Insider.

Lehigh University

College of Business & Economics
2007 Ranking: 1st in the Mid-Atlantic
Rauch Business Center
621 Taylor St.
Bethlehem, PA 18015
E-mail address:
    mba.admissions@lehigh.edu
Web address: www.lehighmba.com
For more info: Call the MBA program
    at (610) 758-3418

Why Lehigh?

Lehigh proves that you don't have to be expensive to be good. It is both low cost and highly ranked, regionally and nationally, owing to smart and experienced students, small classes, and accessible faculty. A choice of six concentrations, a capstone experience that requires students to tackle real company problems, and a "team teaching" approach that brings complementary approaches to each class set this program apart. Students are free to take as many or as few courses as they want and to take a quarter off if necessary.

Lehigh is a private institution. Established in 1953, Lehigh's part-time MBA program is accredited by the Association to Advance Collegiate Schools of Business (AACSB). Lehigh also offers a full-time MBA.

☑ B4UGO

Applicants accepted: 63%
Average GMAT score: 637
Average years' work experience: 7.5
**Average time to complete the
    program:** 36 months
Completion rate: 64%

🔵 Who Are My Classmates?

Part-time enrollment: 233
Women: 27%
International: 10%
Minority: 12%
Average age: 33
Average base salary at admission:
    $62,857*
Reason for getting an MBA: Career
    advancement with current employer
    (69.4%), career advancement with
    new employer (11.3%), change
    industries/functional areas
    (19.4%)*

*Estimates based on *BusinessWeek* survey data.

> *"A challenging, highly participative MBA program."*

Where Do They Come From?

Top functional areas: Operations/Production (54%), Management Information Systems (20%), Consulting (8%), Marketing/Sales (8%)

Top industries: Healthcare (29%), Manufacturing (23%), Petroleum/Energy (18%)

Top companies: Merck & Co., Air Products and Chemicals, Lutron Electronics, sanofi pasteur, PPL Corp.

"Would have liked to see more leadership and strategy work."

The 411

Maximum time to complete the program: 72 months

Can PT students switch to the FT MBA program: Yes

Tuition per credit hour: $630

Classes begin: August, January, May, July

Application deadlines: July 15 (fall), December 1 (spring), April 30, May 30 (summer)

Application fee: $65

Getting In

Relative importance of:
GMAT scores: Very important
Work experience: Very important

Application essay: Important
Interview: Considered
Recommendations: Important
Transcripts: Important

Getting Out

Number of credits required for degree: 36

Access to Career Services for part-timers: Yes

Access to alumni database for part-timers: Yes

Part-timers permitted to interview on campus for internships: Yes

Part-timers permitted to interview on campus for full-time jobs: Yes

Graduates reporting post-MBA salary increase: 48.7%*

Average increase: 31.6%*

*Estimate based on *BusinessWeek* survey data.

Cliff Notes

Leading areas of study: Entrepreneurship, Finance, Marketing, Supply Chain Management

Average class size, core courses: 19

Average class size, electives: 13

Number of electives: 83

Teaching methods: Lectures (35%), case studies (25%), experiential learning (16%)

Faculty sharing with FT program: 100%

Classes meet: Weeknights, weeklong sessions

Average workload per week: 10 hours

But What's It *Really* Like?

Program quality, graded by students:
Overall: **A**
Teaching quality: **A**
Caliber of classmates: **B**
Facilities: **B**
Support: **A+**

Curriculum, graded by students:
Overall: **A**
E-business: **A+**
Entrepreneurship: **A+**
Ethics: **B**
Finance: **C**
International business: **C**
Marketing: **B**
Strategy: **B**
Teamwork: **A**

 The Good, the Bad, and the Ugly: Students Speak Out

"Lehigh offers a challenging, highly participative MBA program. This program is definitely not for someone who is just seeking the sheepskin. It requires a lot of effort, but the effort has paid dividends in both acquiring new skills applicable to my career and producing research projects and tools that my company can use."

> ## *"Every course contains information that helps me with my job."*

"I would have liked to see more leadership and strategy work and fewer academic functions such as accounting and finance."

"Every course that I've taken at Lehigh contains information that helps me with my current job and information that will be useful in positions that I hope to pursue in the future."

"The instructors were top notch, and I was able to work the classes into my busy schedule through the distance-learning program that Lehigh University offers."

> ## *"Instructors were top notch."*

"I found that some of the coursework was more undergraduate-focused (the professors also treated us like undergraduates at times). Also, I felt that I didn't gain more incremental knowledge than what I had going into the program."

"The professors worked very hard to make themselves completely available at any time. The videotaped sessions were well done. The live online sessions were well attended and engaging. The 'homework' was applicable to work. The theory taught was cutting edge."

Where to Stay

Historic Hotel Bethlehem
437 Main St.
Bethlehem, PA 18018
(610) 625-5000

Comfort Suites University
120 W. Third St.
Bethlehem, PA 18015
(610) 882-9700

Ramada Inn
1500 MacArthur Rd.
Whitehall, PA 18052
(610) 439-1037

 ## Where to Eat

Deja Brew Coffeehouse & Deli
101 W. Fourth St.
Bethlehem, PA 18015
(610) 865-2739

The Green Café
22 W. Fourth St.
Bethlehem, PA 18015
(610) 694-0192

The Grotto
336 Adams St.
Bethlehem, PA 18015
(610) 867-1741

 ## Things to Do

Tally Ho Tavern
205 W. Fourth St.
Bethlehem, PA 18015
(610) 865-2591

Town & Country Bowling Lanes
1770 Stefko Blvd.
Bethlehem, PA 18017
(610) 867-0586

CHECK OUT BUSINESSWEEK.COM FOR MORE:

Expanded Profile: Find more details on Lehigh's part-time MBA program in its online profile.

Search & Compare: See how Lehigh stacks up against other part-time MBA programs using this interactive tool.

School Tour: Planning a visit? Check out Lehigh's Bethlehem campus before you go.

Forums: Connect with other Lehigh hopefuls using our online forums.

Access all the B-schools content on BusinessWeek.com by subscribing to MBA Insider.

Loyola Marymount University

College of Business Administration
2007 Ranking: 3rd in the West
Hilton Center for Business, Room 233
1 LMU Dr., MS 8387
Los Angeles, CA 90045-2659
E-mail address: mbapc@lmu.edu
Web address: www.lmu.edu/
Page20338.aspx
For more info: Call the MBA program
at (310) 338-2848

Why Loyola Marymount?

If speed is what you want, look no further. Loyola Marymount, which has one program for full-time and part-time students, can be finished in as little as one year—if you have enough recent undergraduate coursework in business to waive the nine required core courses. Ten electives—including three in an "area of emphasis" and five outside of it—are also required, as is a year-long integrative experience that includes travel to Europe or Asia. Students who move mid-degree can complete their studies at any of the 23 schools in the Jesuit Transfer Network.

Loyola Marymount is a private institution. Established in 1974, LMU's part-time MBA program is accredited by the Association to Advance Collegiate Schools of Business (AACSB). LMU also offers an executive MBA.

 **B4UGO**

Applicants accepted: 43%
Average GMAT score: 572
Average years' work experience: 6
Average time to complete the program: 24 months
Completion rate: 85%

 Who Are My Classmates?

Part-time enrollment: 231
Women: 48%
International: 2%
Minority: 33%
Average age: 27
Average base salary at admission: $77,000
Reason for getting an MBA: Career advancement with current employer (28.6%), career advancement with new employer (33.3%), change industries/functional areas (38.1%)*

*Estimates based on *BusinessWeek* survey data.

> *"I found a perfect environment for learning."*

Where Do They Come From?

Top functional areas: General Management (24%), Finance/Accounting (20%), Operations/Production (15%)

Top industries: Government (20%), Technology (13%), Consumer products (13%)

Top companies: Northrop Grumman, Boeing, Electronic Arts, NBC Universal, Weyerhaeuser

---

"I was not challenged enough."

The 411

Maximum time to complete the program: 60 months

Can PT students switch to the FT MBA program: Separate FT MBA not offered

Tuition per credit hour: $982

Classes begin: August, January

Application deadlines: None

Application fee: $50

Getting In

Relative importance of:
GMAT scores: Very important
Work experience: Considered
Application essay: Important
Interview: Considered
Recommendations: Important
Transcripts: Very important

Getting Out

Number of credits required for degree: 54

Access to Career Services for part-timers: Yes

Access to alumni database for part-timers: Yes

Part-timers permitted to interview on campus for internships: Yes

Part-timers permitted to interview on campus for full-time jobs: Yes

Graduates reporting post-MBA salary increase: 65.2%*

Average increase: 37%*

*Estimate based on *Business Week* survey data.

Cliff Notes

Leading areas of study: Entrepreneurship, Finance, International Business, Marketing

Average class size, core courses: 23

Average class size, electives: 17

Number of electives: 49

Teaching methods: Lectures (30%), case studies (24%), team projects (20%)

Faculty sharing with FT program: N/A

Classes meet: Weeknights

Average workload per week: 18 hours

"Recruiting events are a joke."

But What's It *Really* Like?

Program quality, graded by students:
Overall: **A**
Teaching quality: **C**
Caliber of classmates: **C**
Facilities: **B**
Support: **C**

Curriculum, graded by students:
Overall: **B**
E-business: **C**
Entrepreneurship: **A+**
Ethics: **A**
Finance: **B**
International business: **B**
Marketing: **C**
Strategy: **C**
Teamwork: **C**

 ### The Good, the Bad, and the Ugly: Students Speak Out

"I found a perfect environment for learning. The teachers are very knowledgeable and know how to make the class interesting for people like me who went to class right after working for eight hours."

"*The student body was extremely diverse.*"

"I feel as though I was not challenged enough."

"The student body was extremely diverse, bringing a lot of depth to class discussions. In one of my groups I had a JD/MBA, a fireman, a soldier back from Iraq, a small business owner, a financial analyst, and an art historian. I don't think this happens in most programs."

"*I left the program feeling much more confident.*"

"While at LMU, I had an opportunity to travel both nationally and internationally to represent the university at three new venture competitions. For aspiring entrepreneurs, I am absolutely certain that there is no finer university in the country than Loyola Marymount."

"LMU suited my needs perfectly. Working full-time, I was able to immediately implement new skills and ideas at my workplace and to tailor my learning to meet my specific interests. I left the program feeling much more confident and prepared not only to manage my career, but to manage others."

"Plan on doing your own recruiting. The career office is worthless and has given bad advice. Career recruiting events are a joke."

Where to Stay

Embassy Suites Los Angeles International Airport North
9801 Airport Blvd.
Los Angeles, CA 90045
(310) 215-1000

Hilton Garden Inn LAX/El Segundo
2100 E. Mariposa Ave.
El Segundo, CA 90245
(310) 726-0100

Courtyard Los Angeles Marina del Rey
13480 Maxella Ave.
Marina Del Rey, CA 90292
(310) 822-8555

 Where to Eat

Alejo's Presto Italian Restaurant
8343 Lincoln Blvd.
Los Angeles, CA 90045
(310) 670-6677

Fireside Restaurant
8522 Lincoln Blvd.
Los Angeles, CA 90045
(310) 670-1212

Korner Delicatessen & Restaurant
8836 S. Sepulveda Blvd.
Los Angeles, CA 90045
(310) 645-5188

Things to Do

Universal Studios Hollywood
100 Universal City Plaza
Universal City, CA 91608
(818) 622-3801

Venice Beach
1800 Ocean Front Walk
Venice, CA 90291

CHECK OUT BUSINESSWEEK.COM FOR MORE:

Expanded Profile: Find more details on Loyola's part-time MBA program in its online profile.

Search & Compare: See how Loyola stacks up against other part-time MBA programs using this interactive tool.

Forums: Connect with other Loyola hopefuls using our online forums.

Access all the B-schools content on BusinessWeek.com by subscribing to MBA Insider.

Loyola University Chicago

Graduate School of Business
2007 Ranking: 2nd in the Midwest
1 E. Pearson Ave.
Maguire Hall
Chicago, IL 60611
E-mail address: gsb@luc.edu
Web address: www.luc.edu/gsb/
For more info: Call the main
  switchboard at (312) 915-6124

Why Loyola?

At Loyola, part-time students get the white-glove treatment: classes are small, 80% of them are taught by full-time faculty, and opportunities for hands-on learning abound. The curriculum focuses on business ethics, social responsibility, and leadership. Students may choose from 13 concentrations, including four—accountancy, human resources, integrated marketing communications, and information systems management—that offer dual degrees and expanded course offerings. Although the degree is typically completed in 18 courses, up to 4 courses can be waived depending on academic background and grades.

Loyola University Chicago is a private institution. Established in 1969, Loyola's part-time MBA program is accredited by the Association to Advance Collegiate Schools of Business (AACSB).

☑ B4UGO

Applicants accepted: 81%
Average GMAT score: 550
Average years' work experience: 4.6
**Average time to complete the
  program:** 27 months
Completion rate: 85%

⬤ Who Are My Classmates?

Part-time enrollment: 361
Women: 56%
International: 19%
Minority: 21%
Average age: 27
Average base salary at admission:
  $46,470*
Reason for getting an MBA: Career advancement with current employer (29.1%), career advancement with new employer (27.3%), change industries/functional areas (43.6%)*

*Estimates based on *BusinessWeek* survey data.

"Loyola exceeded my expectations . . . an exceptional value."

Where Do They Come From?

Top functional areas: Finance/
Accounting, Human Resources,
Marketing/Sales
Top industries: Financial services,
Consumer products, Education
Top companies: Loyola University
Chicago, Accenture, Abbott
Laboratories, JPMorgan Chase,
Northern Trust

"I do not feel that I had to try very hard."

The 411

Maximum time to complete the
program: 60 months
Can PT students switch to the FT
MBA program: FT MBA not
offered
Tuition per credit hour: $1,047
Classes begin: August, November,
February, May
Application deadlines: July 15 (fall),
October 1 (winter), January 15
(spring), April 1 (summer)
Application fee: $50

Getting In

Relative importance of:
GMAT scores: Very important
Work experience: Very important
Application essay: Important
Interview: Considered
Recommendations: Important
Transcripts: Very important

Getting Out

Number of credits required for degree:
54
Access to Career Services for part-
timers: Yes
Access to alumni database for part-
timers: No
Part-timers permitted to interview on
campus for internships: N/A
Part-timers permitted to interview on
campus for full-time jobs: N/A
Graduates reporting post-MBA salary
increase: 70.6%*
Average increase: 32.6%*
*Estimate based on *Business Week* survey data.

Cliff Notes

Leading areas of study: Accounting,
Finance, Human Resources,
International Business, Marketing
Average class size, core courses: 40
Average class size, electives: 30
Number of electives: 88
Teaching methods: Lectures (25%),
case studies (20%), team projects
(20%)
Faculty sharing with FT program:
N/A
Classes meet: Weeknights, weekends
Average workload per week: 20 hours

"The accounting department is amazing."

But What's It *Really* Like?

Program quality, graded by students:
Overall: A
Teaching quality: B
Caliber of classmates: C
Facilities: B
Support: B

Curriculum, graded by students:
Overall: A
E-business: B
Entrepreneurship: C
Ethics: A+
Finance: C
International business: B
Marketing: A+
Strategy: C
Teamwork: A+

 The Good, the Bad, and the Ugly: Students Speak Out

"Loyola exceeded my expectations in the quality and variety of courses offered. I think it is an exceptional value."

"Professors take the extra step to get to know you."

"My MBA experience at Loyola has been fantastic. There is a pretty good selection of classes and options for concentration, and there are many opportunities to study abroad. Professors are very knowledgeable and take the extra step to get to know you. Ethics are regularly incorporated into lectures/discussions."

"The business career center is underperforming."

"Overall, I had a good experience; however, I do not feel that I had to try very hard or truly learned much that I hadn't already learned in my undergraduate education."

"The accounting department at Loyola is amazing. I was impressed with the faculty members. They are caring, yet also demanding. They are excellent in their fields, and they are wonderful teachers."

"I thought the quality of the classes was poor and the business career center was, and still is, underperforming."

"Great sense of community, Jesuit tradition, comprehensive core curriculum, and unparalleled foreign-study programs."

"I was impressed with the quality of the professors and the amount of material we were able to cover in 10 weeks. The capstone class, where we created a business plan, was invaluable and tied up the program nicely."

 **Where to Stay**

Sofitel Hotel
20 E. Chestnut St.
Chicago, IL 60611
(312) 324-4000

The Talbott Hotel
20 E. Delaware Pl.
Chicago, IL 60611
(312) 944-4970

Residence Inn by Marriott
201 E. Walton Pl.
Chicago, IL 60611
(312) 475-1924

 Where to Eat

Giordano's
6836 N. Sheridan Rd.
Chicago, IL 60626
(773) 262-1313

Heartland Café
7000 N. Glenwood Ave.
Chicago, IL 60626
(773) 465-8005

Tiffin: The India Kitchen
2536 W. Devon Ave.
Chicago, IL 60659
(773) 338-2143

 Things to Do

Millennium Park
55 Michigan Ave.
Chicago, IL 60602
(312) 742-5222

Signature Lounge
875 N. Michigan Ave.
Chicago, IL 60611
(312) 787-7230

CHECK OUT BUSINESSWEEK.COM FOR MORE:

Expanded Profile: Find more details on Loyola's part-time MBA program in its online profile.

Search & Compare: See how Loyola stacks up against other part-time MBA programs using this interactive tool.

Forums: Connect with other Loyola hopefuls using our online forums.

Access all the B-schools content on BusinessWeek.com by subscribing to MBA Insider.

New York University

Leonard N. Stern School of Business
2007 Ranking: 3rd in the Northeast
Langone Part-Time MBA Program
Henry Kaufman Management Center
44 W. 4th St.
New York, NY 10012
E-mail address:
  sternmba@stern.nyu.edu
Web address: www.w4.stern.nyu.edu/
  admissions/langone/
For more info: Call the MBA admissions
  office at (212) 998-0600

☑ B4UGO

Applicants accepted: 46%
Average GMAT score: 675
Average years' work experience: 5.5
**Average time to complete the
  program:** 36 months
Completion rate: 90%

program, see page 73. For details on its
executive MBA program, see page 249.

🔘 Who Are My Classmates?

Part-time enrollment: 2,030
Women: 36%
International: 24%
Minority: 36%
Average age: 28
Average base salary at admission:
  $81,432
Reason for getting an MBA: Career
  advancement with current employer
  (46.7%), career advancement with
  new employer (20.6%), change
  industries/functional areas (32.7%)*
*Estimates based on *Business Week* survey data.

Why NYU?

Whether it's a course on volatility
taught by a Nobel Prize winner or a
class on managing in the performing
arts led by the general manager of the
Metropolitan Opera, part-timers at
Stern reap all the benefits of studying in
one of the world's great capitals of
finance and culture. The academic
smorgasbord on offer includes 21 specializations, of which students can
choose up to three. Courses are held in
Manhattan and Westchester, and students can finish in as little as two years.
Stern also has a separate career center
for part-time students.

NYU is a private institution. Established in 1916, Stern's part-time MBA
program is accredited by the Association to Advance Collegiate Schools of
Business (AACSB). Stern also offers
full-time and executive MBA programs.
For details on Stern's full-time MBA

*"We have access to the
best professors at the
university."*

Where Do They Come From?

Top functional areas: Finance/Accounting (33%), Management Information Systems (14%), Marketing/Sales (12%)

Top industries: Financial services (41%), Technology (8%), Media/Entertainment (6%)

Top companies: Citigroup, Goldman Sachs, Morgan Stanley, JPMorgan Chase, UBS

"Worth the time and effort, but not the money."

The 411

Maximum time to complete the program: 72 months

Can PT students switch to the FT MBA program: No

Tuition per credit hour: $1,440

Classes begin: September

Application deadline: May 15

Application fee: $175

Getting In

Relative importance of:

GMAT scores: Important

Work experience: Very important

Application essay: Important

Interview: Considered

Recommendations: Important

Transcripts: Very important

Getting Out

Number of credits required for degree: 60

Access to Career Services for part-timers: Yes

Access to alumni database for part-timers: Yes

Part-timers permitted to interview on campus for internships: No

Part-timers permitted to interview on campus for full-time jobs: Yes

Graduates reporting post-MBA salary increase: 51.7%*

Average increase: 38.3%*

*Estimate based on *BusinessWeek* survey data.

Cliff Notes

Leading areas of study: Entrepreneurship, Finance, General Management, International Business, Marketing

Average class size, core courses: 52

Average class size, electives: 43

Number of electives: 137

Teaching methods: Team projects (30%), case studies (25%), lectures (20%)

Faculty sharing with FT program: 100%

Classes meet: Weeknights, weekends, weeklong sessions

Average workload per week: 20 hours

"The school prohibited us from on-campus recruiting."

But What's It *Really* Like?

Program quality, graded by students:
Overall: A
Teaching quality: B
Caliber of classmates: A
Facilities: B
Support: C

Curriculum, graded by students:
Overall: A
E-business: B
Entrepreneurship: A
Ethics: B
Finance: A+
International business: A
Marketing: C
Strategy: B
Teamwork: C

The Good, the Bad, and the Ugly: Students Speak Out

"I had some skepticism about attending a part-time program—that it might not be viewed as highly as a full-time MBA in the professional world—but for the most part that hasn't been my experience."

"My only issue with the program was the availability of career services assistance for the part-timers. We had access to interview training and résumé workshops, but the school explicitly prohibited us from attending corporate presentations and on-campus recruiting events, which was discouraging and annoying."

"This is by far the best part-time program. Our electives are mixed with the full-timers' so that we have access to the best professors at the university. The program offers intensives during January and August, allowing part-timers to finish a three-credit course in less than a month. The caliber of students is fantastic, as many are pursuing their second or third master's degree."

> *"NYU has a fantastic study-abroad program."*

"The program was worth the time and effort, but not the money."

"NYU has a fantastic study-abroad program. I attended Doing Business in China (in Beijing), and it was one of the best parts of my graduate experience."

"The Finance faculty is outstanding, however members of the Strategy, International Business, Marketing, and Information Systems departments were also excellent."

> *"The Finance faculty is outstanding."*

 **Where to Stay**

W New York—Union Square
201 Park Ave. S.
New York, NY 10003
(212) 979-5052

Holiday Inn Manhattan Downtown
138 Lafayette St.
New York, NY 10013
(212) 966-8898

Washington Square Hotel
103 Waverly Pl.
New York, NY 10011
(212) 777-9515

 Where to Eat

Mamoun's Falafel
119 MacDougal St.
New York, NY 10012
(212) 674-8685

Patsy's Pizzeria
67 University Pl.
New York, NY 10003
(212) 533-3500

Spice
60 University Pl.
New York, NY 10003
(212) 982-3758

 Things to Do

Sing Sing Karaoke
9 St. Mark's Pl.
New York, NY 10003
(212) 387-7800

Washington Square Park
Fifth Ave. at Waverly Pl.
New York, NY 10003

CHECK OUT BUSINESSWEEK.COM FOR MORE:

School Tour: Get a glimpse of Stern's Washington Square campus and all that it has to offer with this photo essay.

Admissions Q&A: Former Admissions Director Isser Gallogly discusses the relationship between full-time and part-time students, what perks to expect, and credentials that Stern hopefuls need if they are to get in.

Sample Application Essays and Interview Tips: If getting into Stern is a priority, these sample essays and interview tips will help.

Search & Compare: Find out how the Langone program stacks up against others in the Northeast.

Access all the B-schools content on BusinessWeek.com by subscribing to MBA Insider.

Ohio State University

Max M. Fisher College of Business
2007 Ranking: 5th in the Midwest
100 Gerlach Hall
2108 Neil Ave.
Columbus, OH 43209
E-mail address:
  fisherptmba@cob.osu.edu
Web address: www.fisher.osu.edu
For more info: Call the part-time MBA
  program at (614) 292-8511

 B4UGO

Applicants accepted: 72%
Average GMAT score: 610
Average years' work experience: 6.8
**Average time to complete the
  program:** 25 months
Completion rate: 93%

Why Ohio State?

Part-time students at Ohio State enjoy access to the same world-class faculty, courses, and extracurricular activities offered to full-time MBA students, with the added benefit of flexibility. They can begin their studies in any quarter and take up to five years to complete the program, with most doing so in less than half that time. Fisher offers 50 business electives exclusively in the evening, and opportunities for hands-on learning include international study trips and project-based classes. Two out of three career switchers surveyed by *BusinessWeek* credit the program with launching them into a new industry or functional area.

OSU is a public institution. Established in 1933, Fisher's part-time MBA program is accredited by the Association to Advance Collegiate Schools of Business (AACSB). Fisher also offers full-time and executive MBA programs. For details on Fisher's full-time MBA

program, see page 81. For details on its executive MBA program, see page 257.

Who Are My Classmates?

Part-time enrollment: 328
Women: 27%
International: 10%
Minority: 24%
Average age: 29
Average base salary at admission: $58,226*
Reason for getting an MBA: Career advancement with current employer (41.3%), career advancement with new employer (19.6%), change industries/functional areas (39.1%)*

*Estimates based on *BusinessWeek* survey data.

"A huge boost for my career."

Where Do They Come From?

Top functional areas: Management Information Systems (29%), Finance/Accounting (19%), Marketing/Sales (13%), Operations/Production (13%)

Top industries: Manufacturing (19%), Nonprofit (18%), Technology (15%)

Top companies: Nationwide, JPMorgan Chase, Battelle, AEP, Limited Brands

---

"Other programs have more online options."

The 411

Maximum time to complete the program: 60 months

Can PT students switch to the FT MBA program: No

Tuition per credit hour: $668 (resident), $1,150 (nonresident)

Classes begin: September, January, March, June

Application deadlines: August 15 (fall), November 15 (winter), February 15 (spring), May 5 (summer)

Application fee: $60 (U.S.), $70 (international)

Getting In

Relative importance of:
GMAT scores: Important

Work experience: Important
Application essay: Important
Interview: Not considered
Recommendations: Important
Transcripts: Important

Getting Out

Number of credits required for degree: 76

Access to Career Services for part-timers: Yes

Access to alumni database for part-timers: Yes

Part-timers permitted to interview on campus for internships: Yes

Part-timers permitted to interview on campus for full-time jobs: Yes

Graduates reporting post-MBA salary increase: 61.5%*

Average increase: 39.3%*

*Estimate based on *BusinessWeek* survey data.

Cliff Notes

Leading areas of study: Corporate Finance, Investments and Portfolio Management, Logistics and Supply Chain, Marketing, Strategy and Consulting

Average class size, core courses: 62

Average class size, electives: 32

Number of electives: 132

Teaching methods: Lectures (25%), case studies (25%), team projects (25%)

Faculty sharing with FT program: 100%

Classes meet: Days, weeknights

Average workload per week: 20 hours

But What's It *Really* Like?

Program quality, graded by students:
Overall: **B**
Teaching quality: **B**
Caliber of classmates: **B**
Facilities: **A+**
Support: **C**

Curriculum, graded by students:
Overall: **B**
E-business: **C**
Entrepreneurship: **C**
Ethics: **C**
Finance: **B**
International business: **C**
Marketing: **B**
Strategy: **A**
Teamwork: **A**

 ### The Good, the Bad, and the Ugly: Students Speak Out

"I was completely impressed by the rigor, quality of the professors, and curriculum at Fisher. The knowledge I've gained has put me well above my peers. It has definitely been a huge boost for my career."

"The program requires 8 to 10 hours of in-class time per week. Other programs have more online options, which help with managing the work/life balance."

> ## *"The work is challenging."*

"It is not an institution where people are showing up just to get a piece of paper for their résumé. The work is challenging, and the people I worked with were top notch."

"It was simply not what I expected. I learn by doing, and in most classes we were reading and working in a group that split the work—not very productive or educational. Also, there were not enough electives in my area of interest (strategic marketing) and not enough flexibility in scheduling."

> ## *"Not enough electives in my area of interest."*

"Some of the courses I wanted to take were very difficult to fit into a nighttime schedule."

"Ohio State was far more expensive than I originally had intended. A degree through a lesser-known MBA program would have given me just as good an education, without emptying my bank account."

"The strength of any MBA program lies in the quality, integrity, and business acumen of the teaching staff. I found the professors to exceed in all three categories."

 **Where to Stay**

The Blackwell
2110 Tuttle Park Pl.
Columbus, OH 43210
(614) 247-4000

**University Plaza Hotel &
Conference Center**
3110 Olentangy River Rd.
Columbus, OH 43202
(614) 267-7461

Fairfield Inn and Suites
3031 Olentangy River Rd.
Columbus, OH 43202
(614) 267-1111

 Where to Eat

The Buckeye Hall of Fame Café
1421 Olentangy River Rd.
Columbus, OH 43212
(614) 291-2233

The Happy Greek
1554 N. High St.
Columbus, OH 43201
(614) 291-7777

Bistro 2110
2110 Tuttle Park Pl.
Columbus, OH 43210
(614) 247-4000

 Things to Do

Wexner Center for the Arts
1871 N. High St.
Columbus, OH 43201
(614) 292-3535

Union Station Video Café
630 N. High St.
Columbus, OH 43201
(614) 228-3546

CHECK OUT BUSINESSWEEK.COM FOR MORE:

Expanded Profile: Find more details on Fisher's part-time MBA program in its online profile.

Search & Compare: See how Fisher stacks up against other part-time MBA programs using this interactive tool.

School Tour: Planning a visit? Check out Fisher's Columbus campus before you go.

Forums: Connect with other Fisher hopefuls using our online forums.

Sample Application Essays: Trying to write an essay that impresses? Check out three that opened doors at Fisher.

Admissions Q&A: Michelle Jacobson, head of admissions at Fisher, describes what the B-school is looking for in an applicant.

Access all the B-schools content on BusinessWeek.com by subscribing to MBA Insider.

Rollins College

Roy E. Crummer Graduate School of
Business
2007 Ranking: 5th in the South
1000 Holt Ave.
Winter Park, FL 32789
E-mail address:
mbaadmissions@rollins.edu
Web address: www.crummer.rollins.edu/
pmba/index.shtml
For more info: Call the MBA program
at (407) 646-2405

Why Rollins?

At Rollins, part-timers complete all
their core classes together in cohorts,
much like a full-time program, and are
taught by the same faculty that teaches
Crummer's full-timers. As a result, students give the program high marks for
teaching quality. There are 12 required
courses, including 2 intensives (a few
days each) and a capstone course that
requires students to integrate everything they've learned. Five concentrations are offered, and students may take
up to two. Global consulting projects
are also available. Career switchers rate
the program highly.

Rollins is a private institution. Estab-
lished in 1957, Crummer's part-time
MBA program is accredited by the
Association to Advance Collegiate
Schools of Business (AACSB). Crum-
mer also offers full-time and executive
MBA programs.

☑ B4UGO

Applicants accepted: 65%
Average GMAT score: 548
Average years' work experience: 6.2
**Average time to complete the
program:** 29 months
Completion rate: 85%

🗨 Who Are My Classmates?

Part-time enrollment: 240
Women: 40%
International: 0%
Minority: 20%
Average age: 27
Average base salary at admission:
$38,458
Reason for getting an MBA: Career
advancement with current employer
(57.1%), career advancement with
new employer (7.1%), change
industries/functional areas
(35.7%)*

*Estimates based on *BusinessWeek* survey data.

*"My MBA completely
changed how I look at
the world."*

Where Do They Come From?

Top functional areas:
Finance/Accounting (23%),
Operations/Production (23%),
Marketing/Sales (14%)

Top industries: Manufacturing (23%),
Nonprofit (16%), Financial services
(14%)

Top companies: Walt Disney World,
Lockheed Martin, Siemens, Bank of
New York

"The school has no brand value."

The 411

Maximum time to complete the
program: 72 months

Can PT students switch to the FT
MBA program: Yes

Tuition per credit hour: $966

Classes begin: September, January

Application deadlines: None

Application fee: $50

Getting In

Relative importance of:
GMAT scores: Very important
Work experience: Very important
Application essay: Important
Interview: Important
Recommendations: Important
Transcripts: Very important

Getting Out

Number of credits required for degree:
53

Access to Career Services for part-
timers: Yes

Access to alumni database for part-
timers: Yes

Part-timers permitted to interview on
campus for internships: No

Part-timers permitted to interview on
campus for full-time jobs: No

Graduates reporting post-MBA salary
increase: 54.8%*

Average increase: 32%*

*Estimate based on *Business Week* survey data.

Cliff Notes

Leading areas of study: Entrepreneurship, Finance, General Management, International Business,
Marketing

Average class size, core courses: 40

Average class size, electives: 33

Number of electives: 28

Teaching methods: Case studies
(40%), team projects (30%),
lectures (20%)

Faculty sharing with FT program:
100%

Classes meet: Weeknights

Average workload per week: 20 hours

"I was awarded a huge promotion."

But What's It *Really* Like?

Program quality, graded by students:
Overall: **A**
Teaching quality: **A+**
Caliber of classmates: **A**
Facilities: **A**
Support: **B**

Curriculum, graded by students:
Overall: **A**
E-business: **B**
Entrepreneurship: **A**
Ethics: **B**
Finance: **A**
International business: **A+**
Marketing: **A+**
Strategy: **C**
Teamwork: **C**

 The Good, the Bad, and the Ugly: Students Speak Out

"My Crummer MBA completely changed how I look at the world and has given me higher aspirations than I would have ever dared to dream before."

"We needed more variety in the summer class offerings."

"I think Rollins relies too much on its name, which outside of central Florida means little to nothing. The school has no brand value, contrary to what the local alumni might believe."

"I was awarded a huge promotion within my company based on finishing my MBA degree, and the hiring manager recognized and respected Rollins."

"I wasn't just another student; I was important."

"We needed a bit more variety in the summer class offerings as well as more events in the evening for the part-time students. Many of the networking and guest speaker events were during the day when we were working or in the evenings during class time."

"The faculty members have the right mix of real-world experience with academic background. They were truly interested in making sure that we mastered the material we were learning, and they were available every day for questions. I had a great time learning. . . . I wasn't just another student to the faculty; I was an individual who was important."

"For students who are paying for the program out of pocket, it would be great if the school offered a job placement service."

Where to Stay

Best Western Mt. Vernon Inn
110 S. Orlando Ave.
Winter Park, FL 32789
(407) 647-1166

Homewood Suites Orlando North
290 Southhall Ln.
Maitland, FL 32751
(407) 875-8777

Park Plaza Hotel
307 S. Park Ave.
Winter Park, FL 32789
(407) 647-1072

 Where to Eat

Boston's Fish House
6860 Aloma Ave.
Winter Park, FL 32792
(407) 678-2107

Houston's
215 S. Orlando Ave.
Winter Park, FL 32789
(407) 740-4005

Siam Garden
1111 W. Webster Ave.
Winter Park, FL 32789
(407) 599-7443

Things to Do

Charles Hosmer Morse Museum of American Art
445 N. Park Ave.
Winter Park, FL 32789
(407) 645-5311

Park Avenue Walking Tour
200 W. New England Ave.
Winter Park, FL 32789
(407) 647-8180

CHECK OUT BUSINESSWEEK.COM FOR MORE:

Expanded Profile: Find more details on the Rollins part-time MBA program in its online profile.

Search & Compare: See how Rollins stacks up against other part-time MBA programs using this interactive tool.

School Tour: Planning a visit? Check out Rollins's Winter Park campus before you go.

Forums: Connect with other Rollins hopefuls using our online forums.

Access all the B-schools content on BusinessWeek.com by subscribing to MBA Insider.

Southern Methodist University

Edwin L. Cox School of Business
2007 Ranking: 2nd in the Southwest
6212 Bishop Blvd.
Dallas, TX 75275-0333
E-mail address:
   mbainfo@mail.cox.smu.edu
Web address: www.cox.smu.edu/grad/
   mba/pmba
For more info: Call professional MBA
   admissions at (800) 472-3622

✓ B4UGO

Applicants accepted: 78%
Average GMAT score: 596
Average years' work experience: 6
**Average time to complete the
   program:** 24 months
Completion rate: 92%

Why Southern Methodist?

Unlike many part-time programs, SMU offers concentrations—including entrepreneurship, finance, and marketing—that require students to take a minimum of 14 half-term electives, giving graduates deep functional-area expertise. At least one elective must have an international focus, a requirement that can be fulfilled through study-abroad programs in China, France, and Germany. Part-time students may attend classes in Plano or Dallas. When not in class, they may receive leadership training from area executives or take advantage of career services, including networking events and on-campus recruiting.

Southern Methodist is a private institution. Established in 1973, Cox's part-time MBA program is accredited by the Association to Advance Collegiate Schools of Business (AACSB). Cox also offers full-time and executive MBA programs. For details on Cox's executive MBA program, see page 265.

 Who Are My Classmates?

Part-time enrollment: 433
Women: 27%
International: 0%
Minority: 27%
Average age: 29
Average base salary at admission: $70,134
Reason for getting an MBA: Career advancement with current employer (46.5%), career advancement with new employer (23.3%), change industries/functional areas (30.2%)*

*Estimates based on *BusinessWeek* survey data.

> *"I feel more confident in my decisions after attending."*

Where Do They Come From?

Top functional areas: Finance/ Accounting (30%), Marketing/ Sales (23%), Operations/ Production (21%)

Top industries: Financial services (26%), Consumer products (18%), Consulting (17%)

Top companies: Lockheed Martin, Texas Instruments, Verizon, Capital One, Countrywide

> ## *"I give the entrepreneurship program very high marks."*

The 411

Maximum time to complete the program: 72 months

Can PT students switch to the FT MBA program: No

Tuition per credit hour: $1,358

Classes begin: August, January

Application deadlines: March 17, May 19 (fall); October 14, November 18 (spring)

Application fee: $75

Getting In

Relative importance of:
GMAT scores: Very important
Work experience: Very important
Application essay: Very important

Interview: Very important
Recommendations: Very important
Transcripts: Very important

Getting Out

Number of credits required for degree: 48

Access to Career Services for part-timers: Yes

Access to alumni database for part-timers: Yes

Part-timers permitted to interview on campus for internships: No

Part-timers permitted to interview on campus for full-time jobs: Yes

Graduates reporting post-MBA salary increase: 56.8%*

Average increase: 37.4%*

*Estimate based on *BusinessWeek* survey data.

Cliff Notes

Leading areas of study: Entrepreneur-ship, Finance, Leadership, Market-ing, Strategy

Average class size, core courses: 55

Average class size, electives: 37

Number of electives: 94

Teaching methods: Case studies (30%), team projects (25%), lectures (25%)

Faculty sharing with FT program: 100%

Classes meet: Days, weeknights, weekends

Average workload per week: 17 hours

But What's It *Really* Like?

Program quality, graded by students:
Overall: **A**
Teaching quality: **A**
Caliber of classmates: **C**
Facilities: **B**
Support: **B**

Curriculum, graded by students:
Overall: **A+**
E-business: **C**
Entrepreneurship: **A+**
Ethics: **C**
Finance: **A**
International business: **A**
Marketing: **A+**
Strategy: **A+**
Teamwork: **C**

 ### The Good, the Bad, and the Ugly: Students Speak Out

"SMU has a fantastic program. I was surprised at how much I learned about myself and from my fellow students more than anything else. I feel more confident in my decisions after attending."

"The career center focuses on full-time students."

"I would give the entrepreneurship program very high marks for the quality of the classes, instructors, and guest lecturers. I wish I had had the time to take some of the additional courses that were offered."

"The career center does not offer enough help for part-time students and focuses its time on full-time MBA students. There needs to be either a dedicated career office for part-time students or a couple of dedicated counselors."

"Now I work on Wall Street, and I have SMU to thank."

"Without my SMU MBA, I would still be doing my same old boring engineering job. Now I work on Wall Street, and I have SMU to thank for that. SMU is a hidden gem in Texas, especially for someone looking for a part-time program that offers everything a full-time program does."

"The program provided me with the intellectual capital and personal confidence to start my own business."

"For the Dallas area and even for the state of Texas, you can't get a better education. The opportunity to learn from industry people is unmatched."

 **Where to Stay**

Radisson Hotel
6060 N. Central Expy.
Dallas, TX 75206
(214) 750-6060

Doubletree—Campbell Center
8250 N. Central Expy.
Dallas, TX 75206
(214) 691-8700

Hilton Park Cities
5954 Luther Ln.
Dallas, TX 75225
(214) 368-0400

 Where to Eat

Peggy Sue BBQ
6600 Snider Plaza
Dallas, TX 75205
(214) 987-9188

Kuby's Sausage House
6601 Snider Plaza
Dallas, TX 75205
(214) 363-2231

Trinity Hall Irish Pub & Restaurant
5321 E. Mockingbird Ln.
Dallas, TX 75206
(214) 887-3600

 Things to Do

Dallas Museum of Art
1717 N. Hardwood St.
Dallas, TX 75201
(214) 922-1200

Addison Improv Comedy Club
4890 Belt Line Rd.
Dallas, TX 75254
(972) 404-8501

CHECK OUT BUSINESSWEEK.COM FOR MORE:

Making the Grade: SMU's MBA admissions director, Patti Cudney, shares her pointers on résumés, essays, interviews, and more.

School Tour: Walk the halls, peak into classrooms, and see where students hang out and study on this photo tour of SMU's Cox campus.

Search & Compare: Find out how Cox compares to other part-time programs based on specialties and other criteria.

Expanded Profile: Check out more details on the Cox part-time program and all it has to offer with our in-depth online profile.

Career Q&A: Assistant Dean George Johnson talks about career services available to students at Cox.

Access all the B-schools content on BusinessWeek.com by subscribing to MBA Insider.

U. of California at Los Angeles

John E. Anderson Graduate School of
    Management
2007 Ranking: 1st in the West
Fully Employed MBA (FEMBA) Program
110 Westwood Plaza
Los Angeles, CA 90095-1481
E-mail address: femba.admissions@
    anderson.ucla.edu
Web address: www.anderson.ucla.edu/
    x119.xml
For more info: Call FEMBA admissions
    at (310) 825-2632

Why UCLA?

With discipline offerings comparable to
those of its full-time counterpart, and
high expectations to match, Anderson's
FEMBA program is not for the faint of
heart. The ten core classes, eight electives, and capstone project required for
graduation; a cohort system similar to
many full-time programs; and on-campus recruiting for part-timers give the
program a full-time feel. The capstone
project, which requires students to log
about 500 hours over six months,
matches part-time students with international technology companies; students are then responsible for helping
these companies develop a business
plan for expansion.

UCLA is a public institution. Estab-
lished in 1988, Anderson's part-time
MBA program is accredited by the
Association to Advance Collegiate
Schools of Business (AACSB). Ander-

☑ **B4UGO**

Applicants accepted: 42%
Average GMAT score: 686
Average years' work experience: 6
**Average time to complete the
    program:** 33 months
Completion rate: 97%

son also offers full-time and executive
MBA programs. For details on Anderson's full-time MBA program, see page
117. For details on its executive MBA
program, see page 273.

 Who Are My Classmates?

Part-time enrollment: 725
Women: 31%
International: 1%
Minority: 61%
Average age: 30
Average base salary at admission:
    $84,000
Reason for getting an MBA: Career
    advancement with current employer
    (52.4%), career advancement with
    new employer (4.8%), change
    industries/functional areas (42.9%)*

*Estimates based on *Business Week* survey data.

*"Good ROI? Yeah, you
could say that."*

Where Do They Come From?

Top functional areas: Operations/
Production (32%), Finance/
Accounting (14%), Marketing/Sales
(13%)

Top industries: Technology (18%),
Media/Entertainment (10%),
Healthcare (9%)

Top companies: Northrop Grumman,
Boeing, Amgen, Walt Disney,
Qualcomm

---

*"Electives were tough
to get into."*

The 411

Maximum time to complete the
program: 72 months

Can PT students switch to the FT
MBA program: No

Tuition per credit hour: $945

Classes begin: September

Application deadlines: November 7,
January 23, April 2

Application fee: $175

Getting In

Relative importance of:
GMAT scores: Very important
Work experience: Very important
Application essay: Very important
Interview: Important
Recommendations: Very important
Transcripts: Important

Getting Out

Number of credits required for degree:
84

Access to Career Services for part-
timers: Yes

Access to alumni database for part-
timers: No

Part-timers permitted to interview on
campus for internships: No

Part-timers permitted to interview on
campus for full-time jobs: Yes

Graduates reporting post-MBA salary
increase: 68.2%*

Average increase: 33.5%*

*Estimate based on *Business Week* survey data.

Cliff Notes

Leading areas of study: Entrepreneurship, Finance, General Management, Marketing, Operations
Management

Average class size, core courses: 65

Average class size, electives: 34

Number of electives: 48

Teaching methods: Lectures (45%),
case studies (30%), experiential
learning (20%)

Faculty sharing with FT program:
100%

Classes meet: Days, weeknights,
weekends

Average workload per week: 20 hours

---

*"Classes I wanted were
during the day."*

But What's It *Really* Like?

Program quality, graded by students:
Overall: **A+**
Teaching quality: **A+**
Caliber of classmates: **A+**
Facilities: **A+**
Support: **A+**

Curriculum, graded by students:
Overall: **A**
E-business: **A**
Entrepreneurship: **A+**
Ethics: **C**
Finance: **A+**
International business: **A+**
Marketing: **A+**
Strategy: **A**
Teamwork: **B**

 The Good, the Bad, and the Ugly: Students Speak Out

"The part-time program is hard. I was worried that it would be a watered-down version of the full-time program, but I found it to be a concentrated version instead."

"Electives were tough to get into for my class. There are some professors who are very highly regarded at Anderson who still do not offer classes for the part-time program."

"The part-time program is hard."

"The true success of the UCLA Anderson part-time program is the international field study, which serves as the culmination of all lectures, coursework, and classroom education in a real-world, hands-on consulting engagement."

"As soon as people hear Anderson, they give me a bit more respect."

"As soon as people hear I'm attending Anderson, they give me a bit more respect and pay more attention to what I have to say."

"I received two promotions during my three years, and my base salary increased by 35%. I have an offer at another company for a further 18% increase. And I will be in a bonus pool that I wasn't in three years ago. Good ROI? Yeah, you could say that."

"Too many times I had to choose a class I really wasn't that interested in because the classes I wanted were offered on weekday afternoons or during the day. Very unfair."

"It's a fantastic way to get practical experience and immediately apply it to the real world. UCLA's professors and the caliber of students are outstanding."

Where to Stay

UCLA Guest House
330 Charles E. Young Dr. E.
Los Angeles, CA 90095
(310) 825-2923

Luxe Hotel Sunset Boulevard
11461 Sunset Blvd.
Los Angeles, CA 90049
(310) 476-6571

W Hotel Los Angeles—Westwood
930 Hilgard Ave.
Los Angeles, CA 90024
(310) 208-8765

 Where to Eat

Westwood Brewing Co.
1097 Glendon Ave.
Los Angeles, CA 90024
(310) 209-2739

Napa Valley Grille
1100 Glendon Ave.
Los Angeles, CA 90024
(310) 824-3322

In-N-Out Burger
922 Gayley Ave.
Los Angeles, CA 90024
(800) 786-1000

 Things to Do

Mildred E. Mathias Botanical Garden
777 Tiverton Ave.
Los Angeles, CA 90095
(310) 206-6707

Geffen Playhouse
10886 Le Conte Ave.
Los Angeles, CA 90024
(310) 208-5454

CHECK OUT BUSINESSWEEK.COM FOR MORE:

Admissions Q&A: The former director of admissions, Linda Baldwin, talks about what UCLA is looking for in an applicant.

Sample Application Essays and Interview Tips: Get the scoop on what it takes to get admitted to Anderson.

Video View: Listen to former Dean Judy Olian explain what's driving the growing interest in part-time MBA studies at Anderson and what jobs are hot.

Best Schools by Specialty: Learn why Anderson is one of the top B-schools for entrepreneurship and marketing.

Access all the B-schools content on BusinessWeek.com by subscribing to MBA Insider.

University of Chicago

Graduate School of Business
2007 Ranking: 1st in the Midwest
450 N. Cityfront Plaza
Chicago, IL 60611
E-mail address: eveningweekend-admissions@ChicagoGSB.edu
Web address: www.chicagogsb.edu/parttime/
For more info: Call part-time MBA admissions at (312) 464-8700

Why Chicago?

Prospective students looking for a high-quality, quant-heavy part-time MBA program in the Chicago area can do no better than GSB, where they'll get exposure to award-winning faculty and some of the smartest classmates anywhere. Unlike those in some other programs, part-timers can participate in and receive training for on-campus recruiting interviews. And for young professionals in their first three years on the job, the Chicago Business Fellow Program offers an evening MBA with the added benefit of peer mentors, a faculty adviser, and a professional skills development seminar.

The University of Chicago is a private institution. Established in 1947, Chicago's part-time MBA program is accredited by the Association to Advance Collegiate Schools of Business (AACSB). Chicago also offers full-time and executive MBA programs. For details on Chicago's full-time MBA pro-

☑ B4UGO

Applicants accepted: N/A
Average GMAT score: 685
Average years' work experience: 6.6
Average time to complete the program: 30 months
Completion rate: 93%

gram, see page 125. For details on its executive MBA program, see page 277.

 Who Are My Classmates?

Part-time enrollment: 1,575
Women: 21%
International: 20%
Minority: 38%
Average age: 30
Average base salary at admission: $65,278*
Reason for getting an MBA: Career advancement with current employer (38.4%), career advancement with new employer (18.4%), change industries/functional areas (43.2%)*

*Estimates based on *BusinessWeek* survey data.

"The best quantitative marketing program around."

Where Do They Come From?

Top functional areas: Consulting (20%), Management Information Systems (20%), Engineering (20%)
Top industries: Investment management (16%), Financial services (16%), Consulting (16%)
Top companies: Motorola, Morningstar, Northern Trust, General Electric, Procter & Gamble

---

"Chicago GSB was worth every penny of my money."

The 411

Maximum time to complete the program: 60 months
Can PT students switch to the FT MBA program: No
Tuition per course: $4,365
Classes begin: September, January, June
Application deadlines: July 11, October 11, January 16, April 17
Application fee: $175

Getting In

Relative importance of:
GMAT scores: Important
Work experience: Important
Application essay: Important
Interview: Important
Recommendations: Important
Transcripts: Important

Getting Out

Number of courses required for degree: 20
Access to Career Services for part-timers: Yes
Access to alumni database for part-timers: Yes
Part-timers permitted to interview on campus for internships: No
Part-timers permitted to interview on campus for full-time jobs: Yes
Graduates reporting post-MBA salary increase: 59.5%*
Average increase: 41.8%*

*Estimate based on *BusinessWeek* survey data.

Cliff Notes

Leading areas of study: Economics, Entrepreneurship, Finance/Accounting, General Management, Marketing
Average class size, core courses: 60
Average class size, electives: 47
Number of electives: 68
Teaching methods: Case studies, lectures, team projects
Faculty sharing with FT program: 100%
Classes meet: Weeknights, weekends
Average workload per week: 20 hours

"The reputation of the school is well deserved."

But What's It *Really* Like?

Program quality, graded by students:
Overall: **A+**
Teaching quality: **A+**
Caliber of classmates: **A+**
Facilities: **A+**
Support: **A+**

Curriculum, graded by students:
Overall: **A+**
E-business: **C**
Entrepreneurship: **A+**
Ethics: **C**
Finance: **A+**
International business: **A**
Marketing: **A**
Strategy: **A+**
Teamwork: **B**

The Good, the Bad, and the Ugly: Students Speak Out

"Even though the GSB is one of the few very prestigious names in the business world, top jobs are still extremely competitive."

"I really think that the Chicago GSB has the best quantitative marketing program around. I don't think I would have been exposed to so many useful quantitative techniques at Kellogg."

"Top jobs are extremely competitive."

"The Chicago GSB was worth every penny of my money. It prepared me to think analytically about problems and to show leadership in tough times. You really become the person people go to to ask hard questions."

"Chicago GSB is awesome. The reputation of the school is well deserved, and I certainly feel that my nearly $100K out-of-pocket expense is a steal relative to the knowledge I have gained."

"The outstanding faculty exceeded my expectations."

"With the tuition the GSB is charging, the program should make a very meaningful difference in a student's career. However, I think the program fails to deliver on such expectations."

"I liked the fact that part-time students can participate in on-campus recruiting with full-time MBA students."

"I am thoroughly impressed with the program. The caliber of students, their collective work experiences, and the outstanding faculty met, and in many cases exceeded, my expectations."

 **Where to Stay**

Hotel Sax Chicago
333 Dearborn St.
Chicago, IL 60610
(312) 245-0333

Hard Rock Hotel
230 N. Michigan Ave.
Chicago, IL 60601
(312) 345-1000

International House
1414 E. 59th St.
Chicago, IL 60637
(773) 753-2270

 Where to Eat

La Petite Folie
1504 E. 55th St.
Chicago, IL 60615
(773) 493-1394

Opera
1301 S. Wabash
Chicago, IL 60605
(312) 461-0161

Medici on 57th
1327 E. 57th St.
Chicago, IL 60637
(773) 667-7394

 Things to Do

Museum of Science and Industry
57th St. and Lake Shore Dr.
Chicago, IL 60637
(773) 684-1414

Art Institute of Chicago
111 S. Michigan Ave.
Chicago, IL 60603
(312) 443-3600

CHECK OUT BUSINESSWEEK.COM FOR MORE:

Admissions Q&A: Stacy Kole, former deputy dean, discusses common essay blunders, important courses to have on your transcript, and other admissions essentials.

Search & Compare: See how Chicago's part-time MBA program measures up against other area schools.

Sample Application Essays and Interview Tips: Get the lowdown on what it takes to get in.

Video View: Listen to Dean Ted Snyder explain how Chicago's teaching style distinguishes itself from that of other MBA programs.

Careers Q&A: Julie Morton, associate dean for MBA Career Services, sheds light on the kinds of career support part-time students can expect to find.

Access all the B-schools content on BusinessWeek.com by subscribing to MBA Insider.

University of Denver

Daniels College of Business
2007 Ranking: 1st in the Southwest
2101 S. University Blvd.
Denver, CO 80208
E-mail address: daniels@du.edu
Web address: www.daniels.du.edu/
 Parttime-Part-time-MBA.aspx
For more info: Call general information
 at (303) 871-3416

Why Denver?

With its newly revised curriculum, Daniels is aiming for a part-time MBA that creates principled leaders. In addition to 44 credits in core courses and 16 in electives, students must now take the Daniels Compass, 20 hours of courses devoted to ethics, value-based leadership, and sustainability. Flexibility is also a major new thrust. In addition to the program's 17 concentration options and joint degrees in law and international studies, students can customize their MBA by choosing a more inter-disciplinary path such as bioenterprise, sports management, or not-for-profit management.

Denver is a private institution. Established in 1982, Daniels's part-time MBA program is accredited by the Association to Advance Collegiate Schools of Business (AACSB). Daniels also offers full-time and executive MBA programs.

☑ B4UGO

Applicants accepted: 76%
Average GMAT score: 597
Average years' work experience: 6.5
**Average time to complete the
 program:** 42 months
Completion rate: 96%

 Who Are My Classmates?

Part-time enrollment: 245
Women: 37%
International: 2%
Minority: 8%
Average age: 29
Average base salary at admission:
 $59,586
Reason for getting an MBA: Career advancement with current employer (46.7%), career advancement with new employer (26.7%), change industries/functional areas (26.7%)*

*Estimates based on *Business Week* survey data.

"The courses were rigorous."

Where Do They Come From?

Top functional areas: Finance/
Accounting (32%), General
Management (24%), Marketing/
Sales (15%)
Top industries: Financial services
(24%), Nonprofit (19%), Technol-
ogy (11%)
Top companies: Charles Schwab,
ICON Advisors, Lockheed Martin,
SpectraLink, Peace Corps

"The instructors were hit or miss."

The 411

Maximum time to complete the
program: 60 months
Can PT students switch to the FT
MBA program: No
Tuition per credit hour: $873
Classes begin: September
Application deadlines: January 15,
March 15, May 15
Application fee: $100

Getting In

Relative importance of:
GMAT scores: Important
Work experience: Important
Application essay: Important
Interview: Very important
Recommendations: Important
Transcripts: Very important

Getting Out

Number of credits required for degree:
80
Access to Career Services for part-
timers: Yes
Access to alumni database for part-
timers: Yes
Part-timers permitted to interview on
campus for internships: Yes
Part-timers permitted to interview on
campus for full-time jobs: Yes
Graduates reporting post-MBA salary
increase: 68.8%*
Average increase: 29.7%*
*Estimate based on *BusinessWeek* survey data.

Cliff Notes

Leading areas of study: Corporate
Social Responsibility, Ethics,
Finance, General Management,
Leadership
Average class size, core courses: 33
Average class size, electives: 27
Number of electives: 87
Teaching methods: Case studies
(25%), team projects (25%),
lectures (20%), experiential learn-
ing (20%)
Faculty sharing with FT program:
100%
Classes meet: Weeknights, weeklong
sessions
Average workload per week: 16 hours

But What's It *Really* Like?

Program quality, graded by students:
Overall: **B**
Teaching quality: **C**
Caliber of classmates: **C**
Facilities: **A**
Support: **C**

Curriculum, graded by students:
Overall: **B**
E-business: **C**
Entrepreneurship: **C**
Ethics: **A+**
Finance: **C**
International business: **A**
Marketing: **B**
Strategy: **C**
Teamwork: **A**

 The Good, the Bad, and the Ugly: Students Speak Out

"Daniels has provided me with a strong academic foundation. The courses were rigorous and pushed students to produce high-quality work. Many students had prior experience that added to the overall learning environment."

"The cost is way too high."

"The instructors were hit or miss. When there was a good instructor, the courses were great. When there was a poor instructor, they were tedious.

The courses were nowhere near as challenging as those in my undergraduate degree."

"The program at DU is excellent, with strong professors, good connections, and real-life education."

"Strong professors, good connections, and real-life education."

"Part of what I liked about it was the diverse backgrounds of the students and faculty. Also, it was the perfect size—small enough to get to know a lot of people, but large enough to be challenging and offer a variety of perspectives."

"The cost is way too high for the actual value received from the courses. If my employer was not paying, I would not have gone to the University of Denver."

"I like the flexibility of the program and the ability to not only customize your degree, but also take a quarter off if you hit a period of high workload at work. I probably would not have been able to finish a program requiring you to go straight through with no delays."

Where to Stay

JW Marriott at Cherry Creek
150 Clayton Ln.
Denver, CO 80206
(303) 316-2700

Burnsley All Suite Hotel
1000 Grant St.
Denver, CO 80203
(303) 830-1000

Loews Denver Hotel
4150 E. Mississippi Ave.
Denver, CO 80246
(800) 345-9172

 Where to Eat

Café Cero
1446 S. Broadway
Denver, CO 80210
(303) 282-1446

Jerusalem Restaurant
1890 E. Evans Ave.
Denver, CO 80210
(303) 777-8828

Sushi Den
1487 S. Pearl St.
Denver, CO 80210
(303) 777-0826

 Things to Do

**The Denver Center for
the Performing Arts**
1101 13th St.
Denver, CO 80204
(303) 893-4000

Coors Brewery Tour
13th & Ford Sts.
Golden, CO 80401
(866) 812-2337

CHECK OUT BUSINESSWEEK.COM FOR MORE:

Interview Tips: See what the interview process is like from students with firsthand experience in the Denver admissions hot seat.

Search & Compare: Find out how Denver compares to other part-time MBA programs based on specialties and other criteria.

Expanded Profile: Check out more details on Denver's part-time MBA program and all it has to offer with our in-depth online profile.

Access all the B-schools content on BusinessWeek.com by subscribing to MBA Insider.

University of Houston

C. T. Bauer College of Business
2007 Ranking: 4th in the Southwest
334 Melcher Hall, Suite 330
Houston, TX 77204-6021
E-mail address: houstonmba@uh.edu
Web address: www.bauer.uh.edu/MBA/
index.asp
For more info: Call the main
switchboard at (713) 743-0700

Why Houston?

With more company headquarters than almost anywhere else in the United States, Houston draws smart, ambitious people from all over, and many of them end up at Bauer. The program focuses on critical thinking skills, ethics, and a multidisciplinary approach to problem solving. As a result, it's rated well by career switchers—nearly all of those surveyed by *Business Week* credit the program with launching them down a new path. The program includes 30 hours in core courses—delivered in a cohort format, much like a full-time program—and 18 in electives. Evening classes meet once a week in the fall and spring, twice a week in the summer.

The University of Houston is a public institution. Established in 1939, Bauer's part-time MBA program is accredited by the Association to Advance Collegiate Schools of Business (AACSB). Bauer also offers full-time and executive MBA programs.

☑ B4UGO

Applicants accepted: 87%
Average GMAT score: 576
Average years' work experience: 6.1
**Average time to complete the
program:** 30 months
Completion rate: 82%

🔘 Who Are My Classmates?

Part-time enrollment: 515
Women: 38%
International: 19%
Minority: 38%
Average age: 28
Average base salary at admission:
$58,561
Reason for getting an MBA: Career advancement with current employer (53.2%), career advancement with new employer (14.9%), change industries/functional areas (31.9%)*

*Estimates based on *Business Week* survey data.

> *"I was taught by former CEOs and CFOs."*

Where Do They Come From?

Top functional areas: Operations/ Production (26%), Finance/ Accounting (21%), General Management (19%)

Top industries: Petroleum/energy (24%), Manufacturing (15%), Financial services (13%)

Top companies: Halliburton, National Oilwell Varco, JPMorgan Chase, Exxon Mobil, AIM Investments

---

"More students are being accepted without work experience."

The 411

Maximum time to complete the program: 60 months

Can PT students switch to the FT MBA program: No

Tuition per credit hour: $352 (resident), $630 (nonresident)

Classes begin: August, January

Application deadlines: June 1, November 15 (U.S.); April 1, October 1 (international)

Application fee: $75 (U.S.), $150 (international)

Getting In

Relative importance of:
GMAT scores: Very important
Work experience: Important

Application essay: Important
Interview: Not considered
Recommendations: Very important
Transcripts: Very important

Getting Out

Number of credits required for degree: 48

Access to Career Services for part-timers: Yes

Access to alumni database for part-timers: No

Part-timers permitted to interview on campus for internships: Yes

Part-timers permitted to interview on campus for full-time jobs: Yes

Graduates reporting post-MBA salary increase: 52.9%*

Average increase: 35.8%*

*Estimate based on *Business Week* survey data.

Cliff Notes

Leading areas of study: Accounting, Finance, General Management, Management Information Systems, Marketing

Average class size, core courses: 51

Average class size, electives: 20

Number of electives: 86

Teaching methods: Team projects (35%), lectures (20%), experiential learning (20%)

Faculty sharing with FT program: 88%

Classes meet: Weeknights

Average workload per week: 25 hours

But What's It *Really* Like?

Program quality, graded by students:
Overall: C
Teaching quality: B
Caliber of classmates: C
Facilities: C
Support: C

Curriculum, graded by students:
Overall: C
E-business: C
Entrepreneurship: C
Ethics: C
Finance: A
International business: C
Marketing: B
Strategy: B
Teamwork: C

 The Good, the Bad, and the Ugly: Students Speak Out

"The professors offer a great deal of industry experience, which I much prefer to theory. I was taught by former CEOs and CFOs of Shell and Exxon and got to meet and interact with many others as guest speakers. I find it hard to imagine that other schools offer a higher-level industry experience."

"A great collection of electives."

"More and more students are being accepted without having the real-world work experience that was once a requirement. This takes away from the overall experience and contribution that students can make in their classes."

"The UH Bauer MBA offers a great collection of electives. The quality of the program is very good, and the cost is low compared to other options in the region."

"The program was not challenging."

"The program was not challenging, and the Bauer School of Business treated us, the paying customers, as if we owed it something at all times. It was frustrating to have to beg at every turn, especially for required classes to be offered!"

"The program's biggest attraction is its cohort-based system where you stay with your group throughout the program."

"We learned from the textbooks, but I don't think there was a lot of emphasis on how to apply the knowledge to our current jobs."

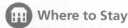 **Where to Stay**

Hilton University of Houston
4800 Calhoun St.
Houston, TX 77204
(713) 741-2447

Marriott Courtyard Houston Downtown
916 Dallas St.
Houston, TX 77002
(832) 366-1600

Residence Inn Houston Downtown
904 Dallas St.
Houston, TX 77002
(832) 366-1000

 Where to Eat

Brasil
2604 Dunlavy St.
Houston, TX 77006
(713) 528-1993

Eric's Restaurant
4800 Calhoun Rd.
Houston, TX 77004
(713) 743-2513

Rainbow Lodge
2011 Ella Blvd.
Houston, TX 77008
(713) 861-8666

 Things to Do

Sambuca Jazz Café
909 Texas St.
Houston, TX 77002
(713) 224-5295

Space Center Houston
1601 NASA Pkwy.
Houston, TX 77058
(281) 244-2100

CHECK OUT BUSINESSWEEK.COM FOR MORE:

Expanded Profile: Find more details on Houston's part-time MBA program in its online profile.

Search & Compare: See how Bauer stacks up against other part-time MBA programs using this interactive tool.

School Tour: Planning a visit? Check out the Houston campus before you go.

Forums: Connect with other Bauer hopefuls using our online forums.

Access all the B-schools content on BusinessWeek.com by subscribing to MBA Insider.

U. of Massachusetts at Amherst

Isenberg School of Management
2007 Ranking: 5th in the Northeast
Graduate Programs Office, Room 305
121 Presidents Dr.
Amherst, MA 01003
E-mail address:
gradprog@som.umass.edu
Web address:
www.isenberg.umass.edu/mba/
For more info: Call the MBA program
at **(413) 545-5608**

☑ B4UGO

Applicants accepted: 92%
Average GMAT score: 557
Average years' work experience: 7.3
**Average time to complete the
    program:** 32 months
Completion rate: 97%

Why UMass Amherst?

Ideal for individuals in career transition, the part-time program at Isenberg offers a flexible schedule and two formats: evenings in Holyoke or Shrewsbury, or weekends in Pittsfield. Students may also take courses online, where the entire core curriculum is offered every spring, summer, and fall semester. Although students have up to four years to complete the degree, many do so in half that time. UMass students have more experience than those in most part-time MBA programs, and they're taught by the same faculty that teaches in the full-time program. All this and a bargain too: the program is about half the cost of higher-ranked programs.

The University of Massachusetts at Amherst is a public institution. Established in 1990, Isenberg's part-time MBA program is accredited by the Association to Advance Collegiate Schools of Business (AACSB). Isenberg also offers a full-time MBA.

Who Are My Classmates?

Part-time enrollment: 235
Women: 35%
International: 0%
Minority: N/A
Average age: 33
Average base salary at admission: $58,529*
Reason for getting an MBA: Career advancement with current employer (60.6%), career advancement with new employer (18.2%), change industries/functional areas (21.2%)*

*Estimates based on *BusinessWeek* survey data.

"Flexibility, low credit requirements, and competitive cost."

Where Do They Come From?

Top functional areas: Healthcare Management (27%), General Management (20%), Engineering (12%)

Top industries: Healthcare (27%), Technology (15%), Financial services (12%)

Top companies: MassMutual, UTC, Bay State Medical, Fidelity, Phoenix

---

> *"A little limited on the electives."*

The 411

Maximum time to complete the program: 48 months

Can PT students switch to the FT MBA program: No

Tuition per credit hour: $540 to $670 depending on venue and format

Classes begin: September, January, February, June

Application deadlines: December 1, May 1, July 1

Application fee: $40 (Mass. residents), $50 (U.S.), $65 (international)

Getting In

Relative importance of:
GMAT scores: Important
Work experience: Very important
Application essay: Considered
Interview: Not considered
Recommendations: Important
Transcripts: Very important

Getting Out

Number of credits required for degree: 37

Access to Career Services for part-timers: Yes

Access to alumni database for part-timers: Yes

Part-timers permitted to interview on campus for internships: Yes

Part-timers permitted to interview on campus for full-time jobs: Yes

Graduates reporting post-MBA salary increase: 41.5%*

Average increase: 36.2%*

*Estimate based on *BusinessWeek* survey data.

Cliff Notes

Leading area of study: General Management

Average class size, core courses: 19

Average class size, electives: 10

Number of electives: 35

Teaching methods: Case studies (30%), team projects (20%), lectures (20%), distance learning (20%)

Faculty sharing with FT program: 55%

Classes meet: Weeknights, weekends, online

Average workload per week: 9 hours

> *"Some professors were a little full of themselves."*

But What's It *Really* Like?

Program quality, graded by students:
Overall: C
Teaching quality: A
Caliber of classmates: A
Facilities: B
Support: A

Curriculum, graded by students:
Overall: A
E-business: A+
Entrepreneurship: C
Ethics: A
Finance: C
International business: C
Marketing: B
Strategy: B
Teamwork: B

 ### The Good, the Bad, and the Ugly: Students Speak Out

"I like the flexibility, the low credit requirements, and the competitive cost of the UMass professional MBA program."

"[If I were to get my MBA now] I would go full-time to a top 50 school. It would have made a significant difference in my ability to get a great job upon graduation."

> ## *"Instructors do a great job of keeping students engaged."*

"I was not in a position to spend 4 to 5 years earning an MBA. I was able to finish this program in 2½ years. Some graduate programs are too long (in my opinion). This program was short and sweet, and I learned a lot. I've been very happy with my choice."

> ## *"This program was short and sweet, and I learned a lot."*

"Most professors were great, encouraging class discussions. And all made themselves available. But a couple were a little full of themselves and were quite removed from the business world."

"The UMass professional MBA program provides the flexibility of online and in-class courses so that I could proceed at my own pace. I was able to attend classes online while traveling for business. The program is a little limited on the electives but provides the fundamental business courses in a concise program at a very competitive cost. The instructors do a great job of keeping the students engaged with the online courses."

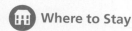 **Where to Stay**

Campus Center Hotel
University of Massachusetts
1 Campus Center Way
Amherst, MA 01003
(413) 549-6000

Marriott Courtyard Hadley Amherst
423 Russell St.
Hadley, MA 01035
(413) 256-5454

Howard Johnson Express Inn—Hadley
401 Russell St.
Hadley, MA 01035
(413) 586-0114

 Where to Eat

Amherst Brewing Co.
24 N. Pleasant St.
Amherst, MA 01002
(413) 253-4400

Black Sheep Deli
79 Main St.
Amherst, MA 01002
(413) 253-3442

Judie's
51 N. Pleasant St.
Amherst, MA 01002
(413) 253-3491

 Things to Do

Emily Dickinson Museum
280 Main St.
Amherst, MA 01002
(413) 542-8161

Fine Arts Center
151 Presidents Dr.
Amherst, MA 01003
(413) 545-2511

U. of Nevada at Reno

College of Business Administration
2007 Ranking: 5th in the West
Ansari Business Building, MS 024
Reno, NV 89557-0016
E-mail address:
  gradadmissions@unr.edu
Web address: www.coba.unr.edu/mba/
For more info: Call graduate admissions
  at (775) 784-6869

☑ B4UGO

Applicants accepted: 63%
Average GMAT score: 577
Average years' work experience: 6
**Average time to complete the
  program:** 36 months
Completion rate: 98%

⬤ Who Are My Classmates?

Part-time enrollment: 249
Women: 51%
International: 13%
Minority: 19%
Average age: 29
Average base salary at admission:
  $45,000
Reason for getting an MBA: Career
  advancement with current employer
  (39.4%), career advancement with
  new employer (33.3%), change
  industries/functional areas
  (27.3%)*

*Estimates based on *BusinessWeek* survey data.

Why Nevada?

Just minutes from the giant hotel casinos that are Reno's claim to fame, it makes sense that Nevada's full-time/part-time hybrid MBA program would offer a specialization in gaming management. But the choices don't end there—accounting, finance, information technology, and supply chain management are also available. Students complete 21 core credits and 18 credits in what the program calls "breadth" courses—seminars in a range of business areas such as investment management and marketing. Nine elective credits allow them to develop a specialization, and a strategic management course integrating all the material they've learned caps off the program. Tuition is the lowest of any ranked program.

University of Nevada at Reno is a public institution. Established in 1965, UNR's part-time MBA program is accredited by the Association to Advance Collegiate Schools of Business (AACSB).

"Flexible and affordable."

Where Do They Come From?

Top functional areas: Operations/ Production (30%), Management Information Systems (30%), Marketing/Sales (20%)

Top industries: Technology (25%), Financial services (20%), Manufacturing (20%)

Top companies: General Electric, International Game Technology, Microsoft Licensing, Sierra Pacific Power, Wells Fargo Bank

---

"We did not get any entrepreneurship classes."

The 411

Maximum time to complete the program: 72 months

Can PT students switch to the FT MBA program: Separate FT MBA not offered

Tuition per credit hour: $176 (resident), $365 (nonresident)

Classes begin: August, January

Application deadlines: October 15, March 15

Application fee: $60 (U.S.), $100 (international)

Getting In

Relative importance of:
GMAT scores: Very important
Work experience: Very important

Application essay: Very important
Interview: Not considered
Recommendations: Important
Transcripts: Very important

Getting Out

Number of credits required for degree: 51

Access to Career Services for part-timers: Yes

Access to alumni database for part-timers: No

Part-timers permitted to interview on campus for internships: N/A

Part-timers permitted to interview on campus for full-time jobs: N/A

Graduates reporting post-MBA salary increase: 65.6%*

Average increase: 44.9%*

*Estimate based on *BusinessWeek* survey data.

Cliff Notes

Leading areas of study: Finance, Marketing, Supply Chain Management

Average class size, core courses: 28

Average class size, electives: 24

Number of electives: 61

Teaching methods: Lectures (65%), case studies (15%), simulations (10%), team projects (10%)

Faculty sharing with FT program: N/A

Classes meet: Weeknights

Average workload per week: 24 hours

But What's It *Really* Like?

Program quality, graded by students:
Overall: **B**
Teaching quality: **B**
Caliber of classmates: **B**
Facilities: **C**
Support: **C**

Curriculum, graded by students:
Overall: **A**
E-business: **B**
Entrepreneurship: **C**
Ethics: **A**
Finance: **A**
International business: **B**
Marketing: **C**
Strategy: **B**
Teamwork: **A**

 ### The Good, the Bad, and the Ugly: Students Speak Out

"The UNR MBA program has excellent professors and an extensive selection of relevant subjects from which to choose. I strongly feel that the education I received at UNR is on a par with that of any well-ranked business school, but with the additional attributes of being both flexible and affordable."

"I became more competent in areas I knew little about."

"I would have liked to have had some choice in the programs we took. We did not get any entrepreneurship classes, and now that I have started the process of owning two businesses of my own, I think they would have been very useful."

"The professors have a good background and understanding of the business world as well as pure academics. I was able to successfully broaden my horizons to become more competent in areas I knew little about."

"Overall, the faculty was top notch."

"One of the biggest issues I have with the program is the acceptance of young, green students straight out of undergraduate programs who have no real-world experience. Most of these students do not have valid comments/ideas to offer in class discussions."

"Overall, the faculty was top notch, and the courses quite quantitative in nature. Faculty members also brought outside experiences—such as working with Harvard Business School faculty, working with the Nevada Supreme Court, and even having worked with Mother Teresa and with Enron—into the classroom."

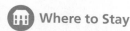 **Where to Stay**

Circus Circus Hotel & Casino
500 N. Sierra St.
Reno, NV 89503
(800) 648-5010

Eldorado Hotel Casino
345 N. Virginia St.
Reno, NV 89501
(775) 954-4050

Silver Legacy Resort Casino
407 N. Virginia St.
Reno, NV 89501
(800) 687-8733

 Where to Eat

Lulou's Restaurant
1470 S. Virginia St.
Reno, NV 89502
(775) 329-9979

Skyline Café
3005 Skyline Blvd., Suite 160
Reno, NV 89509
(775) 825-5611

The Steakhouse Grill
1100 Nugget Ave.
Sparks, NV 89431
(775) 356-3300

 Things to Do

210 North (nightclub)
210 N. Sierra St.
Reno, NV 89501
(775) 786-6210

Eldorado Casino
345 N. Virginia St.
Reno, NV 89501
(775) 954-4050

CHECK OUT BUSINESSWEEK.COM FOR MORE:

Expanded Profile: Find more details on UNR's part-time MBA program in its online profile.

Search & Compare: See how UNR stacks up against other part-time MBA programs using this interactive tool.

Forums: Connect with other UNR hopefuls using our online forums.

Access all the B-schools content on BusinessWeek.com by subscribing to MBA Insider.

University of Richmond

Robins School of Business
2007 Ranking: 4th in the Mid-Atlantic
1 Gateway Rd.
Richmond, VA 23173
E-mail address: mba@richmond.edu
Web address:
    www.business.richmond.edu
For more info: Call the MBA program
    at (804) 289-8553

Why Richmond?

The part-time program at Robins proves that a high-quality program doesn't have to result in sticker shock. At $770 per credit hour, it's half the price of some rival programs in the region, but it gets high marks from students for individualized attention from faculty and a high-caliber student body. The program requires 11 core courses, 4 electives, an international residency, and a capstone project that brings previously acquired skills to bear on a complex business problem. Another plus: actively involved alumni, who return for speaking engagements, provide career opportunities for graduates, and help shape the curriculum.

The University of Richmond is a private institution. Established in 1976, Robins's part-time MBA program is accredited by the Association to Advance Collegiate Schools of Business (AACSB).

☑ B4UGO

Applicants accepted: 77%
Average GMAT score: 592
Average years' work experience: 5.1
**Average time to complete the
    program:** 36 months
Completion rate: 83%

🗩 Who Are My Classmates?

Part-time enrollment: 148
Women: 47%
International: 6%
Minority: 19%
Average age: 28
Average base salary at admission:
    $42,143*
Reason for getting an MBA: Career advancement with current employer (50%), career advancement with new employer (10%), change industries/functional areas (40%)*

*Estimates based on *BusinessWeek* survey data.

> *"Very personal approach and small class sizes."*

Where Do They Come From?

Top functional areas: Finance/ Accounting (25%), Operations/ Production (25%), Marketing/Sales (21%)

Top industries: Manufacturing (34%), Financial services (25%), Health-care (9%), Nonprofit (9%)

Top companies: Philip Morris, Capital One, Circuit City, Genworth Financial, Honeywell

"The program needs greater variety in electives."

The 411

Maximum time to complete the program: 60 months

Can PT students switch to the FT MBA program: FT MBA not offered

Tuition per credit hour: $770

Classes begin: August

Application deadline: May 1

Application fee: $50

Getting In

Relative importance of:
GMAT scores: Very important
Work experience: Very important
Application essay: Not considered
Interview: Considered
Recommendations: Considered
Transcripts: Very important

Getting Out

Number of credits required for degree: 54

Access to Career Services for part-timers: Yes

Access to alumni database for part-timers: Yes

Part-timers permitted to interview on campus for internships: N/A

Part-timers permitted to interview on campus for full-time jobs: N/A

Graduates reporting post-MBA salary increase: 35%*

Average increase: 50.8%*

*Estimate based on *Business Week* survey data.

Cliff Notes

Leading areas of study: Finance, General Management, Leadership, Marketing, Strategy

Average class size, core courses: 23

Average class size, electives: 12

Number of electives: 12

Teaching methods: Lectures (25%), case studies (25%), experiential learning (25%), team projects (25%)

Faculty sharing with FT program: N/A

Classes meet: Weeknights

Average workload per week: 12 hours

"Innovative in its curriculum."

But What's It *Really* Like?

Program quality, graded by students:
Overall: **A+**
Teaching quality: **A**
Caliber of classmates: **A+**
Facilities: **A**
Support: **A+**

Curriculum, graded by students:
Overall: **B**
E-business: **A+**
Entrepreneurship: **C**
Ethics: **A+**
Finance: **A**
International business: **B**
Marketing: **C**
Strategy: **A+**
Teamwork: **C**

 The Good, the Bad, and the Ugly: Students Speak Out

"Very personal approach and small class sizes. I got the attention I needed from my professors."

"The faculty was sometimes frustrated by the quality of students. A few stragglers held back classes, particularly in the core courses, such as managerial economics."

> ## *"I would prefer more students with business experience."*

"The program needs a greater variety in concentrations and electives, greater reliance on case studies, increased homework, and more class discussions."

"The University of Richmond is innovative in its curriculum, as it focuses more on leadership than do traditional MBA schools. For those of us who choose not to follow the finance path, having the option to pursue a leadership path that includes creativity and design classes allows for a rich diversity of learning that helps to wholly round out the education."

> ## *"The varied coursework kept me from getting bored."*

"I would prefer more students with several years of business experience. Most of the time a majority of the students had a long history of experience, but a few classes contained JD/MBAs and Masters of Accounting undergraduates who didn't add much to the dialogue."

"The workload was doable with a full-time job, and I feel that just about anyone would benefit from the program. The teachers were great, and the varied coursework kept me from getting bored with it."

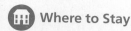 **Where to Stay**

Comfort Inn Executive Center
7201 W. Broad St.
Richmond, VA 23294
(804) 672-1108

Courtyard by Marriott West
6400 W. Broad St.
Richmond, VA 23230
(804) 282-1881

Sheraton Richmond West
6624 W. Broad St.
Richmond, VA 23230
(804) 285-2000

 Where to Eat

The Tobacco Company Restaurant
1201 E. Cary St.
Richmond, VA 23219
(804) 782-9555

Carytown Burgers and Fries
3500½ W. Cary St.
Richmond, VA 23221
(804) 358-5225

Buffalo Wild Wings Grill & Bar
1501 E. Cary St.
Richmond, VA 23219
(804) 648-8900

 Things to Do

Short Pump Town Center
11800 W. Broad St.
Richmond, VA 23233
(804) 364-9500

Richbrau Brewing Company
1214 E. Cary St.
Richmond, VA 23219
(804) 644-3018

CHECK OUT BUSINESSWEEK.COM FOR MORE:

Expanded Profile: Find more details on Richmond's part-time MBA program in its online profile.

Search & Compare: See how Richmond stacks up against other part-time MBA programs using this interactive tool.

Forums: Connect with other Richmond hopefuls using our online forums.

Access all the B-schools content on BusinessWeek.com by subscribing to MBA Insider.

U. of Southern California

Marshall School of Business
2007 Ranking: 2nd in the West
MBA for Professionals and Managers
611 Exposition Blvd.
Popovich Hall, Room 308
Los Angeles, CA 90089
E-mail address:
   uscmbapm@marshall.usc.edu
Web address: www.marshall.usc.edu/
   web/MBAPM.cfm
For more info: Call admissions at (213)
   740-6166

☑ B4UGO

Applicants accepted: 61%
Average GMAT score: 624
Average years' work experience: 6
**Average time to complete the
   program:** 33 months
Completion rate: 98%

Why USC?

Few programs serve the diverse needs of part-time MBA students better than USC's, which ranked No. 1 in post-MBA outcomes. A challenging curriculum allows students to choose from more than a dozen concentrations and certificate programs—from the Business of Creative Industries to Product Innovation and Brand Management—and a weeklong international trip adds a global flavor. Classes are offered in twice-a-week evening sessions at the University Park campus in Los Angeles or the Orange County Center in Irvine.

USC is a private institution. Established in 1922, Marshall's part-time MBA program is accredited by the Association to Advance Collegiate Schools of Business (AACSB). Marshall also offers full-time and executive MBA programs. For details on Marshall's full-time MBA program, see page 169. For details on its executive MBA program, see page 301.

🔘 Who Are My Classmates?

Part-time enrollment: 790
Women: 29%
International: 0%
Minority: 49%
Average age: 28
Average base salary at admission:
   $76,000
Reason for getting an MBA: Career advancement with current employer (37%), career advancement with new employer (25.9%), change industries/functional areas (37%)*

*Estimates based on *Business Week* survey data.

"The program was very challenging, but worth it."

Where Do They Come From?

Top functional areas: Finance/ Accounting (22%), Operations/ Production (18%), General Management (10%), Human Resources (10%)

Top industries: Manufacturing (23%), Financial services (13%), Real estate (13%)

Top companies: N/A

"It was my first choice and the right choice."

The 411

Maximum time to complete the program: 60 months

Can PT students switch to the FT MBA program: No

Tuition per credit hour: $1,217

Classes begin: August

Application deadlines: October 1 to May 1

Application fee: $150

Getting In

Relative importance of:
GMAT scores: Very important
Work experience: Very important
Application essay: Very important
Interview: Not considered
Recommendations: Very important
Transcripts: Very important

Getting Out

Number of credits required for degree: 63

Access to Career Services for part-timers: Yes

Access to alumni database for part-timers: Yes

Part-timers permitted to interview on campus for internships: No

Part-timers permitted to interview on campus for full-time jobs: Yes

Graduates reporting post-MBA salary increase: 62.5%*

Average increase: 40.9%*

*Estimate based on *Business Week* survey data.

Cliff Notes

Leading areas of study: Entrepreneurship, Finance, Marketing, Portfolio Management, Real Estate

Average class size, core courses: 65

Average class size, electives: 36

Number of electives: 83

Teaching methods: Case studies (30%), team projects (30%), lectures (25%)

Faculty sharing with FT program: 100%

Classes meet: Weeknights

Average workload per week: 20 hours

"Teachers and peers were all exceptional."

But What's It *Really* Like?

Program quality, graded by students:
Overall: **A+**
Teaching quality: **B**
Caliber of classmates: **B**
Facilities: **A+**
Support: **A**

Curriculum, graded by students:
Overall: **B**
E-business: **B**
Entrepreneurship: **A+**
Ethics: **C**
Finance: **A**
International business: **B**
Marketing: **A**
Strategy: **A+**
Teamwork: **A+**

 ### The Good, the Bad, and the Ugly: Students Speak Out

"The program was very challenging, but I feel that it was worth it. Both the education and the relationships with students and faculty will be with me forever."

"USC has so much more going for it than just a great education—the atmosphere, networking, friendships, etc. are all a part of the experience. It was my first choice and the right choice."

"The school offers many important courses only during the day, from noon to 4:00 p.m., and that makes it impossible for part-time students to attend."

"USC has hundreds of speakers—including former presidents Clinton and Bush, the Dalai Lama, George Will, Maya Angelou, and so many others."

"I am very disappointed in the Career Resource Center. There are obvious discrepancies between the caliber of support that full-time MBAs and evening MBAs receive."

"The career center was the only bad part about the program. I found the career center employees and director to be very inaccessible."

"Teachers, curriculum, and peers were all exceptional. The study-abroad experience was extremely well structured and valuable. Networking opportunities were amazing."

"Between the tailgates, parties, social events at bars, bowling nights, poker tournaments, career days, lectures, and industry events, networking was pretty well covered!"

> *"I am very disappointed in the Career Resource Center."*

 **Where to Stay**

Los Angeles Radisson Hotel
3540 S. Figueroa St.
Los Angeles, CA 90007
(213) 748-4141

Omni Los Angeles Hotel
251 S. Olive St.
Los Angeles, CA 90012
(213) 617-3300

Westin Bonaventure
404 S. Figueroa St.
Los Angeles, CA 90071
(213) 624-1000

 Where to Eat

Philippe the Original
1001 N. Alameda St.
Los Angeles, CA 90012
(213) 628-3781

Water Grill
544 S. Grand St.
Los Angeles, CA 90071
(213) 891-0900

El Cholo Restaurant
1121 S. Western Ave.
Los Angeles, CA 90006
(323) 734-2773

 Things to Do

Getty Museum
1200 Getty Center Dr.
Los Angeles, CA 90265
(310) 440-7300

Venice Boardwalk
Pacific Ave. & Windward Ave.
Venice, CA 90291

CHECK OUT BUSINESSWEEK.COM FOR MORE:

School Tour: Take a virtual tour of Popovich Hall at the Marshall school's main campus to see students and faculty at work.

Sample Application Essays and Interview Tips: Examples of how to approach the daunting application process and tips on how to tackle the Marshall interview.

Expanded Profile: Find out more about the campus, students, and admissions criteria with our extensive online school profile.

Search & Compare: How does USC compare to other programs? Find out using this handy interactive tool.

Access all the B-schools content on BusinessWeek.com by subscribing to MBA Insider.

University of Texas at Austin

McCombs School of Business
2007 Ranking: 5th in the Southwest
Texas Evening MBA (TEMBA)
2100 Speedway GSB 5.132
Austin, TX 78712
E-mail address:
TEMBA@mccombs.utexas.edu
Web address: www.mccombs.utexas.edu/
temba/
For more info: Call MBA admissions at
(512) 471-5893

☑ B4UGO

Applicants accepted: 51%
Average GMAT score: 659
Average years' work experience: 6
**Average time to complete the
program:** 33 months
Completion rate: 95%

Why McCombs?

Unlike other part-time programs, McCombs's TEMBA program has many features of a full-time MBA. Students are assigned to small teams that take classes together for three years. Students are assigned consulting projects at nearby companies, and a one-week immersion course each August includes an introduction to upcoming courses. The program also gives evening students a chance to work with far more experienced executive MBA students. You'll pay a pretty penny—eight times more than higher-ranked UT San Antonio—but three out of four career switchers surveyed by *BusinessWeek* credit this program for helping them achieve their goals.

Texas–Austin is a public institution. Established in 1999, McCombs's part-time MBA program is accredited by the Association to Advance Collegiate Schools of Business (AACSB). McCombs also offers full-time and executive MBA programs. For details on McCombs's full-time MBA program, see page 173.

 Who Are My Classmates?

Part-time enrollment: 217
Women: 22%
International: 19%
Minority: 22%
Average age: 29
Average base salary at admission:
$60,000*
Reason for getting an MBA: Career advancement with current employer (46.2%), career advancement with new employer (7.7%), change industries/functional areas (46.2%)*

*Estimates based on *BusinessWeek* survey data.

"Now that I am done, I will be starting my own business."

Where Do They Come From?

Top functional areas: Management Information Systems (41%), Operations/Production (16%), Consulting (14%)

Top industries: Consumer products (49%), Technology (20%), Financial services (13%)

Top companies: Dell, IBM, National Instruments, Cisco Systems, Advanced Micro Devices

---

"Just as rigorous as the full-time program."

The 411

Maximum time to complete the program: 60 months

Can PT students switch to the FT MBA program: No

Tuition per credit hour: $1,523 (resident), $2,086 (nonresident)

Classes begin: August

Application deadlines: November 1, January 18, March 17, May 5, June 2

Application fee: $125

Getting In

Relative importance of:
GMAT scores: Important
Work experience: Important
Application essay: Important
Interview: Important

Recommendations: Important
Transcripts: Important

Getting Out

Number of credits required for degree: 48

Access to Career Services for part-timers: Yes

Access to alumni database for part-timers: Yes

Part-timers permitted to interview on campus for internships: No

Part-timers permitted to interview on campus for full-time jobs: Yes

Graduates reporting post-MBA salary increase: 58.6%*

Average increase: 51.5%*

*Estimate based on *BusinessWeek* survey data.

Cliff Notes

Leading area of study: General Management

Average class size, core courses: 77

Average class size, electives: N/A

Number of electives: 0

Teaching methods: Lectures (25%), case studies (25%), simulations (25%), team projects (25%)

Faculty sharing with FT program: 100%

Classes meet: Weeknights

Average workload per week: 20 hours

"Not enough practical coursework."

But What's It *Really* Like?

Program quality, graded by students:
Overall: C
Teaching quality: A+
Caliber of classmates: A+
Facilities: B
Support: C

Curriculum, graded by students:
Overall: C
E-business: C
Entrepreneurship: A
Ethics: C
Finance: C
International business: C
Marketing: C
Strategy: C
Teamwork: C

 The Good, the Bad, and the Ugly: Students Speak Out

"I went into the program expecting to learn about entrepreneurship, and I did. Now that I am done, I will be starting my own business on the side."

"There was an element of camaraderie and competitiveness."

"UT is a first-class institution. The quality of the education and the relationships I built with professors will pay off far more than I could have ever imagined."

"Our UT McCombs part-time program was just as rigorous as the full-time program, with the same instructors and the same workload for all the core courses and electives. The summer ENHANCE program substitutes for the traditional summer internship undertaken by full-time MBAs."

"The scope of the program was way more than I expected."

"The scope of the program was way more than I expected. B-school was not just about money or capitalism. I participated in deep debates on how to treat people, what employee benefits are fair, and the responsibility of business in our society."

"High-quality, rigorous education at an affordable price in a friendly atmosphere. I was amazed at the open-door policies of the professors. There was an element of camaraderie and competitiveness in a good sort of way."

"The resources aren't devoted to the part-time program to make it as beneficial as the full-time program."

"The curriculum was disappointing, and I feel it did not offer enough practical coursework."

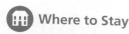 **Where to Stay**

DoubleTree Guest Suites
303 W. 15th St.
Austin, TX 78701
(512) 478-7000

Hilton Austin
500 E. 4th St.
Austin, TX 78701
(512) 482-8000

Hotel San Jose
1316 Congress Ave.
Austin, TX 78704
(512) 444-7322

 Where to Eat

Güero's Taco Bar
1412 S. Congress Ave.
Austin, TX 78704
(512) 447-7688

Trudy's Texas Star
409 W. 30th St.
Austin, TX 78705
(512) 477-2935

Shady Grove Restaurant
1624 Barton Springs Rd.
Austin, TX 78704
(512) 474-9991

 Things to Do

Bob Bullock Texas State History Museum
1800 N. Congress Ave.
Austin, TX 78711
(512) 936-8746

Blanton Museum of Art
The University of Texas at Austin
Martin Luther King Jr. Blvd.
at Congress Ave.
Austin, TX 78701
(512) 471-5482

CHECK OUT BUSINESSWEEK.COM FOR MORE:

Expanded Profile: Still not satisfied? Check out Texas–Austin's online profile for more details on what to expect from the part-time program.

Search & Compare: See how Texas–Austin measures up to other part-time programs when it comes to cost, competitiveness, and other important considerations.

Interview Tips: Suggestions on how to handle the Texas–Austin admissions process.

Access all the B-schools content on BusinessWeek.com by subscribing to MBA Insider.

U. of Texas at San Antonio

College of Business
2007 Ranking: 3rd in the Southwest
One UTSA Circle
San Antonio, TX 78249-1644
E-mail address: mbainfo@utsa.edu
Web address: www.business.utsa.edu/
graduate/
For more info: Call the main
switchboard at (210) 458-4011

Why UT–San Antonio?

UT–San Antonio's full-time/part-time hybrid MBA offers the ultimate in flexibility, allowing students to switch back and forth between formats as their schedules require. Students choose from three options: a general MBA nonthesis path including 12 credit hours of electives, a thesis option that replaces half the electives with a thesis project, or a concentration option where students can focus in on one area of interest. A laundry list of concentrations includes standards such as accounting and finance, but also more esoteric subjects such as real estate finance and tourism destination development. An MBA in international business is also available.

The University of Texas at San Antonio is a public institution. Established in 1969, the College of Business's part-time MBA program is accredited by the Association to Advance Collegiate Schools of Business (AACSB). UTSA also offers an executive MBA program.

☑ B4UGO

Applicants accepted: 58%
Average GMAT score: 558
Average years' work experience: 4.1
Average time to complete the program: 24 months
Completion rate: 75%

💬 Who Are My Classmates?

Part-time enrollment: 360
Women: 39%
International: 17%
Minority: 39%
Average age: 29
Average base salary at admission: $54,000
Reason for getting an MBA: Career advancement with current employer (30%), career advancement with new employer (30%), change industries/functional areas (40%)*

*Estimates based on *BusinessWeek* survey data.

> *"There is a ton of experience in each classroom."*

Where Do They Come From?

Top functional areas: General Management (23%), Marketing/Sales (23%), Operations/Production (15%), Finance/Accounting (15%)

Top industries: Financial services (32%), Government (15%), Consulting (12%), Real estate (12%)

Top companies: United Services Automobile Assn., City Public Service Energy, The Hartford, University of Texas at San Antonio, Valero Energy

---

"I wanted more interaction with faculty than just in the classroom."

The 411

Maximum time to complete the program: 72 months

Can PT students switch to the FT MBA program: FT MBA not offered

Tuition per credit hour: $201 (resident), $757 (nonresident)

Classes begin: August, January, June

Application deadlines: May 1 to November 1 (U.S.), March 1 to September 1 (international)

Application fee: $45 (U.S.), $80 (international)

Getting In

Relative importance of:

GMAT scores: Very important

Work experience: Considered

Application essay: Important

Interview: Not considered

Recommendations: Considered

Transcripts: Very important

Getting Out

Number of credits required for degree: 33

Access to Career Services for part-timers: Yes

Access to alumni database for part-timers: No

Part-timers permitted to interview on campus for internships: N/A

Part-timers permitted to interview on campus for full-time jobs: N/A

Graduates reporting post-MBA salary increase: 21.4%*

Average increase: 22.9%*

*Estimate based on *Business Week* survey data.

Cliff Notes

Leading areas of study: Finance, Healthcare Management, Management Accounting, Marketing, Project Management

Average class size, core courses: 26

Average class size, electives: 15

Number of electives: 67

Teaching methods: Lectures (50%), team projects (25%), case studies (20%)

Faculty sharing with FT program: N/A

Classes meet: Days, weeknights

Average workload per week: 15 hours

But What's It *Really* Like?

Program quality, graded by students:
Overall: **A**
Teaching quality: **B**
Caliber of classmates: **B**
Facilities: **A**
Support: **A**

Curriculum, graded by students:
Overall: **C**
E-business: **B**
Entrepreneurship: **C**
Ethics: **B**
Finance: **B**
International business: **A**
Marketing: **B**
Strategy: **C**
Teamwork: **C**

 ### The Good, the Bad, and the Ugly: Students Speak Out

"I liked the mix of professionals (part-time) and full-time students. There is a ton of experience that gathers weekly in each classroom."

"I really wanted more interaction with faculty than just in the classroom. I have many unanswered questions, and now I am out of the program. Also, career services for MBA students are very limited."

"One of the best decisions in my life."

"My professors' strengths were rooted in their subject matter expertise coupled with their industry and academic experience. Many integrated current events into the course material to demonstrate how to make use of the information to make better decisions. Many professors also worked hard to teach students to think for themselves by challenging their assumptions."

"The instructors' only weakness was not having an abundant amount of office hours to select from after 5 p.m. for working professionals."

"There was too much emphasis on group work."

"I understand the importance of working as a team. However, there was too much emphasis on group work inside and outside of the classroom."

"I chose this program because it allowed me to finish my CPA requirements within the MBA degree plan. I also participated in a study-abroad program that enhanced my experience, making it one of the best decisions I have made in my life."

 **Where to Stay**

Best Western Fiesta Six Flags
13535 Interstate Highway 10 W.
San Antonio, TX 78249
(210) 696-2400

Comfort Inn Fiesta Park
6755 N. Loop 1604 W.
San Antonio, TX 78249
(210) 696-4766

The Westin La Cantera Resort
16641 La Cantera Pkwy.
San Antonio, TX 78256
(210) 558-6500

 Where to Eat

Rome's Pizza & Greek Food
5999 De Zavala Rd., Suite 111
San Antonio, TX 78249
(210) 691-2070

Rudy's Country Store & Bar-B-Q
24152 Interstate Highway 10 W.
San Antonio, TX 78257
(210) 698-2141

Silo's Elevated Cuisine
434 N. Loop 1604 E.
San Antonio, TX 78232
(210) 483-8989

 Things to Do

Far West Rodeo
3030 N.E. Loop 410
San Antonio, TX 78218
(210) 646-9378

River Walk
110 Broadway, Suite 440
San Antonio, TX 78205
(210) 227-4262

University of Washington

Michael G. Foster School of Business
2007 Ranking: 4th in the West
110 Mackenzie Hall
Box 353200
Seattle, WA 98195-3200
E-mail address:
mba@u.washington.edu
Web address: www.bschool.washington.edu/evemba/
For more info: Call the MBA program at (206) 543-4661

Why Washington?

The evening MBA program promises students an experience of the same caliber as the school's full-time program. Students can choose to customize their MBA with a certificate in areas including real estate studies, environmental management, and global business, among others. Alternatively, students can choose to earn a dual degree, coupling their MBA with a degree in law, public health and community medicine, auditing and assurance, taxation, international studies, or Japan studies. In a hurry? Qualified students are allowed to waive up to two core courses.

The University of Washington is a public institution. Established in 1996, Foster's part-time MBA program is accredited by the Association to Advance Collegiate Schools of Business (AACSB). Foster also offers full-time and executive MBA programs.

☑ B4UGO

Applicants accepted: 59%
Average GMAT score: 669
Average years' work experience: 6.1
Average time to complete the program: 30 months
Completion rate: 98%

🔵 Who Are My Classmates?

Part-time enrollment: 225
Women: 30%
International: 17%
Minority: 19%
Average age: 30
Average base salary at admission: $75,200
Reason for getting an MBA: Career advancement with current employer (33.3%), career advancement with new employer (44.4%), change industries/functional areas (22.2%)*

*Estimates based on *BusinessWeek* survey data.

"Constantly looking to improve."

Where Do They Come From?

Top functional areas: Operations/
Production (20%), Finance/
Accounting (18%), Marketing/Sales
(18%)

Top industries: Technology (20%),
Manufacturing (19%), Financial
services (16%)

Top companies: Microsoft, Boeing,
Amazon.com, Washington Mutual,
T-Mobile

"Does not get the attention of recruiters."

The 411

Maximum time to complete the
program: 72 months
Can PT students switch to the FT
MBA program: Yes
Tuition per credit hour: $689
Classes begin: September
Application deadline: April 15
Application fee: $75

Getting In

Relative importance of:
GMAT scores: Important
Work experience: Very important
Application essay: Very important
Interview: Very important
Recommendations: Important
Transcripts: Important

Getting Out

Number of credits required for degree:
74
Access to Career Services for part-
timers: Yes
Access to alumni database for part-
timers: Yes
Part-timers permitted to interview on
campus for internships: Yes
Part-timers permitted to interview on
campus for full-time jobs: Yes
Graduates reporting post-MBA salary
increase: 57.9%*
Average increase: 25%*

*Estimate based on *Business Week* survey data.

Cliff Notes

Leading areas of study: Entrepreneur-
ship, Finance, General Manage-
ment, International Business,
Marketing
Average class size, core courses: 60
Average class size, electives: 32
Number of electives: 64
Teaching methods: Case studies
(35%), lectures (25%), team
projects (20%)
Faculty sharing with FT program:
82%
Classes meet: Days, weeknights
Average workload per week: 22 hours

But What's It *Really* Like?

Program quality, graded by students:
Overall: B
Teaching quality: C
Caliber of classmates: A+
Facilities: C
Support: B

Curriculum, graded by students:
Overall: C
E-business: A+
Entrepreneurship: A
Ethics: C
Finance: B
International business: C
Marketing: C
Strategy: C
Teamwork: C

 The Good, the Bad, and the Ugly: Students Speak Out

"The UW evening MBA program does everything it can to meet the needs of students and understands the unique stresses that working students with families face. It is constantly looking to improve the program and is willing to adjust the curriculum to accommodate the students' needs."

"Professors were very passionate about teaching."

"The only downside of UW is that it does not get the attention of recruiters the way other schools do."

"Most professors were engaging. But some were really dull."

"Overall, the professors were very passionate about teaching and imparting a great education. This was visible in all their interactions. They also cared that the students learned and took the extra time to make sure that we did."

"The strengths of the UW evening MBA are really the accounting/finance and entrepreneurship programs. The instructors all had real-world experiences that they brought to the classroom."

"Most of the professors were engaging. But some of them were really dull. I wish many of them had real-world business experience instead of just the academic or consulting side."

"Overall, I thought it was a good program. I felt that this was a better program than the more compressed 18-month program, even though it took three years to complete. I felt that I had more options to choose more electives than with the 18-month program."

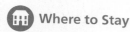 **Where to Stay**

Hotel Deca
4507 Brooklyn Ave. N.E.
Seattle, WA 98105
(800) 899-0251

Travelodge Seattle University
4725 25th Ave. N.E.
Seattle, WA 98105
(206) 525-4612

Watertown Hotel
4242 Roosevelt Way N.E.
Seattle, WA 98105
(206) 826-4242

 Where to Eat

Schultzy's Sausage
4114 University Way N.E.
Seattle, WA 98105
(206) 548-9461

Shalimar Restaurant
1401 N.E. 42nd St.
Seattle, WA 98105
(206) 633-3854

Thaiger Room
4228 University Way N.E.
Seattle, WA 98105
(206) 632-9299

 Things to Do

College Inn Pub
4006 University Way N.E.
Seattle, WA 98105
(206) 634-2307

University District
4114 University Way N.E. (at 45th St.)
Seattle, WA 98105
(206) 526-9000

CHECK OUT BUSINESSWEEK.COM FOR MORE:

Expanded Profile: Find more details on the University of Washington's part-time MBA program in its online profile.

Search & Compare: See how Washington stacks up against other part-time MBA programs using this interactive tool.

School Tour: Planning a visit? Before you go, check out the University of Washington campus, where cherry trees blossom in the spring.

Forums: Connect with other Washington hopefuls using our online forums.

Access all the B-schools content on BusinessWeek.com by subscribing to MBA Insider.

Villanova University

School of Business
2007 Ranking: 3rd in the Mid-Atlantic
Bartley Hall, Room 1054
800 Lancaster Ave.
Villanova, PA 19085
E-mail address: mba@villanova.edu
Web address: www.villanova.edu/
business/graduate/mba/
For more info: Call the MBA program
at (610) 519-4330

Why Villanova?

Part-timers at Villanova have a choice of MBAs—a self-paced program and a two-year "full-time equivalent" version. The former has a revamped curriculum emphasizing teamwork and strategic decision making, and offers five specializations, including healthcare management and international business. The latter is built around a dozen core courses—no electives—that take a cross-functional approach, using multiple disciplines to tackle complex problems. A one-week international trip gives that program a global flavor. The information in this profile is for the two-year program only.

Villanova is a private institution. Established in 2003, Villanova's part-time MBA program is accredited by the Association to Advance Collegiate Schools of Business (AACSB). Villanova also offers an executive MBA program. For details on the executive MBA program, see page 305.

☑ B4UGO

Applicants accepted: N/A
Average GMAT score: 590
Average years' work experience: 6.3
**Average time to complete the
program:** 24 months
Completion rate: 97%

Who Are My Classmates?

Part-time enrollment: 433
Women: 24%
International: 0%
Minority: 24%
Average age: 30
Average base salary at admission: $58,636*
Reason for getting an MBA: Career advancement with current employer (93.3%), career advancement with new employer (0%), change industries/functional areas (6.7%)*

*Estimates based on *BusinessWeek* survey data.

"My experiences have been nothing but exceptional."

Where Do They Come From?

Top functional areas: Operations/Production (34%), Finance/Accounting (20%), General Management (18%)

Top industries: Healthcare (35%), Technology (17%), Financial services (14%)

Top companies: GlaxoSmithKline, Lockheed Martin, Johnson & Johnson, Vanguard, Siemens

> *"I hope that my children will go to Villanova."*

The 411

Maximum time to complete the program: 24 months

Can PT students switch to the FT MBA program: FT MBA not offered

Tuition per credit hour: $885

Classes begin: August

Application deadline: June 30

Application fee: $50

Getting In

Relative importance of:
GMAT scores: Very important
Work experience: Very important
Application essay: Important
Interview: Not considered
Recommendations: Important
Transcripts: Important

Getting Out

Number of credits required for degree: 44

Access to Career Services for part-timers: Yes

Access to alumni database for part-timers: Yes

Part-timers permitted to interview on campus for internships: N/A

Part-timers permitted to interview on campus for full-time jobs: N/A

Graduates reporting post-MBA salary increase: 68.4%*

Average increase: 24.8%*

*Estimate based on *Business Week* survey data.

Cliff Notes

Leading areas of study: Accounting, Corporate Strategy, Finance, General Management, Technology Management

Average class size, core courses: 19

Average class size, electives: N/A

Number of electives: 0

Teaching methods: Lectures (25%), case studies (25%), team projects (20%)

Faculty sharing with FT program: N/A

Classes meet: Weeknights

Average workload per week: 13 hours

> *"The 'pure academics' need to get out into the real world."*

But What's It *Really* Like?

Program quality, graded by students:
Overall: **B**
Teaching quality: **C**
Caliber of classmates: **A**
Facilities: **A**
Support: **B**

Curriculum, graded by students:
Overall: **C**
E-business: **A+**
Entrepreneurship: **B**
Ethics: **A**
Finance: **B**
International business: **A+**
Marketing: **A+**
Strategy: **A+**
Teamwork: **A+**

 The Good, the Bad, and the Ugly: Students Speak Out

"My experiences at Villanova have been nothing but exceptional. My advisers are available, teachers adjust to our needs, and my classmates have become friends."

"I have developed personal relationships with all of my professors to the point where it seems as if I have numerous mentors. I hope that my children will go to Villanova."

"You can't develop a specialization."

"The faculty consisted mostly of academics with very little industry experience. This made discussion of industry trends and real-life examples rare. The use of case studies became very repetitive. For those with a business undergraduate degree, this program would be considerably less useful because of the amount of time spent covering undergraduate topics (basic accounting, finance, economics, and statistics, for example)."

"The faculty has very little industry experience."

"Now that I am nearly done with the program, I wish it had an option to specialize in a given area. The primary disadvantage of cohort programs is that you typically can't develop a specialization."

"I have had only six instructors. Some of the 'pure academics' need to get out into the real world. They seem to have trouble relating to working professionals."

"The professors are eager to share their knowledge as well as to apply their expertise in helping individual students to address/solve problems that they may be facing in their businesses."

Where to Stay

The Radnor Hotel
591 E. Lancaster Ave.
St. Davids, PA 19087
(610) 688-5800

Philadelphia Marriott West
111 Crawford Ave.
W. Conshohocken, PA 19428
(610) 941-5600

Radisson Hotel Valley Forge
1160 First Ave.
King of Prussia, PA 19406
(610) 337-2000

 Where to Eat

Wild Onion
900 Conestoga Rd.
Rosemont, PA 19010
(610) 527-4826

Blush
24 N. Merion Ave.
Bryn Mawr, PA 19010
(610) 527-7700

Fuji Mountain Restaurant
14 N. Merion Ave.
Bryn Mawr, PA 19010
(610) 527-7777

 Things to Do

Lights of Liberty Show
600 Chestnut St.
Philadelphia, PA 19106
(215) 925-8077

The Franklin Institute Science Museum
222 N. 20th St.
Philadelphia, PA 19103
(215) 448-1200

Wake Forest University

Babcock Graduate School of
  Management
2007 Ranking: 4th in the South
Worrell Professional Center
1834 Wake Forest Rd.
Winston-Salem, NC 27106
E-mail address: clt.mba@mba.wfu.edu
Web address: www.mba.wfu.edu
For more info: Call part-time MBA
  admissions at (704) 365-1717

☑ B4UGO

Applicants accepted: N/A
Average GMAT score: 570
Average years' work experience: 7.5
**Average time to complete the
  program:** 24 months
Completion rate: 88%

 Who Are My Classmates?

Part-time enrollment: 237
Women: 28%
International: 0%
Minority: 24%
Average age: 30
Average base salary at admission:
  $65,141
Reason for getting an MBA: Career
  advancement with current employer
  (68.5%), career advancement with
  new employer (12.6%), change
  industries/functional areas
  (18.9%)*

*Estimates based on *Business Week* survey data.

Why Wake Forest?

The Wake Forest part-time MBA has much more in common with full-time MBAs than other part-time programs. Small classes with an experienced student body are taught by the program's full-time MBA faculty. And students can take part in a two-week international study tour offered each summer, and a second-year management consulting practicum. The part-time MBA—15 core courses and 3 electives—takes two years to complete. It's offered two evenings per week in Winston-Salem and either two evenings per week or Saturdays only in Charlotte.

Wake Forest is a private institution. Established in 1987, Babcock's part-time MBA program is accredited by the Association to Advance Collegiate Schools of Business (AACSB). Babcock also offers full-time and executive MBA programs. For details of the full-time MBA program, see page 197.

> *"The instruction leaves me wanting to learn more."*

Where Do They Come From?

Top functional areas: Marketing/Sales (31%), Finance/Accounting (26%), Operations/Production (13%)

Top industries: Financial services (32%), Healthcare (10%), Technology (6%)

Top companies: Wachovia, Bank of America, R.J. Reynolds Tobacco, BB&T, BASF

"The relationships I built are priceless."

The 411

Maximum time to complete the program: 24 months

Can PT students switch to the FT MBA program: No

Tuition per credit hour: $1,104

Classes begin: August, January

Application deadlines: None

Application fee: $75

Getting In

Relative importance of:
GMAT scores: Important
Work experience: Important
Application essay: Considered
Interview: Very important
Recommendations: Important
Transcripts: Considered

Getting Out

Number of credits required for degree: 55

Access to Career Services for part-timers: Yes

Access to alumni database for part-timers: Yes

Part-timers permitted to interview on campus for internships: Yes

Part-timers permitted to interview on campus for full-time jobs: Yes

Graduates reporting post-MBA salary increase: 69.8%*

Average increase: 34.1%*

*Estimate based on *Business Week* survey data.

Cliff Notes

Leading area of study: General Management

Average class size, core courses: 42

Average class size, electives: 23

Number of electives: 19

Teaching methods: Case studies (45%), lectures (15%), experiential learning (15%), team projects (15%)

Faculty sharing with FT program: 100%

Classes meet: Weeknights, weekends

Average workload per week: 20 hours

"I was very disappointed."

But What's It *Really* Like?

Program quality, graded by students:
Overall: **B**
Teaching quality: **B**
Caliber of classmates: **B**
Facilities: **B**
Support: **A**

Curriculum, graded by students:
Overall: **B**
E-business: **B**
Entrepreneurship: **B**
Ethics: **B**
Finance: **C**
International business: **A**
Marketing: **B**
Strategy: **A**
Teamwork: **A**

 The Good, the Bad, and the Ugly: Students Speak Out

"The instruction is top notch, relevant, and interesting, and leaves me wanting to learn more. Many of us feel as if we are getting more out of our experience than we are paying for."

"I was promoted twice."

"I was very disappointed. I will return to another school to obtain my MBA. However, it will be a school that is better organized and managed."

"Grades are not easy at Wake."

"The knowledge I obtained was very helpful in letting me be more productive on the job. The relationships I built during the program are priceless."

"It is definitely worth completing an MBA at Wake Forest. I was promoted twice. My soft skills and analytical skills have improved significantly. And the faculty did a great job of teaching fundamental management skills."

"Unless you act as though you are in a full-time program, you will wash out. Many students assumed that they had a B average just for showing up. They were shocked (and bitter) when they received an F or a C–. Grades are not easy at Wake."

"I believe some of the professors we had forgot that we were part-time students. Staying up until 2 a.m. to finish preparing for a class, and then getting up at 6 a.m. to go to work can be taxing."

 **Where to Stay**

Holiday Inn Select
5790 University Pkwy.
Winston-Salem, NC 27105
(336) 767-9595

Courtyard by Marriott
3111 University Pkwy.
Winston-Salem, NC 27105
(336) 727-1277

Hampton Inn
5719 University Pkwy.
Winston-Salem, NC 27105
(336) 767-9009

 Where to Eat

Ryan's Restaurant
719 Coliseum Dr.
Winston-Salem, NC 27106
(336) 724-6132

Twin City Chop House
115 S. Main St.
Winston-Salem, NC 27101
(336) 748-8600

La Carreta
725 Coliseum Dr.
Winston-Salem, NC 27106
(336) 722-3709

 Things to Do

Germanton Art Gallery & Winery
3530 Hwy. 8 & 65
Germanton, NC 27019
(800) 322-2894

Winston Cup Museum
1355 N. Martin Luther King Jr. Dr.
Winston-Salem, NC 27101
(336) 724-4557

CHECK OUT BUSINESSWEEK.COM FOR MORE:

School Tour: Take a peek at the campus, its classrooms, and its facilities with this online photo essay.

Search & Compare: Find out how Wake Forest compares to other part-time MBA programs with our interactive tool.

Expanded Profile: Learn more about the student body, what it takes to get in, and what to expect in the classroom using our online school profile.

Access all the B-schools content on BusinessWeek.com by subscribing to MBA Insider.

Washington University

Olin School of Business
2007 Ranking: 4th in the Midwest
Campus Box 1133
1 Brookings Dr.
Saint Louis, MO 63130
E-mail address: mba@olin.wustl.edu
Web address: www.olin.wustl.edu/
prospective/pmba.cfm
For more info: Call the MBA program
at (314) 935-7301

Why Wash U?

There's a lot to like about Wash U. Students attend core courses as part of a cohort, much like a full-time program. Semesters are divided into two "mini-terms," allowing most students to finish faster. And electives make up two-thirds of the course load, with a rich offering of concentrations that include entrepreneurship and strategy. Part-timers also are free to take courses in other graduate programs, as well as a two-week international trip. Part-timers can also switch into Olin's highly ranked, and highly selective, full-time program.

Washington University is a private institution. Established in 1975, Olin's part-time MBA program is accredited by the Association to Advance Collegiate Schools of Business (AACSB). Olin also offers full-time and executive MBA programs. For details on Olin's full-time MBA program, see page 201. For details on its executive MBA program, see page 309.

 **B4UGO**

Applicants accepted: 78%
Average GMAT score: 601
Average years' work experience: 5.5
**Average time to complete the
program:** 33 months
Completion rate: 91%

 Who Are My Classmates?

Part-time enrollment: 380
Women: 28%
International: 7%
Minority: 15%
Average age: 29
Average base salary at admission:
$62,085
Reason for getting an MBA: Career advancement with current employer (66.7%), career advancement with new employer (11.1%), change industries/functional areas (22.2%)*

*Estimates based on *BusinessWeek* survey data.

> *"A lot of resources for very few students."*

Where Do They Come From?

Top functional areas: Operations/ Production (35%), Finance/ Accounting (25%), Marketing (15%)

Top industries: Manufacturing (35%), Financial services (25%), Health-care (15%)

Top companies: Boeing, Anheuser-Busch, Emerson, Monsanto, MasterCard

---

"Anyone would be hard-pressed to find a better faculty."

The 411

Maximum time to complete the program: 84 months
Can PT students switch to the FT MBA program: Yes
Tuition per credit hour: $1,150
Classes begin: August, January
Application deadlines: None
Application fee: $100

Getting In

Relative importance of:
GMAT scores: Important
Work experience: Important
Application essay: Important
Interview: Important
Recommendations: Important
Transcripts: Important

Getting Out

Number of credits required for degree: 54
Access to Career Services for part-timers: Yes
Access to alumni database for part-timers: Yes
Part-timers permitted to interview on campus for internships: No
Part-timers permitted to interview on campus for full-time jobs: Yes
Graduates reporting post-MBA salary increase: 53.3%*
Average increase: 41.6%*
*Estimate based on *Business Week* survey data.

Cliff Notes

Leading areas of study: Finance, General Management, Marketing, Strategy, Supply Chain Management
Average class size, core courses: 57
Average class size, electives: 28
Number of electives: 75
Teaching methods: Case studies (40%), team projects (25%), lectures (20%)
Faculty sharing with FT program: 100%
Classes meet: Days, weeknights, weekends, weeklong sessions
Average workload per week: 18 hours

"There needs to be more variety."

But What's It *Really* Like?

Program quality, graded by students:
Overall: A
Teaching quality: A
Caliber of classmates: B
Facilities: A
Support: A

Curriculum, graded by students:
Overall: A+
E-business: C
Entrepreneurship: B
Ethics: C
Finance: B
International business: A
Marketing: C
Strategy: B
Teamwork: B

 ### The Good, the Bad, and the Ugly: Students Speak Out

"This school has a lot of resources for very few students, which makes you feel like you get more than your money's worth. It also has counselors waiting in the halls each night so that students can meet with them on the fly before class—it's awesome."

> *"You have the same professors as the full-time students."*

"I feel this program was challenging, but did a really great job of tying conceptual learning to real-world application. Cases were never studied in a vacuum, and I believe anyone would be hard-pressed to find any program with a better faculty teaching part-time students."

"They made it difficult for part-time students to have access to the same resources as full-time students, such as the career center."

> *"I could immediately apply the concepts to my current job."*

"As a I neared completion of my MBA, I got stuck taking some classes that I never would have chosen. There needs to be more variety."

"My experience at Wash U was fantastic. I was concerned that by attending a part-time program, I was not going to have access to the best professors, but that is not true at the Olin School of Business—you have the same professors as the full-time students."

"I could take what I learned from my professors and classmates and immediately apply the concepts to my current job."

 **Where to Stay**

Clayton on the Park
8025 Bonhomme Ave.
St. Louis, MO 63105
(314) 721-8588

Seven Gables Inn
26 N. Meramec St.
Clayton, MO 63135
(314) 863-8400

Crowne Plaza Hotel St. Louis—Clayton
7750 Carondelet Ave.
Clayton, MO 63105
(314) 726-5400

 Where to Eat

J Bucks
101 S. Hanley Rd.
Clayton, MO 63105
(314) 725-4700

Miss Saigon
6101 Delmar in the Loop
St. Louis, MO 63112
(314) 863-4949

BARcelona
34 N. Central Ave.
Clayton, MO 63105
(314) 863-9909

 Things to Do

Anheuser-Busch Brewery
12th & Lynch Sts.
St. Louis, MO 63118
(314) 577-2626

St. Louis Art Museum
One Fine Arts Dr., Forest Park
St. Louis, MO 63110-1380
(314) 721-0072

CHECK OUT BUSINESSWEEK.COM FOR MORE:

School Tour: Take a closer look at Olin's B-school campus with this photo tour.

Expanded Profile: Olin's online part-time MBA profile offers more information on the program, its students, and what to expect.

Search & Compare: How does Olin measure up to other part-time programs? Find out using our interactive tool.

Sample Application Essays and Interview Tips: Check out our advice for navigating the admissions process at Olin.

Access all the B-schools content on BusinessWeek.com by subscribing to MBA Insider.

Worcester Polytechnic Institute

Department of Management
2007 Ranking: 1st in the Northeast
100 Institute Rd.
Worcester, MA 01609
E-mail address: mgt@wpi.edu
Web address: www.mgt.wpi.edu
For more info: Call the MBA program
at (508) 831-5218

☑ B4UGO

Applicants accepted: 70%
Average GMAT score: 620
Average years' work experience: 7.3
**Average time to complete the
program:** 48 months
Completion rate: 92%

Why WPI?

With a unique focus that integrates business and technology, WPI's part-time MBA is ideal for students coming from science and engineering backgrounds. Students can concentrate in areas such as information technology, supply chain management, technology innovation, and information security. A graduate qualifying project, in which students analyze real company problems and propose solutions, challenges them to use all the skills they've learned. In the *BusinessWeek* ranking, WPI scored highly in student satisfaction and academic quality. Part-time students attend classes on weeknights, online, or both.

Worcester Polytechnic Institute is a private institution. Established in 1970, Worcester's part-time MBA program is accredited by the Association to Advance Collegiate Schools of Business (AACSB). Worcester also offers a full-time MBA.

 Who Are My Classmates?

Part-time enrollment: 121
Women: 30%
International: 1%
Minority: 19%
Average age: 34
Average base salary at admission:
$81,000
Reason for getting an MBA: Career advancement with current employer (69.6%), career advancement with new employer (13%), change industries/functional areas (17.4%)*

*Estimates based on *BusinessWeek* survey data.

"I feel like a much bigger contributor at work."

Where Do They Come From?

Top functional areas: Operations/
Production (25%), Management
Information Systems (25%),
Consulting (15%), Finance/
Accounting (15%)

Top industries: Technology (35%),
Healthcare (25%), Financial
ervices (15%), Consulting (15%)

Top companies: Hewlett-Packard,
EMC, Raytheon, Teradyne, Intel

---

*"An online class for
12 or 13 weekends
is a drag."*

The 411

Maximum time to complete the
program: 96 months

Can PT students switch to the FT
MBA program: Yes

Tuition per credit hour: $1,042

Classes begin: September, January

Application deadlines: July 1 (fall),
November 1 (spring)

Application fee: $70

Getting In

Relative importance of:
GMAT scores: Very important
Work experience: Very important
Application essay: Important
Interview: Considered
Recommendations: Important
Transcripts: Very important

Getting Out

Number of credits required for degree:
49

Access to Career Services for part-
timers: Yes

Access to alumni database for part-
timers: Yes

Part-timers permitted to interview on
campus for internships: Yes

Part-timers permitted to interview on
campus for full-time jobs: Yes

Graduates reporting post-MBA salary
increase: 40%*

Average increase: 46.2%*

*Estimate based on *Business Week* survey data.

Cliff Notes

Leading areas of study: Information
Technology, Innovation, Opera-
tions Management, Supply Chain,
Technology Marketing

Average class size, core courses: 10

Average class size, electives: 13

Number of electives: 17

Teaching methods: Case studies
(45%), lectures (25%), team
projects (15%)

Faculty sharing with FT program:
100%

Classes meet: Weeknights, online

Average workload per week: 12 hours

---

*"The '101' classes were
staffed by adjuncts."*

But What's It *Really* Like?

Program quality, graded by students:
Overall: A+
Teaching quality: A+
Caliber of classmates: B
Facilities: A
Support: B

Curriculum, graded by students:
Overall: A
E-business: A+
Entrepreneurship: A
Ethics: A
Finance: C
International business: C
Marketing: A+
Strategy: A
Teamwork: A+

 ### The Good, the Bad, and the Ugly: Students Speak Out

"This program has enabled me to improve my business acumen and has prepared me to interact with people of all different backgrounds and cultures. I feel like a much bigger contributor at work because of my increased knowledge base and level of confidence."

"All of our classes included hands-on exercises."

"Some of the '101' classes were staffed by adjuncts who, while they offered a lot of direct business and workplace knowledge, were not as deeply rooted in the course material as I would have liked."

"I need a faster-paced online format, like that of the University of Phoenix, to fit my schedule. An online class for 12 or 13 weekends is a drag."

"WPI needs more focus on teamwork and leadership."

"In general, I would say that WPI needs to have more focus on teamwork and leadership skills as part of the core/required components. I ended up taking a number of classes that focused on these topics (leadership mainly) and found them to be some of the most useful."

"WPI has provided me not only with a quality education, but also with a great opportunity to apply the concepts being taught in class. All of our classes included hands-on exercises and group work that really gave me a sense of what it's like out in the world of business."

"The schools is good for a student who has a busy job. The classes are not too intense, and professors understand when it comes to work/school conflicts."

 **Where to Stay**

Crowne Plaza Hotel Worcester
10 Lincoln Square
Worcester, MA 01608
(508) 791-1600

Hampton Inn Worcester
110 Summer St.
Worcester, MA 01608
(508) 757-0400

Hilton Garden Inn Hotel
35 Major Taylor Blvd.
Worcester, MA 01608
(508) 753-5700

 Where to Eat

The Boynton Restaurant
117 Highland St.
Worcester, MA 01609
(508) 746-5432

Peppercorns Grille & Bar
455 Park Ave.
Worcester, MA 01610
(508) 752-7711

The Sole Proprietor
118 Highland St.
Worcester, MA 01609
(508) 798-3474

 Things to Do

Worcester Art Museum
55 Salisbury St.
Worcester, MA 01609
(508) 799-4406

Worcester's Centrum Centre
50 Foster St.
Worcester, MA 01608
(508) 755-6800

CHECK OUT BUSINESSWEEK.COM FOR MORE:

Expanded Profile: Find more details on WPI's part-time MBA program in its online profile.

Search & Compare: See how WPI stacks up against other part-time MBA programs using this interactive tool.

Forums: Connect with other WPI hopefuls using our online forums.

Access all the B-schools content on BusinessWeek.com by subscribing to MBA Insider.